VOICES UNHEARD

VOICES UNHEARD

A Socio, Economic and Political Investigation in the Countryside

Vidyasagar Sriadibhatla

KALPAZ

ISBN : 978-93-5128-049-1

Price : ₹ 1050

First Published, 2014

Published by

Kalpaz Publications
C-30, Satyawati Nagar,
Delhi-110052
Ph. : 9212142040
E-mail: kalpaz@hotmail.com

Laser Typesetting: Gyan Prints (AB-II), Delhi
Printed at: G. Print Process, Delhi

Cataloging in Publication Data—DK
Courtesy: D.K. Agencies (P) Ltd. <docinfo@dkagencies.com>

Sriadibhatla, Vidyasagar.
Voices unheard : a socio, economic and political investigation in the countryside / Vidyasagar Sriadibhatla.
p. cm.
Includes index.
ISBN 9789351280491

1. Vizianagaram (India : District)—Social conditions. 2. Vizianagaram (India : District)—Economic conditions. 3. Vizianagaram (India : District)—Politics and government. I. Title.

DDC 306.095484 23

Dedication

To my Parents

My father late Sriadibhatla Venkata Chayanulu an activist of Andhra Pradesh Teachers Federation (APTF) who inculcated in me the sense of social responsibility and habit of extensive reading. Constantly encouraged me to look beyond but not bothered about my academic track record.

My mother, Smt. Surya Jyoti Sriadibhatla who is a constant source of inspiration for me to follow ethics in life.

Contents

PART–II

CFIR Project:

Centre for Independent Researchers (CFIR) is an independent and non-commercial social sciences forum to promote research in social sciences with highest standards. It encourages critical analysis in every stage. It shall work with public and private research institutes, policy makers and independent researchers. CFIR organises programmes which are designed to create awareness for people who want to pursue research in social sciences. It will work with national and international research networks to learn from one another.

CFIR would like to thanks Gyan Books (New Delhi) for publishing the book which will enable us to reach a wider audiane.

B. Rama Naidu

Centre For Independent Researchers (India)
Flat 8, Olney House,
1 Wynter Street,
London SW11 2QH
bramanaidu@hotmail.com

Preface

In the last two decades, I consistently kept hearing from friends and close circles that 'the villages are in decadence reflecting in human relationships based increasinglyon selfish gains'. Telugu literature, either fiction or non-fiction and art forms swamped with stories about the decadence of villages. I too carried away with these impressions and even I argued in support of this line of thinking for some time at least. My early study and field observations about how the transformation of the villages came into effect during the late nineties raised many doubts about the popular perception spread among the progressive circles. Gradually, my questions challenged the very basis of these arguments, *which led me to this adventure though I am not a trained economist or researcher. Whatever the drawbacks or limitations, I could not resist to start my 'pilgrimage' to villages to quest for answers.*

I cannot say that all sections among the economists, public intellectuals, writers and social activists have opined the village as a monolithic and plain unit, but I had that impression because of this incessant propaganda unleashed in the literary and political spectrums. To my surprise, the government agencies and the government constituted committees and commissions have had the most realistic assessment and fore thought about the changing conditions in the villages.

During my investigations, I understood that the agriculture wasprimarily labour intensive, therefore mutual co-operation was the pre-condition for the early agriculture. In the absence of mechanisation, wooden plough was the prime instrument, while human and animal labour was the primary inputs. Due to the necessity of many ploughs, cattle and labour, interdependence and co-operation must have beenthe pre-requisites for the smooth functioning of the production line in agriculture. In other words, the mode of production necessitated the co-operation among the masses. Introduction of the tractor brought in a sea change in the agricultural operations of the country side. Wooden ploughs are now almost entirely replaced by these labour and time saving machines. Hence, in one sense the pre-requisite was abolished and so the unity and co-operation too. This change not only reflected in the tractorisation of agriculture, but also, the other old modes of production. Mostly the machines now replace the invariable unity of personnel in the earlier modes of production.

Another aspect of propaganda is on the relations between the landowners and agrarian labour. Apart from the mythological glorification and legends about the Indian village and its community life, some of the sections are mournful that the cordial and fraternal relations that existed previously between the owners and labour have become extinct. In fact, innumerable masses for their paltry wages and minimum needs were inevitably tied up with these sections in the absence of alternate livelihood opportunities. These sections got some 'privilege' in the shape of urban wage labour. Evan a lay analyst or a sensible observer can find a new human being, liberated from the remnants of the Indian feudalism not 'sacrificing' his seat in the bus to his old master. It is a paradox to complain about this defiance by the Sudra uppercaste farmers who hadnever been civilised towards the poorer sections from the time immemorial. The transport and communication system eased the way and the masses have gone in search of alternate livelihood. Probably this appears to be the disappearance of "human relations".

Yet at times, some opinions appear to be universal but those are not entirely reflecting the universal character. The changes in rural production re-defined the productive relations and this change in the productive relations almost dismantled the old structures. However, each social group and class understood these changes differently as per their perceptions.

In order to get a firsthand account of the situation and widen my understanding, I have travelled through the selected villages in all fifty-six Mandals and met people of diverse social and economic backgrounds. Gathering information from people has been a very enlightening experience. They allowed me to enquire about the changes they had undergone in their day-to-day lives. It became obvious to me that different social groups have different experiences in this process.

Were all these changes unplanned? Did they happen through intervention or none at all? Were they policy driven? What are the logical conclusions that can be drawn from these consequences? Were all the supposed dismantled relations filled with love and affection? Such were the questions that motivated me to undertake this and find convincing answers.

I have observed that the rural masses are lost confidence on all the persons those who are in public life and they are continuously believing that all are deceptive. It was an utter disappointment and concern on people's psyche, which bothered me during my conversations. Of course, I understand that this is also one of the social and cultural reflections of the transformation that swept the economic structure. However, this will become a temporary hurdle for the genuine forces those who try to emancipate the masses from the drudgery.

Further, I found it difficult to convince the rural masses that there are people who will live and work without selfish motives. Though these perceptions are not new in the society, they are gaining wider social acceptance. I understand that, the roots of these cultural phenomena are in the changing productive relations. Almost in every village of the plains that I have visited, I have encountered a question, "*What will be the people gain from this exercise?*" My reply was always a negative. Then, they would ask mehow I would profit from this work. My answer would again be negative.

In the course of my travels, I once visited Malliveedu, a villagein Palakonda Mandal. After conducting an interactive session with the people there and ceremoniously being asked the same questions about gains and profits, I started my journey back to the city, definitely not with a sense of accomplishment. At that time, a farmer approached me, about 35 years of age, and from what I could remember, he never spoke a word during the group interaction. He looked fully composed and said to mein a sage-like manner (and I translate)–"you are sowing a seed; let us wait for the result". At that moment, my despair was replaced with hope and reassurance. It was one of the most cherished and memorable moments during my research.

This book would not have been possible without the advice, support and good wishes of many. I have to mention two persons exclusively for their valuable contributions. They are B. Ramanaidu (London) and Veluri Ramarao of Visakhapatnam. They almost equally endeavoured in this research all along these five years. Mr. Ramanaidu has also extended financial support to this research. I am grateful to them for their partaking in this research.

Last but not the least, I wrote an essay with the findings on three villages in the surveyed district and sent the essay to the prominent journal Economic and Political weekly. The editorial team published the essay titled with "The saga of three villages". Within no time, Amit Garg, The Director, Gyan publishers New Delhi congratulated me for my work and gave a fabulous offer for me. He offered to publish my work though it was at a nascent stage by that time. He kept his promise and published this book. I am very much thankful to the Editorial team of EPW and Gyan Publishers for their co-operation in making **"the voices unheard"** as audible. I am indebted to them.

I am grateful to my mother, wife and my daughter who extended their moral support in times of despair. I am especially grateful to my daughter Kiranmai for lending a patient ear while I incessantly narrated my experiences all these years.

All the opinions expressed in this book are my personal.

Vidyasagar Sriadibhatla
Vidyasagarsriadibhatla@gmail.com
09492340651

A Brief Synopsis of All Chapters

PART—I

1. Villages

The book chiefly aims at understanding the changes in the countryside that has undergone over a period of time. Its objective is to establish the changes in modes of production-from feudal to semi feudal and then on to capitalistic. In this endeavour, the writer set his job in such a way that classical theories are substantiated with findings at ground level. He chooses a particular district, Srikakulam of Andhra Pradesh, for his field study. Though the district has undergone some geographical changes owing to reorganisation of districts by Government, he chose the erstwhile district to make things easily understandable and with the rationale of studying the same for a fairly long period, say half a century. He selected two villages from each of 56 mandals of the district and visited the villages. He prepared a questionnaire and went on probing. He spoke to people, administration, machinery etc.

The subject has been classified, for clarity, into various chapters. In the first chapter, a briefing is given about the history of the human race and formation of various groups. How, aborigines started to settle and settlements grew up into villages. Statistics have been given on demographic distribution and changes in the same. To establish that the capital that has flown into the villages brought with it, inevitably, inequalities within and among various groups, examples have been given from various villages. In addition, examples have been given to buttress the above, how and where the capital flew and changes brought about by it in the periphery-habits, culture, and politics etc.

Then he goes on to explode the popular historical myth about the "Golden Era" or the glorious past. Excerpts have been given from historians like Henry Mein, Bernier, Peter Mundey, W. Foster, Theodor Morrison, Alexander Tytler, and others. Also there are proofs produced from various Government reports and surveys, e.g., reports on famines in India and Population Census. Writer also quotes M.K. Gandhi and B.R. Ambedkar to prove the point that changes in the face and texture of villages are not only a necessity but also a historical dialectic. At the end, it is aimed to prove that village structure has never been permanent, and it is certain to explode and vanish. Like nomads, like groups, like communes, like tribes, like settlements, villages too change and the agent of change is no other than *capital*. Still there shall be some remnants, and they have been cited with all the idiosyncrasies.

2. Land

The chapter Land begins with History of Land ownership in India. In their journey of life people settled down wherever they found virgin lands. They cultivated land and built a dwelling. Collided and collaborated with one another in raising crops. Agriculture at that time was only a source and means for living. There were no owners or proprietors. People raised crops and lived. The role of state was confined to collecting a part of the crop as Cess. The British, through enactment, installed some persons as proprietors or owners. A new word Zamindar was added to the glossary. However, that was only in the territory ruled directly by the British crown. India had 500 plus princely states in which the status quo continued. Land came to be recognised as a commodity, and the first ever registration of land transaction was in 1802 in Madras, a presidency area.

Land became a commodity, and trading started. Inheritance aided the process. The exit of the British and abolition of Zamindari and Inamdari speeded up the same. There were a lot of transactions, transferring in the name of trusts, charities etc. on the one hand, and "selling" to kith and kin on the other. The Act saw the transfer of land from the then ruling castes to peasant castes. The large parcels of land in the names of Zamindars and inamdars got fragmented and changed hands. Cultivators as of then were able to secure ownership of land, in varying extents. This process saw replacement of ruling castes, i.e., Brahmins, Kshatriyas, Velama Doras, and hill Zamindars by peasant castes chiefly koppula velama, toorpu kapu and others. They became new owners and assumed the role of rural rulers. Dalits and other rural labour castes were only the mute witnesses. There was no change in the life of castes of servitude, but for that the rulers have changed.

The land ceiling Act made little impact on the scenario. However, land got further fragmented. Large holdings became many small and marginal holdings. The number of small land holdings increased many-fold. There were not any significant movements for transfer of land to actual tillers. The catchy slogan remained so and the act and the movements had no impact.

Now the Government, proper owner of all land in the country even today is making use of the land as a commodity. It is allocating large chunks of land to various industrial houses unmindful of consequences and effects on environment. It is not ready to consider the pauperisation and loss of livelihood of masses. This has driven the peasantry into conflict with the state. Rural proletarian are also joining them. In many cases, land remains fallow and in many cases, land is put to uses other than agriculture. Speculation in the name of real estate has taken large areas of land into it. It appears that land, after the fragmentation, is ready for consolidation in the hands of industrial houses.

The writer narrated the above based on his field study and interactions. He provided statistics to prove every sentence of his. There are quotations from various books by western and Indian social scientists and historians, from pre British era till date. There are excerpts from various Government reports, surveys. There are quotes from Marxist theoreticians Marx, Engels, Karl Kautsky. There are quotes from M.K. Gandhi and B.R. Ambedkar. The quotations and excerpts prove the conclusions of the writer, beyond any doubt.The reader gets convinced of the compelling logic, substantiated by facts and figures.

The writer dutifully records the conflicts at Sompeta and Kakarapalli where there were firings and loss of life. People are revolting against the proposed power plants. The movement has caught the attention of national and international media and the Government is in the process of undoing. All this is recorded. There was a massacre on Dalits, in a village called Lakshmipeta and it has been recorded here in.

3. Agriculture

Settled cultivation necessitated changes in implementation and it resulted in surplus production. The very advent of plough increased need for live stock. Still primitive implements and methods of productions persist, as vestiges. Changes in ownership and tenancy brought about changes in relations. Fragmentation of land has ultimately led to migration. Contract farming by sugar and paper industries has been in vogue in the district. All these have been affecting the use of land. Land is being put to non agriculture purposes and more and more land is lying fallow, each year. Net sown area is consistently decreasing. Though the area under cultivation is decreasing, the production is increasing. But the same has further aggravated the situation of the small peasants. Policy makers suggested shift of cultivation from food grains to commercial crops. Majority of suicides are from cotton farmers and cotton is a purely commercial crop. Capitalist production has increased cost of inputs and incomes of the peasantry dwindled more so in case of small peasants. Production is aimed and targeted at supplying food items to the urban rich. Milk, marine food, fruits etc. do get graded and the best of them find their way to market while rural areas are famished and malnourished. Public investment in agriculture is on decline while private investment is on the rise. Allocations to agriculture leave much to be desired. First ever policy on agriculture was formed only in 2000 half a century after self-rule. In the process, peasantry is abandoning agriculture and lands are remaining fallow. Tenancy rules make things more complicated. For many an apprehension, persons do not lease out land to others and leasing out is confined to kith and kin. Tenancy has to be in two ways. One is absentee landlords and the other is peasant proletarians. The former are those who inherited large tracts of land and can not cultivate it themselves for the reasons that they reside in towns elsewhere because of their gainful employment. They are willing to lease out only to confidants. The other is one with small and uneconomical piece of land who can not stay in the village for want of incomes, and become foot loose. They lease out land to their own clan and leave in search of work. Even the tenants are not blessed, as the input costs, pervasive rains, lack of water resources, market manipulation spell their doom. Eventually land is left fallow and is aimed at non agricultural use to fetch a good price.

Simultaneously consumerism, an offshoot of capitalism generates a fetish of goods and this takes away all the earnings of the peasantry. It also creates hype and aura about grandeur in life styles. State for the mere sake of revenue encourages alcoholism. Maxim Gorky puts it that the State gives a rupee and takes away rupee and a half. The half is the debt burden.

All this is narrated with the help of examples from villages and interactions with peasantry. All this process has been explained in the light of classic writing. Karl Kautsky said that the hunt for markets is not amongst the proletarian but among rural masses. Karl Marx wrote that agriculture deteriorates under one government and revives again under some other government.

Some historians, Campbell, D.D. Kosambietc have also been quoted to emphasise the point wherever necessary. Reports by Government and its wings such as sub group on land related matters, etc., have been quoted to establish the accuracy of the derivations.

Statistics from official sources and also statistics complied from the facts gathered have been provided in tabular form.

4. Cropping Pattern

Production in India was barely sufficient to meet the growing food needs. As a panacea to famines, low production and malnutrition, Government embarked upon infusing capital into agriculture euphemistically naming it *Green Revolution* which in its natural course, resulted in uneven growth and further perpetrated inequalities. Food grains gave way to commercial crops. Use of pesticides and fertilisers has been rampant, and soil became infertile. Government is trying to thrust the blame on the farmers, but the fact is that the shift was not merely deliberate but engineered and propagated as well.

Production of conventional oil seeds such as groundnut, sesamum etc., has decreased, and land under cultivation of palm oil has multiplied. Production of jute has dwindled owing tactics pursued by jute factories in the area, while production of maize has increased. This way the very cropping pattern has come to be dependent on industry and market.

While exodus out of agriculture is a reality, Government as a counter has come out with the bogey of food security.

All this has been proved by ground level survey. Tables about costs of production for various crops, oil seeds, maize, mesta, sugar cane, palm oil, cotton have been given. Likewise, crop-wise usage of fertilisers has been tabulated. Excerpts from budget speeches, Government reports, have been given. Quotes from Marx have been given to substantiate.

Agricultural workers are decreasing in absolute terms and also in percentage. Though the percentage reduction is not reflected in the population of the countryside, yet the complaint by the peasants about non-availability of labour for agricultural operation speaks volumes of the freed labour turning to nearby urban areas for work. Cost of accommodation in the urban areas and increased transportation still keep the people in the villages. Capitalism results in breaking of families and nuclear families are a common sight even in the countryside. Migration to distant areas is also increasing, and population of urban areas is swelling. 2011 census recorded that percentage growth in population is higher in urban areas than in rural areas, for the first time. Even Government has become conscious of the same and trying to arrest the migration. NREGP is one such measure, and rural housing scheme is one. Chief Minister himself spoke vehemently about creating employment and incomes in the rural areas.

Tables have been provided to show the decrease in agricultural workers, decreased percentage growth of the rural population, decrease in total workers in rural areas, increased migration.

Derivations have been proved through interactions with persons in villages. Excerpts from various Government reports and speeches in the legislature have been given. Instances have been given from internet, newspapers and media. Quotes from classics of Marx, Engels and Kautsky and writings of Ambedkar, Kosambi have been given to prove the point.

5. Human Resources

Human labour was an integral part of cultivation. However, of late cultivation as a profession lost its glory. People are disinterested in continuing in the cultivation. The census and the field level studies have proved this fact in a formidable manner. The capital not only grabbed the input market but also it grabbed the working hands from the countryside. This is all dealt with the help of census reports and with the current field visits.

6. Livestock and Mechanisation

Livestock has always been a part of peasant's family. Agriculture was dependant on livestock and each peasant reared them and even revered them. Fragmentation of land and increased holdings should have resulted in increase in the number of livestock. I have collected Figures of livestock from various livestock surveys for the country and from district handbook for the district and gave in tabular form. As a result of flow of capital into agriculture, machinery in the form of tractors, etc., came into being and it proved to be a cheaper and quicker alternative to the livestock. People switched over and livestock has slowly walked out of peasants' family. This can be seen in the statistics of he buffaloes. However, in the name of pink revolution, production of beef has been encouraged. Beef is a major earner of foreign exchange for the country and we have surpassed countries like Brazil and Australia who have been dominating market for a long time. I supported the same from interactions with villagers and from input survey 2006, national commission on cattle, GAIN report prepared by Deepa Dhinkar, basic animal husbandry statistics 2010, national commission on livestock 2010, daid.nic.in, and agricultural ministry of USA. This way the mute cattle have helped the rural folk both in their life and in death.

Villages have also been places of industry. Craftsmen stationed in the villages prepared all the tools and implements necessary for agriculture. Slowly, capital crept in and mechanisation of tools and implements started. Tata Agrico the oldest brand of Tata Steel started making agricultural implements way back in 1925 and the production increased. System changed from making to manufacture and it cheapened the implements. Heavy machinery followed. Number of tractors in the villages is increasing and other machinery like thrashers, harvesters, etc. did not lag behind. Sugarcane crushers, drip irrigation systems, reapers, seed drillers, chaff cutters, earth movers and the list is end less. I quoted from Karl Kautsky, and Karl Marx, I relied on Director CIAE, www.tataagrico.com, Andhra Pradesh crop reports, Gyanendra Singh and Indra Mani, FAO, Agricultural engineering data book, India tractor manufacturer association, FICCI, etc., data was compiled for the district and presented in tabular form. Export and import values of agricultural machinery from ministry of commerce presented in tabular form.

Mechanisation of agriculture as it is euphemistically called has displaced not only animals but also men from agriculture. While male labour left the agriculture,it is substituted by the female one.

7. Irrigation

India, as has been rightly identified by Karl Marx, is a semi arid area and providing artificial irrigation is a crucial factor for agriculture. Colonial rulers paid no heed to this. Nor did the Zamindars and Inamdars do. This resulted in frequent famines and loss of life. About only 0.5 per cent of gross revenue was spent on irrigation in Madras presidency. This district was a Zamindari area and situation was worse. There is a consistent demand for irrigation schemes. Many schemes that were announced remained on paper and many are in ever-continuing stage.

Irrigation through surface water has been neglected. Area under cultivation through tanks as percentage to total irrigated has been decreasing. Tanks, which are main source of surface irrigation, are depleting and neglected. Local powerful castes and sections are occupying tanks and in stray cases dalits too. Many tanks are closed in the name of public works. Neither the government nor the people undertake any repairs. Flows, canals, streams, dams saw no investment and the area cultivated under these is decreasing. There is no investment in lift irrigation schemes, regulators etc.

Flow of capital into ground water resulted in increase in tube wells and bore wells. Land under irrigation from tube wells has increased. Investment in irrigation by settlers from other districts and availability of institutional credit has resulted in indiscriminate exploitation of ground water. Off late it is observed that though the number of tube or bore wells is increasing, the area under their irrigation is decreasing. This is attributed to low output owing to depleting water tables.

People, for centuries, dug wells on common well, for irrigation. With fragmentation, investment in digging of wells became cost ineffective. Not merely the land but the fragmentation of social fabric an offshoot of capital, also is responsible and the practice of digging of new wells has stopped and even those are existing are not repaired.

To summarise flow of capital has replaced the natural process of irrigation into a mechanical one. Instead of storing of renewable water resource, non-renewable water resource is exploited. Machinery and money replaced collective will and labour. Many examples from some villages. Interactions with farmers have been given to drive home the point. I provided the history of reservoirs and dams announced and not completed. I provided tables for irrigation through canals, tanks, wells and tube wells. Statements of the government and its wings and from various reports as the evidence for the same process is quoted in this chapter.

8. Seed

For ages, seed, the vital most input in agriculture, has been prepared locally. Sure, the yields were low but there were about 30,000 varieties of seed. People grew a variety of food crops like Paddy, Ragi, Maize, Bajra, Jowar, Varige, Korralu, Samalu etc. Based on their economic strata people ate one or many of these. Capital entered into seed business post green revolution and it changed the scene. In this district the HYV entered in late 70s. Government through its organs encouraged and advocated use HYV and gave seeds free of cost. Peasantry ran after the HYV on seeing sparkling results in yield. Then the government subsidised seed cost and as of now there are no subsidies. People have almost forgotten that seed can be prepared locally and they totally became dependent on seed market. Though government claims that it is supplying entire seed, facts speak otherwise. There are many market players. Their turnover is increasing consistently.

Lured by the production people shifted to production of only a few varieties. Growing Ragi, Bajra, Jowar is almost absent. More and more area is going under cultivation of cotton, maize and paddy. BT cotton drove local seed out of sight. So is the case with maize.

Dependence on others and market for seeds is playing havoc with the lives of peasantry. Non availability of seeds, in the name of market operations, is pushing their price high. Local greedy millers and other seed traders are selling sub-standard and spurious seeds. End of the day the, peasantry is doomed. It can be proverbially said, seed dies to give birth to a plant but the spurious seed is born to kill the planter.

All these are proved this point with quotes from government departments, web sites, and also from inter actions with villagers. Also I provided statistics of business of various giants like Mahyco, Nuzvid Seeds, Emergent, Monsanto etc.

It is proved that while seeds are adding to the riches of millionnaire companies, the peasantry are losing ground.

9. Fertilisers and Pesticides

Until almost 70s, peasants used organic manure. Menace of pests was more or less confined to rodents and so use of pesticides was never in their minds. Green revolution has changed all this. It was a scheme advertised as a panacea to all the ills of agriculture. But it was proved to be the birth bed of capitalism in agriculture. In the name of increasing productivity HYV were thrust on the peasantry. These HYV are highly fertiliser intensive. Hence, farmers queued up for fertiliser. Initially government subsidised for fertilisers and the subsidies have been withdrawn in a phased manner. This has increased the cost of fertilisers. Besides, the process of in fertilisation of soil necessitated more and more fertilisers leading to further infertility. This way it is cause and effect of infertility of soil, now government wishes pass on the blame on the innocent peasantry, and advocates return to organic fertilisers. The entire process has been merely a facilitator for capital in agriculture. Fertiliser companies have swelled in both capital and strength. The lobby has become so powerful. Profits soared. Sales leaped. Government departments spoke differently at different times. In 1972, they spoke of use of judicious use of fertilisers and in 1975 the rhetoric was to increase the nutrition of soil.

All this went on despite the cautions aired by various scientists.

This is proved this with the help of various government reports, speeches of political parties, department notes etc., also I provided statistics of capital flow into fertiliser industry and its profits. Tables for consumption of fertilisers in India, fertiliser consumption vis-à-vis food grain production, subsidies given to fertiliser companies, share of public private foreign companies in production and the production pattern have been incorporated.

With HYV and indiscriminate use of fertilisers, pests and insects have become a major problem to agriculture. Protection became a necessity for production. Government embarked on use of pesticides. Locally made organic pesticides could not meet the demand, naturally. Pesticides have been introduced and people have been cajoled into the use through persuasion, propaganda and subsidies. Phasing out of subsidies made pesticides costly. Now government and its machinery speak against the use of pesticides. In the meanwhile, profits of pesticide companies knew no bounds. Most of these companies are foreign. It is proved through interactions with villagers and various government reports, and other sources.

10. Credit

History does not discriminate. Germany or France or India, peasantry have always groaned under the weight of debt burden. During the colonial rule, the era of Zamindars and Inamdars, peasants have been literally producing for the usury. In the studied district there are two methods of lending. One is "fayida" system in which the money borrowed during investment season is paid in grain after the harvest with some addition as Fayida (gain). The other is money is borrowed at a predetermined price of the future harvest. In both the cases usury made abnormal gains at the cost of peasantry.

The penetration of capital into agriculture started in the form of co-operative credit societies–in which state itself played the role of moneylender. The structure of the system was so designed that only a few—local powerful affluent sections—have access to the same. The societies used to be governed by a body elected locally which decided the whole of lending exercise and elections, as they are, always kept the common man at bay. Armed with political power, this rich peasantry never cared to repay the dues and it spelt the doom to the system. Then came commercial banks, in the name of nationalisation and social responsibility. These "institutions" are manned by beauracracy that tries to be more loyal than the king. It pinned its lending philosophy—in contrast with its own policies—to security and title documents. Majority of the peasants either lacked documents or could not offer any security for that they already been sucked out by the usury. Statistics and reports clearly indicate that credit flowed only into the hands of local powers. The much advertised lending to allied activities has only resulted in depletion of not only the financial resources but also physical resources of the small and marginal farmers and the landless. Non availability of inputs and market manipulations turned these allied activities a drenching exercise. These banks, rightly named commercial banks, raised hue and cry of defaults. However, the peasantry was a bit relieved from the clutches of the local usury. The very activity has almost stopped.

A section of the locals who had migrated to urban areas and secured employment and who are working as teachers in the villages have today took the role of money-lenders. Interestingly enough, in some cases, the dalits that migrated to urban places are saving money and they are lending in the village to the peasantry. Those who contributed labour for a long time are today supplying capital, to rural economy. This way though the method and machinery of debt changed yet the devil is not dead.

All this process is proved with the help of interactions with natives and local employees, teachers, bank employees etc. I provided tables and statistics of credit from co-operative societies from 1971 to 1976 and table of asset holding vs. loans to various sections of peasants. There are quotes and references from S.C. Ray, NSSO, P.S. Badal, survey for assessment of situations, Sir G. Wingate, etc.

11. Market

This chapter dealt with the output market. Largely the market is controlled by private individuals barring Sugar cane. Earlier as per tradition, Vysya community had the saying in the rural market whereas; now the peasantry castes took over the reins. The government market yards are not catering to the needs of the cultivators. Citing the inflexible objections of the market yards the peasantry prefers private traders to the market yards.

12. Rural Industry

Agriculture, like any other industry, is in a way, a composite economic activity that necessitates some occupations as smith or a carpenter etc. Settlements necessitated other vocations such as washermen, barber, and weaver and so on. In India, these occupations became solidified as castes. Professions too have become hereditary rather than of choice. We can learn a lot about this caste system in the writings of Manu. He denoted duties for various castes. Spiritual needs and the philosophical well being of the villagers is the duty of the Brahmin while Vysya has to do cultivation. Other Sudra castes are to serve the three upper varnas, i.e., Brahmin, Kshatriya and Vaisya. Campbell who surveyed and studied villages in India made valuable observations. Caste system served the village economy well. At the same it strangulated those at the bottom of the echelon. They tried in vain to free themselves. They knew not that only in the abandonment of the profession lies their freedom. The upper castes took great care to further fortify the caste system for they knew well that in that lies their well being.

Agriculture survived on co-operation from rural industries.; Barika the village servant, the smith made implements and tools, weaver supplied clothes, potter supplied utensils, etc. Feudalism has further ossified caste system. Gandhi openly supported the varnashrama dharma and looked at it as an engine to rural economy while Ambedkar severely condemned this and wished for dismantling of all existing Hindu dharma.

Entry of capital into agriculture brought about changes in the professions. Machine made tools and implements of agriculture cheapened the same and available readily. This rendered the smith and carpenter redundant and they had to flee villages. Mining of aluminium and other metals and making of utensils on machines made the potter workless. Tractors, etc., deprived the detail labour of work. This way the exodus of people from rural to urban areas accelerated.

Now the rural rich peasantry is facing the heat. They are blaming the rural proletarian for their leaving the villages. The cheap labour in the form of caste based occupations which was a basis for their wealth is eroding. Hence they are making a hue and cry of the bygone golden era.

Caste based occupation system is an axis to feudal mode of production in the Indian context. It is an unparalleled social contract in India. The burden of inhumanity was largely borne by the subdued castes.

Capital and only capital is the medicine to the malady. Capital can not thrive without destroying the feudal base.

Part–II

13. Forests and Adivasis

The British destroyed forests yet they wished to preserve forest tracts. They nationalised forests and made a policy statement that forests are reservoirs of valuable timber and they should be managed on commercial lines as a source of revenue to the state. It extinguished all the natural rights of Adivasis on the forests, and the symbiotic relationship of Adivasis with the forests. As decided in 1976, plantations started to be grown in forests and the area increased multi-fold only to cater to the needs of industries. Production of pulpwood increased but the revenue to government did not. The paper mill lobby is so powerful and pulpwood has no other buyers. However, in the process Adivasis became aliens to the land and the produce. All the acts and actions were aimed at protecting the forests from the Adivasis, not for the Adivasis. All the committees looked at forest as a source of wealth for the investors and revenue to the state. I discussed various provisions of Debar Committee, Centre for Sustainable Development, National Commission on Agriculture etc. Forest Development Corporation chalked out plans for planting of industrial raw material. At the end, they sold coffee, cashew, bamboo and pepper at throwaway prices. This way people are paying the industrial lobby in an indirect manner through taxation and are paying directly to the industrialist from their pocket through purchase of food items. A paper prepared by N.C. Saxena commented, "The arrangement is unlawful. Officers are taking grave risk of prosecution in being a part to such illegal arrangement."

In the studied district, forest area is decreasing because of deforestation for the benefit of industries. Tribes equated title to possession while the law of the land spoke different. This is resulting in agitations. Number of cases booked against Adivasis increased consistently. Government procured some lands in the name of development such as irrigation projects. Committee appointed by prime minister stated that the tribal people have been the biggest victims of displacement due to development projects. The native tribes are now only proletarian without any means of living. Tenancy, land distribution, land ceiling, you name it, no act helped the tribes secure land for living. 91 per cent of Adivasis are surviving on uneconomic land holdings. Estimated land sown by tribes is decreasing.

Girijan corporation set up for helping the Adivasis get a better price for forest produce are no less greedy than the local traders. Other means of earning such as selling of broom, firewood, honey, etc., are withering away.

Lack of titles keeps the tribes away from institutional credit and the result is entanglement with the local usury. This was a prime cause for rebellions and unrest.

The landlessness, the land alienation, debt burden, the primitive mode of production, and the stringent forest polices made them migrants to earn a livelihood. Some if not many or all, often get into the clutches of labour contractors who supply labour to urban works and continue to suffer in a different form.

Employment statistics of tribals leave us gasping. Almost none of the females from tribes are in employment. Among men, it is less than recognisable.

All this is proved with interactions with locals tables are provided to each of my observations. Various observations of social scientists and intelligentsia such as N.C. Saxena have been given to prove the cost of development, excerpts from many committees constituted by government have been given aptly to understand the process. Gist of findings, observations and prescriptions of many committees have been given to understand the dynamics of the process statements of minister for tribal welfare and from speeches in assembly and parliament have been reproduced.

14. Dalits

Ambedkar stood for the cause of dalits. In 1935 the colonial rulers provided reservations to these classes. Andhra Pradesh officially recognised 59 castes as scheduled. Dalits were all rural proletarian. They had no land. But they were the actual tillers. Social oppression added insult to injury. They are allowed to enter even the temples but not to temple lands. Peasant castes were recorded as tenants in these lands while the dalits tilled the same and Brahmins enjoyed the produce. When Brahmins fled villages the peasants became owners and got possession as well. Speeches and proclamations by the government in and outside legislature remained rhetoric and dalits are still a landless lot. They left the trivial small pieces of land allotted to them, for want of capital and time, for what they were given was part of hillocks, uncultivable, shrubby etc. They had no livestock or implements and the pieces were so small and uneconomic.

In many a case the government through its schemes drove the dalits away from the lands, acquiring lands for projects, housing colonies, public works etc. In some cases, the offer of ready cash lured the dalits, poor and famished, into selling out their piece of land. In some cases the local peasant castes used all possible ways to throw the dalits out of land. Loss of life, litigations, luring, there are many ways. National Commission on Scheduled Castes recorded that, "the Allotted of ceiling surplus or government lands are generally the victims of harassment by means of dispossession or obstruction to cultivation etc."

Agriculture work is seasonal and is only a small time livelihood. Therefore, dalits preferred to be attached to labour to eke out a living. Wages were miserably low and not even sufficient for two square meals a day. There was no time limit for work. Work started at 4 am and ended up in the dark. It might have continued into the night, but it was not possible, thanks to the lack of the electricity in the villages. Everybody in the dalits worked for the peasantry, man as attached labour, and children as collectors of dung, herding the cattle and running errands while women worked as house maids and shared the work of her husband. The total family of the attached labour was tied to the rich peasantry only to fetch a permanent livelihood with a minimum guarantee. They were totally unorganised. The rural labour enquiry 1974-75 remarked that only one per cent of agricultural labourers were members of any organisation or union of farm labourers. It should be noted further that dalits were not part of this one per cent.

Entry of capital into villages in the shape of transport, communication, education, and electricity etc. had paved way for the freeing of these semi serfs from the clutches of peasantry. By the end of last century this system of attached labour disappeared.

The rest of dalits worked as agricultural labour. The inroads of capital opened the world for them and the dalits became footloose.

The number of employees from these sections is very low. And also it is confined to some castes and some families who have migrated to urban areas first.

The influential sections of the four peasant castes had enjoyed a lot almost for 30-35 years in the countryside. The cheap labour earned profits in the agricultural sector for them. They could turn this profit as rural capital and at the same time their savings exported the capital to the urban sector.

Experiences of Dalits from some villages are incorporated to prove the point of oppression.

Urbanisation has not opened the doors of heaven for the dalits. Here also they are leading their life in harsh conditions in urban slums. They are working as unskilled labour in construction and transport sectors. Relative guarantee of work and better wages are the sticking agents. Absence of caste discrimination keeps them here, in all ills.

15. The Fishermen and the Sea

The sea is the source of livelihood. The colonial rulers came to the country through the sea ways but fortunately, they had not touched the wealth of the sea. They conducted a comprehensive survey on the wealth of sea and oceans. In India and Burma, Francis Day did a survey and published a report in 1873.

Fishermen used various types of boats for fishing. Raft made of wood from Oleander or Silk cotton tree cost them about a thousand rupees. Each village had about 50 such boats. Catamaran made of wood with good buoyancy and bamboo or casuarinas are used by some for fishing in the shore up to 50 m depth. It carried 3-5 persons. Catamaran with thermocool is also used. Government wanted to modernise the fishing sector to increase the catch and introduced fibre boats. Later these fibre boats were fitted with engine. Steadily Raft and Catamaran gave way to fibre boats.

For a long time fishermen used nets made of cotton yarn and jute twine. Nylon nets came into being in 70s and they replaced the cotton yarn and jute twine. When fishermen used boats made of local wood and thread from local crops, they owned the same on collective form. A group of men pooled up small resources required and laboured together for making of them. Fibre boats and nylon nets were made in machinery by industries. Fishermen can not make them on their own and have to buy them. The cost is high and beyond the means of these fishermen. This gave rise to need of capital and non fishing owners came into being. Then came big capital and constant improvements in boats and nets have further alienated fishermen from fish and all of them became labourers, proletarian in other words.

Fishermen did not receive any institutional finance for the life of fishermen is uncertain and there are no securities to back up. So usury had his hey day. Lending terms defy all the laws of land.

Modernisation increased production in simple terms. But this increase had costs too. Sea is being stirred and squeezed by the rapacious capital. Wars are fought for catch. Rules are broken. Agreements between nations and understandings blatantly violated.

Mechanisation breeds in itself and boats are undergoing changes. Fibre boats to mechanised boats, then on to Sona boats etc. Latest boats are capable of fishing far and deep in the sea and even can be harboured in the deep sea. Nets have further improved and today tons of fish can be caught in a single throw. There are separate nets for targeted catch.

This process resulted in contamination and mudding of shore waters and fishermen with primitive implements can not get any catch. Further the mechanised boats and modern nets throw away all other fish than the targeted ones back into the sea, dead. This dead fish are contaminating sea waters. Variety of fish which crossed 1000- has now decreased to less than 100.

Vocational fishermen find no capital and no catch. They join in the mechanised fishing boats as labourers. But they have absolutely no say either in catch or in its selling. They have no rights on the catch. Presently fishing is done with the eye on export and inland fisheries activity is taking better of marine fishing. Women folk of fishermen families sold the catch of their husbands and ran family. But now they have nothing to sell. They work as detail labour. Fishermen left with no other means became foot loose and are today migrating to distant lands.

Fishermen of Srikakulam district travel to Cochin for selling cap, cradles etc. Some men travel even up to Kutch, Paradeep, Goa and Hiravali as either fishing labour or other detail labour. Some of them switched over to other occupations such as auto rickshaw driving. All this is proved with interactions with local people. Excerpts from various committees and reports have been incorporated. Statistics in tabular form about number of rafts, catamaran, fibre boats, Sona boats etc., and trends about fishing, etc., have been provided.

16. Weavers

Cloth is next only to food and in this process, weaving emerged. In the initial phases, like other goods, production and consumption was limited to that village or settlements nearby. As production increased markets expanded. Indian traders exchanged cloth for Gold. This worried the British and they declared embargo on selling Indian textiles in Britain. There was a long debate on this in Young India.

The first blow on the Indian textile industry came not from the foreign capital but it was from Indian manufacturers. It is Indian capital that started making coarse cloth consumed widely by impoverished Indians. The first Indian mill was established in 1851. Gandhi advocated people to wear coarse hand made cloth made by Indian handmade yarn. Mill made cloth could not produce sufficient cloth for a long time. During that period rural industry flourished. As soon as the urban industry dominated the production pattern the looms had become obsolete and the lives of the weavers strained.

The studied district had a large presence of weavers. The implements—heads, pickas, reed, brush, hand brush, shuttle, and charkha—were made locally. The entry of capital started with mechanising the process of manufacture of these implements thus displacing persons from Muslims, Erukula, Singam and carpenters. Likewise the making of yarn in machines spelt doom for the weavers who were eking out their livelihood by making handmade yarn from cotton. Steadily area under cultivation of cotton, production of cotton has increased but since production of yarn is fully in the hands of business, both the peasantry and the weavers perished because yarn, basic raw material for weaving got commoditised and entered market. Yarn producers, the millers, keep their eyes on export of the same for more profit and government is encouraging export for foreign exchange.

Co-operative sector played its own role in the ruin of weavers. The apex body supplies hank yarn to the weavers and pays them up for the labour on piece rate basis. This results in very low wages for a long hard working day. Government policies too have their say in that the raw material is not supplied and work orders for buy back of the product are not given. Nationalisation led to making and breaking of rules. Sops and concessions given in the name of small scale/rural sector found their way into the treasuries of the rich. Now that the very process came in handy to the capital, converting all and whole of the entrepreneurs/artisans into proletariat, industry–state combine is speaking volumes of privatisation in the name of disinvestment.

All these are proved with the help of interactions with many villagers and weavers both individual and co-operatives. Excerpts from various committees are provided. Statistics of production of yarn, export that of, employment etc., are provided.

PART—I

ANDHRA PRADESH
SRIKAKULAM DISTRICT
MILES
KILOMETRES
ORISSA STATE
(EASTERN ZONE)
ORISSA STATE
(EASTERN ZONE)
BAY OF BENGAL
VISAKHAPATNAM DISTRICT
PARVATHIPURAM TALUK
SALUR TALUK
BOBBILI TALUK
PALAKONDA TALUK
PATHAPATNAM TALUK
TEKKALI TALUK
SOMPETA TALUK
NARASANNAPET TALUK
SRIKAKULAM TALUK
CHEEPURUPALLE TALUK
ICHCHAPURAM
ICHCHAPURAM (I. S. T.)
SOMPETA
MANDASA
BARUVA
KAVITI
TEKKALI
PATHAPATNAM
NARASANNAPET
SRIKAKULAM
SINGUPURAM
SRIKURMAM
PALAKONDA
VEERAGHATTAM
RAJAM
PONDURU
CHEEPURUPALLE
MARAPAKA
GARBHAM
BOBBILI
PEDDAPANKI
PARVATHIPURAM
SALUR
RAMABHADRAPURAM
FROM POTTANGI
FROM KORAPUT
TO RAYAGHADA
TO BISSAM CUTTACK
FROM GUNUPURU
TO GUMMA
FROM PARLAKIMIDI
TO CHATRAPUR
FROM VIZIANAGARAM
FROM BHEEMUNIPATNAM
MAP OF INDIA
ANDHRA PRADESH

1

Villages

Many people have studied the origin of villages in our county. Humankind was similar to fauna in being nomadic: Gathered food to survive and subsequently learnt to hunt. Rising crops necessitated living around and this led to settlements. This culture, to live around and work together, close to land, came to be called "agriculture" brought with it a common productive system that cannot be anything else than collective consumption. It inherited the factor of no surplus. There was no scope for exchange since entire produce was for common usage. Astray and miniscule, yet producing for consumption exists in tribal settlements and new areas open up even today.

The role of labour in all these processes is evident. Invention of agricultural implements improved the practices of cultivation and this lead to surplus value and its extraction. In this process, large landholdings formed.There is a strong link between the establishment of settled farming and formation of villages. Still in this area, tribes are changing their cultivation practices and trying to shift to new way of cultivation. In this process, they are building new villages.

Regarding My Research Area

The research on villages is not a new subject. I have selected Srikakulam district for the purpose. This district had geographical boundary changes in 1979. Some parts are carved out of this district and merged with newly formed Vizianagaram District. Prior to this, the district had 10 taluks and one sub-taluk. Out of these, three taluks—Saluru, Parvatipuram and Bobbili are completely merged and 112 villages of Cheepurupalli taluk are merged in Vizianagaram district.

I have taken the undivided district for my research. Now it consists of 56 Mandals and I have selected two villages from each Mandal. The basis for the selection and the list of villages is given in Annexure I. Normally, my research indicates for the undivided district unless I mention it separately.

Indian national leadership has two contrasting views on the life of villages. Gandhi has seen that villages are the backbone of the country. Ambedkar expressed quite different approach and opined "the working plant of the Hindu social order which one could see its operation in full swing" (quoted in: Who will Speak for Village? Agrarian Change and Marginalising ruralitiesin Contemporary India: Prof. Surinder S. Jodhka). He also felt that admiration towards the isolated structures is unnecessary. Marx felt that elimination of this village structure is a prerequisite for transformation.

There are many variations in the villages of this district. More than hundred villages are very near to the seacoast while many villages have come up in hilly terrain. Many villages are not aware of the canal irrigation while some are well irrigated. This district is a den of natural resources with fertile plains, sea besides natural forests. Unfortunately, of late, all these natural resources are targeted for minting money at the cost of existence of very natural resources.

The forest dwellers, scheduled tribes who have led a prolonged isolated life and now the scenario is changing considerably. Interestingly, the fisher folk surviving along the seacoast is living like tribes.

Indian villages conducted a community production method for a long time. It has survived long in spite of repeated wars and annexations on it. Marx said, *"all the civil wars, invasions, revolutions, conquests, famines, strange complex, rapid and destructive as the successive action in Hindoostan may appear, did not go deeper than its surface"* (Marx on India Page-12).

India probably got this power from its caste-linked occupational structure. India made these occupations mandatory and linked it with caste. Agriculture system has resulted in numerous professions as an auxiliary to it and survived for a long time.

The Villages of this District

The evolution of villages in the last four decades can be found from the following table.

Table 1. Change in the Number and Population of the Villages

Census Year	*Uninhabited Villages*	*Inhabited village*							
		less than 200	*200-499*	*500-999*	*1000-1999*	*2000-4999*	*5000-9999*	*above 10000*	*Total Inhabited Villages*
1971	215	656	1228	684	544	217	15	1	3345
1981	182	NA	NA	NA	NA	NA	NA	NA	NA
1991	606	411	623	631	622	330	42	5	2664
2001	156	368	584	614	638	381	52	12	2649
2011	262	341	571	628	637	393	62	7	2639

Source: Primary Census Abstracts of Various Census reports.

As seen in the Table 1, the number of villages dropped from 3345 to 2639 by 2011. In above 10,000 populations category it is increased from one to twelve and further dropped to seven in the latest Census 2011. In the process of urbanisation, many villages have amalgamated into towns. As per the official definition, the number of towns may appear less in number, but the urban lifestyle has annexed almost all the Mandal head quarters. Even the tribal Mandal headquarters are also reflecting the urban life style.

Demography: The changing pattern of the population can be seen from this table below.

As per 1971 census, the population of this district was 25.89 lakhs. In 2011, it has reached 38.55 lakhs. The urban share is steadily increasing till 1991. It has dropped slightly in 2001. However, there is a fundamental shift in the population growth rate in 2011 census. Population growth rate of the present Srikakulam besides Vizianagaram districts (part of the area is in my research) is recorded as 6.38 and 4.10 respectively. One of the lowest growth rates has been recorded in Vizianagaram district. Urban growth has been recorded as 16.31 in the existing Srikakulam District and rural growth rate has been recorded as 4.66. Urban growth has been recorded as 12.39 in Vizianagaram District and rural growth rate has been recorded as 2.25.

Social Composition of the District: Till the proclamation of independence, four caste—Brahmin, Kshatriya, Velama Doras (hereafter upper castes) and Hill zamindars with their power on the means of production ruled the district. This continued for two decades even after independence. Except Hill Zamindars (Kurupam Zamindar was the only exception) all the upper castes exhibited feudal oppression on these peasant castes.

Legal landlordism was abolished with "The Madras estate abolition and conversion into Ryotwari Act, 1948, the A.P. Inam abolition Act, 1956, and Minor Inam abolition Act". Litigations and agitations, sustained as they were, replaced the four ruling castes and Kalingas, Koppulavelama, Toorpukapu and Polinativelama (hereafter peasant castes) usurped into the space. They are numerous and a section of them had ushered into economic hegemony, which led them to the centre of power, local and central. All the four castes are listed

Table 2. Trends in the Urban and Rural Population

Census Year	*Population Break Up*					
	Urban	*Rural*	*Total Male*	*Total Female*	*Grand Total*	*Percentage of Urban*
1971	275720	2314271	1279085	1310906	2589991	10.65
1981	350561	2525299	1425311	1450549	2875860	12.19
1991	458661	2913725	1678784	1693602	3372386	13.60
2001	446343	3213503	1816996	1841850	3658846	12.20
2011	630606	3228629	1913522	1945773	3859235	16.34

Source: Compiled from various census reports of India, Primary census abstracts.

Table 3. Social Composition in Parliament

Sl. No	*Year of the general election*	*Total seats in parliament*	*Reserved seats*	*Net seats*	*Kalinga*	*T.K*	*KV*	*P.V*	*Backward castes other than these 4*	*SC*	*ST*	*St/hill zamindars*	*OC*	*Representation of four peasant castes from general seats*	*Percentage of representation of four peasant castes*
1.	1971	3	1	2	1	1	0	0	0	0	1	0	0	2	100
2.	1977	3	1	2	1	0	0	0	0	0	0	1	1	1	50
3.	1980	3	1	2	1	0	0	0	0	0	0	1	1	1	50
4.	1984	3	1	2	1	0	0	0	0	0	0	1	1	1	50
5.	1989	3	1	2	1	1	0	0	0	0	0	1	0	2	100
6.	1991	3	1	2	1	0	0	0	0	0	0	1	1	1	50
7.	1996	3	1	2	0	1	0	1	0	0	0	1	0	2	100
8.	1998	3	1	2	0	1	0	1	0	0	0	1	0	2	100
9.	1999	3	1	2	0	1	0	1	0	0	1	0	0	2	100
10.	2004	3	1	2	0	1	0	1	0	0	0	1	0	2	100
11.	2009	3	1	2	1	1	0	0	0	0	0	1	0	2	100

Source: Various election results compiled fromwww.eci.gov.in
T.K: Toorpukapu: K.V: Koppulavelama: P.V: Polinativelama

as "backward castes" quite long thereafter in the 70s. Understandably enough, most of the local bodies, some through the "reserved" route aided by law and the other through unreserved route were aided by their numerical strength. A look at the list of people's representatives proves that vast and most majorities of the representative positions were held by these four castes, courtesy, their numerical strength. While ownership on land was the determining factor in those early days, wealth was acquired through education and business decides now, the road to power. The other backward castes lived up to their categorisation and never have been able to touch the wall of majesty.

The representation of these peasant castes can be seen from these tables. The table 3 shows the representation of these peasant castes in various elections.

In all these elections, apart from these peasant castes, only two other castes represented the assembly. Sompeta constituency represented with Gouda caste. Goutu Latchanna and his son represented this constituency until 2009. Latchanna fought for the peasantry and strived hard for the backward caste reservations. Because of this, this seat has almost been reserved to his family till 2009. In the restructuring, this seat has altered and this family lost the election. Now for the first time, another backward community of fisher folk, is representing the seat.

One cannot draw conclusion that all the peasant castes have equal share in representing the legislature irrespective of their class. Micro level analysis reveals that some constituencies are reserved for two families. Therlam, Amudalavalasa, Narasannapeta, Parvatipuram, Vunukuru, Harishchandrapuram, Bobbili are almost reserved for two families. The innumerable backward castes cannot even touch the walls of the legislature.

Inequalities galore at us in the selected villages as well. Lot of uneven development is on the village record. This unevenness is among the villages and the same castes. Many villages are remote even now and do not have an access to reach. The villagers of such village carry the patients in swing cots even today. Many villages are not having safe drinking water. Villagers particularly in tribal areas are perishing because of drinking impure water. Many villages have nominal representation in education and employment. At the same time, there are many villages which are denied to take part in the development sphere. In the coastal areas, some villages are reflecting the Teutonic lifestyle while some are representing the sophisticated urban lifestyle. Adjacent villages, Nuvvularevu is representing the first stream of life while Manchineellapeta is representing the other. Even in plains, these vast differences are prevailing. Piridi and Chitrakotaboddavalasa are situated in Bobbili Mandal. The distance from Bobbili is 10 kilometres to these villages. While one is towards east, the other is towards west. But in the development parlance, those villages have vast differences. While Piridi is considered as one of the developed villages in the district, the other represents the quite opposite stream. Both the villages are representing Koppulavelama caste. Piridi

Table 4. Social Composition in Legislative Assembly

Sl. No.	*Year of General Election*	*Total Seats*	*Reserved Seats*	*Net Seats*	*Kalinga*	*T.K*	*K.V*	*P.V*	*Total*	*Other Backward Castes*	*Percentage of Representation of Four Peasant Castes*
1.	1972	19	5	14	4	3	2	2	11	1	78.57
2.	1978	18	5	13	5	2	3	1	11	1	84.62
3.	1983	18	5	13	3	2	3	3	11	0	84.62
4.	1985	18	5	13	1	3	3	3	10	2	76.92
5.	1989	18	5	13	2	3	3	3	11	1	84.62
6.	1994	18	5	13	1	2	3	3	9	2	69.23
7.	1999	18	5	13	2	2	3	3	10	1	76.92
8.	2004	18	5	13	2	3	1	3	9	1	69.23
9.	2009	15	5	10	3	2	0	2	7	1	70.00

Source: Various election results compiled from:www.eci.gov.in

sent representative to assembly and person from this village got ministerial berth in the cabinet. Education played a crucial role in the village. Quite contrary to this, the peasant castes of Chitrakotaboddavalas even lost their land to settlers and the educated elite of peasant castes. Even in Piridi, the development is uneven. Broadly speaking, Koppulavelama caste has got all the fruits of development. Even in Koppulavelama, 2/3rd of families are out of the ambit of this development. The same situation can be seen in Kalinga dominated villages.

Kanugulavalasa and Chintalapeta are situated in Amudalavalasa Mandal. The distance from Amudalavalasa is two kilometres to Kanugulavalasa and six kilometres to Chintalapeta. But in the development parlance those villages have vast differences. While Kanugulavalasa is considered as one of the developed villages in the Mandal, the other represents the quite opposite stream. Both the villages are representing Kalinga caste. Education played a crucial role in the village. Quite contrary to this, the peasant castes of Chintalapeta could not get their share in education and employment. The political awareness in Kanugulavalasa lifted the village and secured the results.

These are not mere examples but in respect of all these peasant castes, the development process has created class in the caste structure. But in the absence of class awareness, these castes are playing crucial role in the district. The elite are leading "their" masses.

Almost 2/3rd of these peasant castes are languishing. But they are taking part in the social oppression of other backward castes and on dalits. In fact, the sections are becoming a tool in the elite sections of the peasantry to fulfil the aspirations of those sections. Many backward castes are almost out of this development process. Dalits and scheduled tribes did not even dream about this development.

This district is famous for handloom industry. Weaver's community flourished sometime in the history and now they are almost perished in the sense of economic angle. In Korasavada village and in some villages, some parsons developed as local leadership but those are rare examples. As a social group, they are pauperised and left the villages. They have left their houses and migrated. Their houses are in dilapidated condition. In the villages surveyed, the houses of Brahmins and weavers are in similar condition. Those houses were deserted and decayed.

Sir Henry Maine conducted a detailed survey on Indian villages and he made a comparative study with the villages of West. He gave six lectures in Oxford University and those were compiled and a book titled "Village Communities—East and West" was published. He stated that these micro level studies cannot represent the entire situation and proclaimed that this type of research is conducive to understand the macro picture. The Indian Council of Agricultural of Reserach while studying Raebareli district expressed the same opinion. The micro level data of Srikakulam district may help the researchers to understand the situation that prevailed in this District and to compare the data to that of macro level.

The sections of society that was enchained to the feudal, semi-feudal forces had no chance to sell their labour freely and it went on unabated almost till 1948. Velama, Kshatriya and Brahmin castes were the oppressive caste over others which continued legally till 1948. Aided by statute, peasant castes fought against these oppressive castes and started reasoning and questioning. This angered the consciousness the powerful oppressors who resorted to assaults and murders. Lack of numerical strength and the statutory protection to the other side forced the oppressive castes to eat the humble pie willy-nilly. Affluent and powerful sections of the peasant castes that inherited the brahminical order have been able to retain the poor among their own social groups. These new powerful sections continued the legacy of oppression against the other and lower social groups which included Dalits.

Peasant castes have an added advantage because of their number. The verbal section with the support of "their" mass enjoyed the supremacy over the remaining people almost for 30 years.

Barring some, almost all the castes are listed as backward castes in this district. All these peasant castes belong to this category. Lot of inequalities prevailed among these castes and even in the same social group. Though there is lot of class variations among these peasant castes, they have unanimity in crushing the artisans, castes of servitude and dalits.

In 1983, the carpenters requested the Koppulavelama for hike in their wages in Piridi village. They turned down their request and almost implemented social boycott and imported the carpenters from other villages. Both the castes belonged to backward castes (B.C.). Carpenter caste belongs to B.C. "B" category and Koppulavelama belongs to B.C. "D" category. In Karivalasa village during 1990, the barbers asked the peasantry to pay the wages in cash instead of in kind. Here also Piridi story repeated. Barber caste belongs to B.C. "A" category. These are not stray examples. With the massive support from their fellow caste people, the peasant castes humiliated and intimidated the people of these vulnerable castes when they tried to get some genuine share of their labour.

Their intimidation on Dalits has no frontier. This is discussed in a separate chapter.

Agriculture cannot sustain on its own. It is just like an industry. The peasant castes have not exhibited this consciousness and they attributed supremacy to them. Many professions played unsung hero role in this flourishing of the industry. The landowning communities tried to write the history inversely. They thought that all these artisans, agrarian labours are surviving on them. In this process, they have dubbed these sections as insignificant and considered their professions with meanness. The rich peasantry of these peasant castes extracted the huge surplus value. Apart from this, economic and social intimidation has been implemented on these sections. All these processes invariably stimulated the remaining backward castes and in Dalits.

Feudal and semi-feudal setup normally tied the labour with the landlord classes. They are subject to massive social and economic oppression. It suffocates the labour and they have no "freedom" to sell their labour at their will. But the capitalist relations in the form of transport, education, media besides opportunities in service and manufacturing sector rapidly changed the scene. The semi-serf model servant freed him or herself and travelled to unknown places for selling their labour as commodity.

This process hampered the cultivation in the villages. The rich peasantry, the agitators of some streams are christening it as agrarian crisis and expressing dissatisfaction over the dynamics of the development. These streams are arguing for village centred development. They are arguing for rejuvenation of villages in the old model. In this process, they are trying to turn the wheel back. For all these years, the rich peasantry and landlords expropriated the surplus value of these innumerable mass. With this, they have profiteered and they have put part of this investment in education. Thus, these sections converted the education as social capital. The progeny of these sections settled in urban centres initially and subsequently they crossed the national boundaries. On the other hand, the offspring of these vulnerable sections have freed themselves from the clutches of this oppression and travelling to faraway places in search of work. In this process, they are converting their labour as commodity. The rich peasantry is baffled with this and crying desperately to stick to the fields as agrarian labour. They are not even bothering about the migration of their children and they are not requesting them to settle in villages. However, they are more worried about the migration of the children of rural proletarian. They are dubbing them as absconders from the worksite. They are expressing that these workmen have become lethargic and they are not willing to do manual labour in the sunshine. In fact, the progeny of this rich peasantry grabbed the opportunities created by capitalist uneven development and working from air conditioned rooms. On the other hand, the sons of the soil are settling in the urban slums and waiting in the streets to sell their labour.

From all these development processes, some issues have been clarified. Capitalists brought development and inequalities in a large-scale. In fact, these two are Siamese-twins in this process. The fruits of development broadly reached to the rich peasantry of the villages and gravity of inequality has swelled. However, the rural proletarian has broadly relieved from the clutches of semi-feudal oppression. Slave like rural proletarian has been relatively converted as freedmen to sell their only commodity left with them.

Official census records revealed the same fact. In 2011 census, lowest population growth has been recorded in Vangara Mandal of this district. Ironically, highest population growth also has been recorded in Pedagantyada Mandal of adjacent Visakhapatnam district. Though Pedagantyada has been recorded as "Rural Mandal," it is almost a part of Visakhapatnam. This shows that the rural proletarian irrespective of their caste are settling side by side in the slums of Visakhapatnam.

This fact has been proved from the swelling of population in Visakhapatnam. In 1991, the number of official slums in Visakhapatnam was 141. By the turn of 2011 census, it rose to mammoth 741. The city of destiny has infamous title of having highest percentage of slum dwellers in India. 44.1 per cent of the households of the city of destiny are in slums. Official estimates indicate that the total population of Visakhapatnam is 17,30,220. Out of this 8,20,000 are living in slums. Almost half of the people are slum dwellers. Major portion of this population are migratory birds of north Andhra comprising Srikakulam, Vizianagaram and Visakhapatnam districts. There is a saying that "Death is the leveller". The truth of the saying is unknown but the people belonging to various social layers are physically settled alongside to get their livelihood.

The list of surveyed villages and the parameters for selecting the villages are given in Annexure I.

As discussed, there were lot of variations in the development. Development brought unevenness among the villagers and in the villages. It brings unevenness among the social groups. Inter and Intra layer unevenness is the order of the day. However, some villages have specific characteristics even in the rocket age. They resemble almost clan life. In the surveyed villages Nuvvularevu, a coastal village in Vajrapukotturu Mandal resembles almost a clan lifestyle.

Kyoto clan is professionally fisher folk. They speak Odiya. While Odisha state was formed in 1936, these parts remained with the then Vizagapatam district. They decided to not to return to Odisha but settled here only. The population of this village as per national Marine census 2010 is 6,026.

Before the emergence of capitalist methods in the sea-fishing, this clan practically lived on the sea for their livelihood. Mechanisation throws them as fish out of the water. In late 70s, government gave one fibre boat for them for fishing purpose. They rejected the boat and cited that it would bring inequalities among the villagers.

Though there is Panchayati Raj system in the village, the village council plays a vital role in the village administration. People elect this council whenever necessary. The head of this council belongs to Beharas and in fact, it is the Beharas who formed this village. Villagers always have a recall right and they have a right to terminate the head of the village council. This kind of occasions keeps occurring in this village.

On every Independence Day, the president unfurls the National Flag not only at Panchayat building but also at village council meeting hall. In 2008, the president did not unfurl it at village council office. Immediately the village council assembled and terminated him from the post.

Their integration in taking decisions is unique. In 2006, the post of Mandal Parishad territory councillor (MPTC) was reserved for backward castes. Kyoto clan has no reservation. Hence, they gave it to one barber. Subsequently the sarpanch post was also reserved to backward caste. In fact, 99 per cent of the villagers belong to Kyoto. Hence, they boycotted the election and government are managing the village with a special officer.

In fact, there is a reservation in Odisha and Andhra Pradesh government did not recognise them as backward castes. They fought tooth and nail for the reservation. Even the legislature committee of Odisha state toured this village and requested the Andhra Pradesh government to include them in the list but by the conclusionof my survey, they were told that they were not included in the list. Subsequently, the villagers informed that they have been included in the list.

They have their own tradition and culture. Marriage is also not performed as per the wishes of the individuals. Marriages take place for five years. For every five years, they group the youth and perform marriages on one Dias. The village itself get transformed as wedding venue. Now the period is reduced to three years. They will not accept the entry of a bus to the village for 14 days during the marriage. There is no dowry. The acceptance by the parents of the bride is a pre-condition for the marriage. As they lost their occupation, the women of Kyoto clan used to purchase the fish and sell the fish in around the villages. As per the stipulation, the women should reach the village before sunset in any circumstances. Otherwise, the village council will penalise them and council will not allow them to enter the village. Now the time limit has been extended up to 10 pm.

The youth of Kyoto is on the way to migrate due to loss of occupation. The modernity in the shape of migration entered the village. Future will determine the sustainability of this clan type lifestyle in the wake of the modernity.

Village's Self-sufficiency

Lot of stories were heard about village self-sufficiency in fable stories. They told us about the golden age of villages. Bunches of books are available to disseminate about Ramaraajya that prevailed in India. They told us about the welfare state and flourishing of all the people irrespective of their class and creed. As seen from history, it appears that the concept itself is fake and concocted. There is no alternative to condemn this concocted fact except to study the history in an unemotional way. As seen from the various books, it is understood that the golden era is a myth.

Though it is problematic to readers, it is inevitable to quote extensively from various authors and official records to shatter this false conception of self-sufficiency.

Bernier travelled in India during Mogul age and wrote a book. It reads, *"It is certain that the number of these slaves was most unreasonable; he had purchased them extremely cheap on account of the famine, and it is also said that his servants had stolen a great many children."* (Travels in Mogul empire: A.D.1656-1658: Page 151: Francois Bernier)

A civil servant Romesh C. Dutt after studying various official reports compiled a book on famines in India, he gave dateline of the famines that occurred during 1860-1900. He narrated 10 severe famines in a row, and some of the statistics are reproduced here. *"Famine of 1860 in Northern India.: It was a wide-spread famine, and the loss of life was estimated at 200,000, but was probably very much larger. Famine of 1866 in Orissa: One-third of the population of Orissa, or about a million people, died of this famine. Famine of 1869 in Northern India. The loss of life was estimated at 1,200,000. Famine of 1877 in Madras: The Land Tax of Madras is heavy, and is enhanced from time to time, and the people are poor and resource less. Five millions of them perished from this famine. Famine of 1900 in the Punjab, Rajputana, the Central Provinces, and Bombay. The most widespread famine ever known in India. The number of persons relieved rose to six millions in the worst months. In Bombay the sufferers in the famine camps "died like flies," as was remarked by Sir A.P. MacDonnell, President of the Famine Commission."* (Indian famines: their causes and prevention: Page 1 and 2: Romesh C. Dutt)

These were some of the famines pertaining to the British colonial period. The period before the advent of colonial rule was also not an exception. Peter Mundey travelled in India during Mogul period and he recorded the famines and pathetic incidents of that era. He travelled in India in 1630 from Surat to Agra. Theodore Morison quoted extensively from this work in his book titled Economic transition in India. It reads *"14/A November 1630.—Wee came to Kirka, apooretownehalfe burnt upp, and almost voyd of Inhabitants, the most part fledd, the rest dead, lyeing in the Streets and on the Tombes.*

16th November 1630.—In this place (Dayta) the men and women were driven to that extremitie for want of food, that they sold their Children for 12d., 6d. and pence a peace.

18th November 1630.—From Baadoore wee came to Netherbarre (12 Course), a greate place, where wee were much troubled to finde a roome convenient for our little Tent, by reason of the number of dead bodyes that lay scattered in and about the Towne. Att last wee tookeupp our lodginge among the Tombes.

Noelesse lamentable was it to see the poore people scrapeinge on the dunghille for food, yea, in the very excrements of beasts, as horses, oxen, belonginge to Travellers, for graine that perchaunce might come undigested from them." (Economic transition in India: Page 108, 109)

These famines tell about north India. W. Foster wrote a book "English factories in India". It recorded the famines that occurred in South India. Morrison quoted these famines. It reads *"Mesulipatam and Armagore was sorely opprest with famine, the liveinge eating up the dead and men scarsly durst travel in the country for fear they should be killed and eaten." (Ibid:* page 112)

Now the historians praise the Shahjehan rule as a golden age. Abdul Hamidlahri recorded the awful picture of that era. It reads *"In the present year (A.D. 1630) also there had been a deficiency in the bordering countries, and a total want in the Dekhan and Guzarat. The inhabitants of these two countries were reduced to the direst extremity. Life was offered for a loaf (Jane banane), but none would buy; rank was to be sold for a cake, but none cared for it; the ever bounteous hand was now stretched out to beg for food, and the feet which had always trodden the way contentment walked about only in search of sustenance. For a long time dogs flesh was sold for goats flesh, and the pounded bones of the dead were mixed with flour and sold. Destitution at length reached such a pitch that men began to devour each other, and the flesh of a son was preferred to his love. The numbers of the dying caused obstructions in the roads, and every man whose dire sufferings did not terminate in death, and who retained the power to move, wandered off to the towns and villages of other countries." (Ibid:* Page 107,108)

The colonial government appointed many famine commissions to unearth the problems. Calcutta University compiled all these reports and published a work. It reads "*We have found no reason to believe that the agricultural population of India have at any known period of their history been generally free from debt'. The cultivator (in the absence of any power of obtaining loans on the security of his holding) was never deeply involved, he was seldom free from debt, and lived the life of a contented serf, exempt from the risks and responsibilities which accompany the possession of independent rights, but also without any stimulus to raise himself or improve his position".* (Agricultural indebtedness in India: Page: 20 and 21 official reports compiled by S.C. Ray)

As described The Indian peasant was a contended slave at that period. Then it is easy to imagine the life of "the slaves of the slave". The slaves of the slave were none other than rural proletarian.

Alexander Fraser Tytler worked as a judge in West Bengal and he did an extraordinary research on the socio, economic conditions. He wrote, *"In Zillah Kishengharh, in the year 1809, the situation of this Ryots was reqlly shocking. The wretched Ryots pushed their lands to the very utmost, took advances from three or four indigo factors at once, besides those from their own Mahajauns, and when no longer able to borrow money, they were compelled either to steel,in order to subsist their families, or fly their native villages to look for kind masters. A native who has long been resident of a place, or perhaps been borne there, must be very hard pushed before he will leave the village that has become so dear to him: and yet we shall see, that in this Zillah, whole villagers were deserted,—the inhabitants flying they knew not where."* (Considerations on the present political state of India: Page 366 and 367: Alexander Fraser Tytler)

The British colonial government directed the authorities to record the past famines in the Bombay presidency. Colonel Ethiridge recorded that the first famine officially recorded in the books took place in 1527. Every page of this book revealed the dreadful atmosphere that prevailed in India during the pre-colonial and colonial period. The reports recorded that one of the main reasons for the famines were *"The general condition of the country is not favourable for storing grain in large quantities. Its produce is not sufficient for its consumption."* (Report on past famines in Bombay presidency: Page 21)

It recorded, *"1813, was a year of great distress, which was felt in all parts of the country. In the commencement of the famine many died of hunger, and many sold their children for food."* (Report on past famines in Bombay presidency: Page 26)

South was also not an exception to the famines. In one of the incidents it recorded, *Captain (afterwards Colonel) Walter Campbell, who was an eyewitness, describes the horrors of the famine at Masulipatam in the centre of the Kistna delta. He states: "It is dreadful to see what revolting food human beings may be driven to partake of. Dead dogs and horses are greedily devoured by these starving wretches; and the other day an unfortunate donkey having strayed from the fort, they fell upon him like a pack of, wolves, tore him limb from limb and devoured him on the spot."* (Memorandum on the progress of Madras presidency during forty years of British administration: Page 27: S. Srinivas Raghavaiyangar)

Theodor Morrison concluded on the causes of famine and the root cause of the famines and it reads, "*Dearth or famine at irregular intervals was inseparable from the conditions which determined the old economic order. The village was isolated, and therefore entirely dependent for its supplies of food upon the produce of its own fields; as the seasons are nowhere invariably propitious, the harvests occasionally failed, and when they failed the population dependent on them necessarily starved. The industrial revolution has so completely transformed life in Western Europe that we find it hard to realise that such things were, and that our forefathers lived in perpetual fear of famine. It is to a continental country like France that we must look for an exact parallel to India. France continued to suffer from recurring famines until the close of the eighteenth century. If such was the case in France, it is not surprising that India, furnished by nature with far fewer facilities for transport, should have suffered from famine from time immemorial. It is sometimes asserted that famines in the past were less severe and less frequent than in the present. Such an assertion proceeds from sheer ignorance; there is not a title of historical evidence to support it. Famines are recorded from the very dawn of India history. In the Jataka Books they are referred to as one of the incidents of life in those days"* (Economic transition in India: Page 92-125)

Gandhi shattered the arguments about the golden age of Indian villages and he wrote, *"the villages were impoverished in the colonial rule. They were in desperate condition. There was no sufficient food for the villagers and cattle. The death rate is so high in the villages. They had not any resistance power against the diseases."* (Khadi Arthasastram: Page 432: Gandhi)

All these recorded evidences cleared one aspect only. Even if we go back to Vedas, there was no evidence of any golden age. The myriad peasants were engaged to work in their field and in remitting taxes, interests on the principal in different shapes and leading the life with a shortage of food because of the low productivity. The state, the moneylender community and the bureaucracy quelled the peasantry and labour in a ruthless manner. Peasantry used to leave their land to avoid the tax burden. People used to flee from their dwellings to stay away from the feudal oppression. There was no research on agriculture and almost the agriculture runs on rain-gods. In the absence of transportation facility, the people faced famine and deaths.

People invariably took barks and leaves of the trees to sustain in the famine. The assumed golden age created cannibalism. While taking the painful life of the present era, some are preaching about the glory of the past. Nothing prevailed in the past for the immeasurable people of this land. The golden age was only for kings and feudal lords. The digging of layers of history will reveal the fact. The kings, feudal lords and colonial rulers crushed the peasantry and labour alike. We can see the traces of this ruthless exploitation and the music of death from the past. The people of different sections and classes were forced to perish because of the starvation. At the most, we can trace the remnants of skeletons of the oppressed but not the traces of the golden age.

2

Land

History is the conflict for hegemony over the land, replete with long waged battles and feuds for authority over the land, unequal distribution of land, the source of all wealth, has been the prime reason for unrest and wars. Land was synonymous to agriculture for a long time, till land was not a commodity. Some tribes share chunks of land with the new entrant in to the habitation even today when a square yard of land is out of reach in metropolis. Tribes moving out of forests and atop hills are forming new habitations. Paradoxically about a lakh acres of land is lying fallow in the district including land of marginal and small peasantry and land acquired for speculation, amid all the sonorous agitations for distribution of land.

The agrarian structure of India is terribly uneven as seen from the available data. The western scholars exhibited ardent enthusiasm in doing research about the agrarian structure that existed before the advent of colonial rule. Bernier, Elphinstone, Henry Maine, G. Campbel were some of them. A civil servant G. Campbel made extensive research on the issues. He proclaimed that his research area constrained mostly to the northern India. He also touched the south. He made a detailed note on the agrarian structure and agrarian relations that prevailed in India.

He has noted, *"I have formally explained that the Hindoo agriculturists from the first settled together in villages, and that the land, so far as use and possession went, was the property of him who first tilled it, subject to the payment of the proper rent to the government. This property in the land, however, only extending the possession of the soil actually cultivated, gave no right to the remaining waste lands, nor authority over any other cultivators who might be settled in them; and, the rent being excluded from the property, the mere right of cultivating (though it might be prized by those who had it, who had been bred on and were attached to the soil) could have little market value. This then is the lowest description of property in the soil, and amounts to little more than a sort of very strong tenant-right. It appears to have been the tenure of very ancient Hindoo times"* (Modern India: A sketch of the system of civil government, with some account of the natives and native institutions (here after Modern India): G. Campbel Page 82, 83)

He noted on the ownership of the land in the rural tribes, *"The democratic tribes have been mentioned as possessed of much stronger rights. With them the whole land of the country was divided among the different communities. They claimed the proprietor ship not only of the cultivated, but also of the uncultivated land, within their limits, and they had authority over, and certain superior rights in the land of any inferior holders cultivating on the original tenant right just described."* (Modern India: G. Campbel: Page 83)

He concluded from Elphinstone that the people collect the money and collectively pay the tax to the government.

Campbell has a different view on the collective farming of the land, but he expressed that the peasants made their individual cultivation on the parcels of land. He opined that the government has no ownership on the land, but it has a right to collect the tax on the land. He concluded that there were no intermediaries. He stated that there were several occupations prevailed in the villages. However, those people belong to the ancestral occupations have no ownership on land. They have to serve the people to get their livelihood. The communities were protecting their land from others with their combined effort.

Another researcher Sir Henry Maine noted that the British faced a lot of trouble in collecting the tax. *"When first, amid the general discredit of the experiment tried by lord Cornwallis in Bengal proper, The Indian administrators of fifty years or sixty years since began to recognise the village community, as the true proprietary unit of the country, they had very soon face the problem of rent."* (Village communities East and West: Henry Sumner Maine: Page 182, Lecture VI)

The circuit committee observed many aspects of the management in land and concluded that there was no ownership on the land in pre-colonial Indian society. Carmichael in his book Vizagapatam district manual widely quoted Sir Thomas Munro. Carmichael quoted his conclusion *"the revenue system in circars, as described by the committee, has a general resemblance to that of many of her provinces in India. The people had no property in land."* (A manual of the district of Vizagapatam in the Presidency of Madras: compiled and edited by D.F. Carmichael Page: 205): (Emphasis added)

Hence, the British imported European methods in tax collection into India. Usually in the villages, some person takes the role of collecting money to pay the tax. The British had created intermediary system in the land administration consciously. Thus, the permanent settlement paved the way for private ownership in the land. On the other hand, it created Ryotwari system and created many landowners. The essence of both the systems is nothing but creation of private property in land. Marx observed that both the systems jeopardised the life of Indian peasantry and remarked, *"The drawbacks of all these different systems accumulate upon him without his enjoying any of their redeeming features. The Ryot is subject, like the French peasant, to the extortion of the private usurer; but he has no hereditary, no permanent title in his land, like the French peasant. Like the serf he is forced to cultivation, but he is not secured against want like the serf. Like the* métayer *he has to divide his produce with the State, but the State is not obliged, with regard to him, to advance the funds and the stock, as it is obliged to do with regard to the* métayer. *In Bengal, as in Madras and Bombay, under the* Zamindari *as under the* Ryotwari, *the Ryots-and they form 11-12ths of the whole Indian population—have been wretchedly pauperised; and if they are, morally speaking, not sunk as low as the Irish cottiers, they owe it to their climate, the men of the South being possessed of less wants, and of more imagination than the men of the North.*"

Private Property on Land in Vizagapatam District

In Vizagapatam and Ganjam districts the British enforced permanent settlement in 1802 and 1804 respectively. In Vizagapatam district, except Golugonda and Sarvasiddhi taluks the remaining area was entirely settled permanently. In these taluks, also there were Zamindari villages. In Golugonda, there were 92 villages under the control of the Government whereas 65 villages of Sarvasiddhi taluk were under the Government. In Ganjam district excepting 457 villages, the whole land was permanently settled.

The private property on the land created havoc on this land and land was soaked with blood by number of rebellions. The peasants especially the Adivasis organised revolts and almost posed a threat to East India Company. The British crushed all these rebellions in a ruthless manner. Because of the limitations, it is not possible to provide a detailed description on all these revolts. In spite of this ruthless crushing the peasants and Adivasis conducted struggles against the Zamindari, Inamdari and Muttadari systems. With the prolonged agitations, the then Madras presidency government appointed a committee that headed by Tanguturi Prakasham pantulu. The committee extensively toured the presidency and recorded the depositions. Subsequently, the government abolished the Zamindari system in 1948 and Inamdari system in 1956. Because of this dissolution, the land was transferred to "officially recorded tenants" and large chunks of land were kept in the hands of zamindars. Normally these tenants belong to elite layer of the peasant castes. The proviso that prevailed in the Act itself was also a cause of uneven proprietorship on the land.

The clause reads, *"That the Land holdee has cultivated such lands himself, by his own servants, or by hired labour, with his own or hired stock, in the first day of July, 1945 and has been in direct as continuous possession of such lands from that date.*" (www.apland.ap.nic.in)

This clause has not stipulated any upper ceiling on the ownership on the land. The only condition is that he should cultivate land only. In the primitive management practices, nobody can cultivate land in excess of two acres. Hence the word by him or by his servants is incorporated. With this single word, the Zamindars and the large tenants on the "record" could own the vast chunks of land. The agricultural labour in general and the Dalits in particular witnessed the whole process in a hapless manner and remained landless. In essence, the single phrase "by his own servants or by his hired stock" has changed the agrarian relations in a big way. The private ownership on the land conferred on the "intellectual" traditional Zamindars and on the handful prominent tenants on records who are mostly belonging to peasant castes.

The word handful is proved in micro level study of the villages across the district. Since the space is constraint, it is possible to recount some of the examples.

Adavaram is a village under the Bobbili Zamindari settlement. The zamindar was exceptionally harsh and he was merciless in collecting tax. He used to raise the tax on his whims and pressures. The peasants resisted this hike and tried to fight against the rack-renting. The zamindar as usually wanted to crush the movement and in the course of struggle, peasants were imprisoned. The whole village fought against the zamindar, and this struggle was recorded in many history books. After the abolition of zamindaris, the whole land was distributed among 30 families. Out of these 27 families belong to peasant caste Toorpukapu and two titles were conferred on dalits and one was to artisan. Remaining families of all castes remained landless.

Ajjada is Brahmin Inamdari village. Brahmins have rights on the land, and the peasants belong to Koppulavelama caste. Twenty families of Koppulavelama community were the tenants on record. After the abolition of the Inamdaris, the land was transferred to these families, and the whole village excepting these families remained landless.

Mabagam village is situated in Polaki Mandal. This village is an Inamdari village, and Kandukuri satyavatamma was the owner of the Estate. Ten families of Polinativelama were the recorded tenants and the whole land was conferred on these tenants. In this transaction, one tenant got 600 acres of land and nine other tenants got 536 acres of land. Thus in place of one Kandukuri satyavatamma 10 families got complete rights on the land.

In light of this mammoth concentration of land, we must look at the implementation of the land reforms in general and in case of this village.

During my visit, retired village revenue officer told that the particulars of distribution of surplus lands are available with revenue records. To my question under RTI Act 2005, the officers reported that the total land distributed was 1.91 hectares, and out of this Dalits got 0.83 hectares and the peasant castes got 1.07 hectares.

Bontalakoduru is a village in Etcherla Mandal. Ankitam Jaggarao was the zamindar of this village. Interestingly, a Kshatriya named Nadimpalli Lingaraaju is the principal tenant, and he possessed under his tenancy to the tune of 447 hectares of land. Naturally, he got the tenancy rights and yet the whole land is rested with him only. During my visit, a retired revenue officer told that there were distribution of surplus lands in this village, but the person could retain the lands with him only. Surprisingly the revenue officers have stated that no distribution of the land took place in this village to the query under the RTI ACT.

This situation is not an isolated one. This phenomenon prevailed in India. The ministry of Rural development declared, "As per information received from States, 125.86 lakh tenants have got their rights protected over an area of 167.14 lakh acres".

With the abolition of intermediaries, zamindars could keep their lands to some extent, and on the other the recorded tenants of the peasant castes got ownership on the land. This situation is applicable to whole of India and in particular to this district. The zamindars and inamdars of this district belonged to four castes namely Brahmin. Kshatriya, Velamadora and Hill Zamindars. In this process of abolition because of their ignorance Hill zamindars totally lost their dominance on land. Most of the Brahmins also lost their lands. To sum-up the zamindars of Bobbili (Velama Dora) the Zamindar of Vizianagaram (Kshatriya) and the Hill zamindar of Kurupam could retain a portion of assets intact in their account. In this district, the dominant sections of the four peasant castes namely Koppulavelama, Kalinga, Polinativelama and Toorpukapu got ownership rights on the land. In this process majority families of the peasant castes and almost 100 per cent of Dalits could not get a parcel of land to their account.

In fact, in the abolition Act itself there were some exemptions, which were widely discussed in the literature. In fact, these exemptions were made to accumulate capital from the primary sector.

It can be construed from the various investigations that there was no property rights in the land. Now the situation has vastly changed. Because of the colonial policies, the private individual property in the land was established, and it is continuing. After the abolition of intermediaries, the recorded tenants belonging to higher strata of the peasant castes of those areas have become owners of the land. We have to make a microanalysis on the process that took place in this district.

Agrarian Structure

Even after the abolition of intermediaries, the unrest is prevailed and the broad masses are left with no land. It sowed the seeds of dissension among the people. This resulted in the enactment of land reforms in India. These were implemented in two phases. The first phase of land reforms those initiated in 1961 was ended in flake. With these reforms, no significant land was declared surplus and the distribution figures indicate that these were fruitless. The planning commission reports also drew the same conclusion. Again, the Andhra Pradesh government brought forward another round of land reforms in the year 1972. This Act fixed an upper ceiling to the lands. The results of these reforms are widely discussed in the chapter Dalits.

It is a known fact that most of the land holders created fake titles in the name of relatives, friends and even on their attached labour. Hence, the surplus land is very meagre to cater to needs of the needy. Economists expect that the land is being divided for every 15 years by virtue of hereditary rights. Sixty years are passed after this abolition of intermediaries. Hence, it can be drawn that, in those terms the land is divided among the family members for four times in this district. Because of all this immensity of the peasants are remained as marginal and small peasants in this district.

Land Records and Agricultural Statistics

Revenue authorities conducted a comprehensive land survey after the abolition of intermediaries. As seen from the records, the department conducted a survey in 1948 and issued titles. It is understood from this study that was the first and final survey on this land. The peasants secured the record of rights because of this survey only.

In Andhra Pradesh, local officials used to administer land records. The posts are inherited. Karanam and Munsab were the village revenue officers. Karanam used to establish the revenue records, whereas the Munsab used to administer Law and order. The villagers of the surveyed village told that at that time, the maintenance of the records were, in a proper way. As understood from the conversations, these two officers are the tools of the feudal oppression in the villages. The revenue village is the basic unit of in Indian land administration. There are some problems in the ownership of the lands. "In land records there are three categories of entries. These are called L1, L2 and L3. If peasant A of B village has land in the Village B his name is entered in L1 register. If the peasant A has land in C village his name is entered in L2 register. If peasant D of E village has lands in this village B his name is entered in the L3 register." (Interview with T. Prakasharao, Retired deputy Tehsildar)

The Andhra Pradesh government abolished this village administration and now the posts are on selection basis. Villagers told that the correctness in the records is lacking after this abolition. At the same time people are expressing that, they are relieved from the clutches of feudal oppression. I have also observed that the land records and the particulars in the records are not reflecting the actual position. 1B register is one of the basic records in the revenue administration. Officers are not updating the records time to time. Even the peoples who are no more are also being shown as landowners in these records. The information provided by the revenue authorities to the question under RTI Act has not reflected the ground level reality in any of the village. The authorities are not updating the records time to time. It appears that even the villagers are disinterested to disclose the changes to the machinery. It appears that the employees are not sufficient in number.

The state government appointed Koneru Rangarao committee to look into the land related matters. The Committee had expressed deep concern about this lacuna and commented, *"The Land committee notes with regret that the*

Land administration over the last decade has gradually weakened to a virtual state of paralysis today". (Land committee report: Koneru Rangarao committee: Page 5)

The central government appointed an expert committee, and it has submitted report namely "Report of the Committee on state agrarian relations and the unfinished task in land reforms". In this report, the committee expressed concern about dire condition that prevailed all over India. It commented, *"To further aggravate the situation is the inconsistencies in land records. Thus, there is visible lack of a long-term perspective towards land. In the present context of aggressive market forces, the absence of a clear land policy addressing the multiple uses of land is bound to jeopardize the interests of landless and the land poor"*. (Report of the Committee on state agrarian relations and the unfinished task in land reforms Page: 13)

The same committee added further, *"The land management continues largely in the pre-independence mode, and it is the common experience that the record-of-rights do not reflect the ground situation. The purpose of the revisional survey and settlement operations was to update the record-of-rights and revise the rent rolls to extract the maximum for the State. Even where the survey operations have been conducted, instead of being completed in the stipulated four years, they have dragged on for more than 40 years in some cases thereby rendering the new records already obsolete. The need for mapping of land parcels and for accurate and updated land records to support the rights of the weak, and for a host of other reasons that facilitate effective land reforms, systematic management of land records is very essential."* (Report of the Committee on state agrarian relations and the unfinished task in land reforms Page: 14)

As seen from the available statistics one can draw two logical conclusions. The systematic process of division of the land by virtue of law of inheritance majority of land holdings is marginal and small. Interestingly, this process leads to the concentration of land in few hands. The first aspect is glaring, and the second aspect is in concealment. The regular process of this division made the peasantry of this district to reach a state of hapless situation. This situation is warranting them to sell their land. From this situation, land has become a commodity. The land is transferring to the hands those who have the capital to manage the agriculture. Many people are purchasing the land. Migrants from coastal districts and the people of natives particularly from peasant castes who transformed the education as social capital are among them. However, the vast chunks of land holding are concealed because of the land reform Acts in vogue. The persons who have the requisite logistic strength to carry out the cultivation could keep the land, and in the absence of the required logistical support, the land is being alienated from the hands of the peasantry. Largely as seen from the villages the peasants belong to four peasant castes namely Kalinga, Koppulavelama, Toorpukapu and Polinativelama are the landowners. The immeasurable people belong to numerous castes are remained landless.

The magnitude of the alienated land cannot be ascertained from the available records in the case of peasant castes as in dalits and tribes since there are no separate statistics for these castes.

Changing Landholding Pattern in the National Level

In the colonial period broadly there were three types of land holding. In the princely states the entire rule was being carried out by the princely Rulers. In the British India, the rights on the land rested with Zamindars in Zamindari areas and the rights on the land rested with Ryots in Ryotwari areas. The concentration of land in the few hands can be seen from the writings of M.N. Roy, *"Of the 17,328 big landowners, 700 are classed in the category of Native States. Their chiefs are called Feudatory or Protected Wards of the British Government. One-third of the area of the entire country or 709,555 square miles, is governed by these Chiefs, and is known as Native India. The biggest of these States is Hyderabad, or the Nizam's Dominions, which equals Italy in area, with 13,500,000 population. The smallest is limited to only five villages."* (India in Transition : Page 18: M.N. Roy)

The census of 1911 puts the number of the first class at 224,000,000. Of these, only eight and a half million lived on agricultural rent; i.e., belonged to the landholding class who took no part in actual production. All the rest were cultivators of the soil. (India in Transition: Page 51: M.N. Roy)

In British India alone, 195,000,000 acres are held by Zemindars (temporary) 122,000,000 acres (permanent) of the entire area of 614,000,000 acres." (India in Transition: Page 64: M.N. Roy)

The merger of the princely states and Zamindars changed this concentration in other way round. New forces emerged in the agrarian sector and the concentration of land has taken a new shape. The first official landholding statistics have come into existence in 1970. The Table is giving a comprehensive picture about the changing landholding pattern in India in the last 40 years.

As seen from the table the marginal holdings have shown a steady increase in the number. In the year 1970 itself they were half in the total number. By 2011, their percentage rose to 67.05 in other words 67.05 per cent of the peasantry is making their livelihood on a mere 22.43 per cent of land. On the other, the extreme end the large holders appear to be decreased in number and in percentage. They formed 3.90 per cent in 1970 and they controlled a whooping 30.88 per cent of land. By 2011, their percentage dropped to 0.71. However, the land concentration is increased when compared with 1970 in the year 2011 they were controlling 10.25 per cent.

On the other the medium and semi-medium peasantry is enjoying good portions of land in a consistent manner. Their duo is maintaining their share in an unswerving manner. In fact this layer is strengthened in a period of 40 years in the countryside. The medium holdings are dropped from 11.17 in 1970 to a mere 4.24 per cent in 2011. However, their share in the land is gone unabated. They are controlling almost a quarter of total land in the year 2011.

Table 1: Changing Land Holding Pattern in India From 1970-2011

All India AGL Census data from 1970-2005:[Holdings in '000][Land in '000 hectares]

	Medium (4 to 10 Hectares)				*Large (>10 Hectares)*				*Total Holdings*		*Total Land*	
Years	*Holdings*	*Per cent*	*Land*	*Per cent*	*Holdings*	*Per cent*	*Land*	*Per cent*		*Per cent*		*Per cent*
1970	36200	50.24	14559	8.98	13432	18.91	19282	11.89	10681	15.04	29999	18.50
1975	44523	54.58	17509	10.72	14728	18.06	20905	12.80	11666	14.30	32428	19.85
1980	50122	56.40	19735	12.05	16072	18.08	23169	14.14	12455	13.99	34645	21.15
1985	56147	57.79	22042	13.39	17922	18.45	25708	15.62	13252	13.64	36666	22.28
1990	63389	59.44	24894	15.04	20092	18.84	28827	17.42	13923	13.06	38375	23.19
1995	71179	62.88	28121	17.21	21643	18.73	30722	18.81	14261	12.34	38953	23.85
2000	75408	62.88	29814	18.70	22695	18.92	32139	20.16	14021	11.69	38193	23.96
2005	83694	64.77	32026	20.23	23930	18.52	33101	20.91	14127	10.93	37898	23.94
2011	92217	67.05	35364	22.43	24670	17.94	35087	22.25	13183	10.04	37471	23.76

All India AGL Census data from 1970-2005:[Holdings in '000][Land in '000 hectares]

	Medium (4 to 10 Hectares)				*Large (>10 Hectares)*				*Total Holdings*	*Total Land*
Years	*Holdings*	*Per cent*	*Land*	*Per cent*	*Holdings*	*Per cent*	*Land*	*Per cent*		
1970	7932	11.17	48234	29.75	2766	3.90	50064	30.88	71011	162138
1975	8212	10.07	49628	30.38	2440	2.99	42873	26.25	81569	163343
1980	8068	9.08	48543	29.64	2166	2.44	37705	23.02	88883	163797
1985	7916	8.15	47144	28.65	1918	1.97	33002	20.05	97155	164562
1990	7580	7.11	44752	26.93	1654	1.55	28659	17.32	106638	165507
1995	7092	6.14	41398	25.34	1404	1.21	24160	14.79	115579	163354
2000	6577	5.48	38217	23.97	1230	1.03	21072	13.22	119931	159435
2005	6375	4.93	36583	23.11	1096	0.85	18715	11.82	129222	158323
2011	5834	4.24	33575	21.29	981	0.71	16174	10.25	137515	157671

Source: Compiled from Agl census data 2005-06,www.agcensus.nic.in.

Changing Landholding Pattern in Andhra Pradesh

Andhra Pradesh was formed in 1956 by merging Nizam Ruled Telangana and Andhra area of Madras Presidency. In one word all the three forms of land management had prevailed in this area. The Telangana area was under the control of Princely state while in Andhra area two types of land ownership prevailed. The Andhra area was part of British India. The pattern of land ownership can be seen from the works of S. Srinivasa Raghayaiyangar.

Out of the 90 millions of acres forming the area of this Presidency, 27 1/2| millions, or between one-third and one-fourth, are held by 849 zemindars; 15 of these zemindars hold 6 3/4 million acres, or nearly half a million each, paying to Government a peshcush of two lakhs of rupees on an average 128 zemindars hold 9 ½ millions of acres and pay to Government an average peshcush of 18,100 rupees and 706 zemindars and mittadars hold 2 3/4 million acres and pay a peshcush, which averages 1,300 rupees.

The next class of landowners are the inamdars who number 438,659 and hold between them 8*2 millions of acres or 19 acres each on an average. Out of this area, a little more than three millions of acres are comprised in entire inam villages and the remainder consists of petty holdings originally held on service tenure in ryotwar villages and recently enfranchised. (Page 133)

The holders of whole inam villages, who generally belong to the sacerdotal and non-cultivating classes, are in an impoverished condition, their property having got sub-divided into minute portions.

The fifth and by far the most numerous class comprises the Ryotwari puttadars or peasant proprietors. The total number of estates on this tenure is 2,850,000 and the number of owners including shareholders is 4,600,000. The total area of Ryotwari villages is 59.3 million acres, from which 31 million acres must be deducted on account of unculturable waste and lands held on inam tenure and lying interspersed with Ryotwari holdings, leaving 28.3 millions which, at present, are considered fit for cultivation. (*Source:* Memorandum on the progress of the Madras Presidency during the last forty years of British administration Page 132 to 134)

Both the national and Presidency statistics revealed similar facts. Huge chunks of land were concentrated in a few hands. They conducted that cultivation in a feudal mode. However, M.N. Roy pointed that even by that time the feudal base was eroding.

The changing pattern of land holding can be observed from the agricultural Census with regard to Andhra Pradesh.

The land holding pattern almost resembles the national trends. In the year 1970 the large landholdings stood at 4.32 per cent and 30.73 per cent of total land was under the control of them. By 2011 the percentage is dropped to 0.27 but 3.86 per cent of total land is being under the control of mere 0.27 per cent of large land holders. Even the land is more concentrated in the few hands when compare with 1970.

Table 2. Changing Land Holding Pattern in Andhra Pradesh From 1970-2011

Andhra Pradesh AGL Census data from 1970-2005:[Holdings in '000][Land in '000 hectares]

	Marginal [< 1 Hectare]				Small[1 to 2 Hectares				Semi-Medium [2 to 4 Hectares]			
Year	Holdings	Per cent	Land	Per cent	Holdings	Per cent	Land	Per cent	Holdings	Per cent	Land	Per cent
1970	2492	45.96	1085	7.99	1065	19.64	1533	11.28	942	17.37	2607	19.19
1975	N.A	N.A	N.A	N.A	N.A	N.A	N.A	N.A	N.A	N.A	N.A	N.A
1980	3804	49.21	1887	13.17	1951	25.24	2412	16.83	1174	15.19	3261	22.75
1985	4461	54.19	2053	14.5	1714	20.82	2454	17.33	1254	15.23	3391	23.95
1990	5211	56.09	2369	16.38	1972	21.23	2827	19.55	1345	14.48	3640	25.17
1995	6299	59.42	2904	20.2	2262	21.34	3229	22.46	1395	13.16	3737	26.00
2000	7023	60.89	3104	21.56	2518	21.83	3565	24.76	1424	12.35	3795	26.36
2005	7418	61.59	3287	22.68	2639	21.91	3730	25.74	1445	12.00	3836	26.47
2011	8425	63.94	3727	26.07	2918	22.14	4120	28.82	1399	10.61	3685	25.78

Andhra Pradesh AGL Census data from 1970-2011:[Holdings in '000][Land in '000 hectares]										
	Medium [4 to 10 Hectares]				Large [> 10 Hectares]				Total holdings	Total Land
Year	Holdings	Per cent	Land	Per cent	Holdings	Per cent	Land	Per cent		
1970	689	12.71	4186	30.81	234	4.32	4174	30.73	5422	13585
1975	N.A	N.A	N.A	N.A	N.A	N.A	N.A	N.A	######	#####
1980	646	8.36	3978	27.75	155	2.01	2795	19.50	7730	14333
1985	657	7.98	3865	27.30	146	1.77	2394	16.91	8232	14157
1990	644	6.93	3777	26.12	118	1.27	1848	12.78	9290	14461
1995	563	5.31	3231	22.48	82	0.77	1273	8.86	10601	14374
2000	502	4.35	2855	19.83	66	0.57	1079	7.49	11533	14398
2005	486	4.04	2759	19.04	56	0.46	878	6.06	12044	14490
2011	397	3.01	2209	15.45	36	0.27	552	3.86	13175	14293

Source: Compiled from various Agl Census: www.agcensus.nic.in

On the other, marginal landholding showed a rapid increase. They have increased from 45.95 per cent to 63.94 per cent. The land under this category is increased from 7.99 per cent to 26.07 per cent. In other words 63.94 per cent of peasantry is contended with a mere 22.68 per cent of Land.

The bulwark between marginal and large is strengthened in the state also. The medium land holdings were accounted for 12.71 per cent in the year 1970 and the land under their possession was 30.81 per cent. By 2011 their number of holdings was cut short to 3.01. However, the land under their control was stood at 15.45 per cent. In other words 3 per cent of Medium layer is controlling almost 16 per cent of land with all resources.

Land Holding Pattern in the District

In the period under review, no lands struggles are being carried out. The struggles are limited to catchphrases and to wall-writings. The land struggles are gained the sense that the struggles for land are nothing but occupation of government poramboku and forestlands. Even this is also not carried out in this district. Prior to 1970, dalits carried out land struggles under the banner of the then communist party of India in some villages in Patapatnam taluk. Now these villages are in Bhamini and Kothuru Mandals. At any point, no systematic land struggles have been carried out against landlords and rich peasantry.

In the last five years, 7000 acres of Adivasi land has been alienated in Saluru Mandal. Neither a systematic study nor a consistent campaign has been built on this process. The peasantry of small and marginal layers are continuously and uninterruptedly losing their land. Peasantry is being thrown out of their profession and being converted as labour. In the period during 1961-71 two lakhs of peasantry lost their occupation. In between 1971-91, this process has a brief intermission and again from 1991 it gains momentum. The occupational pattern of the people is discussed in later passages. In essence, these movements have played no role in transformation of the agrarian structure of this district.

"The Adivasi movement popularly known as Srikakulam uprising in its early days it started the land struggle in Panasabhadra village. Actually all the land in Bhadragiri block is protected under Laws relating to scheduled areas. The Sahukar-money lender combine have occupied all the lands and violated all the protective laws in vogue. The Girijan Sangham (union of Adivasis) vehemently fought against this. The struggles gradually converted in to wage rate struggles. Broadly, the associations and the communist party restricted the struggles for a long time to just economic struggles. The agenda for the land has been taken back-foot. It appears that the association felt that these economic struggles would pave the way for the ultimate struggle for land. On the other hand, the same organisation tried to occupy government lands in some parts of the district by organising Dalits. The same organisation has not continued its struggle in Adivasi areas though they have legal protection for their lands. As seen from the record it looks quite contradictory" (Srikakulam Girijan rytanga udyamam: Venkat)

Table 3: Trends in Landholding Pattern in Srikakulam District (others)

TABLE 5: LAND HOLDING PATTERN in the Srikakulam District												
	Marginal (<2.46 acres)				Small (2.47 - 4.92 acres)				Semi Medium (4.93-9.87 acre Medium			
Year	No	Per cent	Extent	Per cent	No	Per cent	Extent	Per cent	No	Per cent	Extent	Per cent
1985	322545	70.75	348993.7	30.27	75832	16.63	268851.3	23.32	N.A	N.A	N.A	N.A
1990	379495	73.32	366840.9	31.23	81300	15.71	284494.2	24.22	38711	7.48	281647.5	23.98
2001	451511	76.49	422549.3	37.12	91968	15.58	314457.6	27.62	36359	6.16	241306.3	21.20
2005	475294	76.72	448143.6	38.16	97590	15.75	331935.4	28.27	36861	5.95	243989.1	20.78
2011	507726	79.00	471308.9	38.69	94233	14.66	320127.6	26.28	31812	4.95	291866.7	23.96

LAND HOLDING PATTERN in the Srikakulam District										
	MEDIUM (9.88 to 24.70)				Large (> 24.71 acres)				Total all classes	
Year	No	Per cent	Extent	Per cent	No	Per cent	Extent	Per cent	No	Extent
1985	57066	12.52	517183.3	44.86	461	0.10	17966.67	1.56	455904	1152995
1990	16703	3.23	191103	16.27	1384	0.27	50565.76	4.30	517593	1174651
2001	9766	1.65	132138.9	11.61	660	0.11	28019.4	2.46	590264	1138472
2005	9200	1.48	129130.6	11.00	589	0.10	21138.09	1.80	619534	1174337
2011	8360	1.30	111361.7	9.14	574	0.09	23470.86	1.93	642705	121835

Source: District hand books of Srikakulam, Vizianagaram, and agcensus.nic.in

Ownership rights on land are continuing as debatable aspect even now. The Land acquisition Act 1894, which has come into force in the colonial government, gave impression that the state has ownership on the land. This Act widely used the term in the interest of companies for acquiring land. Subsequently the term has been replaced with Public interest. This Act proved that whoever having the titles on the land, the real owner of the land is none other than the State. This Act is with slight modifications still in vogue.

In the titles, revenue authorities use G. Ryti term to indicate the nature of ownership. Revenue authorities stated that this word G indicates the Government.

The changing agrarian structure can be assessed through the agricultural census that took place for every five years and with the micro level studies. Agricultural census figures from 1977 to 2011 have been used for this research. These statistics may be seen from this tabular form.

In 1977, the agricultural census has accounted only 7.67,200.20 Acres of land, but the district hand book of statistics have shown 12,19,305 acres as net sown area. Hence, I believe that the census of 1977 has not reflected the actual figures. I have restricted myself to compare the 1986-87 to 2011 census reports.

In the year 1986-87, the land holding of this district stood at 4,55,904. The share of marginal land holdings was 70.74 per cent, and the land rested with them was 30.26 per cent only. The share of small land holdings was 16.63 per cent. They have 23.31 per cent of land only 87.73 per cent of landholders are compelled to content with merely 39.94 per cent of primary natural resource. On the other hand, 12.5 per cent per cent of rich peasantry is enjoying 44.8 per cent of land. The upper strata are reduced to mere 0.1 per cent, and they are controlling 1.55 per cent of the total land. The picture is so obvious that instead of handful feudal lords 12 per cent of rich peasantry are controlling the entire resources.

By the turn of 2005, the number of marginal and small peasants is swelled. The number of marginal peasants rose to 4,75,294, and their share in land accounted to 38.15 per cent of the total land. The number of small peasants rose to 97,590 and their part in land accounted to 28.26 per cent of the total land. The number of rich peasantry stood at 46,061 their share in land accounted to 31.77 per cent of the total land. Their share in number is mere 7.74 per cent.

By the turn of 2011, the marginal and small peasants further increased to 6,01,590. Out of this, marginal peasantry stood at 5,07,726 and constituted 79 per cent of the whole of the peasantry and small peasantry stood at 14.7. In other words, 93.7 per cent of peasantry is getting their "livelihood" on 52 per cent of land. It is very painful to note that 79 per cent of marginal peasantry is eking their livelihood on a mere 38.69 per cent of land. On the other hand the medium and large peasantry is consolidating their position.

In reality, the traditional property owners doomed because of these abolition Acts. The space is replaced by the rich peasantry belong to the four peasants castes. On the other hand, marginal and small peasantry is continuing in agriculture with tremendous hardship.

As seen from the historical process, there is a lot of change occurred in the land holding class pattern. Up to 1948, handful Zamindars and Inamdars had a full-fledged control over land. Those belonged to Brahman, Kshatriya, Velamadora and Hill zamindar castes. The elimination of intermediaries brought a change in the then existing framework. The sporadic struggles and judicial intervention have changed the scenario. The Tenants belong to peasant castes namely Kalinga, Koppulavelama, Toorpukapu; Polinativelama largely replaced these monopoly landlords. This situation prevailed roughly until 1990's. In the post 1990 period, the iand is being slowly alienated from the small and marginal peasants to the settlers and to the rich peasantry of these four castes.

As of now, majority dalits are landless. Though they have land majority are marginal. The artisans castes and castes of servitude have no saying in land. Almost 92 per cent of the peasants of the peasant-castes are marginal and small.

Land Holding Marginal and Small

As seen from the agricultural census majority of the land holdings are marginal and small. The fact remains from the district to national level. In my observation, all the villages of this district majority land holding are either marginal or small. As per the government statistics, the frequency of the marginal land is 0.01 acres to 2.46 acres. In other words, the smallest land holding varies from 0.01 acres to 2.45 acres. As seen from the 2011 agricultural census of this district, the marginal land holdings stood at 4,75,294. The lion's share had gone to this category. 76.72 per cent of ranks and file of peasantry are marginal, and they are leading their life in a difficult manner on these land holdings.

The farming is painfully processing on these tiny land holdings.The peasantry has no wherewithal support to cater to the needs of the agriculture. The marginal peasantry are continuing in the operations with meagre incomes almost every minute of his life is dedicated to conducting the farming operations. In this process, the peasants are unaware of the situation that took place in the country. At the same time, they are even ignorant about the policies that took place even about them.

Agricultural Operations in a Small Land Holding an Example in Villages :

Nandabalaga is a village situated in Therlam Mandal. M.R. Kandi Venkata Naidu is a marginal peasant having 0.80 acres of land. He totally relies upon his family labour. The sugarcane cropping has needed much labour force. The statistics of the labour needed is given below:

Table 4. Labour Needed to Cultivate Sugarcane per Acre (2.46 acres = 1 hectare)

Operation	*Men*	*Women*
Planting the seed	5	5
To make Ridges and furrows	5	0
Weeding (1st time)	0	15
Weeding (2nd time)	0	15
Weeding (3rd time)	10	0
To make Ridges and furrows	8	0
double line propping	8	0
double line propping	10	0
To apply fertilizers	40	80
Watering the plant	6	4
To harvesting	12	0
To loading and unloading	40	40
Total	152	159

Source: Kandi Venkatanaidu, a marginal peasant of Nandabalaga village.

Sugarcane is an annual crop. Peasants plant sugarcane in December/ January/February. It will be harvested in the following year. As seen from the table, 311 agricultural labourers needed for the cultivation of sugarcane. In present case for 0.80 acres of land, 249 agrarian labours are needed. Kandi Venkatanaidu with his wife is continuing this cultivation without hiring any labour. They work in the fields from 4.00 am to 8.00 pm. Family labour has been continuing almost by 76 per centof total peasantry. In this process, Kandi Venkatanaidu and his family will not go for any work. Thus, they saved Rs. 37,069. On an average, the couple earned Rs. 101.55 per day. It is understandable that these marginal and small "owners" cannot sell their labour elsewhere as commodity nor do they have time or energy to think of plight and problems either of their own or those of co-habitants around them, having enslaved and tied themselves to the small piece of land for the glory and aura of proprietorship and it is thinkable whether they are owners in the real sense or slaves in guise.

The factory management is not usually giving cutting orders for them in time, which reflects the loss of net weight in the crop. Even the orders given, the management would not pay the bills in time. There is a stipulation that the management should pay the amounts along with applicable interests in case of late payments. Majority of peasants do not know about the stipulations. Even they are in a position to claim the interest, the factory owner will not pay it. On the other hand, the peasantry has to bear the burden of interests on their loans. When I have asked the peasants about this proviso, the peasants unanimously told, "when we are in a hectic schedule in our agricultural operations how can we know all about these Acts and how can we fight against this formidable owner". This expression makes it clear that how the large proportion of peasants have been tied to their piece of land.

The economists of different streams are busy in describing this situation in a sophisticated manner. The sub-group of planning commission has described this situation, *"The small farmers continue to be more productive as compared to their large counterparts most ostensibly in terms of productivity per acre of net operated area, primarily because of higher cropping intensity and more intensive use of family labour"*. (Report of sub-group on land related issues for the Eleventh five year plan: Planning commission: Page: 119,120). (Emphasis added) 92.47 per cent of this district peasantry are conducting their agricultural in a laborious manner, and they are not in a position to care about anything that harmed them in one way or other. The term "owner" is reflecting mockery of the peasantry. In fact, these people can be called as slaves who are unceasingly working on their patch of land.

Land Allocations

Almost all the political parties and voluntary organisations are pronouncing that the redistribution of the land is the salvation for the problems. Plenty of official and unofficial reports are available about the redistribution that took place in country. On the other hand, the governments are allocating large chunk of lands to industrialists. The governments are allocating common property resources and even the private land to the industrialists with a nominal price. The land concentration is going towards corporatisation of the land.

In India, the land is acquiring under 1894-land acquisition Act. Even the official organs are proclaiming that the process of the land acquisition is not pro-people and is not according to the needs of the public. C and AG has made strong remarks against these land allocations in general and in particular with regard to the Andhra Pradesh. The C and AG has made performance audit report on these land allocations in Andhra Pradesh for the period of 5 years that reflects 2006 to 2011. It has elicited so many irregularities in the process of allocation. The Commissioner, Land Administration has accepted almost all these objections. In these 5 years, the government has allocated 88,492 acres to the corporate empire. 1207 beneficiaries got these lands. Audit has condemned these allocations in stringent words. It reads, *"Audit found that land allotments for commercial purpose were not made in a fair, consistent and transparent manner so as to serve the public interest" (Performance audit report on Land allotment).*

The report further stated that the government has overruled many of the Acts and Rules in vogue while allocating these lands. The government has turned down the recommendations of the district collectors and empowerment committees in fixing the price of the land. In this process, the government has allotted the lands at through away prices. Audit observed that some companies not even paid the meagre price even after the allocation. On the other hand, the companies took control over the land. The companies promised jobs for getting the land at cheaper rates, but no company has given any job.

The report says that 11 companies have promised 5,92,507 jobs to get 17,911.48 acres of land. Out of this 11companies have taken 10528.60 acres of land and promised 3, 26,000 jobs. In practice, they have not created even a single job. Lepakshi Knowledge Park has promised 1, 50,000 jobs and took over 8,844.01 acres of land but not created even a single job. In all these 11 cases, only five companies created 25,582 jobs (Audit report page number 30).

Villagers told that the companies have annexed the assignment lands in Pydibhimavaram village of Ranasthalam Mandal. Even the audit report has taken one example of M/s Aurobinda Pharma of this village. It reads, "*M/s. Aurobinda Pharma Ltd., Hyderabad (APL), in 2008 requested for alienation of 25.72 acres of land in Pydibhimavaram and Chittivalasa villages of Ranasthalam (M), Srikakulam district. Out of 25.72 acres requested for, 20.48 acres were already under encroachment by APL since 2002. To discourage such encroachment and keeping in view the prevailing market value, the District Collector, in his recommendation however, alienated (March 2010) the land at five lakh per acre, resulting in undue benefit of 5.14 crores to the Company. Thus, instead of penalising APL for encroaching upon Government land and resuming the same, the encroached land was regularised/alienated at a meager amount, which would only encourage further encroachment of Government land." (ibid)*

The government are allocating lands to the companies even in this district. The government has acquired land in Latchayyapeta village of Seetanagaram Mandal for construction of Nizam sugar factory in the public sector. Almost all the dry land has been acquired, and it comprises assigned land that allocated to dalits. While acquiring, the government has given Rs. 20,000 as compensation per an acre and Rs. 17,000 for the assigned land. Thus, the government has acquired 162 acres land at the rate of Rs. 32,40,000. This happened in the decade of 90s. The government has sold this factory along with machinery and land to a private company for a meagre amount of Rs. 25,00,00,000. Now the price of land has reached to Rs. 20,00,000 per acre. The cost of the land itself gone up to Rs. 32,00,00,000. Thus, a private owner gainfully managed to get the land of the peasantry through government.

The Andhra Pradesh government has started *Jalayajnam* in a fanfare. It has planned so many projects and reservoirs in the state. For this, the government has acquired so much of land and tunnelled the canals. Ironically, no canal is carrying a single drop of water to the intended purpose.

The government intends to construct a reservoir across Suvarnamukhi at Madduvalasa in 1976. By that time, the peasantry was ignorant about the compensations acts in vogue. The government decided to give Rs. 8900 for wet land per an acre and Rs. 2500 for dry land per acre. In fact by that time the market price of the land was Rs.15,000. The government did not bother about and heeds to its proclamation. The peasants got peanuts as compensation and could not buy a piece of land with the compensation since the price of land is spiralled. In this process owner of 20 acres land is now remained as a labour.

Government intends to build Thotapalli Balancing reservoir at Thotapalli. Government has proclaimed that they will give water to drought stricken Cheepurupalli Mandal. The government has procured land in Cheepurupalli Mandal and dug the canals. As per official estimates, 10,097 acres are needed to build this reservoir, which comprises private land to the tune of 6876 acres. "The government has already procured 2839.90 acres of wet land and 3471.15 acres of dry land from peasantry". (*Source:* Reply under RTI ACT, 2005) This procurement is continuing. The minimum payment for this land was in Therlam Mandal. In the year 2005 the government has paid Rs. 60, 000 per an acre of dry land. The government has paid Rs. 1,00,000 per an acre of wet land. This minimum payment has also been made in Therlam Mandal. The peasantry is fighting tooth and nail to get their rightful compensation amounts. In the year 2008, the government has paid Rs.1,33,000 per an acre of dry land in Cheepurupalli Mandal Hqrs. In fact, the market price is much higher in this Mandal Headquarters when compared to this government price.

In case of Vamshadhara reservoir, the government has not paid a reasonable price for these lands. Duggipuram village people told that the government has not paid any compensation to the dalits who have assigned lands. In fact the original price of the wet land per acre is Rs. 3,50,000 while an acre of dry land cost is Rs. 1,40,000. The government fixed the compensation at Rs. 1, 29,800 and Rs. 80, 000 respectively. The peasantry is still knocking doors of the judiciary to get a genuine verdict. The proclamation of the land acquisition Act regarding compensations reads:

1. "first the market value of the land at the date of the publication of the {subs, by act 38 of 1923, S-7 for declaration relating thereto under S.6} (notification under Section 4, sub section (1)).

2. in addition to the market value of the land as above provided, the court shall in every case award a sum of fifteen per cent on such market value, in consideration of the compulsory nature of the acquisition."

The commentary reads, "*If the sale deeds on found to be genuine the market value mentioned therein must be presumed to be relied upon. Proper tests and principles laid down by the court must be applied to determine compensation." (Hookier Sing vs. Special land acquisition offices, Moradabad AIR 1996 supreme Land Acquisition act, 1894)*

Though the judgment and Act settled the position, the government did not come forward to implement these provisions, though the peasantry had shown the documentary proof for the land transaction for Rs. 3,50,000 the government turned down their requests. Inevitably, they were forced to plunge into legal litigations. As seen from the audit report that the government has indiscriminately allocated thousands of acres at throw off prices. On the other hand the government has grabbed the piece of land that owned by the marginal and small peasantry by cutting the market price to the tune of 50 per cent.

Agricultural rural development notes of World Bank has also noted that the fraud that took place in allocating and maintaining the land records. It reads

"In India, bribes paid annually by users of land administration services are estimated at $700 million (Transparency International, 2006), three-quarters of total public spending on science, technology, and environment". (A strategy for improving land administration in India: Klaus Deininger).

The Land Problem

Ever since national movement strated, the national leadership thought of and spoke of solution to the issue of land. Section of the leadership of national movement thought that it is an impediment to the main cause to speak about the problem of Ryots amid national movement another stream took it as advantage to the national movement to enlighten the rights. The country had more than 500 princely states and the British ruled the remaining part. Ownership on the entire land in the princely states was rested in the princes and in the remaining British India, land belonged to zamindars as name itself denotes. Only in the Ryotwari areas, ownerships were with the Ryots. Consequent to pitched battles fought over changing the conditions necessitated abolition of intermediaries. This abolition of much Adore served a little, if not no purpose of transferring the ownership to the tenants, and purposely excluded the sub-tenants for; there was no record of tenancy. The number of tenants, as recorded was very few in number and the sub-tenants were kept at bay angered and hopeful.

Land to Tiller Slogan a Miserable Failure

Ironically enough, the slogan land to the tiller occupied the forefront as a solution of the land issue. The slogan is must necessarily have had at the least elementary idea, as to what extent of land can be tilled by a family, comprising man, woman and children. It is a common estimation that in the absence of commercial crops and mechanisation a family, as above can cultivate 0.4 hectares of land. However, to expect of abolition Act to such an extent of land distribution is more than a dreaming. All this has resulted in land to the cultivator not to the tiller. There are no evidences of any agitations against these Acts and the exemptions there in. Let us understand that the forces that led the fight that the Zamindars were only the recorded tenants taking along the sub-tenants and rural proletarian who were to be betrayed and bereft.

The princes and Zamindars belonged to minority castes and the tenants belonged to the majority peasant castes. The Dalits and the artisans were to seen nowhere in the hierarchy and these castes are large in number, tilling and toiling. The history and the happenings lead us to conclusion that the much fancied slogan land to the tiller, with all its sway and glory helped only a few tenants of the peasant castes secure ownership on the land while majority of the very same peasant castes and the castes of servitude were left in the lurch meant only for sacrifices, trials and punishments. These few tenants usurped in to the place of Zamindars and princes.

Economists used to laud the land reforms those took place in Kerala under the regime of communist party. However, the first communist chief minister of

Kerala Sri E.M.S. Nambudripad has expressed his concern in other way. It reads, *"The old Janmi System was replaced by Land Lordism of another type"of Land Lords who get their lands cultivated through wage labour and those who live by lending money and dominated rural Trade."* (Reversing land reforms: R.K. Krishnakumar: Frontline)

It is a trillion dollar question for the *hoi polloi* has to expect of other governments while the most illustrious and acclaimed chief minister who came to power through ballot spoke thus of land reforms implemented by himself.

The only one word that incorporated in the abolition act "that the land holdee has cultivated such lands himself by his own servants" has completely changed the scenario of Indian agrarian structure. This phrase helped influential sections of peasantry that belongs to peasant castes to get hold majority share of primary means of production. The term by his own servants, itself is a horrible word, which has not been taken into consideration either by the writers of the Act or by the agitators who are agitating for judicious redistribution of the land.

The sixty years process of land reforms transformed feudal latifundium into multiple strata of land holdings. Normally the large landholders are none other than those belong to influential peasant castes those spread across under various names. Kautsky remarked the small land holding are the manifestation of capitalist mode of production. In other words, the reform acts that took place in postcolonial India transformed the agrarian relations from feudal to capitalistic. By showing this large scale, marginal and small holding economists are vehemently arguing for consolidation of these holdings. Marx rightly expressed this process while reviewing an article and it reads *"and finally, if in France the tide has already begun to turn from fragmentation to concentration, in Britain the large landed estates are making giant strides towards renewed disintegration, conclusively proving that agriculture necessarily proceeds in an incessant cycle of concentration and fragmentation of the land, as long as bourgeois conditions as a whole continue to exist" (Marx, 'Discussion of "Le sodalisme et l'impot"* www.marxists.org*)*

The Indian economists are putting their feet in shoes of France now. They are now continuously arguing for consolidation of land holdings to make capitalist estates. The economists are arguing for modification in laws of tenancy to allow the capitalist farmers to take over the holding of marginal and small peasants in the peaceful way.

The sub-group report on the land related matters for the eleventh five year plan stressed that the stringent stipulations of tenancy Acts are hindering the process of consolidation of the land holdings. They opined that because of the stipulations, the small and marginal peasants are afraid of leasing their lands. It observed, *"More recent studies also show that the small and marginal farmers have started leasing-out land primarily due to an increase in the cost of production, growing scarcity of water, falling returns and increasing uncertainty on account of erratic weather conditions. There is also an anecdotal evidence to suggest that many farmers, including small and marginal ones, are leaving their land fallow in view of restrictive tenancy laws."* (Report of sub group on land related matters: 11th five-year plan: Page 122)

The protective measures in the tenancy Act are acting as a tool to left the land fallow. The acts should be regulated for freely letting of the lands to the forces that are interested conducting agriculture on commercial basis.

The same report has clearly come out with these words, *"The amendments of the existing laws allowing leasing-in and leasing-out with explicit provisions for protection of ownership rights, fixed tenure of lease, recording of lease and allowing landowners to resume land for self-cultivation after the expiry of lease shall enable the tenants to obtain credit from the financial institutions. The protection of ownership rights shall provide incentives for different categories of farmer households to move out of agriculture and seek employment elsewhere without the fear of losing their land. It shall also help in consolidation of holdings as the farmers shall prefer to lease out rather than sell the piece of land that is inconveniently located. The legalisation of tenancy is expected to give rise to long-term tenancy contracts, which have important implications towards improving agricultural productivity. Given other things, long term tenancy contracts offer more incentives to the tenants for undertaking productivity enhancement measure."* (Report of sub group on land related matters:11th five-year plan: Page 123)

It is clear from these, that the land will be transferred from the small players to big players in the shape of lease initially. This logical process will ultimately lead to the ownership of the big capital forms.

Agrarian Question and its Solution

Economists across the globe have made so many thoughts for the solution of the agrarian question.The problem lies in the private property on the land. German economist *Frithj of Kuhnen*in his work *Man and Land* as certained, *"Private ownership of land is a Western concept that was first introduced into many developing countries by Europeans. It arose under a specific legal order by original acquisitioning of land (occupying and making the land arable) or changes in ownership (conquest, contract, inheritance). Until today, some societies have still not developed any forms of personal, private rights to land that would grant a right of disposition. This economist has come to a definite conclusion the concept of private property on land is itself is a bread of western mode of production".*

His theory can be proved from the Indian records itself. The legality to the land transactions is very new concept. British colonial rulers introduced this aspect in India.

"At last on 1st February 1865, the first Government approved Sub Registry office commenced operation from his bungalow. Lord Murdoch Brown assumed charge as Deputy Registrar and stated to register documents. Though stamp papers and stamp laws were not in vogue at that point of time, Lord Murdoch

Brown's sharp intellect had a solution for everything. He brought the stamp papers from Madras specially prepared by the stamp office there and he himself donned the mantle of stamp vendor and affixed signature on stamp papers in that capacity also and sold it to the needy." (*Source*: www.keralaregistration.gov.in)

The same sources further added, "Though oblivious of it, Lord Murdoch Brown was creating history at Ancharakkandy in Kannur District a century and of half ago while demarcating boundaries of landed properties of local people. He might not have thought that this demarcation was the starting point of a new model of administration or Department of its kind not only in Kerala or India but also in Asia."

The colonial government introduced land registration Act For whole of India excluding Jammu and Kashmir in 1908 which is still in vogue.

The individual property on the land is the primary cause of conflicts between individuals, between groups, between villagers and even between countries. Property owner belongs to Annavaram village of Palkonda have surplus lands. However, his surplus land is situated in another village, viz., Vadama. The government tried to distribute his surplus land to the landless and dalits of that village. The landless and Dalits of Annavaram village claimed that these lands should be distributed in them because the landlord belongs to that village. However, dalits and land less of Vadama village claimed the right since the lands is in their revenue boundary. Thus, the distribution of land has led to conflict like situation between same classes of people of two villages. The root cause of this lies in the individual property rights on the land. Finally, the revenue administration distributed the land to the people of Vadama village and the people of Annavaram remained land less.

The land has definite character. It cannot be transferred from one place to another. Normally the agronomists claim that India has this much of surplus land and it can be distributed among this much of people, but these macro level statistics are futile when go to ground level reality. These kinds of calculations indicate utopian attitude only.

The villagers who have 400 acres of surplus land would not come forward to share the land with their counterparts in the adjacent villagers where there is no land for distribution. The Marxist teachers all over the planet described the selfishness of peasants those who are tied with their patch of land.

History categorically proved that individual property rights on the land could not pave the way for attaining equality. Hence, economists of different streams advocated for the abolition of individual property on land. Fabien socialists, Marxists along with Marx, and Ambedkar vehemently argued for the abolition of individual property. All these expressed unanimity for the nationalisation of land. Ambedkar in his book "State and Minorities expressed" *"That agriculture shall be State Industry"*.

Ambedkar suggested that the government can give debentures to the land holders which many criticised. While amalgamating princely states, Indian

Government promised and gave pensions to large magnitude to the princely state chiefs. The successive government, however, abolished those pensions. Had the state accepted the proposal of Ambedkar, the debentures would have been cancelled.

Fabien socialists argued for nationalising land besides arguing in favour of giving the land to the people's counsels. Marx made an in-depth study on the agrarian question and made appropriate proposals even in 1872. In Brussels conference, one of Marx's friends proposed which reads, "*Small private property in land is doomed by the verdict of science, large land property by the justice. There remains then but one alternative. The soil must become the property of rural associations or the property of the whole nation. The future will decide that question.*" Marx rejected this proposal and said, *"I say on the contrary—the social movement will lead to this decision that the land can but be owned by the nation itself. To give up the soil to the hands of associated rural labourers, would be to surrender society to one exclusive class of producers. The nationalisation of land will work a complete change in the relations between labour and capital, and finally, do away with the capitalist form of production, whether industrial or rural."* (The Nationalisation of the Land: Published in The International Herald No. 11, June 15, 1872)

As seen from history, economists who have thought for genuine distribution of resources correctly argued that the nationalising means of production is the only solution to establish egalitarian society. Thus, for primary means of production, the land should be nationalised. Engels expressed that a small proprietorship in the land would create many obstacles in clinching the problem efficiently. He expressed, *"More the difficult it is for him to defend his endangered patch of land, the more desperately he clings to it, the more he regards the Social-Democrats, who speak of transferring landed property to the whole of society, as just as dangerous a foe as the usurer and lawyer."* (Engels: The Peasant Question in France and Germany: www.marxist.org)

It is clear that the right path is to nationalise the land but not to make a landowner a hapless proprietor of a small piece of land. Yet, paradoxically the issue of land has further been complicated by the slogan 'land to the tiller', which resulted in inequalities. Land and self-respect were projected as complimentary and it was believed and campaigned that in order to attain self-respect, one should be a proprietor. Dr. B.R. Ambedkar quoted Seleucus as saying that the Indian farmer continued to till his miniscule piece of land unmindful of the soldiers fighting for their own country land.

With history, presenting as clear as this, philosophers everywhere advocated that there should be no private ownership on the land if the literature says so. The campaigners of 'land to tiller' have conveniently forgotten that it is a commercial art to campaign that land and self-respect are complimentary. Let us understand very clearly that this campaign resulted in our earth to bleed to have become the property of individuals instead of being a source of cultivation and food to the masses at large.

Lands Struggles in the District

In this district too during the colonial rule, the tenants under the banner of Krushikar Lok party, communist party fought for their rights. Peasants took a rally from Itchapuram of this district to then capital of Madras presidency by consistently fighting for their rights and the reference was mainly drawn from peasant castes. In this district, four-peasant castes run the show. The dominant section and the recorded tenants fought for their share of economic and social respects against the upper caste strata though the landless and the dalits who played a role in the struggles, could not get their righteous share in the land.

The general picture has repeated again in this district too. The verbal section of these four castes gained control over the land because of these movements. Here too, the majority of people remained landless. Based on the castes, the feudal sections of these peasant castes could gather greater masses of their castes to build their leadership. As in national scenario, here too, no land struggles were carried out to eliminate this rich peasantry ownership by mobilising greater masses that were landless. In other words, the rural proletarian centred movements did not take place.

The period under review, i.e., since 1970, there were no land struggles in this district. However, during this decade, there were two types of land struggles emerged. People are fighting against the indiscriminate allotment of lands to the corporate companies. The second set of struggle is reflecting the genuine aspirations of the dalits. In this district, government allocated community property resources for the establishment of thermal power plants in Sompeta and Kakarapalli. Some argued that these struggles again brought the land question into agenda. It was necessary to investigate the cause and the effects of these struggles dispassionately.

Sompeta Struggle against Nagarjuna Construction Company (NCC)

People claimed, "The government allocated 900 acre and the company purchased nearly 500 acres of land from the peasantry and never disclosed the purpose of the purchase. Company argued, *"The land identified for the proposed project site was 762-ha., barren and uncultivable waste land" (Environment impact assessment (EIA) report submitted in a public hearing). The census 2001 particulars show, "the 10-km study area admeasured to about 27570-ha. In that area, irrigation land consisted of 7293.22-ha (26.46 per cent), un-irrigated land about 12458.40-ha (45.19 per cent), cultivable waste land of 1045.34-ha (3.79 per cent), land unavailable for cultivation was about 6770.69-ha (24.56 per cent). The study area consisted of 1,55,107 persons who inhabited in the study area".*

"As per the census records the study area consists of 155107 persons inhabited in the study area of 10 km radial distance from the periphery of the proposed plant. The males and females constitute 48.05 per cent and 51.95 per cent of the study area population respectively. The average household size of the study area is 4.3 persons. The density of population reveals that the

study area has an overall density of 102 persons per km^2. In the study area, 6.61 per cent of the population belongs to Scheduled Castes (S.C) and 11.13 per cent of the population belongs to Scheduled Tribes (S.T)". (*Source:* EIA report of NCC Company)

As seen from the village surveys, water from Beela was the lifeline for a two-crop paddy in over 5,000 acres. In land fishing sustained the Kandra and Agnikulakshatriya communities, while fisher folk from Kaviti Mandal were leased out to fishing rights by the fisheries department every year. Apart from this, government has built three lift irrigation schemes on this water body to supply water for cultivation. Interestingly, the government authorities reported that the Beela was a wasteland. In the parlance of international language, this was not wasteland but a wet land.

While summing up the agitation, The Times of India reported, "*The National Green Tribunal accepted the apex environment body's recommendation that the location of the thermal plant in question was a wetland and not for commercial use. Wetland expert S. Kaul has also faulted the alienation of 973 acres of government land for transfer to NCC. "The government showed fertile land as banjaru (barren land) to benefit the company at the cost of fishermen and farmers," The NEAA said the wetland was of great ecological value and an important source of water for several villages. Beela, as it is known, was also the last surviving wetland in coastal Andhra."* (June 5, 2012 The Times of India)

Table 7. Demand Forecast for Power

Sl. No.	*Plan*	*Demand (MW)*
1.	10th Plan (2000-07)	1,15,705
2.	11th Plan (2007-12)	1,57,107
3.	12th Plan (2012-17)	2,12,725

Source: Working plan document, The Ministry of Power

Taking cue on these estimates, the private power plant companies swing into action and as per the NCC Annual report, "*The Eleventh Plan document envisaged a capacity addition of around 78,000 MW during the Eleventh Plan period (Around 58,000 megawatts under construction). This created a huge opportunity for the private sector to capitalise upon."* the annual report further added, "*We embarked upon the construction of our thermal merchant power plant with a targeted capacity of 2,640 MW to be executed across two phases. Located in Srikakulam, this project entailed investments of Rs. 7,000 crores in Phase (1320 MW)"*

As per the report of NCC Company, it entered one-Billion dollar club in 2009-10. It has 38 per cent of shares of foreign institutional investors. The famous financial giant namely Blackstone had 21,375,135 shares. It accounted for 8.33 per cent of all the shares. It is the single largest shareholder in the company.

The fisher folk who had the fishing rights on Beela first sensed the danger and tried to resist the move. The peasant castes are not interested, and in fact, in the initial phase they did not give ear to these fisher folks. Fisher folks knocked the doors of judiciary. Subsequently the peasant castes started the agitation and the semi-urban Sompeta people took the lead. The company tried to start civil work in July 2010. The residents of surrounding villages gathered to protest. The situation lead to firing and two villagers died instantaneously with one succumbing to injuries.

After this bizarre incident, the ministry of environment has proclaimed, *"further representations against the site were received by the MoE&F in view of which the Regional Chief Conservator of Forests from Bangalore was asked to carry out a site inspection in Srikakulam district. His report was expected over the next two weeks. Once this report was received, the matter was again to be considered by the EAC. Meanwhile, in view of the unfortunate incident that took place at Sompeta yesterday and keeping in mind the public sentiment, the environmental clearance for this project stood suspended and the project proponent was directed not to go ahead with the implementation of the project till the EAC gave its decision based on the RCCF's site report".* (Press release of Ministry of Environment and forests Dated 15th July 2010)

Kakarapalli Struggle against East Coast Thermal Plant: The government allotted nearly 2500 acres of the swamp to East Coast Energy private Limited at throwaway price. Government allotted this land for a mere 80,000 rupees for an acre. In this swamp, the fisher folk belong to Kandra caste had lease rights for fishing. They registered a fisherman society even prior to independence. Here, they almost lead Teutonic type culture. In this swamp, the fishermen used to carry brackish water for fishing and distributed the catchment among them. The catching fish took place in three places. Here too the government authorities reported that it was a wasteland.

Kandra fisher folk immediately recognised this threat and tried to resist the plant and in the process, they urged the peasant castes to join the fight. As usual, the peasantry did not understand the threat and even part of the peasantry supported the construction. The fisher folk tried to pursue the peasantry against the plant but failed. In 2009, the factory built a retaining wall thus obstructing the course of rainwater. Due to water logging, the entire harvest of the year submerged into sea. It was only then the peasant castes realized the threat and came out to street in a bid to stop the on-going work, which resulted in police firing. Here too, the Sompeta story repeated where three persons were killed.

Back in 1982, Bay of Bengal programme conducted a survey to explore coastal aquaculture development in Andhra Pradesh. It submitted a report in the same year post-recording the practice prevailed in Kakarapalli and said,

"The mission visited a brackish water site in Kakarapalli, Tekali Taluk covering 1236 ha and was owned by the East Coast Chemical Ltd., a state corporation. It was located 10 km inland and was only slightly influenced by the rise and fall of tide at 0.3-0.35 m. The saltwater creek, which was cutting across the land, harboured the seed of milkfish and mullet from May to September. Some fishermen practiced traditional fish culture in saltwater reservoirs which they filled by pumping water from the nearby creek. The shrimp and fish seeds got into the reservoirs along with the incoming water and grew there for 4-6 months after which the crop was harvested. The farmers found this culture practice quite profitable because of the low costs". (Source: Exploration of possibilities of coastal aquaculture development in Andhra Pradesh: Bay of Bengal programme: BOBP/WP/17)

Apart from this, rich fauna surrounded the swamp site. Wild Life Institute of India revealed and reported, *"The Nowapada Swamp area was an excellent habitat for migratory birds, and was classified as Important Bird Area. The entire area within the bounds of the projects starting from the approach road to project site was a marshland. The State Forest Department had erected a watchtower and bird observatory after acquiring land. Environment Impact Assessment report had ignored the bio-diversity value of the area". (Source:* Minutes of the 17th Meeting of the Standing Committee of National Board for Wildlife (NBWL) held on 22nd December, 2009 in Paryavaran Bhavan, CGO Complex)

The Comptroller and Auditor General of India (hereinafter C&AG) had strongly indicted these allocations in general and particularly in the case of Sompeta. It has quoted the apex court judgment, "*The Supreme Court of India in Civil Appeal No. 4787/200119 ordered (25th July 2001) that forests, tanks, ponds, etc., which are nature's bounty, maintain delicate ecological balance and hence needed to be protected for a proper and healthy environment."*

It indicted that the government had violated the norms and allocated the swamps for construction of thermal power plants. It noted, "*Contrary to these orders, Government of Andhra Pradesh in September 2008, alienated 1046.21 acres of land in Sompeta Mandal of Srikakulam district to Nagarjuna Construction Company Infrastructure Holdings Ltd (NCC) for establishing a 1980 MW thermal power project. Out of this land, 972.69 acres constituted a water body. The area was a huge swamp submerged throughout the year and was used by fishermen for inland fishing and as a source of drinking water. The swamp was a natural habitat for more than 120 resident/migratory birds and was internationally recognised as wet land ecosystem. Although Government had prohibited (May 2000) its alienation for any purpose, it gave possession of the site to the company, in violation of its own orders."*

Even now the Special Chief Secretary tried to expose a partial truth to the Auditors and ascertained, *"that the land in question was a swamp but stated that it was being used only by fisherman for catching fish for their livelihood and since it was not considered good enough for any other activity, it was allotted for setting up a thermal plant".*

Auditors came with strong objections and said, *"The reply was not acceptable, because as per the National Environmental Appellate Authority (NEAA) quashed (July 2010), the environmental clearance given by EAC20 ordered the State Government not to alienate such lands. Moreover, the Irrigation Department of Government of Andhra Pradesh in response to an RTI application, in November 2009, revealed that three minor irrigation projects were taken up in the area (ayacut of 750 acres). Of these, two were already commissioned (ayacut of 500 acres)."*

The government was a part of Ramsar convention, and it promised that the detailed survey would take place for recognition of wet lands in the country. It is noticed that the government did not take any detailed survey to recognise the wet land. Ramsar convention defined the wet lands. It read, "*Including lakes and rivers, swamps and marshes, wet grasslands and peat lands, oases, estuaries, deltas and tidal flats, near-shore marine areas, mangroves and coral reefs, and human made sites such as fish ponds, rice paddies, reservoirs, and salt pans".*

Interestingly, the Indian government had given a restricted list to the convention. In this list the government did not list these two swamps.

Though the police force took the lives of six persons, both the struggles are continuing peacefully. They are continuing the relay fast camp, which continued for three long years.

Government handed over the common property resources to the giant companies without providing any alternative livelihood to this community. They were protesting against the capitalist penetration. In essence, these struggles were not against the feudal/semi-feudal exploitation. One should not confuse that these struggles were against the feudal/semi-feudal forces to get their rights on land. These struggles appeared as environment struggles, but can be characterised as the struggle against rapacious usage of natural recourses by the capital.

Second Type of Land Struggles

Land acquisition policies and rules were only causing these types of struggles. Government procured land for the construction of various irrigation projects. During 2006-11, the land acquired for the said purpose was enormous. In the name of Jalayajnam, the government procured the land. In many places, the constructions were not yet started. The government had given unjustified compensation to the peasantry. (Irrigation schemes and the status of those schemes separately discussed in the chapter "irrigation")

In some places, government completed the constructions of reservoirs. In those places, some lands were still useful for cultivation. In the study area, such surplus lands were available in Madduvalasa and Peddagedda reservoirs. Government had procured land for Thotapalli reservoir, Vamshadhara Phase II reservoir, and Meliaputti offshore reservoir in a large scale. In many places, the works were not even started though running at a snail pace.

Madduvalasa Reservoir

The write up of the Government in the year 2003 said, "*The project was under construction, across the river Suvarnamukhi near Madduvalasa village, Vangara Mandal to create a total IP of 24,700 acres in the district of Srikakulam. The estimated cost of the project was Rs. 8.47 Crores and an amount of Rs. 120.80 crores was spent to create an Ayacut of 11,900 acres".*

Actually, the declaration for the construction of the reservoir was made in 1976. However, the reservoir was partially incomplete. In the year 1982-83, the price of the land was fixed at Rs 8,900 per an acre of wet land and Rs. 2500 for an acre of dry land. At that time, the cost of an acre was around Rs 15000 for wet land and Rs 5000 for dry land. The aspiration of the contemplated irrigation facility triggered the prices even up to Rs 20,000 in the adjacent villages. Majority of the peasants could not purchase lands. Routu Vasudevarao (should not be confused with the prime accused in Lakshmipeta carnage) said that only 10 families could purchase land in nearby villages.

Even after the commencement of the reservoir, some lands were not entirely submerged in the reservoir. Out of the total 500 acres of land, nearly 250 acres were still cultivable. The large landholder had 20 acres of land before they submerged. Majority was small with marginal landholders in the village. After taking compensation, almost 54 families belonging to Toorpukapu migrated elsewhere in search of livelihood. These migrants "had" 60 acres of land in the land available for cultivation. The 60 families belonged to Dalits (sub-sect mala) were cultivating this land for last 10 years. The peasants who remained in this village had a queasy impression on their cultivation.

For last one year, mostly the atmosphere was spoilt and the Toorpukapu and Dalits knocked the doors of the police several times. A police post was deployed there to avoid the clashes and to maintain law and order situation. Because of these clashes, the revenue department issued orders to both the parties not to cultivate the land. Hence, the lands of the both parties (in fact the Government land) fell vacant with no standing crop anywhere. This situation infuriated the Toorpukapus who hatched a plan to teach a lesson to Dalits. The police picket was lifted (Dalits attributed that it is conspicuous) and the police were sent as a protection force for the by poll at Narasannapeta constituency.

Dalits used to go to work in the nearby towns/villages early in the morning. Hence, the attack started in the morning. The peasant caste people hurled the country made bombs and attacked with conventional arms. They made indiscriminate attacks on selected Dalit persons without showing any mercy on Dalits. Though the Dalit woman were seeking mercy the caste people resorted to unbridled attacks on all the Dalits. In this attack, four male Dalits were murdered almost on the spot and one male succumbed to injuries in King George hospital in Visakhapatnam. This situation prevailed almost in six places in the study area. The rich peasantry is organising the marginal and small peasants against the Dalits and Scheduled tribes who were requesting the tank beds to cultivate. In Madavlasa, the Tribes intended to cultivate the remaining land, but the Toorpukapu were threatening them with dire consequences.

In one word, the government was the *de-jure* owner of the lands. The peasantry was still thinking that they had *de-facto* ownership on the lands. The rich peasantry (who also lost their land) were even leasing these lands and collecting lease amounts from the landless. Even some settlers who bought hundreds of acres in these areas saw their compensation going towards lease. Dalits and landless tried to occupy tank beds in these areas but the peasantry was trying to obstruct them.

Some were trying to characterise that the Lakshmipeta struggle brought again the land issue into the agenda. Here too, the Dalits were not trying to occupy "the private lands". Even they did not try at any point of time to take over the entire land. They took on lease some land and they even stopped paying the lease amount, which infuriated the peasantry caste. This leads to the carnage of Dalits. In fact, there was no owner in the village. The entire land belonged to the state. In other words, the passive attitude of the revenue machinery was the root cause of all these problems.

People's struggles against landlords and feudal/Semi-feudal forces are now a history, which tells us that all the past struggles were tenant centred and they had lands by virtue of various Acts. In this process, the rural proletarian in general and the Dalits in particular could not get their legitimate due. At no point of time, the struggles were carried out in large scale with the help of these people. Hence, these people remained land less.

In course of time, these land holdings had become marginal and small appearing that the peasantry had concluded that this patch of land could not give any assurance to cater to their needs. Hence, the peasantry was fighting to get their legitimate compensation rather than to protect their lands.

In the first set of struggle, the people were losing their livelihood without any compensation. The people are resorting to struggles to protect common property resources against the penetration of capital.

The struggle of Dalits and landless was to take the ownership rights on the government lands, but they were not being organised to take hold of any private land. Even in these areas, they were not trying to occupy the lands as the de-facto owners. They were rather restricting themselves to occupy the tank beds and poramboku lands.

In one word, all these land struggles were meant either against movement of privatisation of common property resource or to occupy the government lands.

Land Holding Pattern in Surveyed Villages

In the surveyed villages, four major peasant castes were residing in 78 villages. In the postcolonial period, the upper strata of these four castes took

Table 8. Land Holding Pattern of Four Major Peasant Castes in the Surveyed Villages

Caste	*Number of families*	*Large*		*Medium/semi medium*		*Marginal and small*		*Landless families*	*Land alienated to settlers*
		Number	*Land in Acres*	*Number*	*Land in Acres*	*Number*	*Land in Acres*		*In acres*
Polinativelama	2627	9	370	31	611	2106	5378.84	524	618
Koppulavelama	2408	1	100	89	568	1854	12525.97	464	1347
Kalinga	2074	2	508	61	452	1618	9996.73	393	183
Toorpu kapu	8121	6	211	300	2500	6117	31529.29	1698	2439
	15230	18	1189	481	4131	11695	59430.83	3079	4587

2.46 acres= one hectare.

over the supremacy from upper castes. As per the government classification, land holdings with a size of 10 ha. And above were large land holdings. In these surveyed villages, thirteen villages were Kalinga dominated, nine villages were Polinativelama dominated, eleven villages were Koppulavelama dominated and thirty-five villages were Toorpukapu dominated.

The agrarian structure of these villages is as given under in a tabular form. As seen from the table, in all these villages, large land holdings stood at 18 and they had 1189 acres in their hands. Out of them, nine belonged to Polinativelama, one belonged to Koppulavelama, two belonged to Kalinga and six belonged to Toorpukapu. Medium and semi-medium (4.92 to 24.6 acres) stood at 481 and they had 4,131 acres in their hands.

In the four Peasant castes 3079 families are landless. Out of them, 524 Polinativelama families, 464 Koppulavelama families, 393 Kalinga families and 1689 Toorpukapu families were landless, 16.90 per cent of Polinativelama, 18.02 per cent of Koppulavelama, 18.95 per cent of Kalinga and 21.36 per cent of Toorpukapu families were landless. As seen from the factual situation, traditional large land holding families disappeared with combined families were the only one with these large land holdings, which were a rare aspect in the villages.

In my observation, traditional families still maintained their hold on the land that prevailed in four villages. In Bontalakoduru and Konuru villages, the traditional landlords belonged to Kshatriya caste still held hundreds of acres. In Kuppili village, two families got hold of the land to the tune of 500 acres. In Kambirigam village, traditional landlord belonging to Kalinga caste still possessed 300 acres. In the village, the peasants belonging to Toorpukapu were fighting for the land for last 40 years. These lands were in legal dispute and fell fallow. Ironically, the government record did not show a single large holding in Kuppili village. In Konuru, the amount of land concentrated as per the records was not a factual figure. In fact, the information of revenue authorities in terms of large land holding is not matched to the statistics of field visit. Interestingly the revenue authorities showed large landholding of 208 acres in Dabaru village. Out of academic interest, I went to the village and observed that the 208 acres in the survey number was nothing but a hill. In all these villages, the landlords had conducted unabated feudal oppression on the masses. Though the land was in their hands, they were unable to conduct that oppression now. The relations of production changed the scenario and the landlords are trying to manage their cultivation by making plantations. However, these types of cases were unique in nature in this District with Kautsky describing this situation, "*Apart from the lease and mortgage system, a third case is possible. This is where the landowner is simultaneously a capitalist— that is, that aside from owning the land, he also possesses enough money to establish a modern farm entirely from his own resources, pocketing as a result not only the profit on enterprise but also the entire ground-rent.*" (The agrarian question: Karl Kautsky Page 93)

He also described it, *"Such a unification of the landowner and capitalist in one person is nevertheless an historical exception"*. (The agrarian question: Karl Kautsky Page 93).

Land Alienation and New Forces as Landowners

Over a period, the land became a commodity and gained a speculative character. In the beginning, the transactions are among the nearby villagers. As Marx told, *"Man has often made man himself, under the form of slaves, serve as the primitive material of money, but has never used land for that purpose. Such an idea could only spring up in an existing well-developed bourgeois society. It dates from the last third of the 17th century, and the first attempt to put it in practice on a national scale was made a century afterwards, during the French bourgeois revolution"*. (Capital Volume I page 61/543 www.marxist.org)

This process took a different shape altogether in this district since the early 90s. The lands were being alienated to individuals and the institutions which included software techies who emerged from these villages, Non-Resident Indians, realtors, people's representatives, companies, doctors, contractors, etc. In the villages surveyed, nearly 4,587 acres were alienated to such forces.

Land alienation was a common feature in almost every village but the alienation was rampant in 20 to 25 Mandals in the district. In some Mandals, the entire village lands were alienated. The process of land alienation can be seen from examples.

In Nandabalaga village, the people sold 340 acres of land to 8 families. In Seebillipeddavalasa village, almost 500 acres were alienated. Gollalapeta in Ramabhadrapuram Mandal and Gochekka in Parvatipuram Mandal were almost sold. In Budumuru, village out of 300 acres of dry land, 110 acres was sold to one single person. In Pydibhimavaram, village, the companies bought almost 1700 acres of land. It is an adjacent village to NH5 but the revenue records were not showing the truth.

In some villages, realtors bought chunks of land. In Ponugutivalasa (nearby village of Rajam), realtors bought 50 acres of land and sold. Ponugutivalasa is a village near to the Industrial centre, and there was a point to buy for real estate. The socalled real-estate boom in 2000 made the realtors buy 80 acres of land in Veerasagaram village of Badangi Mandal. Even the village has no bus facility. Now the land is left fallow. Realtors bought land in Chinabondapalli village and it is left fallow.

Marrapu Suryanarayana is a peasant activist and said, "Maxworth Company bought 300 acres of land at Pujariguda village in Komarada Mandal and carried out plantations. The same company bought 420 acres at Sangamvalasa village of Kurupam Mandal and carried out plantations".

Generally, in drought, prone Mandals and in Cheepurupalli, Garividi, Merakamudidam Mandal, the alienation was rampant and lands were converted to plantations. As Kautsky told, *"More the means of communication develop, easier the link between town and country, more such country seats will encroach into the countryside and drive the peasants off their plots"*.

Normally until the early 90s, people used to buy a small piece of land in the irrigated areas or water available areas. Later, the situation has vastly changed. People were buying the lands not for cultivation but for speculation. A peasant C. H. Venkatanarayana of Vadada village said, "My village is an irrigated village. We can cultivate two crops a year. However, our lands are costing less. In our village, an acre of land is about five lakhs whereas the lands near to highways where there is no facility of irrigation, the land cost had spiralled to Crores for an acre. I cannot understand the reasons for this shift"

Marx explained the reasons behind this process in his work Capitalthat reads, *"We therefore find that speculators make it a rule when such sudden changes in value occur, to speculate in that material on which a least possible quantity of labour has been spent."*

Thus, speculators across the country are grabbing the land where there is no need to add value of labour for speculation purpose. The concentration of the land is an inevitable process. In the name of leases or in the way of sales, this process is continuing in nature. However, one cannot confuse the type of concentration with that of feudal latifundium. In these enlarged farms, agriculture is being conducted in capitalist method. The of production relations represent the capitalist character. Agricultural engineering and chemistry will play higher role than the human labour. Wage labour replaces the old model of feudal oppression.

In the real sense, the original meaning that land is for cultivation in traditional methods has vastly changed. The land has become a commodity with the contenders being no more the marginal and small peasantry. In fact, even the traditional rich peasantry who are living exclusively on the cultivation cannot compete with the contenders. Land is transferring to those forces who own stocks of money. They are buying hundreds of acres. Even the rich peasantry who have surplus value from their cultivation are not in a position to contend them in purchasing the land. Those forces that have no direct link with the agriculture are playing enormous role in these transactions and were becoming estate owners. They were converting these lands for, *"the pursuit of pleasure - mansions, ornamental gardens, parks, game enclosures"*. (The agrarian question: Karl Kautsky Page 210)

In other words, the marginal and small peasantry were leaving room for the powerful lobbies and quietly merging into the crowds of proletarians. Engels described all this process, *"and thus the peasant sinks forever. Taxes, crop failures, divisions of inheritance and litigations drive one peasant after another into the arms of the usurer; the indebtedness becomes more and more general, and steadily increases in amount in each case—in brief, our small peasant, like every other survival of a past mode of production, is hopelessly doomed. He is a future proletarian."* (Engels 1894: The Peasant Question in France and Germany).

3

Agriculture

Humankind went through the phases of shift as well as settled cultivations with the labour having played indispensible role thorough this entire journey. Even the man-made national boundaries could not hinter this process. The process of agriculture transforming to agri-business has to be understood as commoditisation of the basic need of human being, food. It took a long time from food gathering to shift-cultivation, which can be understood as sowing and reaping still prevalent in tribal tracts. Officers of Tribal welfare department said that compared to what prevailed during 70s, the area under shift-cultivation had significantly come down and there was no further enhancement in this regard. Field level observations too confirmed the same. The statutes for Adivasis have been cautious to be confined only among themselves with the Adivasis to the parcel and morsel of land being uneconomical and in many cases unproductive and not to accede even an inch further. Filing of cases against those intending to start shift-cultivation in new areas resultantly both because of the incessant campaign by the government machinery, as the shift cultivation was not viable and because of the new generations disinclination for the shift-cultivation to come to a halt.

The people of earlier period of human life would not have even dreamt of the settled cultivation. They thought that development of agrarian society was itself difficult and that human society was nomadic in nature. D.D. Kosambi described this transformation as, "*the older problem of transition to an agricultural society had been so completely solved that people forgot it as if it had ever existed in history.*" (The culture and civilisation of ancient India in historical outline: D.D. Kosambi)

Agricultural implements played a greater role in the transformation. People devised the implements to suit their needs according to time. Kanka and Jiggi played a greater role in Podu. In the plains, the plough replaced these. Even now in tribal areas, tribals use Kanka and Jiggi. Plough played a crucial role in improving the agricultural practices. It appeared that the timeline of plough was shorter than Kanka and Jiggi. However, plough annexed the primitive implements and its vital role in Indian agriculture is significant. European researches exclaimed about the methods of ploughing in British India and noted, "*the fields are manipulated to a very great degree, ploughed and reploughed a dozen times, and reduced to a powder without a clod or a knot.*" (Modern India a sketch of the system of civil government: Page: 65 G. Campbell)

Plough helped in surplus produce and the surplus prompted certain people to bring large chunks of land and declare themselves as owners. The surplus production got exchange value to agricultural produce in place of mere use value. Surplus necessarily searched markets and market determined the production. The district was no exception for this process. Necessary production techniques, mechanisation and market exploration came into being. The general principle was that the capital originating from this surplus systematically replaced labour with machines, which were seen in agricultural sector. Tractor replaced plough and yet Kanka and Jiggi (primitive implements in tribal tracts) still existed in remote tribe habitations. Similarly, plough did its job, cantered by tractors. Plough was used more in preparation of seedbeds than in mere fields.

Changing Pattern in Agriculture

The ancient people were not in a position to produce even to cater to their own needs. The concept of surplus had not entered the arena for a long time. Hence, commoditisation of agriculture produce did not come into picture.

Permanent settlement system paved the way for the advent of zamindari system. Handful zamindars gained control over the land. This system evolved with a pen stroke in this area. With a pen stroke, innumerable peasants turned as tenants. With this evolution, the peasant community faced the oppression from the zamindars along with the economic exploitation. The produce had been expropriated by the zamindars in the shape of rent. The remaining part went to the traders and moneylenders combine. The cash-commodity form (here it is called fayida) that prevailed in money lending robbed the peasantry. At the end of every agriculture season, the peasantry remained with bare hands. Thus, the zamindari system made the peasantry as mere paupers. In political parlance, this system can be christened as feudal and semi-feudal oppression. Even the working group of eleventh five year plan also expressed in the same way, "*Rural India, on the eve of independence was characterised by feudal and semi feudal agrarian relations. The peasantry under all varieties of land settlements was exploited in terms of rack renting, insecurity of tenure, forced labour, usuary and so on.*" (Sub group on land related matters, 11th Five-year plan: Page 118)

The situation in the district was almost similar to the above description during until 1948. Huge tracts of land were concentrated with few families. Only a handful of people lived as tenants. Many people were living as unrecorded tenants who suffered from economic and social oppression. The abolition of landlordism led to disintegration of feudal latifundium. In this process, medium to large holdings were formed with the law of inheritance being conducive to disintegration of land. Over a period of 65 years, these land holdings had become marginal and small. In majority of villages, 80 per cent were living with sub-marginal land holdings. The agriculture survived a long time primarily on family labour, attached labour (majority were Dalits) and on agricultural labour.

Human resources were the primary motive power for the agriculture. The changing pattern in this factor had led to effective changes in the agrarian relations. Large tenants had a history of fighting for their rights on the tenancy lands. These large tenants led the peasant movement in this district during the colonial period. The Rytu Rakshana yatra (March to save the peasantry) from Itchapuram to Chennai was nothing but the reflection of the aspirations of these sections. Though the participation was sizeable, the composition of leadership belonged to these affluent recorded tenants. In fact, in that process, the aspirations of rural labour did not reflect.

Tenancy

The leasing out of land had two features. (With regard to local intervention) The sections, which had the rights on the land, got benefitted from the public capital in the agriculture and even retained their lands intact. The children of these sections reaped the benefits from the education and in the initial stage, most of them were settled as teachers. They lived in their original places and conducted the cultivations on their "own" with hired labour. This situation continued until early 90s. The progeny of these sections entered the new fields and became techno savvies and even bureaucrats. These sections lost the advantage of supervising the agriculture. Hence, those who were leasing out their lands, it did not mean that these were large landholdings. Whatever land they had in their villages, they gave it on lease to their fellowmen of their own caste. Dalits were not playing any significant role in this process. In the surveyed villages, leasing by Dalits was almost a rare feature. Even some rich peasants though stayed in the village too were leasing out their lands. When asked about this in Yaragam village, a rich peasant said, "We are leasing the land to avoid the risk". In the surveyed villages, leasing-out of lands varies from 10 per cent to 50 per cent. It represents one type of tenancy.

The second set of tenancy reflects the dark side of tenancy. Many sub-marginal, marginal and small peasants are not in a position to manage the agriculture in the old model. Factors like escalation of costs, non-profitability in the agriculture, the increased spending on health and education, interest payments, crop failures, etc., made difficult for these small entrepreneurs to conduct their business. Hence, they were leaving their villages in search of livelihood. They were letting their tiny holdings to their fellow marginal and small players for lease. One cannot equate this tenancy to the old feudal mode of tenancy. Instead, one should classify it as losing the right of entrepreneurship of these marginalised sections. On the other hand, some are exhibiting this right and taking the land for tenancy. In this process, some more people are becoming insolvent to migrate to other areas in search of livelihood.

In the surveyed villages, many examples were unearthed for this process of marginalisation. Burujola is a village situated in Bhamini Mandal. Bodepu Rajarao is a marginal peasant. He tried to cultivate land on lease basis. In 2010, in this district, due to flood, the crop failed. He took five acres of land on lease and spent Rs. 40, 000. He lost all his investment and became indebted. He along with his son migrated only to pay the debt. In this process, he gave his own piece of land 0.80 acres to another on lease and migrated. Now he is working in Chennai, and his son is working in Bangalore as construction workers. This has become a regular feature in this district.

Contract Farming

North Andhra (comprises Srikakulam, Vizianagaram, Visakhapatnam) peasantry are supplying pulpwood to J.K. Paper mill that is situated in Rayaghada of Odisha state. As per annual report of that mill, they have only 35,764 hectares under their control on contract basis. As per the CDM project titled 'Improving Rural Livelihoods through Carbon Sequestration by Adopting Environment Friendly Technology Based Agro forestry Practices, 15,578 hectares were under control of this paper mill in Andhra Pradesh. J.K. Paper's Managing Director, Harsh Pati Singhania said, *"We provide high quality seedlings/clones to private farmers located within the vicinity of our manufacturing units and source wood back from such farmers. In the past 15 years, we have covered 80,000 hectares of land under this programme, and this constitutes our 80-85 per cent of the raw material requirements. We believe that this would reduce uncertainty in the availability of raw materials,"* (Interview to Press Trust of India dated 20/07/2011)

The International Finance Corporation is giving US$120 million loan to four paper companies for planting plantations in the private lands. (I.F.C. document: Long-term partnerships with emerging players).

As seen from the factual position, in this area, Zamindar of Bobbili conducted contract farming from 1936 and it continued until 1978. Further, it was converted as public sector contract and back as private contract. Paper mills were encouraging plantations for the constant supply of raw material. In this district, jute was one of the major crops. In this district as of now, a dozen jute mills were functioning. However, there is no written agreement but the total produce is processing in these mills only. Of late, cottonseed companies were making agreements with peasantry and cultivated cottonseed on contract. The IFFRI research paper indicated that even the paddy and wheat are under contract system since the government was procuring the product with minimum support price.

A remarkable fact in this system was most of the suppliers were marginal comprising small peasantry. In case of sugarcane, in the year 2011-12, 14,200 peasants supplied the cane. The total area was 19,800 acres with the average landholding being 1.39 acre. In 2006-07, during the season, sugarcane was being cultivated in 30,000 acres. The number of peasants during that season was 20,000. This was in the case of NCS Sugars, Bobbili. Parry's sugar mill situated in Sankili, which GMR Company started and Parry's group taking it over. Here too, the majority of suppliers were marginal and small.

Even in the forest areas, massive tracts of land were being cultivated to provide the raw material to handful of companies. In this process, the projects resorted to a form of contract system.

As noted by the sub-group of the planning commission, the characteristics of the Indian agriculture that prevailed during 1948 had disappeared. However, the crisis in agriculture come to an end. Economists of every stream, every report of the government besides every report of voluntary organisation unanimously declared that agriculture was in crisis. The two terms-agriculture and crisis are entangled.

Land Usage Pattern

Soil and labour are the source of wealth. Land is a habitat to humans. It is also a feeding source to all the human beings. Hence, the primitive man brought the land into usage only to provide food. Even now, people considered land as a source of producing food. However, the concept of visualising land as a commodity is remote to the common person. The development paradigm has transformed the source of livelihood as a commodity. World Bank affiliated magazine—The Rural Development Notes, described the Indian land policy, *"This importance of land together with the central institutional role of land administration dating back to colonial days, implies that land policy has long been the subject of animated debate. There is consensus that land administration—which was neglected after independence—is in urgent need of improvement.* (A strategy for improving land administration in India: Klaus Deininger: Agricultural rural development and notes: Issue 33, Feb. 2008)

It indicates (whatever the intentions of the WB. May be to get some more land to other than agriculture purpose) that there is no rational land use policy prevailed in India.

That magazine also added, *"Most of the institutions and processes for administering land in India were adopted from the British at Independence and have been modified only slightly since. The principal purpose of those institutions was to generate tax revenues, and as such they focused on productive rural areas, leaving 'marginal' rural and urban areas outside the system."* (A strategy for improving land administration in India: Klaus Deininger: Agricultural rural development and notes: Issue 33, Feb 2008)

As per the official classification, the government classified the land usage under ten heads. Those are:

(1) Forest, (2) barren and uncultivable land, (3) Land put to non- agricultural usage, (4) Permanent pastures and other grazing lands, (5) Misc. crops and groves not included in net area sown, (6) Cultivable waste, (7) other fallow

lands, (8) current fallow lands, (9) net area sown, (10) area sown more than once, (11) fishponds.

There is a need to consider the seventh and eighth categories. The official definition of these categories is given below.

(7) *Fallow Land other than Current Fallows:* This includes all land, which was taken up for cultivation but is temporarily out of cultivation for a period of not less than one year and not more than five years.

(8) *Current Fallows:* This represents cropped area, which is kept fallow during the current year (Source: www.dacnet.nic.in)

Hence, it is an undeniable fact that these lands were ready to use for cultivation and people cultivated this land for a long time.

Land Usage Pattern in Andhra Pradesh

The land usage pattern of Andhra Pradesh is given below in tabular form. This table shows the trends in the land usage pattern. Andhra Pradesh as a state formed in 1956. This table shows that in 1956, the net area sown in that year was 113.74 lakh hectares and constituted 42.26 per cent. At no point of time, the net area sown was increased. Moreover, this area was decreasing sharply. By the year 2009-10, the net area sown had dwindled to 99.92 lakh hectares. In 2009-10, its share constituted only 36.28 per cent. In real terms 13.82 lakh hectares productive land was not being utilised for the prime purpose.

On the other hand, the area under other fallows and current fallows were showed a drastic increasing trend. Over a period of 55 years, the area under these categories was almost doubled. In 1956, the area under both the categories was 25.91 lakh hectares. By the turn of 2009-10, this area had reached an

Table 1. Land Use Pattern in Andhra Pradesh

Sl. No.	*Year*	*Geographical Area (in Lakh hectares)*	*Net Area Sown (area in lakh hectares)*	*Per cent of net area sown*	*Other Fallows*	*Current Fallows*
1.	1956-57	269.12	113.74	42.26	8.06	17.85
3.	1968-69	274.75	109.19	39.74	9.18	24.82
4.	1976-77	274.4	106.02	38.64	12.16	26.47
5.	1981-82	274.4	113.25	41.27	13.19	20.66
6.	1985-86	274.4	104.27	38.00	14.92	31.58
7.	1990-91	274.4	110.22	40.17	13.77	24.85
8.	1995-96	274.4	106.37	38.76	16.58	25.39
9.	2000-01	274.4	111.15	40.51	14.17	23.12
10.	2005-06	274.4	107.45	39.16	16.23	24.34
11.	2009-10	275.4	99.92	36.28	16.26	33.6

(Area in Lakh Hectares)

Source: 50 years of Andhra Pradesh and data compiled from the publications of directorate of statistics of Andhra Pradesh.

alarming figure of 49.86 lakh hectares. In the last five years, the growth in current fallows had increased from 24.34 lakh hectares to 33.6 lakh hectares recording a growth of 38 per cent. It is interesting to note that in all these five years, rain gods showered their blessings on the state.

As seen from the available data, the net area sown more than once had increased from 10.7 lakh hectares to 25.69 lakh hectares. However, there was a lot of however, there is a lot of inter-district and intra district variations in the availability of irrigation sources which results in the variations in the net sown area. This growth had occurred in irrigated areas. The rich peasantry of this irrigated belt declared crop holiday. Some are even calling those as "peasant movements".

Land Usage Pattern in Srikakulam District

The land usage pattern of Srikakulam District is given below in tabular form. This table almost reflects the macro level trends. Srikakulam as a district was formed in 1950. This table shows that during 1957-58, the net area sown in that year was 9.08 lakh acres and constituted 36.46 per cent. By 1967-68, the net sown area had increased sharply reaching 11.08 lakh acres. There was no substantial improvement in the net sown area for the last 42 years. Interestingly, the net sown area was decreasing from the last decade. The season 2009-10 showed that it had again almost touched the figures of 1967-68.

On the other hand, the area under other fallows and current fallows were in increasing trend. Previously, the area under other fallows is in decreasing trend. At one stage, it had even fallen to 24,630 acres, and it had further rose to 95,551.32 acres. At the same time, current fallows recorded 89 per cent growth in the reviewed period. In 1957-58, there was 99,498 acres of land under this category, but it reached 1,88,704.10 acres. In 1968-69, there was 1, 22,306 acres of land under the category of land used for the non-agricultural purpose, but it reached to 3, 39,888 acres in 2009-10. Almost 177 per cent of growth was recorded in this category.

Table 2. Land Usage Pattern in Srikakulam District

Sl. No.	*Year*	*Geographical*	*Other Fallows*	*Current Fallows*	*Net Area Sown*	*Percentage of net area sown*
1.	1957-58	2491076	153342	99498	908323	36.46
2.	1968-69	2477828	89093.82	122306.3	1103723	44.54
3.	1976-77	2389939	44596	89128	1219305	51.02
4.	1990-91	2375137	28402.38	67973.88	1238092	52.13
5.	1994-95	2368121	26432.7	104328.6	1247173	52.67
7.	2004-05	2341059	24639.36	149164.6	1209343	51.66
8.	2007-08	2374144	71716.38	57076.92	1253213	52.79
9.	2009-10	2425371	95551.32	188704.1	1118432	46.11

Area in acres :

Source: Compiled from district hand books and crop report of 1957-58.

Thus, the state and district trends show that the primary purpose of the land is taking a back seat. On the one hand, cultivable land is becoming fallow and on the other considerable land is being diverted to Non-agricultural purpose. This shows that land is being slipped away from the cultivators.

As seen from the land usage statistics of the district, there is an extraordinary decrease in the pastoral grounds and the cultivable waste. In 1968-69, there was 49,869 acres of pastoral grounds. For the corresponding period, the land under the category of cultivable waste was 1,21,094 acres and 6,661 acres respectively. In the initial phase, it appeared from the record that these lands were being utilised for agriculture. In the later stage, the statistics proved otherwise.

This is not a distinctive character of either this state or to this district. Planning commission and economic surveys also revealed the same trend for all over the country. Thus, it attained universal character. Economic survey 2009-10 noted, *"The area coverage of 667.84 lakh ha under total food grains during Kharriff 2009-10 compared to714.02 Lakh ha during Kharriff 2008-09 showed a decline of 46.18 lakh ha."* (*Source:* www.finmin.nic.in).

The working group on land related matters for the eleventh five-year plan had expressed deep concern over this unprecedented trend and noted, *"Recent years have seen conversion of large tracks of agricultural land for the purpose of commercial and real estate purposes. Though these conversions were yet to be recorded in the official statistics, the issue of declining net sown area were highlighted as a major concern in the Indian agriculture during the recent months (Alagh, 2006). Though the net sown area fluctuated along with rainfall, it was argued that the recent decline of about one million hectares during 2003-04 was unprecedented. Even severe droughts during the 80s did not experience such a decline."* (Report of sub-group on land related matters: www.plannincommission.nic.in)

The Sub-group anticipated the reasons and said, *"For agriculture, in general, it has become unviable even during the normal monsoon years; hence farmers may be shunning away from taking a greater risk in a below normal monsoon years. Other important reasons could be; (i) degradation of land and (ii) allocation of land for more remunerative purposes like real estate, development activities, special economic zones, etc., (iii) corporate agriculture was also growing though it would not alienate land from agriculture". (Ibid)*

Variations in the Net Sown Area across the District

In 1968-69, the average net sown area recorded in this district was 44.54 per cent, it reached its peak in 2007-08, and it again dropped while the average net sown area of this district stood at 46.11 per cent in 2009-10. However, many Mandals in this district could not reach this average due to lack of irrigation. Mountains and Forest tracts also were one of the reasons for this. Twenty Mandals out of Fifty-six always recorded below average. Gummalakshmipuram and Kurupam Mandals never crossed even 20 per cent. Pachipenta, Seetampeta, Meliaputti and Hiramandalam Mandals were always fluctuating between twenty and twenty-five per cent.

Changing Land Usage Pattern in Mandals

For further investigation of land usage trends, some Mandals had to be taken. In this district, Bobbili and Tekkali Mandal are almost plains.

Table 3. Land Usage Pattern in Bobbili Mandal

Sl. No.	*Year*	*Geographical Area*	*Other Fallows*	*Current Fallows*	*Net Area Sown*	*Percentage of net area sown*	*Rain normal (in mm)*	*Rain actual*
1.	1990-91	50934.3	31.98	24.6	36122.64	70.92	1122.6	945.3
2.	1994-95	50934.3	0	0	37168.14	72.97	1122.6	1256.3
3.	2004-05	50934.3	1289.04	302.58	34398.18	67.53	974.8	1148
4.	2007-08	50934.3	1067.64	1230	33465.84	65.70	1134	1395.2
5.	2009-10	50934.3	0	4437.84	31950.48	62.73	1143.9	1143.9

Source: compiled from District hand books.

As seen from the table, Bobbili is also reflecting the existing trends. Current fallows are increasing. The net area sown had decreased from a peak 72.97 per cent to 62.73 per cent. The percentage of net sown area was consistently declining. In fact, there were almost no forests and mountains in this Mandal. The cultivation was almost rain fed. Though there was a shortage of rain in the year 1990-91, the net sown area was recorded as 36,122.64 acres and it accounted for 70.92 per cent. By the turn of 2009-10, the scene was reversed. Though the rain gods showered optimum rain, the peasants had left the land fallow. Current fallows recorded maximum land over twenty years.

As seen from this table, the net sown area started declining. When compared with 1990-91, net decrease in 2009-10 was 5,771 acres. The percentage of net

Table 4. Land Usage Pattern in Tekkali Mandal

Sl. No.	*Year*	*Geographical Area*	*Other Fallows*	*Current fallows*	*Net area sown*	*Per cent of net sown area*	*Rain normal (in mm)*	*Rain actual*
1.	1990-91	34167	1114	830	22384	67	1110.8	1325.3
2.	1994-95	34014.42	14.76	3057.78	20548.38	60.4	1110.8	1238.6
3.	2004-05	34014.42	14.76	3650.64	18491.82	54.4	1274	1226
4.	2007-08	34014.42	319.8	2322.24	19515.18	57.4	1274	1467.4
5.	2009-10	34014.42	297.66	5247.18	16612.38	48.8	1272.3	925.6

Source: Compiled from District Handbooks.

decrease was recorded as 25.78. Almost 1/4th of the once cultivated area were utilised for other purposes. It appeared from the table that there was a shortage of rain in 2009-10. However, when compared to 1990-91 to 2007-08, the rainfall was almost equal, but the net sown area had declined. As the sub-group noted the paucity of rain is indicating only a partial reason. In fact, many other reasons contributed for this constant decline in the cultivation. The main reason for this decline was people losing faith in that profession.

As observed from the field study, these two Mandals were reflecting the trend of urbanisation. Many employees of surrounding Mandals had shifted from their countryside and settled in these Mandal Head quarters. It is said that most of the employees of 13 to 14 Mandals were residing in Bobbili and performing their duties in the villages. Because of this, the land rates spiralled in Bobbili and over a period of twenty years, the price of land had multiplied.

Agriculture

Gandhi said, *"Agriculture is not a dying profession. However, it needs a change and development. National government can only execute the required reforms in that sector."* (Translated version of Gandhi article in Khadi arthasastram: originally published in Young India Dated 30/7/1925).

Even after the evolution of agrarian society, the productivity and production were in low ebb for a long period. People could not even make the sufficient food grains to cater to their needs. Even in India, the production of food grains in the year 1950-51 stood at 50.8 Million tonnes. At the same time, the area under cultivation was 97.3 Million Hectares.

Table 5. All-India Area, Production and Yield of Food Grains. Along with Coverage under Irrigation

Year	*Area*	*Production*	*Area - Million Hectares* *Production - Million Tonnes* *Yield - kg./Hectare* *Yield*	*Percentage of Area under irrigation*
1970-71	124.32	108.42	872.10	24.1
1980-81	126.67	129.59	1023.05	29.7
1990-91	127.84	176.39	1379.77	35.1
2000-01	121.05	196.81	1626.00	43.4
2007-08	124.07	230.78	1860.00	46.8
2008-09	122.83	234.47	1908.83	48.3
2009-10	121.33	218.11	1797.64	NA
2010-11*	125.73	241.57	1921.38	NA
2011-12**	70.49	123.88	1757.00	NA

* Fourth Advance Estimates as released on 19.07.2011.

**First Advance Estimates released on 14.09.2011.

Source: Directorate of Economics and Statistics, Department of Agriculture and Cooperation.

Note: The yield rates given above have been worked out based on production and area figures taken in '000 units.

The period under review indicated that in 1970-71, the area under food grains was 124.3 million hectares and the production of food grains was 108.40 million metric tonnes. The figures in 2009-10 reached to 121.30 million hectares and 218.10 million tonnes respectively. The decrease in the net sown area was recorded at 2.40 per cent and growth in the production of food grains was recorded at 101.19 per cent. However, the pro-people economists were expressing deep concern over the availability of food grains and they were stating that the situation was again reflecting the early 70s.

Balance of Payment Crisis

Various government reports and agronomists were consistently portraying that the country was facing agrarian crisis. In general, parlance, crisis had occurred in any sector due to stagnation in the production. However, as seen from the statistics, production showed increasing trend constantly. Every crop, whether it is food grain or it is a commercial crop was recording accelerated trend. Still, predominantly the marginal and small peasantry producer were caught in the crisis. The reasons for this crisis required to be examined carefully.

Economists of early 60s were of the opinion that the reason for the crisis was due to the low-productivity. Hence, they tried to solve the crisis by invoking modern methods in the cultivation for increasing the production and productivity. For this purpose, they preferred small-landholdings, high-yielding varieties, irrigation, engineering, fertilisers, pesticides and electricity to increase the production. However, these facilities were available only in selected areas. Briefly, to negate the problems of feudal and semi-feudal pattern, modernity was established. In the initial period, the stimulation had yielded good results and the sections of those areas were flourished along with the agriculture. Irrespective of the irrigation facilities, all these practices were universalised in the country. In this process, the entire inputs for this cultivation were put on sale. People lost control over consumption of inputs and no peasant was in a position to formulate their inputs. Kosambi said about the problems of transition to an agrarian society. The same thing was applied *mutatis mutandis* to the transformation of agrarian society to the modern methods of cultivation. The earlier process of transition had then been completed that people of present generation forgot it as if it never existed in the society. The spiralling cost of these inputs escalated the cost of production. Economists were proclaiming that productivity is not in proportion to the cost of cultivation. Hence, it again led to further round of fresh crisis. A worth observing fact was that this crisis could not be compared with that prevailed in 1947-70 period. The first crisis was a reflection of low production and non-usage of modern methods in the agriculture while the current crisis is showing a reverse trend.

The continuous growth in the production pattern of food grains did not bring any change in the marginal and small peasantry. Policy makers said that the cultivation of food grains was not a profitable business. Policy makers suggested to the peasantry to harvest the crops that could cater to the industrial needs to make profits. Peasantry also shifted their approach accordingly. In spite of that, the crisis was continuing as a riddle. It was a glaring fact that in this country, majority of suicides in the farm sector occurred in the cotton fields. Cotton was exclusively cultivated for industrial production. While the traditional cropping pattern made the peasantry half-starved, the merger of agriculture production pattern to the manufacturing sector was taking the lives of the peasantry in the fields. In such cultivation, Indian fields were either filled with the bodies of peasantry or making them flee to town side. Thus, the peasantry is leading life with bed of nails.

No economist or no government was in a position to say that agriculture was not in crisis even from the early years of independence. Peasantry was getting into crisis proportionately to their produce. This crisis was not a reflection of low production. Though they were continuously starving for higher production, their calamity did not decelerate. The capitalist society had enhanced the expenditure of the peasantry to multi folds and they were entrapped. The difference between their incomes and the expenditure was constantly increasing. Low production, low incomes and low expenditure were the characters of early independence days. The low productivity and low produce created a crisis and in economic parlance, it was called a crisis created by the feudal mode of production. However, now the situation entirely changed but the crisis has not been changed. In economic parlance, the plight of feudal practice was converted to capitalist crisis.

Peasantry Problem is Nothing but Balance of Payments Crisis

Normally economists take the balance of payments as a scale to determine the extent of the crisis. This language used to notify the financial health of a country. It was understood from the available data that the peasantry was entangled in balance of payment crisis.

During the survey of the village in Chinabondapalli village, a peasant Jakku Appalanaidu asserted, *"as production increases, productivity also increases"*. Minimum support price and market guaranteed returns were encouraging. However, they were caught in the debt trap. In the olden days, the children used to study in the village schools. Now they were going to a nearby town even to study lower kindergarten (popularly known as L.K.G). The lowest annual fees structure started from 10,000 even for an average school. Earlier, all the family members used to wear two or three pairs of dresses each. The total luggage of the clothes could be adjusted in a trunk. Now, each of the family was using a large bureau for storage of cloths. All the inputs, which were necessary for conducting agriculture, had slipped from their hands. The cultural onslaught also was playing its part. In their life, they were unaware of birthdays, wedding days or valentine days. The list was endless. They were unaware of even the photography as none had a photo of any old aged departed relatives. However, later, videography was the order of the day for every function. This was the state of the peasantry in the countryside."

A peasant of Chalivendri village described the best example for the cultural onslaught on the rural masses saying, "I have strived hard to harvest sugarcane all the year. I went to get payment to the factory and the factory management paid 10,000 rupees. As I returned with money, my friends reminded me about birthday celebration of my son. Now the only meaning to the party in the villages is nothing but serving alcohol. The total amount perished in an hour. The whole labour of mine has gone."

The peasants of Turakalakota village narrated the other face of the crisis. In their words, "in the olden days family labour, friends and relatives help sharply cut down the cost of the labour. Now the good old practices are perished. The family labour is also considerably decreased. The children are going to school and they are not in a position to extend their help. Hence, the wage labour is increased in the agricultural operations. This is also one of the reasons for the crisis."

When asked about the family labour in an agricultural operation a small peasant of Piridi village gave an account of labour for the paddy crop.

Table 6. Wage Labour versus Family Labour for Paddy Crop

Sl. No	*Work*	*Labour*		*Work Days*	*Coolie*	*Tractor*	*Fertiliser*	*Family Labour*
		male	*female*					
1.	seed	1				0	3250	0
2.	seed bedding	1	0	1/2 day	200	0	0	1
3.	aakupota	2		1/2 day	200	0	0	1
4.	weeding	0	4	1	400	0	0	0
5.	ploughing	1			0	800	0	0
6.	puddling	1			400	0	0	0
7.	Bunding	5		1	1000	0	0	1
8.	transplanting	0	20	1	1000	0	0	1
9.	weeding	0	10	1	1000	0	0	1
10.	weeding	0	10	1	1000	0	0	1
11.	harvesting	0	12	1	1000	0	0	1
12.	loading and unloading	8	0	1	1000	0	0	1
13.	Threshing (tractor)	1	0		0	800		1
14.	coolie threshing	10	0		2000	0	0	1
15.	fan	5			0	50	0	0
16.	water	2		2	0	2000	0	0
17.	packing	5						
	Total	42	56		9200	3650	3250	10

Source: Peasants of Ajjada village.

As seen from this table for 98 coolies the family labour is accounted only for ten coolies. The peasants of Turakalakota village omitted the cheap labour part in their earlier surplus value. The omission of cheap labour is conspicuous in nature.

The national and international capital produces commodities *ad infinitum*. Destination of most of these commodities was the countryside.The incessant propaganda made the public fetish towards these commodities. In one term, the people were the consumers. This process looted the money from the rural people. In the international trade, developing countries were caught in the vicious circle of balance of payment crisis. In the international trade, advanced countries exported products like armaments, technical knowhow, etc., at an exorbitant price. However, the developing block exports agricultural products for cheaper rates. Though the quantum of exports was high from the developing world, they could not fill the gap in the international trade, which led to balance of payment crisis. The same pattern applied to rural masses too. They laboriously toiled in the fields and in their tiny piece of lands only to sell their goods at lower prices. In this way, the urban market made the necessities like education and health as expensive. At the same time, the consumer market exported the trivial goods at exorbitant prices thus reflecting the balance of payment crisis for the marginal and small peasantry. As Mahatma Gandhi said, "the devil surpassed all the boundaries and the rural peasantry were caught in the web". Maxim Gorky said about this process "the city on the one hand, puts one rupee in a pocket and by the evening it will take one rupee twenty five paisa from another pocket." (*Source: Nagaram, Telugu version*)

Karl Kautsky theorised all this process and summed up, *"Their first hunt for markets is not amongst the proletarian but the non-proletarian masses, and in particular, the rural population. We observed how this ruined rural domestic industry and created a large market for the sale of articles of mass consumption."* (Kautsky: The agrarian question: Page 239)

The rural peasantry tried to repay the debt burden by working through the days and nights in the fields and they produced the goods required for urban industrialists and for urban rich. They always tried to get instant cash to reduce the debt burden. This approach invariably led them to merger with urban interests. Their burden proportionately increased with their production. This process brought many changes in the cropping pattern. The revolutions whatever it named like Green, White, Blue and now Pink were all able to increase the production only to sell them at the behest of urban interests. The only goal of urban production was nothing but expropriation of agricultural surplus from the rural masses. In this process, even the rural masses had changed their food habits. They kept on sending higher quality products to the urban market and keeping the inferior quality for their own consumption. Even the rural masses were not using any value added products for their consumption. In the early 20s, Mahatma Gandhi painfully expressed that the rural masses were not in a position to combat malaria because of the low immunity because of non-availability of good food. He particularly named the non-availability of Milk.

However, the white revolution increased the milk production from a mere 28.2 million tonnes in 1970-71 to 121.80 million tonnes in 2010-11. As per the statistics, the per capita "availability" of milk increased. However, in real terms, the consumption pattern in the countryside had decreased. Even the government reports indicated that the consumption of milk among the producers was 14.21 per cent in 2008-09 and it further decreased to 11.76 per cent in 2009-10.

Even in the surveyed villages, the rural mass is considering milk production as an additional source of income. The people said that they give almost total milk to the milk procuring centres without storing milk for their personal consumption. In Veerasagaram village, the rural peasantry and Dalits have milk-yielding animals from which they used to give the entire milk to the centre without retaining a drop of milk with them. They purchase tea from the tea stalls. Kothapeta is a village in Etcherla Mandal nearer to District headquarter Srikakulam. Here, the peasantry cultivates vegetables and send to Srikakulam market. Boddepalli Sudhakar, the former sarpanch of that village told that 99 per cent of the peasantry deliver the finest quality of fresh vegetables to market, and they retain poor quality of vegetable to be added into their dine. The blue revolution is a cause of disappearance of protein-rich fish from the dine of the rural fisher folk. Bhart Dogra, a freelance journalist, exposed the strategy of Blue revolution and told, *"While fish exports have reached very high levels, the per capita availability of fish in coastal villages, where it is the staple protein for the masses is declining."* (*Source: Crisis in Indian fisheries: page: 8: Bharat Dogra*) Further he quoted John Kurien which reads "*The main attraction of the smaller fish (which provide protein for masses) to the deep sea fishing interests is that such fish are available in bulk quantities. Given the spiralling of world market prices for fishmeal, considerable attention will be focussed on the bulk of those smaller, lower price species for this purpose. Here again, given the interests, when controlling the deep-sea operations, the option is between fishmeal for earning foreign exchange and protein for masses. The choice is obvious*" *(Ibid)*

This is not an unusual aspect of development model of India. It has a universal character.

Many historians and political economists wrote about this process. Lenin described this subject with respect to Danish rural masses, which reads, *"It is very simple. The vast majority of the Danish population, like that of any other capitalist country, consists of workers and property less peasant who cannot afford real butter. Even the middle level peasants in Denmark, being in need of money, sell abroad the butter they produce on their farms and buy the cheap margarine for themselves. The wealth of the Danish capitalists is growing, and so are the poverty and want of the Danish workers and peasants"*. (Lenin: Capitalism and popular consumption: *Source:* www. Marxist.org)

Citing the Russian example, "The same thing is happening here in Russia. Very long ago, some forty years back, when it became fashionable to set up cheese dairies and cartels in the countryside, Engelhard, a democratic writer, noted that the peasants, being in need of money, sold their milk and butter while their children starved to death." (Lenin: Capitalism and popular consumption: Source www. Marxist.org)

This process has literary evidence. Pannalal Patel, a Gujarati novelist and the winner of central government awards, described the life of the rural peasantry in his work "Jeevitame Oka naatakarangam". A peasant character Kaala describes the life of the rural peasantry, which reads, "*We (the rural peasantry) are not the patrons of the planet. Instead, we are carrying the burden of the earth. We are just like bullock. Bullock carries rice, ghee. Wheat, Gur and so on. However, nothing is gone in its mouth.*" Another peasant in agreement with this replied *"yes. We harvest wheat, and we eat only the inferior Variga."*

This novel described the rural peasantry life that existed in colonial Rule. It is a melancholy to note that the situation is further aggravated even after the large-scale revolutions in the food sector.

Share of GDP and Public Investment in the Agrarian Sector

Agrarian sector is the foundation for every society. The primary sector contributes substantial share to national income in the initial stages. Lion's share of national income came from this sector for a long period. The surplus accumulated in that sector enters the manufacturing sector and act as an investment to the industrial sector. Agrarian sector plays a vital role in development of capital.

The capital thus born will not be satisfied with the local and geographical boundaries. It travels overseas to develop markets. International trade is not a new concept and history repeatedly proved that this is a natural process of capital penetration.

"There is some historical evidence that a Green Revolution preceded the Industrial Revolution in Europe, its offshoots and Japan. Recent scholarship has excavated the importance of pre-war agricultural growth to the post-war industrialisation of Taiwan and South Korea. Cross-country studies which seek to track the sectorial sources of growth in developing countries unambiguously reported that a dynamic agriculture has the strongest linkage to growth in other sectors and aggregate growth." (*Source:* Locking Private Investment in Indian Agriculture: Rommer Correa).

This process is re-enacted in India. In light of the above proposition, there is a need to observe the trends of public investment in agriculture and simultaneous contribution of primary sector to GDP. In the initial phase to create capital from the primary sector, public investment was poured in the primary sector. Irrigation, high-yielding seeds, subsidies on fertilisers and pesticides, agricultural implements, expansion of the banking sector, creation of jobs in the public sector, etc., an unending list is passing through to villages to stimulate the village economy only to get the accumulation of capital from the primary sector. Because of all these efforts, the share of primary sector increased substantially.As soon as the target achieved, the necessity of capital development has disappeared from the scene. The efforts of the public sector streamlined the flow of capital. Hence, the public investments took a U-turn.

Table 7. Share of Agriculture and Allied Sectors in Total GDP (in Crores at 1993-94)

Sl. No	Year	Agricultural, Forestry and Logging, Fishing, Mining and Quarrying	Total GDP	Increase/ Decrease in GDP	Percentage of Growth in GDP Sector in the Period	Increase/ Decrease in Agl and Allied Sector	Percentage of Growth in Agl and Allied Sectors in the Period	Share percentage of Agriculture and Allied Sectors	At 2004-05 prices
1.	1970-71	142581	296278					48.12	41.7
2.	1974-75	141185	315514	–1396	–0.44	–1396	–0.99	44.75	38.5
3.	1979-80	148663	374591	7478	2.00	7478	5.03	39.69	33.9
4.	1984-85	196353	492077	47690	9.69	47690	24.29	39.90	34.2
5.	1989-90	231389	656331	35036	5.34	35036	15.14	35.25	29.9
6.	1994-95	276049	838031	44660	5.33	44660	16.18	32.94	27.8
7.	1999-00	314253	1148442	38204	3.33	38204	12.16	27.36	23.3
8.	2004-05	565426	2971464						19
9.	2005-06	594487	3254216	282752	8.69	29061	4.89		18.3
10.	2006-07	619190	3566011	311795	8.74	24703	3.99		17.4
11.	2007-08	655080	3898958	332947	8.54	35890	5.48		16.8
12.	2008-09	654118	4162509	263551	6.33	–962	–0.15		15.7
13.	2009-10	656975	4493743	331234	7.37	2857	0.43		14.7
14.	2010-11	700390	4877842	384099	7.87	43415	6.20		14.5

Source: Economic surveys and state of Indian agriculture 2009-10: Figures up to 1999-200 are based on 1993-94 prices: Figures from 2004-05 are based on 2004-05 prices.

Table 8. Public and Private Investments in Agriculture at Current and 1980-81 prices.

Year	Gross capital formation in agriculture (GCFA) At the current price Total	Public	Private	Share of (%) Public	Private
1970-71	1214	329	885	27.1	72.9
1974-75	2089	591	1498	28.29	71.71
1979-80	4976	1618	3358	32.52	67.48
1984-85	7006	1679	5327	23.97	76.03
1989-90	11008	3347	7661	30.41	69.59
1994-95	24520	6022	18498	24.56	75.44

Public and Private investments in agriculture at current and 1999-2000 prices

Year	Gross capital formation in agriculture (GCFA) At the current price Total	Public	Private	Share of (%) Public	Private
1999-00	50151	8668	41483	17.28	82.72
2004-05	49108	12273	36835	24.99	75.01
2005-06	54905	15006	39899	27.33	72.67
2006-07	60762	17749	43013	29.21	70.79

Public and Private investments in agricultural at current and 2004-05 prices

Year	Gross capital formation in agriculture (GCFA) At the current price Total	Public	Private	Share of (%) Public	Private
2007-08	110006	23039	86967	20.94	79.06
2008-09	138597	24452	114145	17.64	82.36

Source: National Accounts Statistics, CSO various issues.
Taken from NCAP, 11th five year plan. Figures in Crores.

As per the 1999-00 prices, the share of primary sector stood at 48.12 per cent in 1970-71. Even at the prices of 2004-05, the percentage of this sector stood at 41.7 per cent. At the same time, the share of public sector in that phase recorded was 27.10. The share of public sector crossed the 30 per cent mark only in 1979-80. From that year, the share was constantly declining and the share of primary sector followed the same trend. By the year 2008-09, the public investment touched ever-low 17.64 per cent. In the same way in that year, the share of primary sector is recorded only 14.7 per cent thus proving that there was a direct proportionate relationship among these trends.

What is the meaning of private investment in the agrarian sector: one cannot obscure that private investment is certainly of the big private entrepreneurs. In fact, the rural peasantry contributes sizeable share in this private investment. All India debt and investment survey defined the private investment and categorised the various categories of investment under eight heads. They are:

1. Land reclamation
2. Bunding and other land improvements
3. Orchards and plantations
4. Wells
5. Other irrigation sources
6. Agricultural implements, machinery and transport equipment etc.
7. Farm houses, barns and animal sheds,
8. Other capital expenditure.

As per the agricultural census, 82 per cent of the peasantry is marginal and small. Their investment contributes to considerable share in this mammoth private investment. Major peasants of this country were making investments with their blood and sweat only to cater to the needs of industrialists by way of harvesting industrial crops or fondly called value added crops. As the governments withdraw the public investments in the agrarian sector, the peasantry is trying more and more to infuse their private capital in the fields to provide the raw materials to the industrial sector. This led them to sink in the ocean. These conditions are only leading them to their ultimate goal of suicides in desperation. As pointed out by the Minister of agriculture in the meeting of National development council *"Of the total number of suicide cases reported, 76 per cent of the victims were dependent on rain-fed agriculture and 78 per cent were small and marginal farmers."*

Table 9. Plan Allocations to Agricultural Sector

Sl. No.	*Plan*	*Plan Period*	*Allocation to agriculture and allied sectors*	*Percentage of allocation*
1.	4th	1969-74	2320.4	14.7
2.	5th	1974-79	4864.9	12.3
3.	annual plan	1979-80	1996.5	16.4
4.	6th plan	1980-85	6623.5	6.1
5.	7th plan	1985-90	12792.6	5.8
6.	annual plan	1990-91	3405.4	5.8
7.	annual plan	1991-92	3850.5	5.9
8.	8th plan	1992-97	22467.2	5.17
9.	9th plan	1997-2002	42462	4.9
10.	10th plan	2002-07	59833	3.9
11.	11th plan	2007-12	50924	2.4

Source: Various planning commission reports, www. planningcommission.nic.in.

Allocations to the agricultural sector in successive five-year plans: This table shows the trend of allocations to the primary sector in the agrarian country.

As seen from the table, there was an obvious deceleration in the allocation to the primary sector. In the fourth five-year plan, the allocations stood at 14.7 per cent. However, the allocation had drastically gone down to just 3.9 per cent during the 10th five-year plan. The plan allocation further deteriorated not only in percentage terms but also in absolute number. The allocation was dropped to 50,924 Crores and the percentage was dropped to a mere 2.4. The approach paper of 11th five-year plan is blaming the state governments for not allocating the adequate amounts to the sector. The strategy paper of the planning commission advised the state governments not to depend on the central funds since the subject of agriculture was, in principle, listed under the state list.

The expenditure of the state governments on agriculture was showing dismal performance. These statistics relates to the period from 1974-77 to 1996-97. For this calculation, the base year was 1980-81. As per the available statistics, while the average spending on agriculture per hectare for all the states stood at Rs. 239 only, Andhra Pradesh spent Rs. 160 per a hectare in that period.

On the other hand, the indirect tax collections were showing positive trends. The indirect taxation appeared to be justifiable, but an ordinary peasant and a billionaire were paying the same tax to the common commodity. They paid equal tax on soap. However, the peasant is not getting his legitimate share in the tax income. The decrease in the public investment on agriculture made the peasant to drain his pocket. On one hand, the peasantry (peasantry comprises marginal and small) was bearing the tax liability at par with the richest sects of this country and on the other hand, they were taking the investment burden. In this way, the peasantry was encountering two large burdens. Either it made them to flee from the countryside to live as urban proletarian or they were taking extreme measures as Shri Sharad Pawar said in his speech at national development council.

During and post colonial Rule, various committees and commissions gave bundles of reports for the welfare of peasantry. Unfortunately, no saviour came to protect the peasantry. Karl Marx commented about the Indian agriculture situation that prevailed in colonial Rule, which read, *"Now, the British in East India accepted from their predecessors the department of finançe and of war, but they had neglected entirely that of public works. Hence, the deterioration of an agriculture which is not capable of being conducted on the British Principle of free Competition, of Laissez faire, alaisseasler. But in Asiatic empires we are quite accustomed to see agriculture deteriorating under one government and revival again under some other government, where the harvests correspond for good or bad governments, as they changed in Europe with good or bad season's."* (Karl Marx on India: Page 13).

Indian agriculture played a pivotal role in developing manufacturing and service sectors, which attained self-sufficiency due to the primary sector. In the initial phase, agriculture played a key role in this process. The panorama then was reversed and the roles became different. The agriculture was running on the mercy of the industrial sector. The transformation of agriculture to agri-business had almost completed. Capital engorged by sucking the rural labour. In this process, agricultural proletariat could not get even the minimum wage. Later, the same capital tied 82 per cent of the peasantry to its chariot. In this process, the capital was continuously thriving with the sweat and blood of these marginalised sections.

In the society too, there were some precedence. A family member who earned job used to look after his entire family. The capitalist relations changed this system and definition of the family was reduced to spouse and children. Then the earning people used all their earnings to the re-defined family interests only.

The same principle applied to the production sector. Industrial and service sectors have reached this stage forgetting the foundation stone they were nurtured and flourished on. Those sectors treated the entire process as a history. These sectors never thought of the welfare of the primary sector. Moreover, they always tried to squeeze the primary sector for continuous growth. In fact, the capital created the crisis in the agrarian sector. Again, they spoke loudly about the crisis and emphasise the salvation. They indicated that massive holdings and capitalist agriculture were the only solution to overcome the crisis. They were managing to determine the policies and schemes towards this end.

However, though this country was declared as an agricultural country, there was no policy evolved to cater to the needs of this sector until 2000. The surprising factor was this country proclaimed industrial policies way back in 1948 and 1956. The first agricultural policy saw the light in 2000. Interestingly, this policy was framed to cater to the needs of the secondary sector.

This policy had put forward the remedial measures preached by the industrial lobby. On one hand, the policy spoke about the land reforms and on the other, it took a road map to consolidate the land holdings.

The policy spoke under the subchapter "Institutional Structure" which read;

(1) Consolidation of holdings all over the country on the pattern of north western States

(2) *Development of lease markets for increasing the size of the holdings by making legal provisions for giving private lands on lease for cultivation and Agri-business;*

(3) *Private sector participation will be promoted through contract farming and land leasing arrangements to allow accelerated technology transfer, capital inflow and assured markets for crop production, especially of oilseeds, cotton and horticultural crops.*

Source: National agricultural policy, Ministry of Agriculture, Government of India.

This is the evolution of Indian agriculture. The abolition of zamindars and Inamdaris paved the way for disintegration of land holdings. This paved the way to create rich peasantry. Broadly, they belonged to the majority peasant castes. Successive governments poured infrastructure to cater to their needs and accumulate capital from the primary sector. The process almost converted the rich peasantry to rural capitalists. As soon as the transformation completed the withdrawal of public capital started and various forces were slowly filling the vacuum. The policy itself stated, "The agriculture was starving of capital". In the absence of such public capital, the burden of filling is transferred mainly to the marginal and small peasants. Now these forces were unable to keep with the pace. Hence, the policy was speaking in favour of handing over the sector to these forces.

However, this does not mean that creation of large landholdings would occupy the whole scene. In fact, the existence of small land holdings was also required for thriving of these large land holdings. Industrialists felt happy in the continuation of small land holdings. A sugar industry owner felt happy to enter into the contract with 14,200 peasants for supply of sugarcane. He could have evaded them in many ways by ignoring the clauses in the contracts or could have postponed the payments at his own will. The suppliers with the average land holding of 1.39 acres could not unify and fight with the mighty forces since they were committed with their tiny land holding. It was not a story of only the sugar industrialist of this area. Contract farming was the best practice to fulfil the needs of these industrialists. In political parlance, the disassociation of this peasantry is a boon to industrialists.

Karl Kautsky summed up the survival of the both types of land holdings. It reads, *"large and small-scale farming are not mutually exclusive. In fact, like capitalist and proletarian, they require each other with the small farm increasingly assuming the latter role"*. (Kautsky: The agrarian Question: Page 166-167)

Contract farming and land alienation were becoming common in this district. The new forces are conducting Agri-business on their large farms. The vernacular dailies Eenadu and Andhra Jyothy published this praising about such practices. As per their story, a tech-savvy Kranti returned from U.S.A. and she left her career to do cultivation. The news stories praised her for conducting the cultivation by compromising a convenient and rewarding career. The stories said that she was conferred awards for taking this profession. The story board advised the rural youth for taking up cultivation since it is also a rewarding job as proved by "Kranti" (literal meaning of Kranti is Revolution). In fact, Eenadu put the title to the story as "Revolution Ushered".

Then what is the truth behind this propaganda? As per the storyline, she bought 50 acres of land, which meant at least 25 to 50 peasants in losing their land holdings to this revolution. What was the cultivation going on? She was cultivating Emu birds and maize in those fields. Since she was getting profits, it was concluded that cultivation was a rewarding business. As understood, 50 acres of land holding was required to earn profits from the cultivation. When

82 per cent of the peasantry was surviving on marginal and small land holdings, how each peasant got 50 acres of land and how it will be called an era of a new revolution. It clarified that the news story reflects the interests of capitalist agriculture.

However, the promotion by the governments, media, and private agencies were influencing the peasantry. Department of Agriculture, Andhra Pradesh conducted a national conference for Rabi campaign on 18th and 19th September 2007 and gave a power point presentation on that occasion. It was a proclaimed effort to educate farmers on contract farming (*Source:* Power point presentation of Department of Agriculture).

The education was not restricted to power point presentations; rather it had already reached the countryside.When asked about the remedy of this crisis, a marginal peasant of Korasavada village of Patapatnam Mandal replied "ah! What is there? Any of the company will come to the countryside and lease-in all these lands. They will remove all these bunds and make them large farms. We have the names in titles, but they will carry the cultivation. If any peasant wants to sell the land, the names will be changed on the paper and the "new" peasant will offer the land to the company. It will appear in the near future".

It indicated that the peasantry was already educated. In economic parlance, this district was considered as a backward area. In this area, too the process of inculcation had been completed.

Briefly, the concept that prevailed indivisibility between the peasantry and cultivation will become invalid. While on one hand, the agricultural production and productivity increased day by day, on the other, the peasantry was thrown out of their fields. Commoditisation of agriculture in the agricultural and non-agricultural sectors was the basis for this crisis. The continuous transformation of the peasantry as urban proletarian was the order of the day. The crisis was in the life of the peasantry but not in the production.

4

Cropping Pattern

Human being considered the soil as a producer of food. This concept has been in vogue for a long time. They were not even in a position to produce sufficient food to cater to their needs. In the tribal tracts of the district, the situation has broadly been prevailing even now.

Even as a country, India too faced this situation. Indian people as a whole faced the shortage of food grains. In one word, the Indians were in a position of "ship to mouth" for a long time. Probably these circumstances led to Malthusian theory. However, an American socialist Simons ridiculed this concept and proclaimed in a tone of self-confidence that the American priorities can produce the wheat that needed for the whole universe.

Indian agriculture broadly continued until early 70s, only to cater to the food needs of the country's citizens. In the name of increasing the food production, successive governments implemented Green Revolution. On one sense, the governments took up irrigation, high yielding seed, requisite loans, market etc. In another sense, not only to increase the production but also to accumulate capital from the primary sector, these revolutions ushered on Indian peasantry. Punjab has become a capital of food grains.

There is a need to observe the proclamations and policies of successive governments of Andhra Pradesh about the cropping pattern. The Budget speech 1972-73 said, *"Our objective has been to diversify agricultural production by emphasising intensive cropping of food crops and encouraging a deliberate shift to high value commercial crops. And it further stated , "Simultaneously, the emphasis has also been on evolving a cropping pattern that will increase production of commercial crops of significance, viz. Oil-seeds, Tobacco, Cotton, and Sugar cane".* (*Source:* Andhra Pradesh budget speech:1972-73)

The government tried to shift the peasantry from cultivation of food grains to the commercial crops. The policy framework is nothing but to cater to the needs of the manufacturing sector. The meaning of changing cropping pattern is nothing but shifting the natural resource to harvest the crops as per the needs of the industrial sector.

The national and state governments educated the peasantry to cultivate those crops needed to the manufacturing sector even from early 70s. The policies advocated that the peasantry could earn profits only by such cultivation. The policies called those crops as value added. However, these policies reflected only in farmers committing suicides. Majority of the victims were the growers of commercial crops. Again the government changed its voice and the Andhra Pradesh budget speech 2000-01 spoke, *"Special emphasis is being laid on increase of area under pulses, particularly, red gram. Similarly, special efforts are being made to increase the area under castor and maize and reduce areas under tobacco, cotton and chillies by diverting the same to food grain and oilseed crops".* (*Source:* Andhra Pradesh budget speech: 2000-01)

Prior to this, the Andhra Pradesh government in its budget speech 1992-93 said, "*The estimated food grains production during the year 1991-92 was 117.05 lakh tonnes compared to 123.30 lakh tonnes during 1990-91. This decline in production was due to reduction in area under food grains which was caused by the deficiencies in rainfall in sowing months and inadequate flows into the reservoirs. The tendency of the farmers to move away from the traditional crops like rice to more remunerative enterprises fish farming could, in the long run,affect food grains production in the State. Therefore, it was necessary to concentrate on increasing productivity of food crops, especially rice".* (*Source:* Andhra Pradesh budget speech: 1992-93)

The budget speech reflected untruthfulness. It commented that the peasantry showed interest in shafting the cropping pattern. As such, the budget speech concealed the fact. In fact, the government itself spoke about "deliberate shift" way back in 1972-73. It is pertinent to note that the peasantry did not shift on their own aspirations. Because of these "shifting" policies only, the peasantry was shifting from their traditional agriculture. In spite of this decrease in the food grain production, the speech did not stress on the diversion of land but had stressed more on the productivity. The meaning of increase in productivity was nothing but to increase the usage of more and more fertilisers, pesticides, new varieties of seeds besides huge loans, etc. Marx commented on these practices, which read "All progress in capitalistic agriculture was a progress in the art, not only robbing the labour, but robbing the soil: all progress in increasing the fertility of the soil for a given time was a progress towards ruining the lasting source of fertility." *(Capital: Page Vol. 475: Marx Karl).*

Not only Marx but also many agronomists said that indiscriminate usage of chemicals in the name of enhancing productivity is causing threat to soil. Indian government conducted many surveys to determine the magnitude of wastelands. The statistics revealed that many lands have become acidic because of the over usage of the chemicals.

Table 1 below indicates the quantum of wastelands in the country, state and the studied District.

Table 1. Degraded and Wasteland in India, Andhra Pradesh and in the Research Area

	Total Geographical Area (km)	*1*	*2*	*3*	*4*	*5*	*6*	*7*	*8*
India	387270	74020	9290	5080	5720	7130	11420	2630	40
Andhra Pradesh	275,045	8050	814	0	0.28	0	0	56	4
Srikakulam District		188	25	0	0	0	0	2	4
Vizianagaram District		337	34	0	0	0	0	0	0

	9	*10*	*11*	*12*	*13*	*14*	*15*	*16*	*17*	*18*	*19*	*Others*	*Total Degrade in '000' Hectare*
India	20	110	60	30	2610	1060	30	20	20	260	860		120410
Andhra Pradesh	0	0	0	17	154	39	0	0	1	39	19		9193.28
Srikakulam District	0	0	0	0	0	0	0	0	0	0	2	363	584
Vizianagaram District	0	0	0	0	0	0	0	0	1	0	0	284	656

Notes: Classes*: 1 Exclusively water erosion (>10 tonnes/ha/yr); 2 Water erosion under open forest; 3 Exclusively acid soils; 4 Acid soils under water erosion; 5 Acid soils under open forest; 7 Exclusively saline soils; 8 Eroded saline soils; 12 Waterlogged saline soils; 13 Exclusively sodic soils; 14 Eroded sodic soils; 17 Eroded sodic soils under open forest; 18 Mining/Industrial waste; 19 Waterlogged area (Permanent).

Others**: Normal agricultural lands, water-bodies, rivers, lakes and habitats etc. (based on the limi ted reconnaisance survey).

Source: NBSS and LUP.

Table 2. Changing Trends in Area of Food Grains Area in Srikakulam District (in Acres)

Year	*Cereals and millets Paddy*	*Jowar/jonna*	*Bajra/sajja*	*Ragi*	*Maize*	*Small millets*	*Total*
1972-73	641987	16653	26509	82467	0	16339	783955
1976-77	672729	14435	35453	115947	0	32273	870837
1986-87	667575	15072	34941	91554	0	16735	825877
1994-95	677134	6782	20583	58833	0	13257	776589
2004-05	652549	1643	11541	21730	8544	0	696007
2007-08	676522	1907	12669	16172	20829	2113	730212
2009-10	608050.5	1530.12	4083.6	11458.68	37052.52	4617.42	666792.8

Source: District hand books: compiled and published: Chief planning officer, Srikakulam and Vizianagaram districts.

As agricultural policy 2000 noted, *"The pattern of growth of agriculture has, however, brought in its wake, uneven development, across regions and crops as also across different sections of farming community and is characterised by low levels of productivity and degradation of natural resources in some areas"*. (*Source:* National Agricultural Policy)

The Hon'ble Prime Minister Manmohan Singh also expressed concern over the unabated degradation of the soil and called for, *"Special efforts will be necessary to control degradation of our land and water resources, which adversely affects the livelihood of millions of small and marginal farmers who live on the edge of subsistence."* [*Source:* Prime minister's speech in National Development Council]

Table 2 indicates the trends in the area of food grains production besides those trends, which took place over a period of last forty years. The striking fact is that the net area is decreased. The area under food grains reached its peak in 1976-77 to 8,70,837 acres. Though the rainfall was normal in the year 2009-10, the area under food grains had been recorded at 6,66,792.80 acres thus showing a net decline of 2,04,044 acres. Even, it fell short when compared to early 70s. Thus, the district reflected the macro trends of the country and state. As the state governments proclaimed that for the enhancement of productivity, the peasantry of this district were caught in the web of chemicals. Turakalakota villagers said in a sarcastic tone, "the productivity was directly proportional to the physical strength of the shoulder. Is this land ask for the stoppage of usage?" Here the "physical strength of the shoulder" meant to make the expenditure on chemicals.

The changing pattern did not only occur in the acreage but also in the varieties. For a long period, paddy and Ragi were the staple food in this district. Jowar and Bajra continued predominantly as a staple food in tribal areas. Ragi cultivation reached its peak in 1976-77 recording 1,15,947 acres. However, it drastically came down to 11,458.68 acres in the year 2009-10.

These two crops have equal importance in the food chart. In the initial years, the productivity of ragi was higher than paddy. There are two reasons for the fall in ragi growth, which were economical and cultural. No Sufficient research was carried out on ragi, and no schemes had been introduced to encourage ragi cultivation. The popular scheme of two rupees per kilogram of rice did not introduce in Ragi. Moreover, taking ragi as food was considered inferior. It was stamped as a food of "labourers" and "down trodden" castes. Hence, the popular schemes replaced the food habit that led to the disappearance of this crop. As seen from the minimum support price structure, now ragi was getting a higher price but there was no crop to sell in this district. Ironically, the capital attracting "aristocrats" for consumption of ragi malt from the departmental stores.

As seen from the statistics, the net sown area of paddy was around six to six and half lakh acres. Over the period of forty years, paddy recorded its peak in 2007-08 to have sown 6,76,522 acres. In 2009-10, the acreage dropped to

Table 3. Cost of Cultivation of Paddy per acre (approx.)

Sl. No.	*Name of the Work*	*Cost*
1.	Seed	600
2.	Preparation seed bed	500
3.	Compost	200
4.	Bunds preparation	1000
5.	Nursing of the plant	1200
6.	Transplanting	1200
7.	Puddlling	1000
8.	fertilisers	2000
9.	Weeding (2 times)	700
10.	threshing	1200
11.	Carrying the crop	2500
12.	Threshing flour	1000
13.	Water tax	450
14.	Total	14,150

Source: Interview with peasants at Nimmada village on 20/10/2011.

6,08,050 acres and recorded a fall of 68,472 acres. Apart from weather, the non-profitability was also the primary reason for this decrease in the acreage.

The cost of cultivation and the poor returns were worrying the peasantry. In my surveyed period (2007-11) it was observed that the cost of cultivation was increasing continuously because of the hike in the prices of chemicals and diesel.

As seen from the table, a peasant was spending Rs. 14,350 for an acre. The average yield in this village was 22 bags with a bag costing Rs. 800 in that year. Hence, a peasant got Rs. 17, 600 per acre on paddy cultivation. The net income was Rs. 3,450 only. When asked about the limited income levels, they said unanimously "if we calculate the expenditure, can we conduct the cultivation?"

This phenomenon was not casual. The policies were to impart education to the peasantry not to plant food grains. The Andhra Pradesh government in its Budget speech 2006-07 proclaimed, "*Farmers are being encouraged to adopt less water intensive crops instead of paddy in order to efficiently utilize the additional irrigation potential to be created under the new projects.*"

Even the budget speech too had philosophical background. International Food Policy Research Institute in its research paper argued that to curb the cultivation of wheat and paddy, fortunes of the peasantry were required to be changed. The research paper stated, "*Once the fortunes from wheat and rice start weakening,traditionalcommodities such as cotton, pulses and maize will rise in importance*". (Agricultural Diversification towards High Value Commodities : A Study in Food Surplus States in India with Focus on Andhra Pradesh and Punjab: IFFRI)

The peasantry got the reply for the cause of low returns on the paddy cultivation in the previously mentioned research paper besides the budget speeches of the state government. In a planned way, the governments and policymakers were trying to discourage the peasantry from making the paddy cultivation to be non-profitable activity. In this way, they were making the peasantry change their cropping pattern to "value added crops." As proclaimed way back in 1972-73, the process had almost completed in Andhra Pradesh. The above policy paper appraised this process and showered praises on the peasantry for their shifting. The report told, *"Farmers are responding to the changing scenario and gradually diversifying production towards high-value commodities (HVCs). But the speed of agricultural diversification has been much faster in Andhra Pradesh than in Punjab."*

The quality of the soil, local weather conditions, the dosage of fertiliser, the seed and irrigation played a vital role in agriculture. However, it appeared that the successive governments did not take into consideration many aspects, which were essential while developing the agriculture. In fact, these policies caused the disappearance of diversity with the peasantry being habituated to cultivate wheat and paddy. The natural rotation system in the cropping pattern had disappeared. Again, the policy institutes are blaming the peasantry for cultivating only food grains. They were calculating the cost pattern in a scientifically by taking the cost of every drop of water and branding paddy as water intensive.

As seen from various reports, it was clear that considerable research were done only on wheat and paddy. Uniformity mostly replaced the diversity. These two crops occupied the entire land that was used to cultivate diversified food crops. The green revolution and the policies thereof almost took out other food grains from the diet. However, the research paper came blatantly with fixing the onus on the peasantry for dampening in agricultural growth. It read, *"Emphasis on cereals production (especially rice and wheat) to achieve food security, which resulted in higher profitability for producers and lower output prices for consumers, is dampening agricultural growth. The food security objective had been achieved. The country has accumulated large foreign exchange reserves if needed, to import food. Alternative options need to be explored to accelerate agricultural growth". (Ibid)*

As seen from this study reports, the target was clear with policy makers trying to replace food grains with value added crops. The budget speeches were also preaching the same. In view of this approach only further research and plateau in the technical support took place. Now the entire direction is towards value added crops. The fields were filled with the commercial crops only. The crux of the diversification was nothing but to transform the fields as cultivating fields of eggs, fish, fruits, flowers and vegetables preferably those catering to the food processing industry. Agriculture was running towards this direction in a swift manner.

The cause of food inflation was lying under these policies. The per capita availability of food grains reached the level of early 70s. The urban proletarian (who once the rural proletarian) was unable to afford the food prices.

The pace of contract and corporate farming in the agriculture could not guarantee the production of food grains. Moreover, the policies were not encouraging cultivation of food grains. This country became so rich that it could import food grains at the cost of foreign exchange. Under such circumstances, the competition for food grains increased enormously. The ordinary food was going to be dearer. Food was available to those who could pay in international currency. As Kautsky told, *"agriculture thrives on the back of urban proletarian"*.

In Visakhapatnam, A.S. Raja Women's College is famous for education. Before corporatizing education, it was a pride to get a seat therein. Thanks to the corporatisation, plenty of the seats were reserved to the children of urban proletarian. The shortage of food causing mal-nourishment could be seen from this example. "Miss Sureswari and Miss Kiranmai studied intermediate (+2) in this college during 2007-09. One day as soon as the lunch bell rang, Sureswari was in a hurry to take her lunch box. Her friend Kiranmai asked, "Why you are running for the box? Had not you taken the breakfast?" Miss Sureswari replied, "The money is not even sufficient to take food for two times? Baby Sureswari replied that she did not have sufficient money to have food twice a day, as her father is not getting the government salary as her friend's father. This was the fate of a girl child of an urban proletarian. In fact, while her parents were working as day labourers, Sureswari herself was working as a house cleaner.

Interestingly, the official reports considered Maize as a food crop. Though it appeared as a food crop, this predominantly was catering to the food needs of the poultry industry. In other words, the poultry used it as food rather than human beings. Maize was being used as bio-fuel. Later, in this district, the cropping had increased. As seen from the district statistics, the area under this crop was consistently growing. Agents of the seed companies were touring this district extensively and selling their seeds. In fact, some poultry companies were making contracts with the peasantry for supply of Maize. It was also interesting to note that in this district hen houses had almost disappeared and poultry farms were running under contract basis. The fields were changing as centres of poultry farms. On the other hand, some more fields were becoming the feeding centres to these poultry farms.

Table 4. Approximate Cost of the Maize Cultivation per an Acre.

Sl.No.	*Name of the Work*	*Cost*
1.	Seed	1,900
2.	Bio-fertilisers	2,000
3.	Chemical fertilisers (3 times)	3,300
4.	Total labour cost	4,880
5.	Milling of Maize	540
6.	Total	12,520

Source: As per the information of Potireddi Srinivasarao Rao a small Peasant of Batuva village.

As seen from the statistics, during the year 2004-05, the peasantry cultivated Maize in 8,544 acres. In 2007-08, it increased to 20,829 acres and further to 37,052 acres during 2009-10. In a span of five years, the area under cultivation showed a drastic increase by 333 per cent. Probably this trend indicated that the agricultural fields here were meant to cater to the needs of the poultry industry. On the other hand, the people of this country were required to wait for the ships to get their food. The policy makers were temporarily making the cultivation of maize profitable. The expenditure and income on Maize is shown hereunder.

The villagers said the average yield in the village was 15 quintals while the maximum crop yield was 20 quintals. As per the official records, the average yield of maize in this district was 18 quintals with the price of a quintal being Rs. 1100. The peasant was getting an income of Rs. 7,280 on this crop. A peasant who was cultivating food for people was getting rupees 3,450 while a peasant who is cultivating food for the poultry industry is getting Rs. 7,280 per an acre. In Andhra Pradesh, it resulted in amending the cropping pattern. Andhra Pradesh got the second place in the production of Maize with 16.51 per cent of total crop of the country and the state produced 2.76 million Metric Tonnes of Maize.

Changing pattern in the oil seed sector: This table shows the Changing pattern of the oil seed sector.

Table 5. Oil Seeds Area in Srikakulam District (in Acres)

Year	*Oil Seeds*					
	Ground Nut	*Sesamum*	*Coconut*	*Caster*	*Sun Flower*	*Total Oil Seeds*
1972-73	162550	16631	17917	59		197157
1976-77	102360	26504	17630	33		146527
1986-87	205814	36029	20300	44		262187
1994-95	195540	48285	28629	0		272454
2004-05	143104	42366	33808	0		219278
2007-08	122009	54829	35449	0		212287
2009-10	116306.3	46110.24	36518.7	0	6172.14	205107.4

Source: Various Dist. Handbooks.

As observed in these statistics, it is clear that the acreage of the oil seed sector was in a decreasing trend from the early 90s. The cultivation of oil seeds reached its zenith in 1994-95 and recorded an acreage of 2,72,454 acres. In that year, it slipped down to 2,05,107 acres and thus there was a net decrease of 67,347 acres. The share of various oil seeds was also being changed. Traditionally, in this district groundnut had a principal share in this sector. In the year 1972-73, it constituted 82.44 percentage of the total sector. Now (in 2009-10) its share had dwindled to 56.70 per cent.

In this district, the peasantry was selling groundnut in bags with every bag consisting 60 kilograms. In 2009-10, each bag cost's was Rs. 1000. The

Table 6. Cost Sheet of Groundnut (Approximate)

Ploughing (3 times)	2000
Compost (5 bullock carts)	1500
seed	2400
Weeding (2 times)	2000
harvesting	1000
To bring the crop	200
Total	9,100

Source: A small peasant, Kolli Simhachalam of Piridi village.

normal yield was 10 bags. Therefore, a peasant was getting Rs. 900 (10000-9,100) from an acre of cultivation. The duration of the crop was three months and fifteen days. This economic reason drove out the groundnut. Not only this, another striking reason was the dry land, which was almost converted to non-agricultural purposes or to plantations. In this village, once the groundnut was one among the principal crops. However, it had almost disappeared with only two families belong to marginal holdings cultivating this on tiny leased-land holdings. Major portion of the same was alienated to Gokul Engineering College in this village. Majority of dry lands have been alienated was not a stray example. The alienation of dry land had also its bearing on the decline in the cultivation of oil seeds in general and particularly in the case of groundnut.

The peasantry stated that the policies were encouraging the cultivation of oil palm in the district with the government giving fertilisers almost free of cost for the first four years. It revealed the deliberate shift from traditional groundnut to expensive oil palm.

As seen from the above Table 7, it shows that there is no usage of chemicals on the land. However, on the other hand, oil palm needs a high dosage of fertilisers. As per the government brochure, the dosage of fertilisers is as given under.

Column 2 to 10 indicates the grams of fertiliser that is needed for planting. Official reports indicated that 57 plants could be planted in an acre. Hence, the column 11 indicates the total dosage of fertilisers in kilograms for an acre. In the first year, the total fertiliser needed was 394 kilograms. Every year, the dosage was progressing and it ultimately reached 1099 kilograms of fertilisers per an acre.

Changing pattern in commercial crops: Table 8 indicates the changing pattern in commercial crops over a period of forty years in this district. Overall, the area under the traditional commercial crops was depleting.

Traditionally in this district, peasantry used to cultivate Mesta on a large scale. Predominance of dry lands and cheap labour were the primary reasons for this cultivation. Now changes occurred in both the factors. Majority of dry lands is alienated to the sections those discussed in the earlier chapter. The physical migration of rural proletarian and changes in their occupation pattern are the reasons for the fall in the acreage.

Table 7. Fertilisers Usage for Oil Palm per an Acre

Period	*Area*	*Ammonium sulphate*	*DAP*	*SSP*	*Rock Phosphate*	*Murate of Potash*	*Magnesium Sulphate*	*Borax*	*Total*	*Total for 57 Plants (in kilograms*
1st year	870	2000	435	1250	1600	607	125	25	6912	393.984
2nd Year	1740	4000	870	2500	2000	1333	250	50	12743	726.351
3rd year	2610	6000	1305	3750	3000	2000	500	100	19265	1098.105
4th year	2610	6000	1305	3750	3000	2000	500	100	19265	1098.105
5th year	2610	6000	1305	3750	3000	2000	500	100	19265	1098.105
6th year	2610	6000	1305	3750	3000	2000	500	100	19265	1098.105

Source: Oil Palm Cultivation: published by National research centre for OIL palm: Pedavegi, West Godavari District.

Table 8. Changing Pattern in Commercial Crops in this District

Year	*Mesta*	*Sugarcane*	*Cotton*	*Total*
1972-73	187828	14466	0	202294
1976-77	205150	23494	0	228644
1986-87	142124	22655.7	0	164779.7
1994-95	162507.6	60014.16	0	222521.8
2004-05	106222.8	68914.44	53933.04	229070.3
2007-08	112242.4	79657.26	20691.06	212590.7
2009-10	50491.05	54095.4	23992.38	128579.3

Source: District handbooks.

As seen from the above table, peasantry cultivated Mesta in 2,05,150 acres in 1976-77. Thereafter, it was very interesting to note that in the Srikakulam district, the acreage was consistently decreasing and reached its lowest in 2009-10 to 50,491 acres. As per the news story of Eenadu, a Telugu Daily dated 18/05/2011, the acreage in the present district is mere 639 acres.

Apart from these two reasons, another principal reason was that in this district, nearly 14 Jute mills played a crucial role in the industrial sector. However, at any point of time they did not enter into any contract with the peasantry as in the case of sugar cane. The owners of these mills always played with the peasantry in determining the price. The price always fluctuated during every second season. If the peasantry cultivated the Mesta on a large scale, the management used to cut down the price and the peasantry always suffered losses in the crop. In that season, the managements purchased Mesta in a large scale and used to store the crop in their warehouses for using this crop for two seasons. The annoyed peasantry had to reduce the acreage in the subsequent year while the managements hiked the price in that season. Thus, there was no crop in the hands of marginal and small peasantry and this became a boon to the rich peasantry to garner the profits. Even the mill management used to proclaim lock-outs claiming shortage of raw material. This practice continued for 30 to 35 years in this district. It was also a prominent cause for the deceleration in the acreage.

In fact, the government-established Jute Corporation of India (a company) was formed in 1971 with the main aim of providing minimum support price (hereinafter referred to as MSP) to the jute farmers and to serve as a stabilising agency in the raw jute sector. The C and AG conducted a performance audit of this corporation and pointed out, *"Audit sample covered 26 Departmental Purchase Centres (DPC) out of 171 DPCs in six major jute growing states. A number of deficiencies mentioned below were noticed in the functioning of the company: The Company procured only 0.99 per cent to 10.4 per cent of available jute in India during the six years (2003-09). Thus, the company could not play any significant role in price stabilisation and in ensuring remunerative prices to the jute farmers."* (*Source:* Annual report 2010-11: Ministry of textiles, page: 276 and 277)

Table 9. The Cost of Mesta Cultivation for the Year 2010-11 (Approximate)

Seed	2000
Ploughing (3 times)	900
Compost	1500
Weeding	2400
To uproot the crop	1600
To carry the crop to nearby Tanks	1700
Retting	500
To take out from the Tanks	500
Fibre extraction	500
To bring the crop	600
Total	12,200

Source: Kolli Simhachalam of Piridi Village

Piridi is a village adjacent to Bobbili town. Three jute mills are functioning in Bobbili. The average yield in this village was three bales. A bale consists of 272 kilograms (in the local dialect it is called "PUTTI"). During that year, the price of that bale was Rs. 4000 with the total earning of the peasant being Rs. 12,000. Thus, the peasant got a net loss of Rs. 200 (12000-12,200) during that season. However, in the subsequent years, an interesting feature was the cost of a bale, which got fixed at Rs. 7,000 when the peasant got a profit of Rs. 8,800 in that year. Thus, the cyclical process is continuing even after large-scale decrease in the acreage.

On the other hand, the acreage of cotton was slowly increasing. As per the statistics of district handbooks, there was no record of cotton cultivation till 2004-05. However, the ground level observations revealed that the cotton cultivation began in early 2000. Initially, the settlers cultivated cotton on their purchased lands. Soon after, hordes of settlers increased and they started taking lands on lease and started cultivating cotton. As per the table, cotton cultivation reached its peak in 2004-05 and subsequently decreased to 23,992 acres. However, as seen from the villages, the statistics regarding cotton appears to have been under-recorded due likely reason pertaining to the lease operations.

With respect to input usage, when compared with Mesta, cotton was more relevant to the industrial sector. Peasantry never used any chemical fertiliser and pesticides for the cultivation of Mesta. However, the situation was just opposite in the case of cotton crop. Cotton needs chemical fertilisers and pesticides thus having links with the industrial sector for its input base. Almost, the peasantry was spending 28.32 per cent on chemical fertilisers and pesticides. The cost sheet of cotton is given hereunder.

The peasantry of Burujola village reported the average yield in the village to be 10 quintals. They told that the pricing pattern was always volatile. During that year, the peasantry got Rs. 2,300 per quintal. Thus, the peasantry was getting Rs. 2,700 per an acre. Policy makers and economists are arguing that

Table 10. The Cost Sheet of Cotton for the Year 2010-11

Ploughing	2000
Seed	1750
Transplanting	800
To uproot the grass (five to six times)	2500
Weeding (Five to six times)	2500
Chemical fertilizers (three times)	3750
Pesticides	2000
To pick up the cotton	5000
Total	20,300

Source: Bodepu Raja Rao of Burujola village a sub-marginal peasant and leased-in peasant.

the peasantry could make the agriculture profitable by wayof shifting the cropping pattern towards commercial/industrial linked crops. These examples were showing a different trend. The consistent propaganda about the value added crops, i.e., the commercial crops ultimately proved fatal in this district.

In this region, the peasantry has been cultivating Sugarcane since early 30s. The then Bobbili zamindar established Sri Rama Sugar Mills in Bobbili and Seetanagaram. These factories were under their control till 1977-78. The management did not pay on time and the management took loans in the name of the peasantry even without their knowledge. This led to turmoil and the peasantry fought against the management and demanded nationalisation. The government agreed to the demands and nationalised the factories they continued under public sector. During the late 90s, the government merged the two mills and built a new unit at Latchayyapeta with a crushing capacity of 2500 Metric Tonnes per day. In 2002, again the government sold the mill to a private management though it is abnormal to hear the ban on liquor during 1994 was also one of the reasons for the sale. In 1994, the Telugu Desam government under the leadership of Sri N.T. Rama Rao banned the liquor because of the popular movement in the state. During that period, the distilleries were affiliated to Nizam Sugars Ltd., which did not buy the molasses resulting in the stocks being piled up. On the contrary, there existed an opportunity to export the molasses for a better price and to earn foreign exchange. The molasses were sold to merchant exporters who earned good profits on the exports. Interestingly, the same merchant exporter M/s N.C.S. Limited of Vizianagaram bought out the mill at a cheap rate in 2002. Yet another feature worth noting was the peasantry were again on the warpath for the same reason that prevailed in 1977-78 during the month of January 2013. The Hindu, a national daily reported the cause of agitations which read, *"The leaders of AP Rythu Sangham, the farmers' association, alleged that the management had taken loans to the tune of Rs. 21 crores from two banks in the name of farmers and they learnt that the amount may unofficially be over Rs. 70 crores from various banks. The farmers wanted the management to come clean on the total loan amount taken in the name of farmers and to give a written undertaking that it would repay the entire loan and that the farmers should not face any harassment*

Table 11. Cost Sheet of Sugarcane (approximate for 2010-11)

Ploughing (4 times)	2400
Seed	6000
To prepare the seed	3000
To carry the seed to field	600
Transplanting	1800
Compost + tractor rent	1600
Weeding (3 times)	4500
To make ridges and furrows (three times)	4800
	4500
Chemical fertilisers (2 times)	3200
Pesticides (5 times)	1500
To cut the plant	11,250
To transport	6000
Total	50,950

Source: Meesala Papinaidu, Allada Apparao marginal peasants of Gollalapeta village.

from the banks. Further, the farmers' association wanted immediate payment of arrears of Rs. 4 crores due to farmers by the management and hiking of cane price from the present Rs. 2,300 to Rs. 3,000 per tonne." (*Source:* The Hindu dated 22/01/13)

This table indicates the cost pattern of Sugarcane in this district. While as per the field staff of NCS factory, the average yield in the factory area was 17 MT, the contention of peasants of Gollalapeta village was that the average crop in that village was 25 MT. The price per MT was Rs. 2000. Hence, the net revenue loss from the cultivation of Sugarcane amounted to Rs. 950 (50,950-50,000). The solace was sugarcane used to yield twice over two years. For the second year, there was no need to sow again. The expenditure on the cane in the 2nd year was Rs. 31,900. Hence the peasant got a positive return of Rs. 8,100 in the 2nd year. For both the years, the net return for a peasant per an acre was considered to be Rs. 7,150 only.

Thus, the peasant ended with a loss of Rs. 200 in a year for his cultivation of Mesta and got a profit of Rs. 8,800 in the subsequent year. In the second year, most of the peasantry did not show interest on the cultivation of Mesta. The peasantry was getting Rs. 2,700 in the cultivation cotton of due to shifting the cropping pattern to another industrial sector. Shifting of the crops to the industrial sector proved the dependence of primary sector on the mercy of the industrial sector.

Conversion of Farm Lands as Plantations

The district is predominantly rain fed. As seen from the cropping pattern, there was not a change in the acreage of paddy. However, the cropping pattern in this district got significant changes over the last forty years. In the food grain sector, only paddy could keep its position with the remaining food grains disappeared from the diet as the poultry feed to be replacing human food. Oilseed sector was facing challenges because of the decrease in the groundnut cultivation.Once, a prominent crop, Mesta also showed decreasing trend. The

Table 12. Area under Horticulture in both the Districts

Year	*Present Srikakulam Dist.*	*Present Vizianagaram Dist.*
2001-02	53636	60687
2002-03	53336	66088
2003-04	55629	69446
2004-05	55919	69110
2005-06	56789	82957
2006-07	71480	84211
2007-08	79953	85567
2008-09	82523	90820
2009-10	72009	91622

Source: Aphorticulture.nic.in.

cultivation of groundnut recorded a decrease of 83,805 acres. Information regarding whereabouts of these lands and the crops occupying these lands were unknown and the answers for these questions could be available with the Andhra Pradesh state Horticulture department.

This table was clear about the direction of agriculture and cropping pattern. In a span of 10 years in the present Srikakulam district, the plantations reached 72,009 hectares. In the acreage, it is 1,77,142 acres. (One Hectare = 2.46 acres). In the present Vizianagaram district, the conversion was more rapid at 2,25,390 acres. During the same period, the area under plantations was 91,622 hectares. Since my research area in Vizianagaram district covered only 18 out of 34 Mandals, only half of the acreage has been considered for the calculation. As per the official statistics, the total land under plantations in the Srikakulam district was recorded as 1,17,820 hectares. Thus, the acreage of the plantations was recorded as 2,89,837.20.

In concurrence with the certificate of research paper, this district also traversed towards "*Value added crops.*"

There were two strong reasons for this shift. First, the land was being alienated from the marginal and small peasantry, and it continued to go to the hands of rich lobby of this district and even to the affluent sections of other areas. These "others" also include other states. Those sections were not in a mood to cultivate oil seeds and food grains. Majority of land transactions was in dry lands only. There was an exclusion clause to the plantations in the land reform Acts. Even the government policy paper recommended that the oil palm was also to be considered as a plantation to exclude the land from the ambit of land ceiling. Plantations were a massive exception to land ceiling Acts due to which only lakhs of acres were transformed as plantations. Even the traditional rich peasantry is also following the suit.

Replacing the labour with capital was the other crucial factor in this transformation. The dry land crops Groundnut and jute were labour intensive crops. To cut the cost on labour, the rich peasantry of this district also changed the cropping pattern by resorting to grow plantations. Moreover, the government policies were subsidizing the expenditure on the plantations.

When asked about this transformation and the disappearance of traditional dry-land crops, a rich peasant Boddepalli Narayanamurty of Kanugulavalasa village said in mordant voice, *"It is good. So many intellectuals are advocating for the protection of the environment. We are making plantations to protect the environment only."*

The vernacular daily Eenadu carried an interview of the horticultural officer of Srikakulam District in a news story dated 03/09/2011. It read, *"horticultural officer M.Venkatramana told that in this District in 22 Mandals, the department is planning to grow plantations in 13,000 acres. These lands belong to marginal and small peasantry. We have already recognised the land in 11 Panchayats of Bhamini Mandal. We are conducting a survey for recognition of the lands in Bhamini, Palasa, Mandasa, Meliaputti, Nandigam, Palakonda, Veeraghattam, Regidi Amudalavalasa, Seetampeta and in other Mandals. We shall give Rupees 34 thousand for cashew plantations per an acre for three years and Rupees 45,000 thousand for Mango plantations per an acre for three years."*

The intention was clear in this district. As seen from the balance sheet, peasantry was not getting an assured income of even Rs five thousand on any crop. On the other hand, the department of Horticulture is pouring huge subsidies in the form of money on the peasantry. Naturally, this situation drives even the marginal and small peasantry towards plantations in the near future. The marginalised sections were compelled to follow the footsteps of the capitalist farmers.

Cut-the-cost theory had occupied the agriculture. Duggeru, a tribal and hamlet village to Panasabhadra Panchayat was the finest example for this theory. As many as 39 Kamma families migrated from Godavari district to this village and settled with purchasing almost the entire lands. Apart from these kamma families, there were some velama Doras families. For a long period, these families treated these tribal families as a cheap labour. Economic oppression was the order of the day. In the early 90s, Rytucooli pedala sangham (a union of the rural peasantry, labour and poor) organised the tribes and fought against the economic oppression in this village. They became a deciding factor in determining the wage rate which were increased from a meagre Rs. 10 to Rs. 80 and 120, Rs. 80 to female labour and Rs. 120 to male labourers thus annoying the rich peasantry. Hence, they searched for an alternative to reduce the human labour.

Paddy crop needed 98 coolies. Marginal and small peasantry used their family labour. Maximum family labour was 10 coolies in the crop. In the existing case, the rich peasantry did not use any family labour but entirely relied upon the hired labour. Due to escalation in the wage rate, the rich peasantry saw the alternative in the cultivation of oil palm. As told earlier, the government was giving subsidies to the cultivation of oil palm. A Velama rich peasant said, *"Majority of settlers had shifted to oil-palm cultivation and there was no need of much labour. For a year, ten labourers were sufficient to oil-palm cultivation. For my ten acres plantation, one "Manager" was sufficient to supervise the fields."*

Thus, it was interesting to see the nature of shifting cultivation besides the tribal peasants too were planting the oil palm in this district.

Division of Labour-Changing Cropping Pattern

Many researchers proposed three-field theory that prevailed in the ancient society. Sir Henry Maine noted, *"The cultivated land of the Teutonic village community appears almost invariably to have been divided into three great fields. A rude rotation of crops was the object of this threefold division, and it was intended that each field should lie fallow once in three years."* (Village communities in the East and West: page: 79: Sir Henry Maine). Further Karl Kautsky described the farming practise reading, "*Each strip owner was therefore obliged to cultivate their plot in each of the open fields in accordance with all the other strips—the Flurzwang. One of the fields was left fallow each year, the second planted with winter grain, and the third with summer grain. What was planted in each field changed annually Apart from stubble and fallow, fodder for animals came from meadows, permanent pasture and forestland":* (The Agrarian question: page: 21: Karl Kautsky).

These researchers tried to elicit the background of the formation of property rights on the land. Whatever way it might have been, feudal large estates replaced this Teutonic culture. In the feudal age, feudal kings and their close associates used these large tracts of lands as hunting grounds. In this process, the peasantry did not have the right to kill the wild animals, which were destroying their standing crop. In this district, many zamindars maintained these hunting grounds and thick forest tracts for this purpose. They did not allow the peasantry even to enter these reserved hunting grounds for a long time. It was a recent history.

After the abolition of legal landlords, these tracts became agricultural fields. The land usage pattern statistics proved this fact. In the initial years, peasantry used these fields for the production of food grains. Gradually, this process was replaced by the commercial crops, which were catering to the needs of manufacturing and service sectors. In this district, this process was taking place from late 90s, and it continued its pace uninterruptedly.

A number of examples proved this process in this district. The process could be observed from one of such examples. "Baguvalasa, a village Garividi Mandal was once under the control of Zamindar of Vizianagaram where cultivation was rain-fed. After the abolition of Zamindaris, for fifty years, the cultivation was conducted on marginal and small-scale land holdings. Later, the process was again going towards consolidation. K.A. Krishnam Raju of Visakhapatnam city purchased 100 acres of land and occupied the village tanks. He planted oil palm in 70 acres and in the remaining 30 acres, he raised mango plantation. In this way, 500 acres belonging to the marginal and small peasantry was alienated and by 1994, this process was completed thus making the peasantry to lose their livelihood. Shodhana, a voluntary organisation, organised these masses and made them buy cows and buffalos besides hybrid animals. Visakha diary established milk-procuring centre. In the olden days, people used to drink milk and sell ghee. However, people did not use even a drop of milk for their consumption and they all became reliable suppliers of milk to the urbanised sector. All the "converted" plantations were being used as pastoral grounds to the animals. The pauperised peasantry were the watch and ward to the plantations, the absentee landowners were not raising any objection." (Interview with Kami Naidu and Appalanaidu of Baguvalasa village. Both are working as volunteers of Shodhana.)

One shot two birds! On one hand, the peasantry lost their land and on the other, plantations replaced the food grains. Moreover, the freedmen who turned as rural proletarian became the reliable suppliers of urban milk industry. This process was becoming a widespread feature in almost every Mandal. Many lands had become a place of poultry industry. National giants were supplying chicken on a contract basis to the peasantry who were establishing poultry farms, which expanded to even hundreds of acres. The pollution from the poultry farms was causing tensions in the village.

In one such tense situation, a poultry farm in Cheepurupalli Mandal was attacked. National daily Pioneer reported the incident, *"The long-drawn protest by the local people against the pollution and the stink emitting from the poultry farm in Karlam village under Cheepurupalli Mandal of Vizianagaram district took an ugly turn when hundreds of people from surrounding villages of Karlam, Alajangi and Mettapalli staged a sit in protest in Karlam demanding the closure of the unit."*

"In a bizarre incident, seven lakh poultry birds died when a mob cut off the power supply to a poultry farm in Vizianagaram district leading to the shutting down of an air conditioning unit and causing asphyxiation. The mob was protesting against stink and the pollution emanating from the farm and demanding its closure. Hundreds of people barged into the Radha Sakku Agrio Bio Pharma and switched off the power supply on Wednesday. When the staff tried to start the generator, they were attacked and beaten up leading to the large-scale death of the birds. The company officials said that it caused a loss amounting to Rs. 21 Crores." (*Source:* Pioneer dated: 08/07/2012)

Thus, the process had turned a full circle with the hunting grounds and the dense forests, which catered to the interests of the feudal landlords becoming a land of small and marginal land holdings. Now again the trend was towards consolidation of land holdings. The agricultural fields were again transforming as plantations to deliver resonance of plantations. While the earlier estates represented the rural feudal interests, the contemporary plantations were representing the capitalist consolidation and urban capitalist economy interests.

Manufacturing sector divided the labour not only within the country but also among the countries. A car industry manufactures spare parts in one country and engine in another country. The same company assembles those parts in the first country. Thus, multiple manufacturing processes wipe outs all the existing geographical boundaries. A similar process embarks on in agriculture industry too.

When asked the settlers for their passage to this area for cultivation of cotton on lease basis they all unanimously replied that the lease amount was much lower than in the other coastal districts. This might also have been one of the factors though they would have been concealing the other important reason. The wage rates were comparatively very low in this district when compared to the same prevailing in Godavari, Krishna and Guntur districts, which showed the wisdom of capitalist farmers.

In fact, the capitalist farmers tried to shift their activity to the areas where the wage rates were low. In the absence of such labour, they shifted the pattern to "high value crops". This shift was not limited just to intra/inter-districts. It rather surpassed the entire national and international boundaries just like its counterpart namely manufacturing sector. Capitalist farmers of this country were conducting cultivation on a large scale in African countries. They were taking thousands of hectares on lease by remitting nominal rent of a dollar per hectare in their country and they were remitting just a fourth as day wage rate here. Andhra Pradesh farmers were also playing a role in this. A capitalist farmer of this state was supplying cut roses to all the international functions across the globe.

Like in manufacturing sector agriculture sector too got internationalised. The countries of the world resemble a chain. Each link was just like a link in that chain. The crisis in a country influenced the other country and it was transforming as a world crises. The Secretary General of World Trade Organisation discussed these crises and explained, *"We live in a world of ever-growing interdependence and interconnectedness. Our interdependence has grown beyond anyone's imagination in fact! Economic and financial shocks spread faster than ever before. With the recent economic crisis we discovered that the collapse of one part of an economy can trigger a chain-reaction across the globe.... The scope of the challenges the world is facing has changed profoundly in the past decades—more profoundly, I suspect, than we fully understand. The world of today is virtually unrecognizable from the world in which we lived one generation ago."* (A lecture delivered in Oxford University in March, 2012)

The primary sector was also heading towards this crisis. The rich peasantry was agitating to get higher prices for their produce and for which, they demanded to lift all inter-state and international barriers. Policies were too traversing towards this direction. Economic survey 2000-01 said, *"For the Indian farmer, it is essential that he looks to the whole country as a single unrestricted market. After further opening up of the trade regime under WTO from April 2001, it is all the more necessary that farmers look not only to the domestic market but also seize opportunities in the global market for improved value added realisation and diversification. Export of processed agri-products would be the key to improved export realisation which is possible only if the domestic polices allow unrestricted movement, storage and liberal trade regime. Thus, for agriculture related products, inputs and services, all restrictions including SSI reservation would have to be removed.*" (*Source:* Economic survey 2000-01 page number 170: www.indiabudget.nic.in)

In the developing paradigm, many advanced countries including UK and USA faced the same situation with the rich peasant lobby demanding free exports. In no time, their demand boomeranged and again they were caught in another crisis. The export market temporarily earned profits to this lobby. However, flooding of imports might have been again a cause of concern and led to slash in prices. Thus, an endless vicious spiral formed in the sector thus the crisis in agriculture was not underlying in the cropping pattern. On the other hand, it lied in its tying up with the national and international trade regime with the crisis in the agriculture being directly proportional to its link with the industrial and service sectors. Unfortunately, many people were searching for the solution in larger tying-up with these sectors by advocating high value crops.

5

Human Resources

The society is progressing based on human labour. Labour plays a vital role in the production process. Basing on this proposition, there is a need to consider the subject. There is a need to examine the part that was played and continuing to play by the human resources in Indian agriculture.

India is the second most populous country in the world. Of late, the country is considering the population as a resource rather than as a problem. The importance of human resources is directly proportional to the number of youth.

Table 1. Population and Agricultural Workers in India

Year	*Total Population*	*Average Annual Exponential Growth Rate (%)*	*Rural Population*	*Cultivators*	*Agricultural Workers Agricultural Labourers*	*(In Millions) Total*
1971	548.2	2.20	439.0 (80.1)	78.2 (62.2)	47.5 (37.8)	125.7
1981	683.3	2.22	523.9 (76.7)	92.5 (62.5)	55.5 (37.5)	148.0
1991	846.4	2.16	628.9 (74.3)	110.7 (59.7)	74.6 (40.3)	185.3
2001	1028.7	1.97	742.6 (72.2)	127.3 (54.4)	106.8 (45.6)	234.1
2011	1210.5	1.64	833.4 (68.8)	95.84 (26.44)	86.16 (23.77)	182

Source: Registrar General of India.
Figures in bracket indicate percentage.

The working youth determine the future of a sector. Advancement or regression of any sector largely depends on the youth in the light of which there is a prerequisite to observe the passage of the youth in the primary sector.

Changing Occupational Pattern: Table 1 indicates the changing occupation pattern in India.

As seen from the table, the population of India in 1971 was 548.2 million. The share of the peasantry was 62.2 per cent with the actual number of the peasantry being 78.2 million. The share of agricultural labour was 37.8 per cent and the net number of the labour was 37.8 million. Over a period of forty years, the percentage of peasantry came down to 26.44 per cent and the share of agricultural workers increased to 45.6 per cent in 2001 only to show a drastic cut in 2011 Census which recorded the percentage as 23.77. The trend clearly indicates the elimination of the peasantry in the agrarian sector. The 2011 census has shown a drastic change in the scenario. The total dependants on agriculture have been dwindled even to the number that prevailed in 1991. In 1991, the total number of dependants stood at 185.3 million while this latest census has shown the figure as 182 millions. The reforms process is nothing but more infusion of capital in the country. Definitely, the capital erodes the rural human base to cater to the needs of the urban capital.

The changing occupation pattern in Srikakulam district: this Table indicates the pattern.

Table 2. Changing Occupational Pattern of the Srikakulam District

Year	*Population*	*Main workers*	*Cultivators*	*Percent of Cultivators Among workers*	*Ag. Labour*	*Percentage of Ag. Labour among workers*
1971	2453209	1060049	423413	39.94	410608	38.73
1981	2871450	1256177	532190	42.37	429185	34.17
1991	3367679	1497248	523273	34.95	604164	40.35
2001	3574846	1344588	429821	31.97	820197	61.00
2011	3859195	1426379	257887	18.07	689239	48.32

Source: Primary census abstracts and District Handbooks.

This table clearly indicates the journey of Srikakulam district. As seen from the table, the population of Srikakulam district in 1971 was 24,53,209. The share of the peasantry was 39.94 per cent, and net number of the peasantry was 4, 23,413. The share of agricultural labour was 38.73 per cent and the net number of the labour was 4, 10,608. Over a span of forty years, the share of peasantry came down to 18.07 per cent and the net peasantry was recorded as 2, 57,887. At the same time, it appears that there was a whopping increase in the agrarian labour up to 2001. Their net number increased to 8,20,197, and their share in the work force increased to 61 per cent. However, the 2011 census shows that the

Table 3. Mandal-wise Occupational Pattern

Sl. No.	Name of the Mandal	*Decrease in the cultivators in two decades* 1991 cultivators	2001 cultivators	Difference	Percentage of decrease	2011 cultivators	Difference	Percentage of decrease from 2001-2011	Galloping capital decades 1991-2011	Percentage of decrease from 1991-2011
1.	Komarada	8658	9067	409	4.72	4059	-5008	-55.23	-4599	-53.12
2.	G.L. Puram	8310	11071	2761	33.23	2366	-8705	-78.63	-5944	-71.53
3.	Kurupam	7528	6933	-595	-7.90	2936	-3997	-57.65	-4592	-61.00
4.	Jiyyammavalasa	10782	8828	-1954	-18.12	5629	-3199	-36.24	-5153	-47.79
5.	Garugubilli	10877	10770	-107	-0.98	7857	-2913	-27.05	-3020	-27.77
6.	Parvatipuram	10984	11182	198	1.80	6326	-4856	-43.43	-4658	-42.41
7.	Makkuva	9181	9065	-116	-1.26	5356	-3709	-40.92	-3825	-41.66
8.	Seetanagaram	11948	12307	359	3.00	7456	-4851	-39.42	-4492	-37.60
9.	Balijipeta	13198	12460	-738	-5.59	8140	-4320	-34.67	-5058	-38.32
10.	Bobbili	13983	12042	-1941	-13.88	11076	-966	-8.02	-2907	-20.79
11.	Saluru	11440	9596	-1844	-16.12	6202	-3394	-35.37	-5238	-45.79
12.	Pachipenta	8195	6063	-2132	-26.02	4034	-2029	-33.47	-4161	-50.77
13.	R.B. Puram	8816	8536	-280	-3.18	4674	-3862	-45.24	-4142	-46.98

(Table Contd.)

(Contd. Table 3)

Sl. No.	Name of the Mandal	Decrease in the cultivators in two decades								
		1991 Cultivators	2001 cultivators	Difference	Percentage of decrease	2011 Cultivators	Difference	Percentage of decrease from 2001-2011	Galloping capital decades 1991-2011	Percentage of decrease from 1991-2011
14.	Badangi	11154	10948	-206	-1.85	9503	-1445	-13.20	-1651	-14.80
15.	Therlam	12358	13079	721	5.83	10434	-2645	-20.22	-1924	-15.57
16.	Merakamudidam	11061	10656	-405	-3.66	5708	-4948	-46.43	-5353	-48.40
17.	Garividi	10699	9021	-1678	-15.68	4448	-4573	-50.69	-6251	-58.43
18.	Cheepurupalli	10275	6006	-4269	-41.55	6107	101	1.68	-4168	-40.56
19.	Ichapuram	7365	5488	-1877	-34.20	2626	-2862	-52.15	-4739	-64.34
20.	Kaviti	5000	2547	-2453	-96.31	2133	-414	-16.25	-2867	-57.34
21.	Kanchili	7750	6297	-1453	-23.07	3787	-2510	-39.86	-3963	-51.14
22.	Sompeta	7588	5123	-2465	-48.12	2086	-3037	-59.28	-5502	-72.51
23.	Mandasa	9451	10534	1083	10.28	4866	-5668	-53.81	-4585	-48.51
24.	Palasa	8451	5890	-2561	-43.48	4947	-943	-16.01	-3504	-41.46
25.	Vajrapukothuru	6993	7948	955	12.02	4084	-3864	-48.62	-2909	-41.60
26.	Nandigam	13561	10396	-3165	-30.44	6792	-3604	-34.67	-6769	-49.92
27.	Tekkali	8337	7542	-795	-10.54	3603	-3939	-52.23	-4734	-56.78
28.	Santabommali	9828	8303	-1525	-18.37	4065	-4238	-51.04	-5763	-58.64
29.	Kotabommali	13060	8839	-4221	-47.75	3934	-4905	-55.49	-9126	-69.88

(Table Contd.)

(Contd. Table 3)

Sl. No.	Name of the Mandal	Decrease in the cultivators in two decades								
		1991 Cultivators	2001 cultivators	Difference	Percentage of decrease	2011 Cultivators	Difference	Percentage of decrease from 2001-2011	Galloping capital decades 1991-2011	Percentage of decrease from 1991-2011
30.	Jalumuru	9922	7891	-2031	-25.74	5105	-2786	-35.31	-4817	-48.55
31.	Saravakota	7869	7157	-712	-9.95	3333	-3824	-53.43	-4536	-57.64
32.	Pathapatnam	7790	5926	-1864	-31.45	2757	-3169	-53.48	-5033	-64.61
33.	Meliaputti	8037	5868	-2169	-36.96	3163	-2705	-46.10	-4874	-60.64
34.	Hiramandalam	6148	5406	-742	-13.73	2718	-2688	-49.72	-3430	-55.79
35.	Kothuru	7013	6873	-140	-2.04	3171	-3702	-53.86	-3842	-54.78
36.	Bhamini	4509	3745	-764	-20.40	2394	-1351	-36.07	-2115	-46.91
37.	Seetampeta	7341	9649	2308	23.92	4511	-5138	-53.25	-2830	-38.55
38.	Veeraghattam	7682	7215	-467	-6.47	3952	-3263	-45.23	-3730	-48.56
39.	Palakonda	7151	5350	-1801	-33.66	2825	-2525	-47.20	-4326	-60.50
40.	Burja	6797	5770	-1027	-17.80	2527	-3243	-56.20	-4270	-62.82
41.	Vangara	9477	8180	-1297	-15.86	4731	-3449	-42.16	-4746	-50.08
42.	R.amadalavalasa	11666	9504	-2162	-22.75	6361	-3143	-33.07	-5305	-45.47
43.	Santakaviti	11690	9242	-2448	-26.49	4613	-4629	-50.09	-7077	-60.54

(Table Contd.)

(Contd. Table 3)

Sl. No.	Name of the Mandal	Decrease in the cultivators in two decades								
		1991 Cultivators	2001 cultivators	Difference	Percentage of decrease	2011 Cultivators	Difference	Percentage of decrease from 2001-2011	Galloping capital decades 1991-2011	Percentage of decrease from 1991-2011
44.	Rajam	10373	7171	-3202	-44.65	5798	-1373	-19.15	-4575	-44.10
45.	Narasannapeta	7249	5291	-1958	-37.01	4019	-1272	-24.04	-3230	-44.56
46.	Polaki	9220	7007	-2213	-31.58	3415	-3592	-51.26	-5805	-62.96
47.	Srikakulam	7951	7106	-845	-11.89	3925	-3181	-44.76	-4026	-50.64
48.	Gara	7226	5401	-1825	-33.79	3152	-2249	-41.64	-4074	-56.38
49.	Amadalavalasa	8674	5456	-3218	-58.98	2983	-2473	-45.33	-5691	-65.61
50.	Sarubujjili	11522	5189	-6333	-122.05	2349	-2840	-54.73	-9173	-79.61
51.	Etcherla	12071	8172	-3899	-47.71	3714	-4458	-54.55	-8357	-69.23
52.	G.sigadam	10217	8259	-1958	-23.71	5055	-3204	-38.79	-5162	-50.52
53.	Ponduru	11505	6821	-4684	-68.67	4648	-2173	-31.86	-6857	-59.60
54.	Ranasthalam	12316	9724	-2592	-26.66	4743	-4981	-51.22	-7573	-61.49
55.	Laveru	15026	10640	-4386	-41.22	4255	-6385	-60.01	-10771	-71.68
56.	L.N. peta	0	3782	3782	100	2436	-1346	-35.59	2436	######
	Carved out area	189447	177630	-11817	-6.2376	112311	-65319	-36.773	-77136	-40.72
	Present Srikakulam	333826	266702	-67124	-20.107	105855	-160847	-60.31	-227971	-68.29
	Total research area	523273	444332	-78941	-15.086	218166	-226166	-50.9	-305107	-58.31

Source: Compiled from District handbook of statistics and from PCA of 2011 Census.

agrarian labour is decreased to 6,89,239. Thus a net decrease in the agrarian labour was 1, 30,958. In a span of ten years the peasantry to the tune of 1, 71,934 and the labour to the tune of 1, 30,958 are vacated the rural livelihood. The share of peasantry showed an increasing trend during 1971-81. As seen from the census data, interestingly during 1961-71, 2.11 lakhs of peasants were eliminated from the agriculture. This trend is arrested in the subsequent decade. The reasons for this arrest can be traced from the stagnation in the secondary and territory sector. Again, this trend was consistently improving from 1981.

The proportion of workers in the population was also diminishing. From 1971 to 1991 census, the share of the working force was constantly recorded as 43 to 44 per cent. In 2011 census, the share of workers drastically dropped to 36.96 per cent. A striking fact is the talented hands were getting migrated in search of work. In other words, this backward district is settled as a net exporter of labour in the period of globalisation of capital.

To know about some more facts, Mandal wise elimination of the peasantry has to be observed. The Table 3 indicates the Mandal wise statistics of the elimination of the peasantry in the period of reforms.

As seen from the table, during 1991-2001, only six Mandals recorded growth with Lakshminarasupeta being a newly formed Mandal. Out of six Mandals, two Mandals were tribal tracts. Vajrapukotturu is a predominantly fisher folk area. In other words, only two Mandals in the plain area recorded the growth. The remaining Mandals recorded the elimination of the peasantry from their profession. The elimination was widespread in dry farming areas and the areas those adjacent to the National highway. The average elimination of the peasantry during that decade was 15.09 per cent. Thirty-two Mandals surpassed this average. Kaviti Mandalnearly recorded fifty per cent of reduction in the population of peasantry.

The current Census 2011 revealed startling facts about the occupation pattern. The capital drove the peasantry out of their occupation in the decade 2001-11, every Mandal recorded the negative figure in the case of cultivators. In the reforms period 68.29 per cent of cultivators left of their profession. The carved out area shows this as 40.72 per cent while the research area shows 58.31 per cent. In other words, more than a half left the fields only to join workshops in the urban centres.

Economists classify the economy based on the occupational pattern. They consider the agrarian based economy as backward. Basing on the definition, this district has become "forward or developed" economy. The current census proved that only 18 per cent of the main workers are in the profession of cultivation, which is even less than national figure in percentage terms. Hence, it can be said that this district has crossed the take-off stage in the parlance of economists' language. However, unfortunately the hapless people have become a part in the capitalist structure as a wage labour where a capital cannot strive without this primary source. In other words, this district is supplying cheap labour to the capital. This can be proved from various socio-economic surveys of the governments. The two districts always have a dubious distinction of getting First and second ranks from the bottom in every parameter.

Marx observed this and concluded, "*on the other hand, these new freedmen became sellers of themselves only after they had been robbed of all their own means of production, and of all the guarantees of existence afforded by the old feudal arrangements. And the history of this, their expropriation, is written in the annals of mankind in letters of blood and fire.*" (Capital, Vol. I page 689)

The study proved in this district that thousands of peasants were leaving their profession and were becoming proletarian. What the statistics were portraying about these freedmen? Where are they settling? It appeared that the de-peasntaisation was leading to swell the agrarian labour.

As observed from the district statistics, barring Kaviti Mandal, the growth in the agrarian labour was glaring. The net increase in the agrarian labourwas 2,16,033. The district average growth is 35.76 per cent. 28 Mandals recorded more than this average growth and even some Mandals showed nearly hundred per cent growth. As discussed in the land alienation chapter, the dry land areas and the Mandals having transport facilities were showing ninety per cent of growth in the labour.

There is an interesting revelation about the enrolment of agricultural labour. As noticed in the villages, many workers from the villages were going daily to the nearby towns to work and earn their daily bread. Almost every Mandal headquarters were jam packed with the daily migrants. Due to lack of even the basic shelter, they were returning home in the night. In other words, the link between earning livelihood and the shelter had almost disappeared from the scene. However, all these were being enrolled in the list of agrarian labour. Temporary and permanent migrants were also being enrolled in the list. As observed, a person who was working as labourer in Visakhapatnam City for the last thirty years too got enrolled in this list.

However, the empirical research was saying a different perspective. These freedmen and even the traditional rural labourers were also leaving their countryside in search of their livelihood. Peasantry of every village were complaining about the shortage of agricultural labour. In fact, had the agrarian labour swelled in this way, cultivation would have become more profitable. Considering the demand and supply theory, the wages would have become cheaper and the rich peasantry could have earned more profits at the cost of labour. However, the ground level was not reflecting the statistics. In the census, these "New" freed persons were being recorded as agrarian labour. Hence, it appeared that the rural agricultural labour to be increasing. No doubt, peasants were becoming labourers day by day. However, they were not remaining in the village for their livelihood. All the earlier census statistics showed that the consistent increase in the agrarian labour. However, the current census shows that this head also is decreasing trend. The current census recorded the number, as 6,89,239, which is a sharp decline from over and above eight lakhs in the previous Census.

Table 4. Changing Pattern in Agrarian Labour

Sl.No.	Name of the Block/ Mandal	1991 Workers	1991 Agl. labour	1991 Percentage of labour	2001 Workers	2001 Agl. labour	2001 Percentage of labour	Difference	Percent
1.	Ichapuram	26550	9343	35.19	22399	12331	55.05	2988	31.98
2.	Kaviti	27560	13853	50.26	19762	11457	57.97	-2396	-17.30
3.	Kanchili	21516	8482	39.42	16070	11476	71.41	2994	35.30
4.	Sompeta	25412	7956	31.31	20545	10401	50.63	2445	30.73
5.	Mandasa	29192	12563	43.04	24984	16300	65.24	3737	29.75
6.	Palasa	29644	7054	23.80	28088	10560	37.60	3506	49.70
7.	Vajrapukothuru	23174	5635	24.32	18325	10018	54.67	4383	77.78
8.	Nandigam	25960	9403	36.22	20808	11311	54.36	1908	20.29
9.	Tekkali	25674	9985	38.89	24589	12942	52.63	2957	29.61
10.	Santabommali	26493	9962	37.60	21742	14058	64.66	4096	41.12
11.	Kotabommali	29488	11270	38.22	21580	16605	76.95	5335	47.34
12.	Jalumuru	27542	13013	47.25	23371	18755	80.25	5742	44.13
13.	Saravakota	23351	10217	43.75	20251	13127	64.82	2910	28.48
14.	Pathapatnam	27166	13024	47.94	21702	15660	72.16	2636	20.24
15.	Meliaputti	24975	8318	33.31	17422	12236	70.23	3918	47.10
16.	Hiramandalam	20129	9708	48.23	17111	12019	70.24	2311	23.81

(Table Contd.)

(Contd. Table 4)

Sl. No.	Name of the Block/ Mandal	1991 Workers	1991 Agl. labour	1991 Percentage of labour	2001 Workers	2001 Agl. labour	2001 Percentage of labour	Difference	Per cent
17.	Kothuru	26335	15326	58.20	24169	17996	74.46	2670	17.42
18.	Bhamini	18872	11570	61.31	15372	13936	90.66	2366	20.45
19.	Seetampeta	24813	15881	64.00	20486	16853	82.27	972	6.12
20.	Veeraghattam	27209	13931	51.20	24647	17593	71.38	3662	26.29
21.	Palakonda	29991	15041	50.15	29789	16850	56.56	1809	12.03
22.	Burja	19796	9721	49.11	17272	11480	66.47	1759	18.09
23.	Vangara	21200	8450	39.86	21192	13442	63.43	4992	59.08
24.	Ramadalavalasa	29778	14016	47.07	27502	19357	70.38	5341	38.11
25.	Santakaviti	30228	13606	45.01	25400	17459	68.74	3853	28.32
26.	Rajam	29736	9830	33.06	26554	13905	52.36	4075	41.45
27.	Narasannapeta	27502	11562	42.04	23070	16391	71.05	4829	41.77
28.	Polaki	29787	14271	47.91	21914	18153	82.84	3882	27.20
29.	Srikakulam	53821	15925	29.59	59753	16839	28.18	914	5.74

(Table Contd.)

(Contd. Table 4)

Sl. No.	Name of the Block/ Mandal	1991 Workers	1991 Agl. labour	1991 Percentage of labour	2001 Workers	2001 Agl. labour	2001 Percentage of labour	Difference	Per cent
30.	Gara	28818	13313	46.20	24207	17675	73.02	4362	32.76
31.	Amadalavalasa	29467	10392	35.27	25008	15187	60.73	4795	46.14
32.	Sarubujjili	28068	13080	46.60	12630	9198	72.83	-3882	-29.68
33.	Etcherla	32035	12462	38.90	28133	20368	72.40	7906	63.44
34.	G.sigadam	24466	10018	40.95	19558	14179	72.50	4161	41.54
35.	Ponduru	32534	13840	42.54	23245	16724	71.95	2884	20.84
36.	Ranasthalam	28558	10040	35.16	25218	17389	68.95	7349	73.20
37.	Laveru	31522	10978	34.83	26165	18671	71.36	7693	70.08
38.	L.N. peta		0	######	10591	8031	75.83	8031	######
39.	Komarada	21639	9685	44.76	26832	14625	54.51	4940	51.01
40.	G.L. Puram	20500	10271	50.10	21860	13103	59.94	2832	27.57
41.	Kurupam	19836	9914	49.98	15660	12119	77.39	2205	22.24
42.	Jiyyammavalasa	23597	9047	38.34	19939	14962	75.04	5915	65.38
43.	Garugubilli	22268	7098	31.88	21830	11153	51.09	4055	57.13

(Table Contd.)

(Contd. Table 4)

Sl. No.	Name of the Block/ Mandal	1991 Workers	1991 Agl. labour	1991 Percentage of labour	2001 Workers	2001 Agl. labour	2001 Percentage of labour	Difference	Per cent
44.	Parvathipuram	38423	11869	30.89	40466	15760	38.95	3891	32.78
45.	Makkuva	20500	7781	37.96	21595	12560	58.16	4779	61.42
46.	Sethanagaram	27268	10388	38.10	28118	13238	47.08	2850	27.44
47.	Balijipeta	30514	11401	37.36	26738	15794	59.07	4393	38.53
48.	Bobbili	45422	15475	34.07	39731	21588	54.34	6113	39.50
49.	Saluru	42312	17932	42.38	41859	21154	50.54	3222	17.97
50.	Pachipenta	19808	9679	48.86	20808	14475	69.56	4796	49.55
51.	R.B. Puram	20808	7759	37.29	21739	12452	57.28	4693	60.48
52.	Badangi	23038	7778	33.76	24060	11827	49.16	4049	52.06
53.	Therlam	27134	10433	38.45	29942	14999	50.09	4566	43.76
54.	Merakamudidam	25714	10229	39.78	26760	16144	60.33	5915	57.83
55.	Garividi	26442	7281	27.54	27584	13259	48.07	5978	82.10
56.	Cheepurupalli	23663	7105	30.03	18443	14053	76.20	6948	97.79
	Total	1497248	604164	22.69	1344588	820197	61.00	216033	35.76

Source: Primary Census abstracts.

As seen from the specific examples, in every village, rich peasantry was complaining about the shortage of labour. A peasant of Kothuru village (Vaddithandra Panchayat) of Santabommali Mandal indicated about the shortage of labour in a complaint voice. By that time, the paddy transplantation season was in progress. The rich peasant asked the labourers to do the work in the paddy field during the afternoon session. In the morning session, they worked in another field. They simply rejected the proposal saying they were anyway expected to work and hence would come the next day despite offering enhanced wages.

As seen from the table, in this Mandal, the growth of agrarian labour recorded 29.14 per cent. However, the above situation enables understanding the real picture. Once in this district, the economic exploitation on the labour had no limit. The labour used to mortgage their labour days well in advance to get the food grains for them in the summer. In the local dialect, it was called "Agaavu coolie". There were no systematic agitations to demand for the wage enhancement. The wage rates were always decided at the whims and pleasures of the rich peasantry. In any case, the labourers used to ask for the wage enhancernent immediately the rich peasantry used to implement social boycott. The rich peasantry used to call the agrarian labour of nearby villages and manage their cultivation in a pride manner. Later, the situation did not reverse because of the united movements of the agrarian labour. The continuous migration of the rural proletarian brought the demand for their labour. In other words, the shortage of agricultural labour in the countryside was an obvious factor.

People with lands and the landless were also on the path of migration. The working group of twelfth planning commission categorically stated that broad sections of the peasantry were expressing anguish and irritation on their profession with most peasants being in a hurry to leave the profession. As per the report, 82 per cent of land holdings were marginal and small. 44.2 per cent of these sections were trying to get rid of the burden of cultivation. 44.2 per cent of marginal peasants and 35.3 per cent of small peasants were ready to leave. Even the medium and largelandholders were not an exception to this trend. 28.1 per cent of that section was disinterested with agriculture and were contemplating to give up. In Andhra Pradesh, 28.3 per cent of marginal peasantry, 19.5 per cent of small peasantry and 15.9 per cent of medium and large sections were in disillusionment and were searching for opportunities.

An interesting thing in the report was the peasantry of West Bengal too pursuing the same path. In fact, leftists, leftist intellectuals and the governments eulogized about the land reforms and its positive impact on the peasantry. Ironically, West Bengal average had exceeded the national average of 40.1 per cent and recorded 45.5 per cent. At National level, on an average 44.2 per cent of the peasantry was disinterested while West Bengal recorded 47.2. In case of small peasantry, these figures were 35.3 and 32.6 respectively. All these clarified one aspect. The peasantry of this country had concluded that this cultivation could not cater to their minimum needs.

Table 5. Share of Urban and Rural Population in India

Sl. No.	*Census year*	*Total Population*	*Rural Population*	*Urban Population*
1.	1971	548,159,652	439,045,675 (80.09)	109,113,977 (19.91)
2.	1981	683,329,097	523,866,550 (76.66)	159,462,547 (23.34)
3.	1991	846,302,688	628,691,676 (74.20)	217,611,012 (25.80)
4.	2001	1,028,737,436	742,490,639 (72.17)	286,119,689 (27.83)
5.	2011	1,210,726,932	833,500,000 (68.84)	377,100,000 (31.16)

Indian census too confirmed these facts. Share of urban population was in a continuous raise from the early 70s. The table is indicating the trends of urbanisation in the country.

In absolute terms, the urban population too increased in the 2011 census. As per the provisional census 2011, "*In absolute numbers, the rural population has increased by 90.47 million and the urban population by 91.00 million in the last decade. For the first time since Independence, the absolute increase in population is more in urban areas that in rural areas*" (Executive summary 2011 census and rural urban ratio in 2011 census).

Education as a Social Capital

The colonial rulers introduced modern education in India to train the people as per its needs. The British introduced the education system only to cut the salary bill. Literature, both the fiction and non-fiction recorded this process and influence that had on the society as a whole. The late governor of Bombay in his work recorded the beginning of education in India. It reads, "*The British government wisely seizes every opportunity of educating under its own auspices, young Native princes. Several sovereigns, now reigning, have in their youth been thus educated. In the next generation, almost every prince will have been educated after the European method, either by private tuition in the palace, or at institutions established for youths of princely degree.*

English has been spontaneously chosen by the Native States as the language for their diplomatic correspondence with the British government. These circumstances induce the chiefs to regard themselves as alumni and the paramount power as the alma mater." [India in 1880: Page 64-65 Sir Richard Temple]

M.N. Roy discussed widely about the economic effect of the modern education in his work. It reads,

"Modern education was introduced by the British Government in the second decade of the 19th century. Since then, the modern intelligentsia has been growing very rapidly, transcending the limits marked out for them by the foreign rulers, and capturing/entirely the professions of medicine, law and teaching - Today, the English are practically ousted from these professions by the Indians. According to the census figures of 1911, the number of people employed in public administration and professions amounted to 7,973,662. This figure does not include the clerks and employees of the commercial firms. These professions proved to be lucrative, and money began to be accumulated in the hands of the upper strata of the intellectual class. In 1850 the total accumulated wealth of this class, as shown in the investments in Government securities, amounted to £ 69,000,000. Since there was no industrial or other profitable means of investment, this whole amount was invested in Government securities. The total capital invested in Native banks at that time amounted to £ 19,000,000/Land offered the only other form of profitable investment at this period, and the accumulated savings of this class were also invested in land-leases, which were in the process of transfer from the hands of the big holders on account of their failure to meet higher government assessments, as well as from the small holders, because of their heavy indebtedness." (Economic Transition in India: M.N. Roy: Page 22) [Emphasis added]

In the earlier period the top layer of India could go to schooling and acquired skills and assimilated in the process of development. In the surveyed district also the Brahmins and Kshatriya and Velama doras could go to schooling and pursued education. In some of the villages, The Brahmins could go to overseas to pursue education and employment. However, the broad masses belonging to innumerable social groups were far away from the ambit of education.

In the colonial period, even some of the Brahmins were not interested to send their children to modern education. The reasons were two fold. Those were economical and cultural. However, some families recognised the necessity of education and its future role as a capital. The famous fiction writer of Andhra Pradesh Gurajada Apparao noted this aspect in his Magnum opus *Kanyashulkam*. He described the future role of education. It reads, *"If our boy becomes a magistrate or gets a police job, he will buy up all the farmlands of this village. We are hesitating to spend a paltry hundred rupees a year. Do you want your son to eke out a living by making shoulder threads like you? If you think his education is such a burden I will sell the farm land my parents gave me as a wedding gift to pay for his schooling"*. (Original: Kanyashulkam: Gurajada Apparao: Girls for sale: translated by Velcheru Narayana Rao page number: 280 scene number 1 Act II)

Early Seeds of Modern Education in this District

The colonial rulers tried to establish modern educational institutions in this district (at that time the studied area was a part of Vizagapatam district).

In A.D. 1813, the court of directors of the East India Company earmarked a sum of one lakh rupees out of their Indian revenues for the encouragement of the "learned natives of India, and for the introduction and promotion of knowledge of the science among the inhabitants". This money, however, remained unspent for want of initiative. The government Anglo-Vernacular school at Srikakulam and the government Taluk School at Itchapuram, both established in 1856, were the earliest institutions." (*Source:* Srikakulam District Gazetteer: Compiled by S.S. Rameshan, I.A.S: Page: 156-157)

Initially, Brahmins who are the ardent supporters of oriental education entered the modern education sector. The affluent sections of the Brahmins entered the modern education and reaped the benefits of the modernity. For a long-time the innumerable castes not even entered the arena because of the economic and cultural reasons.

The educational institutions came into this district on a snail's pace. By 1951 the entire district had only one degree college. It was established in 1951 after the formation of the District under the management of the government. The second college was established under private management at Bobbili. By 1969 there were only two degree colleges and ten junior colleges in the entire district, which showed a dismal performance in the sector. The 1961 Census recorded that only 16,465 males and 945 females were attained matriculation and above matriculation. Their percentage was 1.45 and 0.08 respectively. In other words education was reserved to affluent sections only. As observed from the field survey the early birds were Brahmins and rarely the elite peasantry.

In fact, until late 60s, the peasantry of this district strongly felt that pursuing employment was nothing but slavery. Even in the surveyed villages, many peasants said that they did not accept the employment due to their parent's attitude. S. Raminaidu of Ponugutivalasa got employment in Indian Railways in 1965. When he intimated about his job, his paternal uncle commented in a sarcastic tone "oh! You are becoming an attached labour." "Even during the early 70s, when the chairman of Zillaparishad, Gorle Sriramulunaidu asked a rich peasant of Annavaram village to join as a teacher, the rich peasant replied, "Now you are coming to my house and we are sitting at equal level. If I join as a teacher, I will become a servant of you. Can I stand with you at par? The salary of the teacher is not even equal to my sugarcane bill. Why should I lose my dignity"? During the survey, the same rich peasant revealed the truth and subsequently he was repenting. Piridi was famous for its employment. Even in that village, many peasants rejected the employment during the late 60s.

The literary evidence also showed these examples. Kalindi Charan Panigrahi an Oriya novelist in his novel "Mattimanushulu" described the situation of an old-aged peasant Shamandhanu talking to his employed son, *"we are continuing in this profession for generations. Our fathers and ancestors continued in this profession for last seven generations. We all dig this soil and harvested crops. Can we go to heaven by leaving this plough and adopting pen in that place?"*

Table 6. Employment Pattern in the Surveyed Villages

Sl. No.	Name of the Caste	Reservation Status	Total households	Households got the employment	Percentage of households got employment	State-gov.	Lecturers	Teacher	lady teacher	Software engineer	Software engineer- - USA	Engineer	Engineer lady	Doctor
1.	Barber	B.C.A	360	12	3.33	4	0	2	0	0	0	0	0	0
2.	Dasari	B.C.A	40	3	7.50	0	0	0	1	0	0	0	0	0
3.	Goolla	B.C.A	207	0	0.00	0	0	0	0	0	0	0	0	0
4.	Jangalu	B.C.A	48	1	2.08	0	0	0	0	0	0	0	0	0
5.	Kurakula	B.C.A	167	0	0.00	0	0	0	0	0	0	0	0	0
6.	Medari	B.C.A	45	0	0.00	0	0	0	0	0	0	0	0	0
7.	Vaddi	B.C.A	80	20	25.00	0	0	0	0	0	0	0	0	0
8.	Rajaka	B.C.A	956	39	4.08	6	0	5	0	0	1	0	0	0
9.	Reddika	B.C.A	2620	32	1.22	2	1	4	0	0	1	8	0	0
10.	Dammali	B.C.A	9	2	22.22	0	0	0	0	0	0	0	0	0
11.	Dommari	B.C.A	14	0	0.00	0	0	0	0	0	0	0	0	0
12.	Kalinga	B.C.A	2054	345	16.80	54	22	170	14	14	7	54	1	23
13.	Pondara	B.C.A	207	8	3.86	3	0	1	0	0	0	0	0	0
14.	Potters	B.C.B	107	1	0.93	0	0	1	0	0	0	0	0	0
15.	Telukali	B.C.B	51	2	3.92	2	0	0	0	0	0	0	0	0

(Table Contd.)

(Contd. Table 6)

Sl. No.	Name of the Caste	Reservation Status	Total households	Households got the employment	Percentage of households got employment	State-gov.	Lecturers	Teacher	lady teacher	Software engineer	Software engineer-USA	Engineer	Engineer lady	Doctor
16.	Balija	B.C.B	4	0	0.00	0	0	0	0	0	0	0	0	0
17.	Bevara	B.C.B	120	1	0.83	0	0	1	0	0	0	0	0	0
18.	Carpenter	B.C.B	394	16	4.06	7	1	5	0	1	0	2	0	0
19.	Gouda	B.C.B	773	9	1.16	2	4	0	0	0	0	0	0	0
20.	Nagavamsham	B.C.D	740	39	5.27	1	0	22	2	1	2	0	0	3
21.	Patnaiks	B.C.D	77	6	7.79	1	0	0	0	0	0	1	0	0
22.	Sondi	B.C.D	70	8	11.43	0	0	0	0	0	0	0	0	0
23.	Uppari	B.C.D	8	0	0.00	0	0	0	0	0	0	0	0	0
24.	Yadavs	B.C.D	787	2	0.25	0	0	0	0	0	0	0	0	0
25.	Ayyerukula	B.C.D	20	0	0.00	0	0	1	0	0	0	0	0	0
26.	Bhatraj	B.C.D	1	1	100.00	0	0	0	0	0	0	0	0	0
27.	Satani Vyshnava	B.C.D	4	0	0.00	0	0	0	0	0	0	0	0	0
28.	Polinati Velama	B.C.D	2627	98	3.73	4	4	27	1	3	0	2	0	3
29.	Toorpu kapu	B.C.D	8121	244	3.00	38	0	85	5	11	4	10	0	3
30.	Koppulavelama	B.C.D	2408	287	11.92	67	1	72	5	32	20	34	0	8

(Table Contd.)

(Contd. Table 6)

Sl. No.	Name of the caste	Reservation Status	Total households	Households got the employment	Percentage of households got employment	State-gov	Lecturers	Teacher	lady teacher	Software engineer	Software engineer- -USA	Engineer	Engineer lady	Doctor
31.	Gudia	B.C.D	5	0	0.00	0	0	0	0	0	0	0	0	0
32.	Yajaka	N.A	15	0	0.00	0	0	0	0	0	0	0	0	0
33.	Roulo	O.C	15	0	0.00	0	0	0	0	0	0	0	0	0
34.	Aakula	O.C	15	0	0.00									
35.	Brahmin	O.C	96	2	3.13	0	0	0	0	0	0	0	0	0
36.	Kshatriya	O.C	55	5	9.09	4	0	0	0	0	0	0	0	0
37.	Pandas	O.C	95	9	9.47	1	0	0	0	1	2	1	0	0
38.	Srivaishnava	O.C	12	0	0.00	0	0	0	0	0	0	0	0	0
39.	Telaga	O.C	577	5	0.87	0	0	1	0	0	0	0	0	0
40.	Velamadora	O.C	5	0	0.00	0	0	0	0	0	0	0	0	0
41.	Vysya	O.C	491	23	4.68	1	0	4	0	0	2	0	0	0
42.	Muslims	O.C	6	0	0.00	0	0	0	0	0	0	0	0	0
43.	Majjala	O.C	300	4	1.33	0	0	0	0	0	0	0	0	0
	G. Total		24806	1225	4.94	197	33	401	28	63	39	112	1	40

(Table Contd.)

(Contd. Table 6)

Sl. No.	Name of the Caste	Reservation Status	Doctor Ladies	Doctor USA	Central gov.	Public Sector	Private	Defence	Police	Para-military	Total
1.	Barber	B.C.A	0	0	0	1	0	2	2	0	11
2.	Dasari	B.C.A	0	0	0	0	0	0	0	0	1
3.	Goolla	B.C.A	0	0	0	0	1	0	0	0	1
4.	Jangalu	B.C.A	0	0	0	0	0	0	0	1	1
5.	Kurakula	B.C.A	0	0	0	0	0	0	0	0	0
6.	Medari	B.C.A	0	0	0	0	0	0	0	0	0
7.	Vaddi	B.C.A	0	0	0	0	0	0	0	0	0
8.	Rajaka	B.C.A	0	0	35	2	2	9	0	1	61
9.	Reddika	B.C.A	0	0	21	0	0	51	5	0	93
10.	Dammali	B.C.A	0	0	2	0	0	0	0	0	2
11.	Dommari	B.C.A	0	0	0	0	0	0	0	0	0
12.	Kalinga	B.C.A	6	0	49	29	10	103	63	27	646
13.	Pondara	B.C.A	0	0	1	0	0	4	0	0	9
14.	Potters	B.C.B	0	0	0	0	0	0	0	0	1
15.	Telukali	B.C.B	0	0	1	2	2	1	0	0	8

(Table Contd.)

(Contd. Table 6)

Sl. No.	Name of the Caste	Reservation Status	Doctor Ladies	Doctor USA	Central Gov.	Public Sector	Private	Defence	Police	Para-military	Total
16.	Balija	B.C.B	0	0	0	0	0	0	0	0	0
17.	Bevara	B.C.B	0	0	0		0	0	0	0	1
18.	Carpenter	B.C.B	0	0	0	2	2	4	0	0	24
19.	Gouda	B.C.B	0	0	1	1	0	2	0	0	10
20.	Nagavamsham	B.C.D	0	0	0	4	3	12	3	0	53
21.	Patnaiks	B.C.D	0	0	1	0	0	0	0	0	3
22.	Sondi	B.C.D	0	0	2	1	0	4	0	0	7
23.	Uppari	B.C.D	0	0	0	0	0	0	0	0	0
24.	Yadavs	B.C.D	0	0	0	2	0	3	0	0	5
25.	Ayyerukula	B.C.D	0	0	0	0	0	0	0	0	1
26.	Bhatraj	B.C.D	0	0	1	0	0	0	0	0	1
27.	Satani Vyshnava	B.C.D	0	0	0	0	0	0	0	0	0
28.	Polinati Velama	B.C.D	0	1	6	4	2	34	15	2	108
29.	Toorpu kapu	B.C.D	1	1	18	14	4	82	47	19	342
30.	Koppulavelama	B.C.D	1	1	20	36	92	37	13	0	439

(Table Contd.)

(Contd. Table 6)

Sl. No.	Name of the Caste	Reservation Status	Doctor Ladies	Doctor USA	Central Gov.	Public Sector	Private	Defence	Police	Para-military	Total
31.	Gudia	B.C.D	0	0	0	0	0	0	0	0	0
32.	Yajaka	N.A	0	0	0	0	0	0	0	0	0
33.	Roulo	O.C	0	0	0	0	0	0	0	0	0
34.	Aakula	O.C									
35.	Brahmin	O.C	0	0	0	2	0	0	0	0	2
36.	Kshatriya	O.C	0	0	3	0	0	1	0	0	8
37.	Pandas	O.C	0	0	20	0	6	1	0	0	32
38.	Srivaishnava	O.C	0	0	0	0	0	0	0	0	0
39.	Telaga	O.C	0	0	0	0	0	2	1	0	4
40.	Velamadora	O.C	0	0	0	0	0	0	0	0	0
41.	Vysya	O.C	0	0	0	0	11	6	0	0	24
42.	Muslims	O.C	0	0	0	0	0	0	0	0	0
43.	Majjala	O.C	0	0	0	0	0	3	1	0	4
	G. Total		8	3	181	100	135	361	150	50	1902

This table does not contain the details of Dalits, Adivasis, Weavers and fishermen families since those have been discussed in the separate chapters. Apart from the four castes there are 43 social groups have been tabulated. Out of 43 castes 11 castes are categorised as unreserved. One caste Yajaka is not listed in the backward castes hence it appears that it is also an unreserved. Hence, 31 castes are recognised as backward castes as per the Andhra Pradesh government list of backward castes. Government categorised these castes as A, B, C, D groups. "A" is considered as most back ward while D is considered as less Backward.

As the district gazetteer noted "the only branch of professional education in which the district effords facilities is teacher-training" (Page 166). In the early days people from Brahmins and Patnaiks entered the teaching profession and in those days those were poorly paid. They have to depend on the peasantry to earn their livelihood in the absence of proper wage structure and irregular payment of salaries. There was a proverbial expression in Telugu language "Batakaleka Badipantulu". The literal meaning of the proverb is, "teacher is the last means". This is also one of the reasons for not entering the teacher profession by the remaining castes. As history told, the teacher training institute was shifted from developed Krishna district to backward Srikakulam district in the year 1965-66.

However, things are changed from late 60s and early 70s. The government intervention in the enhancement of education, hostel facilities and creation of employment in the public sector above all the reservation system to the backward classes those introduced in the early 70s changed the situation in a drastic way. Even now, barring the four major peasant castes umpteen people of the other backward castes are not get their genuine share in the education and in employment.

As seen from the Table the sector wise employment clears many things. The sectors were broadly categorised under ten categories. Out of the total employment, interestingly, 21.08 per cent are teachers. One teacher belongs to Brahmin caste who is on the verge of retirement Mantha Raghunadha Sharma, a teacher by profession told, *"There are almost no Brahmin teachers. The stage all set for backward castes"*. The reasons are obvious. The Brahmins almost become urbanised and their children do not have any interest in the profession. The vacated places are being occupied by the backward castes. Even, once the Brahmin dominated villages have no strength of Brahmins now.

Now the same suit is followed in the peasant castes. The children of first generation teachers of the peasant castes are not showing any interest in the profession and they are settling in the higher strata.

The second largest employment is in nothing but in defence sector. During the colonial Rule Gandhi expressed that in the absence of proper livelihood opportunities the poor Indian from the countryside were joining the British army and aiming their guns over the common people in the foreign lands for the sake of British colonial interests. Unfortunately still the district is being a supplier of soldiers. It is interesting to note that all the defence employees are settled in a low-rung position and all these came from marginal and landless families. Some parts of these people are also from small peasant families. As observed no person from the affluent peasant family has joined the army.

As seen from the Table, in the surveyed villages the average employed families are 4.94 only. There are wide differences in the getting of employment in inter and intra social groups. In the Backward castes as a whole the larger benefits have gone in favour of Kalinga and Koppulavelama. In the B.C.A group in the surveyed villages there are 13 social groups. The total employment in this group is 825. Out of this, The Kalingas secured 646 jobs and the share of their employment is 78.30.The remaining 21.70 per cent is shared among 12 social groups. One more interesting thing is sample of Kalinga household are lesser than that of Reddika caste which is also under the category of B.C.A. Their share in the employment is 11.27. The remaining castes of servitude have almost no saying in the employment. As seen from the table, the high earned jobs have been categorised in seven categories. Almost no social group apart from Reddika entered the competition with Kalinga caste. Out of 115 high earned jobs the Kalingas stood with 105 jobs. In percentage terms they got a share of 91.30. The second rank went in favour of Reddika caste and they had 9 high earning jobs. The remaining one high earned job went in favour of Rajaka family. The remaining 10 social groups could not enter this slab. Education is acting as a social capital for these 105 families and they have become entrepreneurs, nursing home owners and neo-capitalist farmers. Kalinga professionals are running almost all the private nursing homes and nearly corporatised hospitals in Srikakulam. Corporatisation of health sector is reaping those heaps of money and this money is becoming a capital for these high earned strata. These sections garnered the entire urban lands of Srikakulam town. Now, a layman cannot even dream of purchasing square yard of land in this town.

The intra layer differences are also disturbing. As observed from the study the Kalinga caste benefitted much from the education. The employment pattern also has its bearing on the landownership. Normally good opportunities knocked the doors of the land holding families. Out of 2054 Kalinga households only 16.79 households could secure jobs whereas the remaining 83.21 per cent of Kalinga households could not touch the doors of regular employment.

When asked about the employment pattern in their Gouda caste, a person belonging to Vanitamandalam Village of Polaki Mandal replied in a sarcastic tone, "By God's grace we have not encountered such a problem in this village." As a whole his words came to true for entire B.C.B group. The B.C.B group has not much benefitted from these reservations. At the most, weavers could get some share in this group.

All the remaining major peasant castes are grouped under B.C.D group. In this group apart from these three there are nine social groups. The major reservation fruits in this group have gone in favour of Koppulavelama. This category got 959 jobs while Koppulavelama got 439 jobs. Out of the total employment. Their share in the employment in this category stood at 45.04 the Polinativelama share is stood at 11.26 while Toorpu kapu share is stood at 35.66. However, when compare with these two social group samples, the sample of Toorpukapus is a larger one. The kapu sample households are 8000 above and the remaining castes are around 2000 only. In this group, Toorpukapus did not get any good share in the employment.As a whole, these three major social groups got 92.69 per cent of jobs while remaining nine social groups were forced to content with 7.31 per cent.

Intra layer differences are also glaring in the Koppulavelama caste. Out of the total 2408 households only 287 household could join the ranks of employment. In other words 88.08 per cent of the Koppulavelama household could not knock the doors of employment. As a whole, the B.C.D group could attain 142 high earning jobs while Koppulavelama got 96 jobs in this sector. They have 67.60 per cent in this cream. Toorpukapus got 30 jobs in this sector and they have 21.12 per cent. Polinativelama caste could get only nine jobs and they had a share of 6.33 per cent. In other words 95.05 per cent of high earning jobs went in favour of three major peasant castes while Koppulavelama dominated the scene.

There is one best example of grabbing lands by the educationally elite sections in the surveyed villages. The educated elites of Piridi village almost purchased half of the village farmlands in another surveyed village Gollalapeta in Ramabhadrapuram and they even stretched out their hands to Odisha state. The Koppulavelama caste people almost purchased Bobbili town with this social capital.

Now, the situation in Andhra Pradesh in general and in this district also changed rapidly in the sphere of education. Almost the education is privatised and corporates occupied the sector. Education has become a commodity and the people prefer private institutions to public institutes. The vehement propaganda against public sector schools from the cross sections influenced the people. Many lands are being sold to get the education in the villages. Marginal and small peasantry are preferring education to their children at the cost of farmlands. Naturally, money-holding sections are getting good education and naturally, they are taking the ladder while remaining is watching the scene in a hapless mood. Thus, education acted as a social capital and helped in widening the gulf in one word the formula is fixed in the region as land-education-land.

Rural Exodus and Withdrawal of Youth

Changing family structure too had its impact on the agriculture. Until the early 90s, combined family system mostly prevailed in this district. The Census of India 2011revealed that 70.1 per cent of households had only one married couple. Interestingly, 11.6 household did not have a single married couple, whereas 14.1 per cent household had two married couples. Family labour played a crucial role in the cultivation. In other words, profit was nothing but extraction of surplus value. The nuclear family had almost replaced the previous type. Nuclear family itself indicated that the disappearance of "unity" was only to cater to the interests of newly "defined" family structure. Hence, the peasantry was depending on hired labour. Invariably, it leads to hike in the wage bill. It was interesting to recollect the history in the words of Campbell regarding the hired labour in Indian agriculture, which read, *"As a general Rule, farming is not carried on by hired labourers. A man has his own little farm, ploughs and cultivates it himself: he generally has sons or brothers to assist. He may occasionally hire labour, and certain services are performed by the inferior inhabitants of the village."* (Modern India.... Page 64-65: G. Campbel).

Indian government conducts input survey for every five years. In that series, 2006-07 was the latest one. As per that survey, "the average family size of a marginal peasant was 4.69. In the case of small peasant, the family size was 4.82. The average family size of medium peasant was 5.11 and in the case of large peasants, the size was 5.28". (*Source: www.dacnet.nic.in*)

Youth has no assurance of livelihood on the primary sector. Hence, they were travelling to town and nearby cities in search of livelihood. As observed from the ground level examples, youth were unaware of many agricultural operations. The young woman of the countryside did not know the skill of transplanting of paddy. Usually in the transplanting season, women go in groups to the fields. In that group, occasionally it was noticed to find the age group of below twenty years. Normally, these women belonged to the middle and old aged group. The progeny of peasant castes was unaware of the agricultural operations though they had the knowledge of the work, as they were disinterested to continue the profession.

The employment generation was diminishing in the primary sector. Swami Nathan committee noted this fact and recorded *"The State-wise data shows that there was overall negative annual growth of rural employment during 1993-94 to 1999-2000 in Goa [-2.90], Himachal Pradesh [-0.13], Tamil Nadu [-1.42], Tripura [-0.67] and Arunachal Pradesh [-2.09]. In following States, the growth rate was positive but below the national level of 0.68 per cent. Andhra Pradesh [0.24], Karnataka [0.17], Maharashtra [0.37], Rajasthan [0.51], West Bengal [0.43] and Meghalaya [0.31]. The negative or extremely low growth rate of employment in some of the larger States like Tamil Nadu, Himachal Pradesh, Andhra Pradesh, Karnataka, Maharashtra, Rajasthan and West Bengal is very disturbing. Incidentally, Maharashtra, Andhra Pradesh and Karnataka which had registered very low rural employment growth during 1993-94 to 1999-2000 had also certain Hot Spots where many farmers have committed suicides during the last five years."* (National commission on farmers: Serving farmers and saving farming fifth and final report, 4 October 2006: Popularly known as Swami Nathan committee: Department of agriculture: GOI).

At the same time, this report aspired for, "*attracting and retaining youth in farming,*" for "*restoring the glory of Indian farmers and farming.*"

NSSO conducted a survey on migration in India in 2007-08 and published a report in 2010, which said, "*Migration of households in both the rural and urban areas was dominated by the migration of households from rural areas. Nearly 57 per cent of urban migrant households migrated from rural areas.Nearly 60 per cent of urban male migrants and 59 per cent of urban female migrants had migrated from rural areas*". (*Source:* Migration in India 2007-08:NSS 64th Round)

However, researchers argued that these statistics were grossly under-estimated. UNDP report research paper strongly remarked that, "*these agencies namely Census and NSSO are not reflecting the magnitude of migration. With wide data, they commented, "It estimates that roughly 1 per cent of the Indian population or 10 million people migrated temporarily (NSSO 2001). But this is also a gross underestimate because the data do not properly count part-time occupations and short-term migrations. The true figure probably lies at around 100 million as we argue later. They tend to underestimate short term movements and thus underestimate or miss altogether, seasonal and circular migration which, according to recent village studies account for the bulk of migratory movements for work*". (Migration and human development in India: Priya Deshingkar and Shaheen akther)

Amrita Sharma made an empirical study of 14 locations covered in 13 states and concluded that the youth was withdrawing from agriculture and Indian agriculture suffering from old age. It reads, "*The regression results suggest that youth who possess non-farm skills are 1.4 times more likely tomove out of agriculture. Age has a significant role as the odds ratio in favour of shifting out of agriculture is high among farmers below 30 years of age. These results are supported by observations from other countries where occupational mobility was found to be higher among younger farmers, and they were found to be more sensitive to income differentials between farm and non-farm occupations, farm prices, and interest rates. Further, this study found that availability of irrigation did not have any significant impact on withdrawal behaviour. The small and marginal farmers expressed a great desire toquit farming possibly because of the low viability of smallholder agriculture. But, as the land sizeincreased the tendency towards withdrawal gained among the large holder category as well thus suggesting a U-shape relationship between farm size and willingness towards withdrawal. Thus, importance of proximity to urban areas for occupational choice seems to be indicated another change was in terms of the age of the farming population. It is expectedthat as young men play a diminishing*". (The changing agricultural demography in India: Evidences from rural youth perspective: http;/ irm.sagepub.com)

The Ministry of Agriculture conducts an input survey for every five years. The latest round survey related to 2006-07. Table 7 indicates the results of the survey with regard to age of the Indian peasantry.

Table 7. Average Age of Peasantry vs. Operational Holdings (years)

Sl. No	*Type of Holding*	*India*	*Andhra Pradesh*	*Srikakulam District*	*Vizianagaram District*
1.	Marginal	47.59	45.51	48.52	47.51
2.	Small	48.10	46.10	49.72	48.67
3.	Semi-medium	49.04	47.21	50.91	49.11
4.	Medium	49.75	48.07	52.14	50.39
5.	Large	50.45	48.83	55.89	51.54
	Total of all groups	47.99	45.96	48.86	47.86

Source: Compiled from agcensus.nic.in.

As observed in the table, it is understood that the researchers had only restrained estimates regarding the ageing of Indian agriculture and the statistics thereby clearly indicating that the working hands had since disappeared from the stage with leaving the platforms for middle-aged men and the woman. The studied districts too revealed this trend and even the average in Srikakulam District was higher than the state and national average.

The youth of the traditional agrarian labour and the children of the peasant castes were also leaving their profession and becoming wage labourers in the urban sector due to which the primary sector lost the primary resource. As seen from the agricultural census, this district had 92 per cent marginal and small land holdings. As seen from the returns of this sector, those incomes were not even catering to their minimum needs. Corporatisation of health and education increased their burden enormously. Hence, the national average age stood at 47.99.

Even culturally too, it was becoming too difficult to get the youth settled in agriculture married. Parents of the bride preferred a security guard in the city to a semi-medium peasant in the village. Almost the entire youth of this district expressed the same opinion. Once, the cultivation was treated as noble and an independent profession. The cultural shift changed this concept and later, agriculture as a profession lost its glory.

When asked about this rampant migration, Vanjarapu Ashok, a peasant of Kandisa village of Regidi Amudalavalasa Mandal said, "Till early 80s, migration was being considered as a great insult. The pauperised were used to leave the village in mid-night. They used to feel ashamed to communicate the matter even to their neighbours. In this village, such things happened in the early 80s. Now, Migration is a regular factor."

There was no dearth for the news stories for this rural exodus. The vernacular daily Eenadu carried a special story on the same. The task force team of the daily gave a comprehensive report on this matter. It titled, *"villages are vacated"*.

"Badangi, Cheepurupalli, Therlam Mandals were showing the higher rate in migration. In every Mandal, 10,000 to 20,000 people were migrating.

Seetarmapuram village of Merakamudidam Mandal got remained with only 20 old aged people. Itikarlapalli, pedanadipalli, chinanadipalli, G. Muragam, Nimmalavalasa, G. Marrivalasa, Paandrangipeta, Pulugummi, Rachapeta, Gollalavalasa, Sheshuvupeta, Jammupeta, Palavalasa, Kondagandredu, Venkupatruni rega and kondadadi villages of Cheepurupalli Mandals were recording higher migration.

Peddimpeta, Palagara, Chilakalapalli, Chellimpeta, Narayanapuram, Ampavalli, Pedapenki, Vengapuram villages of Balijipeta Mandal recorded higher migration.

Tribal tracts were no exception for this migration. Neelakantapuram, Vobbangi, Thittiri, G.Shivada Panchayats of Kurupam Mandal recorded rampant migration. Almost 120 families were on the path of migration. 40 families went on migration in another schedule Mandal Gummalakshmi puram 1000 families of Komarada and Garugubilli Mandals had already left their villages." (Eenadu: Vizianagaram District edition: dated: 19/10/2011).

Today, so many intellectuals including the "pro-people" too are blaming the Mahatma Gandhi National Rural Employment Guarantee Scheme (MGNREGP) for the worsening condition of primary sector while the news stories have something different to reveal.

Shaik Madeena of Itikarlapalli village lamented to the team of reporters "We are getting Rs.70 as our wage in MGNREGP. It is not even sufficient to minimum needs. Hence, I have left the village with my family. We are working as labourers in a brick kiln in Nalgonda District. We could save Rs. 300 per a day. We have come to the village to participate in Diwali festival. After this festival, we will go back again."

Out of 20 Panchayats in Rajam Mandal, migration was intense in Dosali, Amiram, Raminaiduvalasa, Aaguru, Gadimudidam, C.S.R. Puram, D.R.S. Valasa villages. Out of 34 Panchayats in Santakaviti Mandal Bodduru, Gullaseetaramapuram, Mamidipalli, Mandakuriti, Suravram villages were recording migration of a higher magnitude. Out of 27 villages in Vangara Mandal, Kondachaakarapalli, V.V.R. Peta, Bangaruvalasa, Kopparavlasa, Raajulagumada, Chinaraajulagumada, Pattuvardhanam, Baagimpeta villages were on the path of migration. Out of 39 Panchayats of Regidi Amudalavalasa Mandal, Ambhakhandi, Korlavalasa, Vannali, Tunivada, Nayaravalasa, Reddipeta, Ungarada, Munakalavalasa villagers were on the path of migration along with their families. (*Eenadu, Srikakulam District edition*)

There was no shortage of such news stories. Regional and national media were giving coverage to these migrations. However, it showed only the tip of the iceberg. The real picture was much grave. When asked about the enrolment of these migrants in ration cards and voters list and ultimately in the list of agrarian labour, former Sarpanch of Kothapeta village of Etcherla Mandal, Boddepalli Sudhakar said, "the ration of four kilograms rice is not sufficient to a person. Migrants also could get the rice if their names were listed in the ration card. Then the ration of the absentee could cater to the food needs of the remaining old aged persons. They were required to be enrolled invariably in the voters list to keep the village voters' base. Almost all the villages had a vertical split among the political parties. To maintain reliable voters base, the responsibility of keeping the names of migrants was entrusted on the local leadership. In the election of local bodies, every vote was crucial. During the elections, the local leadership had to mobilise all these migrants at the expenditure of local candidates. Regarding his or her profession, the enumerator could write none other than as the agrarian labour. However, the district recorded almost 7,00,000 agrarian labour, the mystery of lack of workforce was lying in the magic of statistics. The de-peasantisation and migration of rural proletarian to the urban centres was a common feature of the development model. Marx categorically stated this process besides the process of grabbing the labour by the greedy capital reading, *"Another prerequisite is the separation of free labour from the objective conditions of its realisation—from the means and material of labour. This means above all that the workers must be separated from the land, which functions as his natural laboratory. This means the dissolution both of free petty landownership and of communal landed property, based on the oriental commune."* (*Source:* Pre-capitalist economic formations: Karl Marx: www. marxist. org)

The urban centres were while filling these proletarian were not in a position to make amenities to these flooded migrants. The alarming rate of migration caused even social tensions. Majority of migrants was settling in unauthorised slums. The United Nations calculated that if this pace of urbanisation continued by 2030, the Indian urban population would reach 634 million. In the initial days, the successive policies encouraged this trend to cater to the needs of urban capital. In this process, the rural infrastructure had limped thus aggravating the problem further.

Even the governments could not cope up with this process and they were looking for alternate policies to stop the influx. As Kautsky said, "*Where self-help fails, state compulsion steps in to assist. Tightening up the Servants Ordinance, punishing breach of contract, making marriage more difficult are all meant to ensure that the farmers can keep their servants. The elimination or obstruction of free movement by banning migration, measures making it more difficult for migrants to settle in towns, increasing the price of rail travel, and similar moves, are meant to keep the migrants at home.*" (*Source:* The agrarian question: page 231: Karl Kautsky)

Kautsky's above observation proved in the case of Delhi state government. The Delhi state government resorted to such measures. A non-government organisation—Centre for Science and Environment criticised the move of Delhi Master Plan and said, "*Delhi's Master Plan is a classic example of the short-sightedness of urban planners. The recent Master Plan for Delhi has a pressing objective: to rid the Capital of migrants. To achieve that end, it suggests populating the city with capital-intensive and sophisticated industries like information technology instead of labour-intensive industries. The logic is that if the city hosts industries requiring high skill, the inflow of migrant labourers would come down. Like Delhi, other metropolitan cities of the country are also trying to regulate migrant inflow, which undoubtedly puts a tremendous pressure on the infrastructure. The migrants end up living in slums, devoid of basic amenities to support a dignified human life. The idea mooted in Delhi's Master Plan, therefore, is just a symptomatic treatment. To tackle the urban chaos before it becomes unmanageable, urban planners have to give due consideration to rural development as well.* (*Source:* Centre for Science and Environment).

On behalf of ODI, a Britain's leading independent think-tank on international development and humanitarian issues conducted in-depth research on the rural-urban migration structure of Andhra Pradesh and noted with pain that the migration was widespread and the rural distress was the primary reason for this distressed migration. It was noted, *"Large scale movement of people from rural AP for manual work was no longer confined to infamous districts such as Mahabubnagar, Anantapur and Srikakulam. Over the years, it became a state-wide phenomenon."* (*Source:* From Survival to Strategy Population Growth and Migration in Semi-Arid Andhra Pradesh, India: Laxman Rao, Priya Deshingkar and John Farrington)

The current Chief Minister of Andhra Pradesh Sri N. Kirankumar Reddy while speaking at a seminar titled , *"Urbanisation in India is preparing for the urban challenges of the 21st century"*, confirmed the same fact *"unless we concentrate on the development of rural areas and start creating job opportunities there and make agriculture more remunerative, it is very difficult to prevent migration from rural to urban areas. He said unless we reduce the migration, the pressure on urban areas will continue. The Chief Minister said we have to decentralise the development and increase the income of the rural people so that migration will not happen.*" (Chief minister's portal)

D.D. Kosambi recorded this process while it was in a low rung and formulated *"Nevertheless, it does remain true that the Indian village is nearly self-contained. Only when over-population forces people from the Konkan or Malabar to labour in distant big cities and to send money back home does the urban control make itself directly felt."* (*Source:* The culture and civilisation of ancient in historical outline: Page 17: D.D. Kosambi)

As observed by the widely acclaimed social scientist, the prime factor of the dependence is its basis in finance. All these examples, reports, daily record of events were confirming one and only feature. The rural industry that was agriculture is losing its manual strength to the secondary and territory sectors. The remaining villagers were surviving on the money of the migrants. As per the above formulation, the urban control on the village economy was completed. On the other hand, the rural industry was depending unconditionally for inputs on the urban industry.

6

Livestock and Mechanisation

"The consumption of meat (is befitting) for sacrifices, that is declared to be a rule made by the Gods; but to persist (in using it) on other (occasions) is said to be a proceeding worthy of Rakshasas. [v.5.31.]" (*Source:* The laws of Manu: page 76: Translation: G. Buhler)

Before the advent of the settled cultivation, the human society predominantly lived on food gathering and hunting. In this process, the mankind inevitably killed the available livestock. Settled cultivation needed the standing army of male buffalos and oxen (hereafter called livestock). Hence, proscribing on indiscriminate killing of these animals came as a pre-requisite. Hence, it appears that the Hindoo Law imposed a conditional ban on the killing of animals.

Changing Pattern of Livestock in the State

In the agrarian sector, the livestock played a crucial role for a long period. They were almost been considered as family members with India occupying the first place in this sector.

Andhra Pradesh was formed in 1956 when the 8th Live stock census was in progress during that year. The table indicated the changing pattern in the livestock during the last 35 years. Now the current round of the census is in progress.

As seen from the Table 1, the role of livestock was decreasing. Almost the entire livestock was stable until 1987. The livestock was continuously decreasing from 1993. When compared with oxen; male buffaloes played a good role in the small-scale farming. Majority of marginal and small peasants relied largely on male-buffaloes. However, as seen from the table, the strength had significantly dropped. In 1972, this strength in the work force was 13.41 lakhs. There was drastic reduction in the number, which fell to just 4.75 lakhs. The percentage of reduction was recorded as 65 with almost 2/3rd of the male buffaloes disappearing away from the scene.

Table 1. Changing Pattern of Livestock in the State

Sl. No.	*Year*	*Oxen (in Lakhs)*	*Male Buffalo (in lakhs)*	*Total*
1.	1972	54.91	13.41	68.32
2.	1977	54.01	12.75	66.76
3.	1983	52.15	11.01	63.16
4.	1987	54.2	9.22	63.42
5.	1993	52.48	6.56	59.04
6.	1999	49.15	6.52	55.67
7.	2003	39.71	5.39	45.1
8.	2007	43.45	4.75	48.2

Source: Compiled from various live stock surveys.

In case of oxen too, the diminishing trend was prevailing. In the year 1972, it recorded a peak 54.91 lakhs, and it came down continuously in every round of survey and in 2003, it revealed 39.71 lakhs only while it showed a slight increase during 2007. Net reduction in all these years was 11.45 lakhs (21 per cent).

On the other hand, the land holdings were consistently increasing. In the year 1972, the total land holdings in the state were 54.20 lakhs. The cattle strength was 68.32 lakhs. By 2005, the land holdings were increased to a mammoth 120.44 lakhs and the cattle strength had decreased to 48.2 lakhs. The percentage of increase in land holdings was recorded as 122.21 and on the other hand, the percentage of reduction recorded in livestock was to the tune of 29.44. These figures clearly indicated that the role played by the livestock was diminishing.

Livestock in the District

Livestock played a vital role in this district until the late 90s. This table indicates the changing pattern in this district over a period.

As seen from the table, the trend was almost the same as in the state. The male buffalo had almost disappeared. In 1977, the figure was 1,80,525 which fell to 53,092. The net decrease in that number was 1, 27,433 with percentages decrease was recorded as 70.59.

Table 2. Livestock in Srikakulam District

Sl. No.		*Oxen*	*Male Buffalo*	*Total*
1.	1977	2,51,977	1,80,525	4,32,502
2.	1987	2,74,729	1,55,928	4,30,657
3.	1992	3,21,561	1,28,029	4,49,590
3.	2003	3,49,492	67,186	4,16,678
4.	2007	3,24,574	53,092	3,77,666

Source: Compiled from district hand books.

The bullock showed an increasing trend till 2003. Interestingly against the state trend, this district recorded a decrease in 2007 when compared with 2003. In a span of 4 years, the number of bullocks decreased to 3, 24,492 while the overall decrease was 24,918. The percentage of reduction was 7.

In the entire livestock industry, the livestock decreased to 3,77,666 during 2007. In the last 30 years, the decrease was 54,836. In the year 1992, (remember the year of reforms) the total number of livestock recorded its peak was 4,49,590. In a span of 15 years, this livestock came down to 3,77,666 with the overall decrease being 71,924.The tipping point started after the peak of the reforms. In other words, 35,962 ploughs devoid with the partners.

The input survey 2006 provided figures of livestock and corresponding landholdings.This table indicates the statistics.

Table 3. Land-holdings vs. Livestock

Sl. No.	*Type of Land Holdings*	*Number (as per 2005 census)*	*Bullocks*	*Buffaloes*	*Total*
1.	Marginal	556071	207733	23677	231410
2.	Small	113,165	66494	9078	75572
3.	Semi-medium	42,206	28491	3683	32174
4.	Medium	10,409	8568.5	916	9485
5.	Large	666	503	231	734
	Total	7,22,517	311790	37585	349375

(***Note:*** The Mandal wise input survey was not available. Hence, only 50 per cent for the research area was taken in respect of the present Vizianagaram District. The input survey mentioned only the category. However, the actual figures have been incorporated from the agricultural census and district handbooks).

The fragmentation of land holdings was following the state and national trends. As per 1977 statistics, the total holdings in this district were 2,85,551. These raised to a whooping 7,22,517 during 2005. The net increase in the holdings was 4,33,966. The percentage of growth itself was 150. On the other hand, the percentage of decrease in the means of implements was (if we see the peak existence) being 16 per cent. As per the input survey, 5,56,071 marginal peasants possessed only 2,31,410 livestock. In other words, this livestock was useful for 1,15,705 ploughs only. It could be assumed that 4,40,306 marginal peasants left with empty hands. If the same formula was applied to small peasantry, it can be concluded that 75,379 peasantry had left with empty hands.

Once, the livestock was continued in the village as a standing army. However, now the feature is almost not visible. Peasantry is using the livestock as mobile army. They are purchasing the draught animals in the beginning of the season and re-selling them immediately after the completion of the season.

Indivisible relation between the peasantry and the livestock had been existed for a long time in Indian agricultural scenario. So much fiction also covered this aspect. When asked about the large-scale decline in the livestock and disappearance of the relationship a rich peasant, Vijayavankusham of Lakhanpuram village told, *"Mostly agricultural operations are in vogue for six months. For six, months, we have to nurture the livestock without getting any work; in the lack of common property resources, it is just impossible to keep the livestock in sheds. It is a tremendous financial burden on the peasantry. More over the disappearance of attached child labourers also was one of the causes for this."*

The empirical research was showing dismal performance in this sector. Official estimates were much better than the ground level reality. As seen from the 78 agrarian villages, it was said that these villages had 7000 pair of livestock, which had fallen to 600 pairs. The net decrease was 6400 and the percentage of decrease was 91. When asked about the making of ploughs, the village carpenters said that the making of ploughs was deteriorating with the trend continuing unabatedly as it appeared that the macro level statistics were not reflecting the ground level reality.

Regarding statistics, the National Commission on Cattle came heavily on the government strongly accusing that, *"The Livestock Census is a quinquennial exercise and every five years, the States are supposed to conduct the Census. The State figures are consolidated at the national level and the last such consolidated figures at the National level are available only for the year 1992. Thereafter, figures at the National level are not available and it is anybody's guess as to what is the livestock population of the country. May be the population has dwindled so much that the Government is wary of publishing the figures! Nonetheless, under the direction of FAO, all Government documents start with the stereotype rhetoric that India has the largest livestock population."* (*Source:* National commission on cattle 2000: www.dahd.nic.in)

When compared with a tractor, a plough had become expensive. Four ploughs were required for ploughing an acre besides taking a day long to complete the work. Hence, for economy of time and money, the peasantry preferred tractor to plough. The shortage of livestock fetched more wages to the plough owners. A peasant of Jadupudi village of Kanchili Mandal said the number of bullocks was decreasing day by day and that they predominantly had cashew plantations for which tractor could not be used and hence they were depending on the bullock drawn ploughs. It was becoming expensive due to shortage of bullocks.

The entire picture clarified the fact that another primary factor was almost disappearing from the scene. Global information network report dated 9/2/2008 commented on the changing scenario of livestock which read, *"Tractors are increasingly replacing bullocks (male cattle) in field operations and dairy farmers are replacing low producing native breeds of cows with a smaller number of high milk-yielding crossbreds and buffalos."* (*Source:* USDA: GAIN report Dated 9/2/2008: Report number IN8098 Prepared by Deepa Dhankar)

Department of Animal Husbandry has stated that there was a need to protect the livestock proclaiming certain schemes in its website. It read, "*Improve India's foreign exchange through export of buffalo meat and leather product. Salvage and rear male buffalo calves for meat production. Increase availability of buffalo meat for export and domestic market."* (*Source:* dahd.nic.in: under the heading Schemes)

At the same time, the meat exports were increasing. *In the year 2007-08, 26 04,000 cattle and 36,30,000 buffaloes were slaughtered and used as meat. In the year 2008-09, the numbers were 24,76,000 and 56,43,000. By 2009-10, this number went up to 24,76,000 and 58 84,000 respectively."* (*Source:* Basic animal husbandry statistics, 2010: Department of animal husbandry: GOI)

Field level observation too confirmed this fact. In Parvatipuram, Manapuram weekly markets, traders were buying livestock only for the consumption purpose. The villagers of Jadupudi (an Andhra-Orissa border village) complained that illicit trafficking of livestock was a persistent feature. A regular trader of livestock, Seepana Neeladri of Chintalapeta village told "earlier the feeble livestock used for consumption purpose. Now the situation is reversed. Even the calves, which have a bit of the flesh, are being purchased for the purpose of meat. Those which are not useful for the consumption are now in the villages."

The National Commission on Livestock 2000 recognised these trends way back in 2000 saying, "*Apart from these indirect blows, there is direct destruction by way of unfettered slaughter. This activity now enjoys state patronage, protection and active encouragement. There are about 4000 authorised slaughter-houses in the country and more than 1,00,000 illegal slaughter houses. The meat export policy of the Government had added fuel to the fire. Let us analyse and interpret some published statistics. In the year 2000-2001, about 2 88,000 M.T. of buffalo meat was exported* (*Source:* Reply to question No. 3313 in Lok Sabha on 10-12-2001) and the Government claims that this is just four per cent of the meat produced in the country (*Source:* Reply to Question No.1112 (H) in Lok Sabha on 23-11-2001), which means that the total buffalo meat production in the country is 72, 00,000 M.T. A grown up buffalo yields 75 kg. Of meat (out of average body weight of 300 kg.). Thus for obtaining 72 lac M.T. about 9, 60, 00,000 buffaloes are slaughtered! (*Source:* dahd.nic.in)

Agricultural Ministry of USA also corroborated these facts in its report which read, "*Export forecasts released by the United States Department of Agriculture (USDA) Foreign Agricultural Service points to Indian beef exports reaching 2.16 million tons cwt in 2013, up from a world leading 1.68 million tons cwt in 2012 – with the next closest nation in 2013, Brazil, shipping 1.45 million tons cwt. Compared to the 29 per cent year-on-year rise forecast in Indian beef exports in 2013, Brazilian and Australian (1.41 million tons cwt) beef exports are only expected to increase 4 per cent and 2 per cent,*

Table 4. Percentage Share of Different Farm Power Sources in Indian Agriculture

Year	*Agricultural Workers*	*Draught Animals*	*Tractors*	*Power Tillers*	*Diesel Engines*	*Electric Motors*	*Power kw/hour*
971-72	10.64	52.86	8.45	0.11	17.16	10.79	0.424
981-82	9.2	33.55	18.46	0.11	22.85	15.82	0.592
991-92	7.22	20.5	26.14	0.16	21.14	24.84	0.097
001-02	5.7	11.76	36.77	0.36	19.1	26.31	1.352
005-06	5.39	9.97	38.45	0.44	20.09	25.66	1.498
009-10	5.12	8.55	41.67	0.52	19.01	25.13	1.658
011-12	5.09	6.37	51.08	NA	NA	NA	NA

Source: State of Indian agriculture: Department of agriculture. GOI Quoted from Singh.

respectively. While the mantle of the world largest beef-exporting nation has traditionally been a three-way race between Australia, Brazil and the US, 2012 has seen India race ahead of the pack, with expectations for Indian beef exports to grow again in 2013." (*Source:* Merco press: dated 7th November, 2012)

All these facts confirmed one thing. Livestock had earned foreign exchange for a long time in an indirect manner by reducing the bill in foreign exchange on diesel and chemical fertilisers. Thus, it stood as a backbone to Indian agriculture. Of late, it is also earning foreign exchange by offering of its own body. Now the process of export of meat is named as pink revolution.

In the light of the above, it was imperative to examine the changing share of different farm power in the last four decades.

As seen from the table, the journey of the Indian agriculture is evident. The draught animal lost its share to tractors with 52.86 per cent share dropped to mere 6.37 per cent, and on contrary, the share of tractor had increased from a meagre 8.45 per cent to 51.08 per cent with halving the share of human power.

In essence, the Indian peasantry had to depend on the market and international market to manage the agricultural operation.

Mechanisation in Agriculture

As Kautsky told, "*Nevertheless, the mechanisation of agriculture faces more obstacles than the mechanisation of industry. Some of these obstacles are technical in nature: the industrial workplace, the factory, is an artificial creation, adapted to the requirements of the machine. In agriculture, most machines have to work in and adapt to natural surroundings. Economic obstacles also block the path to agricultural mechanisation. Whilst industry can use its machinery every day, most machines in agriculture are only required for a short period each year."* (The agrarian Question: Page: 44: Karl Kautsky).

However, Kautsky confirmed after studying the empirical data of different countries, *"Despite all these obstacles, agricultural mechanisation has increased rapidly"*. (The agrarian question: Page: 44: Karl Kautsky)

A peasant of Korasavada said, "even if everything was going well, a peasant used to surrender to the nature" with the nature playing a dominant role in the agricultural sector when compared to the secondary sector. In the secondary sector, the industrialists could work day and night. Despite all these hurdles, as seen from various reports and data, the Indian agriculture swiftly moved to that direction in the last four decades. Director of CIAE wrote, *"The farmers are not afraid of hot/cold desert and vagaries of weather as they have green houses and low tunnel plastic houses technology to grow crops in any place at any time of the year."* (Agricultural machinery industry in India: Gyanendra Singh: Director, Central institute of industrial engineering).

Normally, while discussing the nature of mechanisation in agriculture, many tried to discuss the large-scale industrialisation. They tried to draw the conclusion from the quantum of large-scale machinery. It did not mean that it was not a matter of fact for determining the nature. However, the penetration of industrial inputs in the Indian agriculture had a large dimension. In the form of small implements, the giants were garnering Crores of rupees every year from the countryside but this aspect had almost neglected in the research.

In fact, the colonial rulers tried to mechanise Indian agriculture during their rule. The above paper indicated this process. It read, *"In 1889, Watts and Kaisar introduced ploughs, corn grinders and chaff cutters Cawnpore (now Kanpur) Experimental Farm in Uttar Pradesh. Sardar Joginder Singh (1897-1946), who was the Agriculture Minister in the Punjab Government (1926-37), introduced the steam tractors in India in 1914 for reclamation of wasteland and eradication of 'Kans'. Horse drawn and steam tractor operated implements were imported during the latter part of the 19th century. With the establishment of Allahabad Agricultural Institute, Allahabad in 1942, the development activities in agricultural machinery accelerated and as a result bullock drawn Meston, Shabash and Wah-Wah ploughs were introduced in Uttar Pradesh, manufactured by the Agricultural Development Society, Naini in early forties."*

However, all these trials gained momentum after the green revolution. Entrepreneures always try to cut the cost of production to make more profit. Reducing the cost on labour was a prerequisite for this. Hence, industrialists mechanised their industries. The agricultural industry too followed the same suit. However, the cheap labour prevented this mechanisation. Rural proletariat in nature dispersed and spread in many villages. The disunity among the rural labour fetched them meagre wage rate. The entrepreneurs gained the benefit from this situation. Once the things changed in the manufacturing and service sectors, the vast rural masses removed their shackles and rushed to the urban and semi-urban centres where it opened gates to the industrialisation or mechanisation of the agrarian sector.

In fact, the entire Indian villages were industrial centres. Complete implements required for cultivation were being manufactured in the villages for a long time. Wooden plough (Naagali), spade (Paara), small spade (Borgia), Kastaboriga (a six feet stick having a sharp a spade in one edge), iron crow-bar (Gunapamu), axe (Goddali), sickle (Kodavali), long stick having a type of sickle in one edge (Kontikarra), crowbar (Gaddapaara), a whip (Korada), etc., were being manufactured in the village manufacturing units.

In fact, the entire part of the plough was made of wood. There was a belief that iron part should not touch the mother soil. Hence, no iron was used for a long period. The iron edge replaced the wood in the plough, and subsequently, the iron had almost replaced the wood in many parts though the wood did not totally disappear from the scène. In fact, on the festival of Ugadi (Telugu New Year) the peasantry still use this wooden edge for ploughing as a ritual.

The change of material from stone, wood to iron itself indicated the industrial relations in the agrarian sector. As observed from the villages, the peasantry had shifted their stance towards urban industrial sector for all these small implements.

Janjeti Ramu of Karivalasa village was a leased-in marginal peasant who leased-in two acre of land and was conducting cultivation. As per his calculation, the minimum implements and expenditure for cultivation for marginal peasant were tabulated hereunder.

Table 5. Small Implements and Expenditure

Sl. No.	*Implement*	*Number of Implements*	*Cost of each Implement*	*Total Cost*
1.	Sickle	3	100	300
2.	Spade	2	800	1600
3.	Crowbar	1	300	300
4.	Iron crow-bar	1	350	350
5.	Kastaboriga	1	400	400
6.	Pipe to the leveller	1	300	300
7.	A whip/scourge	2	40	80
	Total	11		3,250

Apart from these, the peasantry had to spend on iron sheets for using them as input for other implements. Thus, the peasantry had to depend on the partial inputs from the urban industry for the final products. As seen from this table, for final products, a marginal peasant was spending Rs. 3,250. Thus, lakhs of the peasantry were remitting money to the industrial sector. As per the calculation of CIAE, the Indian peasantry was remitting Rs. 50,000 crores to the manufacturing industry. (*Source:* Official website of CIAE)

The penetration of implements in the shape of small implements could be seen from Tata Company Brochure, which read, "*TATA Agrico, the oldest brand of TATA Steel, is a pioneer in superior quality agricultural implements. Since 1925, it has been the leading manufacturer of hoes, shovels, sickles, crowbars, pickaxes and hammers. Now, Agrico has also entered the hand tools market launching its own range of files, pliers, spanners, wrenches, screwdrivers and other tools. Agrico has also forayed into the mechanised implements market with the launch of consumables like rotavator blade, tiller shoe, harrow disc, etc., and non-consumable tractor attachments like rotary tiller. For the mechanised agricultural sector, Agrico has introduced the sub brand Grasshopper." (Source:* www.tataagrico.com*)*

In one word, the engineering industry in the shape of small implements invaded the country yard and the peasantry are tiring in remitting their earnings to this sector.

Heavy Machinery in Agriculture

Largely, the economists gave priority for this sector while determining the process of mechanisation in the primary sector. During the national movement, Gandhi spoke about the mechanisation in agriculture, which read—*Let the Indian plough be not replaced by any modern machine.* However, the dynamics of development always paves the way for progress in the machinery. In fact, the Indian wooden plough itself a developed version for the ancient implements. One who cannot understand this development in the process, one would become obsolete in understanding the dynamics.

In Srikakulam district until the early 80s, wooden plough played cent per cent role in this sector. People used to make adverse comments out of superstition on those people who dared to bring a tractor in the field. People used to think that the mother soil cursed those people. If any harm happened in that family, people used to attribute it to the tractor. In some cases, the people even sold their tractors. This scenario almost continued until late 80s in the district.

Andhra Pradesh state crop report 1957-58 said about the mechanisation. It read, "*Under hire purchase scheme 270 tractors, 122 oil engines, and 99 electric motor pump sets were distributed. During the reviewed period 12,357 acres were ploughed by tractors"* (*Source:* Andhra Pradesh state crop report 1957-58, Page 46. Government of Andhra Pradesh)

It was a modest start of this tractor industry in this state.

Tractors in the Country

Indian governments made conscious efforts to introduce heavy machinery in general and particularly tractors in the country. Immediately after the independence, the Indian government borrowed money from the International bank for reconstruction and development (IBRD). As per the Bank report "Up to March 31, 1955 seven loans had been made to India". As per the report, the total loan amount was stood at $126,013,813, out of this a tune of $ 7,203,813 had been given for tractors only. The Bank mission visited the country and gave an appraisal report in the year 1954. The appraisal report reads, "In the initial years of the project the Bank was mainly interested in the mechanical aspects of the project and in the ability of the Central Tractor Organisation (CTO) to do the task of clearing the revised target of 1.6 million acres envisaged for the seven-year programme. For this purpose a Bank engineer visited the project three times, once in 1952 and twice in 1953, to look into such matters as the operational planning, the maintenance of tractors and the adequacy of spare parts. Towards the end of 1954 it was clear that the operational efficiency of the CTO had greatly improved and that most of the problems which had been impeding the progress of the project in the earlier years had been solved. It was also clear that in the remaining years of the project more attention ought to be paid to other aspects of the project, such as the extent to which crop yields have increased, the possibilities of checking erosion, etc. In August 1954, the Bank suggested the sending of a mission to make an assessment of the project with a view to helping the Government in assessing the value of the project to India.

(a) that the project was technically and financially sound and will substantially reach its objectives;

(b) that the tractor fleet of 280 medium and heavy tractors (all except 12 were financed by the Bank loan) was in good sound mechanical condition and maintenance of equipment was efficient;

(c) that deep ploughing, when done at the correct time, was an effective means of destroying kans grass;

(d) that CTM had provided a first-class piece of land reclamation but to obtain-full benefits it would have to be followed by improved farming methods. These will also be necessary tocombat soil erosion which presents an urgent problem

(e) that additional agricultural statistics were needed for a full appraisal of the effects of reclamation". (*Source:* IBRD report number A.S.32.B: India second loan administrative report)

Until 1960, India primarily depended on imports for the tractor. In 1951, the total number of tractors in this country was only 8,500. Indian public sector unit HMT started manufacturing of tractors in 1972. The manufacturing sector of tractor industry developed leaps and bounds from that decade. Subsequently, India succeeded USA in the tractors production. Its annual capacity of production touched 3,43,520 in the year 2008-09. 16 indigenous and 4 multinational companies were producing tractors in the country. Indian agricultural machinery export value touched 457.77 million dollars in 2007-08 themselves wherein tractors had a considerable share.

The vice-chancellor of Doon University co-authored with Indra Mani way back in 2003 and they in their study concluded, "*The increased cropping intensity and higher quantities of inputs and outputs could no longer be effectively managed by animate power alone. Therefore, farmers adopted tractors, irrigation pumps, harvesters and power threshers, extensively. The growth of farm power and agricultural machinery over last 50 years has been phenomenal.* (*Source:* Influence of legislation/subsidies to help agriculture and/or agricultural mechanisation on the market of agricultural machinery in India: Gyanendra Singh and Indra Mani)

Table 6. Availability of Tractors Per 100 sq. Kilometres

Year	*Tractors*	*10000 HA*
1961	31016	1.99
1971	143000	8.96
1981	417769	25.65
1991	1063012	65.48
2000	2091000	128.51

Food and Agricultural Organisation (FAO) released the data in the tractor availability figures which are shown in the tabular form. FAO updated this figures up to 2000. From other sources, I have added the current strength of tractors.

As seen from the table, during 1971, there were only 8.96 tractors and it reached 128.51 in 2000 itself. Tractors manufacturing association was expecting it to be stabilised at 200 per 10,000 hectares.

The production and sale of tractors in the last decade is shown in the following Table.

Table 7. Production and Sales of Tractors in India

Year	*Production of Tractors*	*Sale of Tractors*	*Purchases of Andhra Pradesh*	*Share of Andhra Pradesh*
2000-01	235602	251939	17520	6.95
2001-02	207252	217456	12203	5.61
2002-03	156613	166182	10987	6.61
2003-04	191633	189518	10477	5.52
2004-05	249077	246469	16603	6.73
2005-06	296080	291680	22444	7.39
2006-07	352368	352287	35613	10.10
2007-08	345172	346501	43758	12.62
2008-09	343520	347010	38417	11.07

Source: Agricultural engineering data book: CIAE: GOI.

In fact, the president of tractor manufacturer's association estimated, "*We expect the domestic industry to stabilise at 3,50,000 tractors per year and exports to reach in excess of 60,000 per year by 2010" (Tractor industry in India-Present and future: Ramesh C. Jain: President, India tractor manufacturer's association).*

As expected, the figures reached proclaimed figures. Further, Ramesh C. Jain expressed the goal of automation 2016. It read, "*Automotive mission plan 2016 fix the target for 52 billion dollar investment, 145 billon dollar turnover and an export value 45 billion dollar in the agricultural engineering sector*".

The growth rate in tractor industry continued to stabilise showing increasing trend. The same paper indicated, "*Volume growth rate in the tractor industry in the past four decades shows a compound annual growth rate (CAGR) of ten per cent, despite seasonal variations that cause changes in tractor demand and subsequently impacting industrial volumes*".

Factually, in 2011-12, the Indian tractor industry recorded a 20 per cent growth rate as per the interview of the chairman of tractor industry, to the Economic times.

In one word, mechanisation in the Indian agriculture indicated a rapid pace. However, the process was uneven in the country, which was an essential character for this development pattern. The growth rate figures were compared in 2006 with 1994. FICCI gave the growth of implements over a period of 12 years which read, "*Use of tractors has witnessed an increase of more than 78 per cent since 1994. There are more 13500 tractors per million hectares at present in India. Use of threshers has increase by nearly 20 per cent since 1994. Use of Harvesters has increased by nearly 5 per cent since 1994. Use of Reapers has increased by nearly 315 per cent since 1994. Use of levellers has increased by more than 35 per cent since 1994. Use of Maize Shellers has increased by nearly 61 per cent since 1994.* (Agricultural machinery sector in India: Federation of Indian chambers and commerce: Shortly FICCI)

Gandhi was even afraid to anticipate the repercussions followed by a developed technique of plough in the colonial period, his fears came true, and custom hiring of machinery had no boundaries. Gyanendra Singh described such a practice in his article, which read, "*Custom hiring of combine harvesters has been another remarkable success in mechanisation of Indian agriculture. A village Shyamgarh near Karnal in Haryana owned 135 combines mostly for custom hiring covering almost five states in one crop season and earning on average Rs. 300,000 per annum.*" (Influence of legislation/subsidies to help agriculture and/or agricultural mechanisation on the market of agricultural machinery in India: Gyanendra Singh and Indra Mani)

In the studied district too, custom hiring on a large scale was prevalent. Some persons made Parvatipuram, (Head quarters of a revenue division) to hire the tractors and harvesters. It extended to almost 10 to12 Mandals. It was seen in Makkuva, (broadly tribal dominated) the rich peasantry hired a harvester and conducted his agricultural operation."

When I surveyed Santabommali Mandal, the peasantry said that they heard about this harvester but did not see the same. I went to that Mandal in 2009 but by 2011 season, the peasantry of Kashipuram village, which was adjacent to the surveyed village Brundavanam, brought a harvester on custom hiring. Eenadu news article reported the issue of a tragic event, which read "in Kashipuram village, a peasant migrated to Nellore District for work. His wife was conducting the agriculture. A harvester came from Nellore district and was harvesting. While the activity was going, by mistake she met with an accident because of the harvester and died instantaneously."

Though the paper reported it as crime news, it revealed so many economic angles of the rural scenario indicating that Indian agriculture was being feminised. The rural men were leaving the field for earning a livelihood in other sectors. The studies indicated that accident death rate was alarming in the agrarian sector because of the mechanisation, besides ignoring this aspect. Above all, while this district was exporting labour, the wealthy districts were importing the capital.

As per the report of the president of Indian Tractor Manufacturers Association, Andhra Pradesh played a key role in purchasing tractors accounting for eight per cent share in terms of total purchases occupying 6th place in the market. As per the data of CIAE, in Andhra Pradesh its share of purchasing was steadily increasing. In a span of nine years of the last decade, it had doubled in its purchases.

As seen from Srikakulam District Handbook of Statistics 1977, this district had only 76 tractors. By the turn of 2010, the number swelled to 8,071. As seen from the empirical data, the animal force was being used to seed bedding and in paddling operations. In fact, in some villages, the tractors also replaced these operations. In the villages surveyed, the strength of total tractors was 196 out of which Mabagam alone had 13 tractors. In the Panchayati of Vadada of Gara Mandal, there were 22 tractors and the number was rapidly increasing.

The pace of mechanisation could be seen by this Table, which indicated the total industrial units in India. In fact, this table indicated the figures of 1997. The 2010 data book is yet to incorporate these figures. However, the data book indicated that there was 1,51,655 industrial units across the country which were manufacturing industrial implements for the agriculture.

On the other hand, the expenditure figures on agricultural machinery were rapidly increasing. The imports itself indicated the increasing expenditure on the machinery. The following figures indicate the export and import values of the agricultural machinery.

The stride of mechanisation continues. Some economists argued for stopping the pace to keep the labour in the countryside. However, in real terms it was not expected to be proved successful. An Economist, Goltz argued to restrict the uses of thresher in the fields on the pretext of saving the interests of agrarian labour. Kautsky exposed his true colour by quoting his work, which read, *"will be amply compensated for any disadvantage arising from such a limitation, if not immediately then in the future, by the greater number of workers made available in the summe."*

Kautsky refuted this argument and said, *"Goltz's proposal to obviate the problem is to 'restrict the use of the threshing machine, and in particular the*

Table 8. Status of Farm Machinery in India

Sl. No.	*Equipment Manufacturers*	*No. Units*
1.	Agricultural tractors	13
2.	Power tillers	2
3.	Earth movers	3
4.	Pumps	600
5.	Sprinklerset	35
6.	Drip irrigation system	35
7.	Plant protection equipment	300
8.	Combines	48
9.	Reapers	60
10.	Threshers	6000
11.	Seed drills	2500
12.	Ploughs, cultivator and harrows	5000
13.	Tractor parts and accessories	546
14.	Earthmoving machinery and parts	188
15.	Diesel oil engines	200
16.	Rice processing machinery	300
17.	Sugar cane crusher	50
18.	Chaff cutters	50
19.	Dairy and food industry	500
20.	Village crafts men	1000000

Source: Data book of CIAE, 1997.

steam thresher', apparently in the interests of agricultural workers, but in fact in the interests of the estate owners."

He anticipated the future course of action in the rural agrarian sector, which read, "*Fortunately, this conservative beneficence towards agricultural workers amounts to nothing more than a reactionary utopian dream. The threshing machine is far too profitable a proposition for estate owners to renounce its use 'immediately' in the hope of profits 'in the future'. They will therefore continue with the revolutionary activity of driving workers into the towns, and so function as a powerful force both for raising agricultural wages and encouraging the further development of mechanisation."(The agrarian question: Karl Kautsky: Page 46).*

Table 9. Export and Import Values

Year	*Value of Agri. Machianery Imports (U.S Million $)*	*Value of Agri. Machianery Exports (U.S Million $)*
2001-02	60.97	36.49
2002-03	38.3	40.4
2003-04	51.44	49.13
2004-05	86.24	65.66
2005-06	110.39	92.84
2006-07	193.89	110.11

In the studied area, a rich peasant made an argument of Goltz. He made an intellectual argument for the non-usage of harvester. When surveyed the villages in Kanchili Mandal, the harvesting season was in progress. A rich peasant, Madina Raghavulu of Mandapalli village of Kanchili Mandal accompanied me in going to another village. There was a hint of rain. He was showing indifference to come with me because of the apprehension of rain and possible inundation of harvested crop. He had 20 acres of paddy field and 20 acres of coconut plantation. When asked about the non-usage of harvester for quicker completion of the work to avert the danger, he argued in the steps of the economist. He remarked in a sarcastic tone "oh! Well said! If it is the case, I could not get labour to work in my coconut plantation. If I use a machine for a light operation, then the workers would flee. Even now, the migration was hampering the work."

This aspect clarified that had the rich peasantry equipped with the appropriate technology to work in the plantations, they would not have thought of the labour.

The wage rate for the tractor was stable despite flooding of the tractors. A great experience was received in this aspec. Turakalakota is a village in Nandigam Mandal. A marginal peasant bought a tractor on credit basis and was doing agricultural operations. In that season he demanded Rs. 650 per hour. However, the nearby villager offered a rate of Rs. 600 per hour. When these villagers opted for that, the native person obstructed those tractors and requested them to vacate the fields. They heeded the request and vacated. Previously, the scenario was just the other way round. When the native labour asked for a meagre hike, the rich peasantry could not even digest it. The small in number and unity was keeping the wage rate of tractor stable.

Successive governments were encouraging the mechanisation in the primary sector, *"Replying to a question raised by B. Kamalakar Rao (Congress) that farm labour was not finding work due to mechanisation, Agriculture Minister N. Raghuveera Reddy said in the Council thatmechanisation of agriculture was inevitable due to rising labour costs and to make farming cost-effective for farmers."* (*Source:* The Hindu dated 06/02/2009)

Policies were framed in favour of long-term loans with subsidies to the farming community. In line of this in 2012-13, the Andhra Pradesh government released a subsidy amount of Rs. 250 Crores for this purpose.

7

Irrigation

Irrigation plays a crucial factor in cultivation. India suffered from drought and famine for a long period. Even the colonial rulers were not bothered about a planned irrigation system.Therefore, the death bells were not stopped even during the period of modernity. A civil servant Ramesh Dutt vehemently argued for improvement in this sector and he compiled the data with respect to various famines and resultant deaths. Marx wrote Engels that an artificial irrigation system was a pre-condition for development of agriculture for semi-arid India. Marx criticised colonial rulers for their rampant expropriation of Indian wealth. He made this with statistical support and criticised the rulers for not considering the welfare of the broad masses. Probably, Marx is the first person who proclaimed about the drain of India's wealth.

As economists confirmed, the situation in the then Vizagapatam district was not an exception. Moreover, almost the entire district was under the control of Zamindars. Hence, colonial rulers did not bother about the planned irrigation system. The only irrigation project was built on the river Nagavali at Thotapalli village. In the year 1905, the British started construction of the regulator at Thotapalli, and they completed the construction in 1912-13. The water was available to 12,636 hectares.Tanks and rain gods were supporting all the remaining lands.

Rivers in the District

The chief rivers in this district were the Nagavali, Vamshadhara, Gomukhi, Suvarnamukhi, Vegavathi, Mahendratanaya, Champavathi, Bahuda, and Kmbirikotagedda. As per the District Gazetteer (1969-70) "there is a quite a good number of large tanks commanding Ayacut of 203 hectares and above. There are 155 such tanks." (Page 57: N. Rameshan I.A.S: government of Andhra Pradesh)

Broadly, irrigation sector has two spheres–One, the surface water resources, and the other-ground water resources.

Surface Water: Prior to 1970, there were eight irrigation projects out of these British built only one across Nagavali.

Marx proved the callous attitude of British and wrote, *"If we deduct these actual remittances from India to England, the military charges amount to about two-thirds of the whole of the expenditure available for India or to 66 per cent. While the charges on public works do not amount to more than 2- 3/4 per cent of the general revenue, or for Bengal 1 per cent, Agra 7.3/4 per cent, Punjab 1/8, Madras 1/2 and Bombay 1 per cent of their respective revenues"*. (Marx on India: page 43)

As seen from the above, the British spent 0.5 per cent of their gross the income in Madras presidency can be imagined from these amounts. The amount transferred to Vizagapatam district for the purpose of irrigation. Hence, until 1947, the district largely remained as unirrigated.

Even after 1947, the people of this district were on a warpath for irrigation schemes. Due to the prolonged agitations, the right channel to Thotapalli regulator, Narayanapuram channels came into existence. These were completed before 1970. Even after 1970, the agitations continued. Because of which the government constructed Dabarsingi reservoir and a regulator at Pedaankalam across Suvarnamukhi River.

Irrigation Profile of the District

As seen from the land usage pattern in this district, the net sown area recorded its peak in 2007-08 was 12, 53, 213 acres. However, as seen from the irrigation data, this district received highest irrigation in 2000-01 and the net acreage was 6,59,515.80 acres. Prior to 1990, the total irrigated area had not crossed even fifty per cent to the net sown area. Interestingly in 2010, the irrigated area could record 56.23 per cent. The drastic decrease in the net sown area was the secret behind this percentage.

Almost in every village, the peasants like skilled engineers gave a vivid account of the opportunities available for assured irrigation. Almost in every

Table 1. Irrigation Through Canals

Year	*Total Irrigation Available Land*	*Irrigation by Canals*	*Share of Canal Irrigation in Total Irrigation*
1969-70	515286.5	177117.7	34.37
1975-76	565395	171446	30.32
1985-86	561894	231581	41.21
1990-91	620088	296626	47.84
1994-95	656861.8	277242	42.21
2000-01	659515.8	289386.5	43.88
2004-05	641959.1	318729.9	49.65
2007-08	658549.4	326985.7	49.65
2010	629415.6	317170.3	50.39

Source: District Handbooks.

surveyed village, the peasantry indicated about the opportunities of the irrigation from the rivers, but no such scheme really came out in their lifetime. Though there were ample examples, some were interesting to mention the fact.

Kuppili was a village in Etcherla Mandal. Interestingly the dry land nature itself made the peasantry alienated from the lands. When asked about the irrigation facility, the peasantry replied, "The trader belonged to Reddika caste of this village who was a money lender. In the usurious money lending business, he purchased almost 500 acres of land and a person from this family twice became a Member of Legislature (M.L.A). This village had chances of getting irrigation potential. Ammacheruvu (name of the Tank) was at Dharmavaram village. Water either from Thotapalli reservoir or from Madduvalasa reservoir could pump into that tank. Ammacheruvu had a large area and the government could transform the tank as reservoir. Every time the people used to apply to M.L.A for permission to construct the reservoir. In the private chat, the M.L.A. used to comment that people would not heed him if the project came in realty and because of his attitude, the village remained arid."

There is another story of Murapaka village in Laveru Mandal where Madugula Thavitaiah, aged 85 years, said, "Water from Narayanapuram channel can be pumped to the tank at Shermahammadpuram. A main canal could be taken through Etcherla-Ramapalli-Chinnammapeta. A sub-channel to this main channel could be built at Chinnammapeta. The thirsty villages could get assured water. However, for the last 60 years, the executives were surveying during every election but it has largely remained as a poll promise."

These were not isolated examples in the district. However, the district remained largely semi-arid.

Irrigation from Canals and Disputes on Projects: This table indicates the area irrigated from canals.

As seen from the table, during 1970, the net irrigated area under canals is 1,77,117.70 acres. It reached its peak in the year 2007-08 to 3,26,985.70 acres. Again, it fell short of that figure and recorded 3,17,170.30 acres during 2010. At no point of time, canal irrigation was recorded in excess of fifty per cent.

Contemplated Projects and Disputes

Almost all the rivers of this district rose in the state of Odisha and the majority of projects were facing inter-state disputes. Except Thotapalli balancing reservoir, the remaining projects were all in the long run disputes. Vamshadhara and Janjhavathi projects suffered badly. In fact, the history of inauguration for the construction dated back to 50 years. However, the constructions were continuing.

Vamshadhara Phase II Reservoir

The history of this reservoir had its roots in the colonial period. As per the district Gazetteer 1969-70, "The necessity of this project, as a scheme of insurance against famines in the district, was conceived as early as a century ago by Captain Rundall under the aegis of the East India Company. But the proposal could not take final shape due to the non-cooperative attitude of the Zamindars of the area". (Srikakulam District Gazetteer: S.S. Rameshan: GOAP)

After a long wait the first phase of Vamshadhara was over,the second phase was under dispute, both from the local public of the affected area and Odisha government. The irrigation profile of Srikakulam District indicated, "*The project is proposed to construct across the river Vamshadhara near Neradi village, Srikakulam District at an estimated cost of Rs.739 Crores (99-2000) to create a total IP of 45000 acres in the district of Srikakulam. The detailed Investigation of the Project is in progress and programmed to be completed after obtaining the concurrence of Orissa and clearance from C.W.C (Source:* Irrigation profile of Srikakulam District: Government of Andhra Pradesh) The Annual Report CWC 2008-09 stated the actual position, *"During February 2006, Government of Orissa made a request under Section-3 of the Interstate River Water Disputes Act, 1956 to constitute a Water Dispute Tribunal to adjudicate the water dispute in respect of Inter-state river Vamshadhara and its valley between the state of Orissa and Andhra Pradesh. It was also agreed that the aspect of shifting of river course due to construction of side weir at Katragadashall be studied by CWC/CWPRC".*

However, as per the villagers, the government wanted to construct a channel at Neradi village to channelise the floodwater from the river. They intended to store the water at the proposed reservoir at Singidi Village from where Parapuram village was at six kilometres distance. The government was constructing another reservoir there and was trying to send the water from Singidi to Parapuram by vacating 18 villages.

Villagers of the affected area further said this was altogether an imaginary reservoir since the total plan depended on the flood water only. They also told "the statistics of acreage under this scheme also did not reflecting the real figure. At most, it would stabilise the current irrigated area."

Thotapalli Balancing Reservoir

As per the official report of the Department of Irrigation, Andhra Pradesh, *"Thotapalli Barrage is a major Irrigation Project across Nagavali river proposed at 500 m upstream of the existing Regulator near Thotapalli (v) in Vizianagaram District to stabilise 64,000 Acres and also to provide irrigation facilities to new ayacut of 1,20,000 Acres (I.D) by excavating a new right main canal of 107 km length, covering 287 villages pertaining to 10 Mandals in Srikakulam District and 12 Mandals in Vizianagaram District. It is programmed to ground the Head Works during the current year as the design and drawing for Barrage are finalised. In the foundation ceremony held on 6.11.2003 Hon'ble Chief Minister has announced that the project will be completed within five years period."*

There are no inter-state or intrastate disputes over this project. The land acquisition process was almost over with no considerable protests to hinder the progress. However, project works were not completed on time. As per the government estimates, it is supposed to have been finished by 2008. However, so much of amounts were spent with no significant drop of water reaching the fields. In this project, there was a chance of getting water to the drought prone Mandals Cheepurupalli, Merakamudidam and Garividi. All the people of these Mandals were regularly watching the canals but not a drop of water.

Disparity in the Irrigation Facilities

Even after sixty-six years of independence, out of 56 Mandals of this district, 17 Mandals could not see a drop of water through irrigation. On records, Itchapuram Mandal had a partial irrigation facility because of Bahuda barrage. However, as seen from the ground level reality, the Odisha government increased the height of their barrage at Cheekati village. Therefore, water was not sufficiently carried in the channels. In a short run, it could get listed 18 in the category. Even in the irrigated Mandal, the irrigated area was inconsistent.

Incomplete Reservoirs

While many promises for construction of reservoirs were made in the past, it remained unaccomplished. Even the district handbooks were not speaking about these reservoirs. The ground level survey indicated a lot about such schemes. Due to space problem, certain schemes were considered for the discussion.

Adaru Reservoir

It intends to supply water to the dry lands of Parvatipuram, an unreservedly a dry Mandal besides Makkuva Mandal. The main gate work was completed in 2010. Spending Rs. 3 crores, the government intended to supply water for 650 acres. Due to non-completion of the works on time, the estimated cost of Rs. 3 crores reached Rs. 7 crores. As per the reports of the newspapers, the works were stopped.

Jamparukota Reservoir

This reservoir intended to provide water in Palakonda Mandal. The foundation stone was laid in 1982. Then the estimated cost was 2.51 Crores with contemplated ayacut to be 2,100 acres. So far, the public money spent was Rs. 6 crores but the estimation reached 15.31 crores while not a single acre received any water.

Meliaputti Offshore Reservoir and Mahendratanaya River

Andhra Pradesh state government laid a foundation stone for this reservoir at Regualapadu, a hamlet of Tekkalipatnam village in Palasa Mandal as a part of much proclaimed programme "Jalayajnam" on 4th April 2008. The reservoir was intended to store the flood water of the River Mahendratanaya. Government promised this water for 108 villages. The estimated cost of the project was Rs. 127 Crores and estimated ayacut was 24,600 acres. Many canals were dug and the contractors earned good sum of public money,while the villagers could not get even a drop of water. Interestingly, the district handbooks did not cover this scheme under Jalayajnam.

Irrigation through Tanks

The crop report of Andhra Pradesh for the year 1957-58 stated, *"This source of irrigation is next importance to government canals in the state."* (Page: 10) The same report, confirmed that Srikakulam district was one of the districts in the state, which was getting irrigated water through tanks. The progress under this head may be seen from this Table 2.

Table 2. Irrigation Through Tanks (Area in Acres)

Year	*Total Irrigation Available*	*Tanks*	*Percentage of Tanks*
1969-70	515286.5	326375.6	63.33
1975-76	565395	387801	68.589
1985-86	561894	310323	55.22
1990-91	620088	299861	48.35
1994-95	656861.8	301723.9	45.93
2000-01	659515.8	302523.6	45.87
2004-05	641959.1	267055.1	41.60
2007-08	658549.4	276213.7	41.94
2010	629415.6	251055.3	39.88

The figures on irrigation in the district too confirmed the above crop report. 68.56 per cent of total irrigated area covered under tanks only. In concrete number, the peak acreage was recorded in 1975-76 as 3,87,801 acres. In Concrete number it was dropped to 2,51,055.30 acres in 2010. Hence, a net decrease under this head is recorded as 1,36,745.70 Acres. In percentage terms, it was dropped to 39.88. The net decrease in the percentage terms recorded as 28.68.

For a long time, peasantry used these tanks systematically. These tanks used to have channels and many villages survived because of the same. Ajjada, a village in Balijipeta Mandal is a fine example. The villagers said "Vallaragudaba was a village in Garugubilli Mandal having a tank named Ramasagaram. Though it was rain fed, it had many sources of getting water from hill-streams. The water from this tank passed through a channel into Ithala tank situated in Sumitrapuram village from where the water flowed through channels into Chintala tank and Soorapu tanks of Ajjada village. This system lasted for a century. However, this system got paralysed and finally the peasantry shifted to tube wells."

It was not an isolated example. In this district, many villages had link channel system in tanks.

Reasons for the decline were dual. In every village, occupying the tanks was a common feature. The peasantry used to occupy these tank beds and merge with their adjacent fields. Normally these fields belonged to higher social groups of that village. The remaining peasants put a nelsons eye on this move either because of their social kinship or because of the fear psychosis. In some cases, the Dalits used to occupy the tank beds. Over a period, Dalits sold the land thus; indirectlythese lands were back in the hands of peasant castes only. The revenue machinery did not interfere in these matters.

Many villages including Murapaka stood as examplesfor this modus operandi. Murapaka village had 15 tanks whose area were 152 acres while the Ayacut were 300 acres. As indicated already, it was dry-farm agriculture. However, there too, the peasantry and Dalits occupied the tank bed and in due course, they sold the same. Later, the entire tank bed got vested in the hands of peasant castes.

Another classic example was Chintalapeta, which was a rain-fed village in Amudalavalasa Mandal. Pedada Krishna of that village said, "A Dalit occupied a tank bed and made a bund across it due to which the water was obstructed and peasantry could not get water for the fields. Peasantry complained to the revenue officials and the Tehsildar of that Mandal came and asked the Dalit to provide at least a passage to allow flow of the water. Then the Dalit gave a small passage. The peasantry again asked him to remove the entire bund which the Dalit rejected. When the peasantry warned him about the police action, the Dalit gently threatened about their occupying other tank beds of the village. The peasantry then left the scene".

Even the 4th minor irrigation survey of the state government noted this fact and remarked, *"Further, some of the tank beds wherever dried up are either encroached/assigned to the Non-Agriculture usage. Generally, this is observed in Mahabubnagar, Adilabad and Srikakulam districts."* (Page number 31/177: Directorate of economics and statistics: Government of Andhra Pradesh)

In essence, on one hand, the irrigation schemes for one or other reasonswere running in snail's pace. On the other, many tanks were either occupied or nor renovated due to which the district remained largely rain-fed.

Ground Water Irrigation

This table indicates the irrigation through underground water resources.

Wells

In the initial days, the peasantry used to dig wells in the fields and used as a resource. For this purpose, they used an implement, which was locally called Etaam. (The meaning as per dictionary: apiccotta—a contrivance on the principle of the lever consisting of a long beam with a large bucket hanging from one end. Dictionary Telugu-English Shankarnarauyana). Two people were needed to operate this device. However, this system has disappeared. With great difficulty, the pictures of such device are available. Another implement named

Table 3. Irrigation Through Wells and Tube Wells

Year	*Total Irrigation Available*	*Tube Wells*	*Per-centage of Tube wells*	*Other Wells*	*Per-centage of other wells*
1969-70	515286.5	0	0	11793.24	2.29
1975-76	565395	1152	0.20	4996	0.88
1985-86	561894	5051	0.90	14939	2.66
1990-91	620088	4909	0.79	18692	3.01
1994-95	656861.8	29908.7	4.55	47987.22	7.31
2000-01	659515.8	33615.9	5.10	33989.82	5.15
2004-05	641959.1	27756.2	4.32	28417.92	4.43
2007-08	658549.4	28523.7	4.33	26826.3	4.07
2010	629415.6	41497.7	6.59	19692.3	3.13

Source: District Handbooks.

Guuda was used extensively. (Swing basket for baling water for irrigation: Oxford Telugu-English Dictionary) Under such wells, the peak acreage reached 47,987.22 acres in 1994-95. Gradually, this share had dropped and in 2010, it fell to 19,692.30 acres. The net decrease was recorded as 28,295.42 acres. The percentage of fall was 58.96.

Tube Wells

When asked about the ground water, a tribal woman of Kaspagadabavalasa of Kurupam Mandal replied, "How do we know that water is flowing beneath the ground? We learnt that fact from the Kamma peasants." She told about the settlers who came from Godavari and Krishna districts.

Even the Government of Andhra Pradesh did not resort to use these resources until early 70s. In its web site, the directorate of ground water department stated, "*Groundwater department was established in March-1971, as per the agreement entered into by Government of India with World Bank (IDA) to channelise financing for minor irrigation schemes based on scientific estimation of groundwater resourceto evaluate minor irrigation schemes like sinking of wells and energising of wells with pump sets.* (www.aponline.gov.in: under the head of Introduction)

Further, the Budget speech of Andhra Pradesh government stated in 1977-78 "*For the exploration of our ground water resources, proper surveys are required and for this purpose the Ground Water Department was set up. The allocation for this Department in the current year's plan is Rs. 60 lakhs. The results of survey and exploration carried out by the Ground Water Department in the State emphasise the imperative need for stepping up exploration and exploitation of ground water resources through tube-wells and bore wells. With intensive exploration, it is expected that the exploitation of ground water resources by tube-wells will gain momentum and stabilise the agricultural production of the State. This is one of the purposes for which the*

Andhra Pradesh State Irrigation Development Corporation was set up. The Corporation has a programme of 250 tube-wells at an estimated cost of Rs. 2.93 crores in the State. The irrigation potential expected under the tube-wells is 5,000 hectares Kharif paddy and 10,000 hectares Rabi irrigated dry during 1977-78. An amount of Rs. 1 crore has been provided under plan for release as share capital to the Corporation during 1977-78". (www.apfinance.gov.in)

By the year, 1996-97, the government was suspicious about the availability of actual ground water resources. On this aspect the government in its budget speech 1996-97 said, *"To expand and utilise the irrigation potential of the State, we need to have accurate information base on hydrology. Therefore, we are taking up implementation of the World Bank aided Hydrology Project during 1996-97. This project would help us in installation of modern instruments, equipments, etc., for collection of surface as well as groundwater data."* (Andhra Pradesh Budget speech 1996-97)

The 4th minor irrigation surveyassessed the role of private management in the irrigation sources. It recorded the figures separately for Dalits and Adivasis (S.C/S.T) besides the changing pattern in this sector.

As per this survey, *"The results of the present census revealed that 97.27 per cent of total in use minor irrigation sources are under the proprietorship of private, whereas meagre share of 2.73 per cent were owned by the public. Almost the entire ground water schemes were owned by private and majority of surface water schemes were owned by public. In private category, out of 34.15 lakh hectares of potential area created, 24.53 lakh hectares of area were utilised for underground water schemes which accounted for 71.83 per cent, whereas the negligible area was covered under public category."* (4th minor irrigation Survey: page: 33 and 34)

Table 4. Changing Ground Water Resources

Sl. No.	*3rd Census*	*4th Census*
Dug wells	11, 85,219	10,72,116
Shallow wells (< 70 meters)	6, 56,3,59	9,17,173
Deep tube wells (>70 meters)	87,482	2,75,972

Source: 4th minor irrigation survey.

This census report broadly categorised the ground water resources in three heads. It recorded the changing pattern in these resources in a tabular form that is reproduced partially here. The census gave the changing pattern in the last four surveys for the state. The table reproduced here is only last two census statistics pertaining to the entire state.

The survey further stated, *"It can be observed that, though the deep tube wells have increased in absolute number but the actually irrigated area has decreased. The reason could be decrease in ground water level. It may be observed that the average area irrigated by a deep tube well is worked out to be 1.79 hectares during the present census period whereas it was 2.77 hectares during last census showing a decrease of 35.38 per cent."*

This situation further aggravated the chasm between poor and rich. The rich peasantry with all their resources was digging deep tube wells and exploiting ground water resources. On the other hand, the majority of the peasantry is hapless with the entire situation. A micro level analysis research report too indicated the same fact and it confirmed, *"As a result of degradation, majority of the resource-poor farmers have lost or are losing access to water, as the water tables have gone down. Even when they owned bore wells, they cannot compete with the resource-rich farmers in deepening their wells (Reddy, 2005). That is, the poor were denied their rightful share in the Common Pool Resources (CPR's)."* (Ground water: Development, Degradation and Management A study in Andhra Pradesh: M. Srinivasa Reddy and V. Ratnareddy)

The over usage of ground water resources was alarming. A research report indicated this fact and observed, "*The area irrigated through groundwater has also increased from 0.8 million hectares in 80s to about 3.1 million hectares in 2007-08. The area irrigated per well is either reduced or constant, but water is being drawn from greater depths. The overall stage of ground water development across the state has increased from 28 per cent in 1985 to 41 per cent in 2007. However, this may not be sustainable in the long term. Non-command areas where the groundwater availability is 52 per cent while utilisation is nearly 59 per cent constitute 77 per cent of the area of the state. Over-utilisation is thus creating a wide gap between demand and supply.*(Ground water scenario in Andhra Pradesh: A.K. Jain, B. M. Muralikrishana Rao, M.S. Ramamohanaro and Venkataswamy)

As per the agricultural statistics of 2010-11, the area has since been increased from 3.1 million hectares to 3.343 million hectares.

Rich peasants belonging to Godavari district migrated to these areas, purchased agricultural lands on a large scale, and dug tube wells. It was only because of them that the tube wells were introduced on a large scale in this area. As seen from this table, during the year 1969-70, the area irrigated under this category was nil. It showed increasing trend from mid 90s and reached 41,497.70 acres. As seen from the above report, this trend was a general feature of the state. In view of this, the availability of ground water resources in general besides the disparities in the extraction of the resources increased alarmingly. All these happened due to policy shift that took place during 1972.

Even the peasantry in the irrigation commanding areas was compulsorily pursuing tube wells due to the attitude of the irrigation department. Such incidents happened in Parajapadu village of Jiyyammavalasa Mandal.

Guntreddi Appalanaidu was a former Sarpanch in the village who said, "Vottigedda reservoir gave irrigation facility to this village on paper. The ayacut of this reservoir was 17,364 acres with left and right channels and irrigation facility drawn from this reservoir. Water was available only for five years. Due to silt, the water was not available to 40 per cent of the area under the right channel and 50 per cent of area under the left channel could not get water for irrigation. The attitude of the irrigation department was the prime reason for this."

He further said, "because of the water shortage, the village suffered draught thus compelling the marginal and small peasantry to sell their lands. The settlers purchased lands and introduced tube wells. Now the peasantry also had to follow suit. Earlier, we could get water at 30 to 40 feet. But later it went down to 80 to 100 feet. Due to the attitude of the department on one hand, we pay water tax and on the other, we are in a position to spend money on the bore wells."

The state and the country were relying on ground water resources extensively. The public spending and common usage of the projects took back seat. In that place, the private investments and exploitation of the ground water resources had become rampant. Traditional implements were replaced by electrical engineering industry. Power occupied the fields, but the control was not vested in the hands of the peasantry. Hence, the peasantry was inevitably ramming the sub-stations and national highways for obtaining water.

An additional feature was "power"; policies were changing the fortunes of the political leaders. Free power promises could change the governments. Besides, National Development Council warned every time to scrap those popular schemes and advocated the tariff hike. As seen from the entire situation, the suggestions and appeals of Ramesh Dutt were not being fulfilled even after 66 years. Private spending replaced the public spending in the sector to a large extent due to which, every economic survey and every budget speech of this state government continued to speak volumes about the grace of rain gods.

8

Seed Sector

As seen from the crop report of Andhra Pradesh for the year 1957-58, majority of the crops were food crops. The situation was continuing for a long period in this district. As per that reportduring 1957-58, in this district, the food crops occupied 80.8 per cent. Rice (Oryza Sativa), Ragi (Eleusine Coracana), Jowar (Sorghum Vulgare), Bajra (Pennisteum Typhodeum), Korralu (Seteria Italica), Samai (Panicum milliaceum) and Oodalu (Echinochola funentacea) were the food crops in this district. As seen from the cropping pattern, this diversity had almost disappeared. While only paddy remained, the other crops lost their relevance in the dine of the broad masses.

The seed sector for all these crops was in the hands of the local peasantry with the market not playing any role due to which the yield was poor for all these crops.

The yield per acre is given in a tabular form below. The figures relate to 60s.

By 1967-68, the yield per acre was increased to 351.45 kilograms in case of paddy while in case of ragi; it was increased to 355 kilograms.

Table 1. Yield of Different Crops during Pre-green Revolution in this District

Sl. No.	*Crop*	*Yield per acre (in kilograms)*
1.	Paddy	351.45
2.	Ragi	383.95
3.	Maize	234.00
4.	Bajra	225.05
5.	Jowar	198.00
6.	Variga	315.00
7.	Korralu	270.00
8.	Samai	225.00

Source: Andhra Pradesh crop report 1957-58.

Self-sustainability in the Seed Sector

For all these crops, the peasantry used to make their own arrangements for the seeds. As per the memory of the peasantry and as per the opinion of the agricultural officers, the high yielding variety was introduced in 1978. As seen from the district handbook of statistics, they have declared the acreage under these varieties even during 1976-77. In that year, the acreage in respect of paddy under HYV was 1,41,006 acres. During that year, the total acreage under this crop was 6,66,721 Acres. By then, the percentage of HYV was 21.14. The aggregate yield was increased to 417 kilograms in respect of paddy and 444 kilograms in respect of ragi.

The district authorities used to show the area using this HYV in the handbook. However, this practice disappeared from 1994-95. It was clear that there was no need to show this data separately since the entire area came into the fold of HYV. Hence, the "own seed" has disappeared from the fields during mid 90s.

High Yielding Varieties and Encouragement Policies

Seed is a crucial sector in the cultivation. The peasant was not ready to change the attitude easily in this crucial sector, though the successive governments and the field staff of the department of agriculture strived hard for the replacement of native seed with HYV. A peasant of Brundavanam village of Santabommali Mandal said, "The officer came to my village and (probably in late 70s) requested me to plant the HYV seed. I rejected the offer. However, the officers gave a packet of seeds at free of cost. I kept that pocket in my house. I wanted to make a trial on that seed and planted that seed only in 0.10 acres. It was unbelievable to see that the yield was so powerful and we never saw such an yield. It was just a miracle. The whole villagers rushed to the field to see this miracle. From that year, the whole village went after that seed."

The government of Andhra Pradesh took several steps to introduce this HYV from the early 70s. The budget speech of 1972-73 narrated, "*The strategy has been to improve the per acre yields through a package of improved practices comprising scientific water-management, high yielding varieties of seeds, plant protection and fertilisers. A Crash Programme for additional food production was launched and steps were taken to cover over eight lakh hectares under high yielding varieties of paddy to enable the State to export about 50,000 tonnes of rice to Bangladesh. As an incentive to the farmers for switching over to these varieties, distribution of paddy seeds was also made on a subsidy basis. Quality seeds being produced in 37 State Seed Farms and development of these Farms has been taken up in a planned manner.*" (Andhra Pradesh Budget speech: 1972-73).

Though these efforts of replacement started during early 70s in the state, this district had tasted the replacement only during mid and late 70s. Till then, the eight types of food crops were broadly self-reliant in the seed sector. However, in the case of sugarcane, the management of private sugar mills used to supply the seed and necessary fertiliser.

Seed Sector Private and Public Entrepreneurship

In the name of enhancing the yield, the government introduced green revolution in the agriculture. Initially, the revolution ushered in the irrigated belt. However, subsequently, without considering the local conditions, the same methods have been introduced. It appeared that the primary source of the soil has not been considered in this research. The peasantry said that a seed variety Swarna could yield 60 bags of paddy in Godavari District while the same yielded only 22 to 25 bags in this district.

The government started Andhra Pradesh State Seed Corporation in the public sector for supply of seeds in 1976. In the paddy seed sector, as per its report, it played a major role and it proclaimed a lion's share was resting on it. However, independent researchers opined that private companies also were playing a considerable role in this sector and the figures were not revealing the truth. A research report indicated, *"Public seed corporations still provide the majority of rice seed in Andhra Pradesh, but the private sector is playing an increasingly important role. This shift toward private sector rice seed provision is largely unappreciated, even by many local observers."* (The Private Delivery of Public Crop Varieties: Rice in Andhra Pradesh: Robert Trip and Suresh pal: www.elsevier.com)

The report gave the quantum of private sector operation in the paddy sector to the whole of the state and in particular of Srikakulam District. "The private seed sector in Andhra Pradesh is large, heterogeneous and difficult to characterise in statistical terms. We shall concentrate only on rice seed, but even here, the players range from small farm-level operations to some of the largest seed companies in India. Interviews and a postal questionnaire carried out as part of this study provided evidence from 23 companies that sold a total of 19,370 tons of Rice seed in Andhra Pradesh in 1998. Estimates from the DOA's seed supply planning process indicate 28 companies proposing to supply about 21,000 tons of rice seed in the Kharriff season of 1999."

As per his survey report in Srikakulam district, the peasantry were purchasing 38 per cent of seed from the private sector. Further, the same report stressed, *"Neither the results of our study nor the DOA figures are complete, as some companies prefer not to provide data, nor there are a number of small, unregistered companies that also participate in the rice seed business."*

In essence, the researchers felt that the real statistics were not available. This is proved from the ground level examples. The peasantry of this district said that the replacement rate was extremely high as they are buying the seed from public sector companies. A peasant of Karivalasa village said, "Earlier almost 10 villages adjacent to Ravivalasa village used to purchase seed from a rich peasant Chukka Lakshum Naidu of Ravivalasa village who used to cultivate the seed and was charging twice the amount of normal bag of paddy. Later, the situation changed. The entire peasantry was purchasing HYV from the public stores. The concern for the seed was becoming normal in the peak season."

Netaji, an independent scientist of this district in the seed sector said, "There are no large commercial players in the rice sector in this district. However, numerous small players are supplying the seed. The government machinery is not in a position to anticipate the actual demand. On an average, 1000 lorry loads of the seed were required in this district. As per the estimates, the share of governments sector was 80 per cent. Hence, 800 hundred lorries were needed. However, they were not in a position to supply 800 lorries. They did not draw a plan for the supply mechanism for the supply of such a huge quantity of seeds. Two-year plan was imperative. However, the machinery did not adopt such a long vision. In the last minute, the anxiety-driven peasantry agitated for the supply of seeds. Then the millers lobby faced the wrath of the machinery and they supplied normal paddy in the name of the seed."

India had a rich diversity in the seed sector. It is told that 30,000 varieties were in the presence in the rice sector. However, in this country, the varieties had drastically reduced to hundred to one hundred fifty. The peasantry of this district said that about 100 varieties of paddy were in this district till late 70s. However, HYV replaced the rich diversity and subsequently, four varieties of HVY existed.

When asked about the lack of diversity in the high-yield varieties, Netaji said, "It was true. The varieties in the market were considerably less in number when compared to earlier diversity. The reasons were not only in the pace of research. In Andhra Pradesh, the millers lobby was a powerful one. They designed their mills long back to suit particular varieties of paddy. They were not ready to purchase the new variety of paddy though the researchers were ready to introduce a new HYV. Hence, it was caught in a vicious circle. Since they were not willing to purchase new variety of paddy, the peasantry too were not keen in planting a new variety".

Private participation in the seed sector was growing rapidly. The umbrella organisation of the seed companies, National Seed Association of India in its power point presentation stated, "During 1960 to 1980 period, *minimal private sector participation was in Indian Seed sector. Whereas by the turn of 21st century, private sector accounted for 70 per cent turnover in seed both in domestic and in international market.*" (*Source:* Power point presentation of Sri R.K. Sinha, I.A.S (Retd) Executive Director, National Seed Association of India)

In the 53rd meeting of NDC, a resolution was passed which read, *"Public-private partnership between SAUs, State Departments and the concerned private sector for development of varieties can be considered".*

The seed association was not satisfied with this resolution as it had its own conditions for the development of seed sector in the private sector. The same power point presentation stated that contract production was already existing in seed production to the tune of one million acres and it needed "Contract farming and the retail boom: changing the ways of farming".

Cotton

The acreage was increasing every year. At all India level, the area under cotton cultivation was recorded 58.80 lakhs hectares. The cultivation was conducted using indigenous seed with increase in the area to be 121.90 lakhs hectares in 2011-12 with B.T seed almost replacing the indigenous seed. In this state too, the cropped area was consistently rising. As per the estimation of Mr. Ramakrishna, General Manager in Namdhari Seed Company, the cropped area had increased to 25 lakh hectares in Andhra Pradesh. In fact, so many committees and commissions on handloom sector recommended for enhancement of acreage of cotton.

Successive governments advocated for cultivation of commercial crops. For this purpose, the governments made deliberate attempts. Due to policy decisions, the peasantry shifted to cultivate cotton. However, the governments did not take care of the seed sector and was left to Indian and multinational seed giants.

These companies while producing cotton seeds, entered in contract farming. These companies were producing cotton seeds in those fields and were selling the seeds at exorbitant prices to the peasantry. There was no control on both the activities. It appeared that the successive governments were not in a position to recognise the need of a control over the unabated bad practices. Due to large-scale suicides of cotton growers, the government made an Act 29/2007 and incorporated certain controls.

Almost six companies monopolised the Indian cottonseed sector. Emergent, Mahico, Mansonto, Proagro, Namdhari and Nuziveedu seed companies enjoyed almost 67 per cent of market share in the cotton seed. All these companies were conducting contract farming. Nuziveedu Seeds Company had "*80,000 loyal seed growers" as per its own report. And the company was expecting the seed market to touch Rs.12,000 crores by 2014.* (*Source:* www.nuziveeduseeds.com) as per Mahyco. "Mahyco has more than one lakh registered contract growers in its network, spread all over India for production and multiplication of its proprietary seed material." (*Source:* www.mahyco.com)

All these happenings revealed one fact. Successive governments had encouraged farming community towards commercial farming only for supplying of raw material to the manufacturing sector. At the same time, the seed sector was left to private national and international manufacturing sectors. The end result, people were removed from exercising their control on the market, not only in respect of raw materials but also in determining the price of their final product. Spurious seeds and pesticides increased expenditure on farming with lack of stable price to the final product putting the peasantry in doldrums. The two-way attack drove the peasantry to their ultimate step.

Jonathan cart wrote a detailed research report on the plight of Indian cotton farmer in Wall Street journal titled Deadly crop: Difficult times Indian farmers to desperate action. It reads, *"King Cotton has turned killer cotton in Southern India. The vast majority of them own less than five acres of land, making modern farming difficult."* (*Source:* www. mindfully.org).

Indigenous farmer-based research and public funded research in the seed sector almost became nil. Instead, the private giants were ruling the seed sector. The farming community of India became dependent for the necessary raw materials on the manufacturing sector. The production centre of the basic raw material was giving way to boundless capital. The companies were trying to squeeze Rs.12,000 crores annually from the community to grab the profits. As a natural principle, the seed only negates to give a life to a plant. Unfortunately, the spurious seeds were negating the planter himself.

Maize

Of late, maize was occupying a wider place in the cropping pattern. It was interesting to note that maize found its place in the category of food crops. Though by nature, it was a food crop, it was being used as feedstock of the poultry industry and a bio-fuel. The commercial interests act as a curtain raiser for the cultivation of maize and like an octopus, its share was increasing in the "Food crops head".

In 1983-84, this country needed only 1.44 lakhs quintals of maize seed, but this figure rose to 8.94 lakh quintal by the turn of 2011-12. The production of seed was transferred to multinational companies and their Indian counterpart. The travel of maize seed started from variety to HYV and then completed at Hybrid. Monsanto played a crucial role in this sector. Of late, Pioneer Company of DuPont group occupied the Monsanto market and gained first place in the maize seed market. In the hybrid sector, public capital had no role to play.

In the year 2011-12, Monsanto sold worth of Rs. 367.98 crores maize seed in the country. Five companies, Pioneer and Monsanto of U.S.A. origin and Nuziveedu seeds, Kaveri seeds, Yaganti seeds of Indian origin monopolised the sale of maize seed.

Vegetable farming was a common aspect to the Indian marginal and small peasantry. They used to plant a vegetable for their consumption in a patch of land. Later, the urban interests dominated the vegetable farming and it got transformed as a commercial activity. Government are encouraging the cultivation of vegetables but the seed sector was not taken care of. The Japanese companies Tokita and Sakita annexed the seed market. An Indian company Namdhariseed too is a vital role player.

The entire cropping sector was transformed in the seed sector. Governments were taking responsibility in food crops only, which were restricted to Wheat and Paddy. When asked Netaji, a scientist in the seed sector about non-participation of private players in food crop sector, he replied to say the profits in the paddy and wheat were at low level while in the remaining crops the profits were quite huge. The profit making sectors were left to private manufacturing sector, and the peasantry was leftin lurch at the mercy of the giants.

As observed in the district, in the paddy sector, public capital was playing a key role and in all the remaining crops, the peasantry was desperately looking at market for their basic raw material. In oneword, the decisive power was taken away from the peasantry only to transfer it to capital-intensive industrialists.

9

Fertilisers and Pesticides

Agriculture and Fertilisers

The history of consumption of chemical fertilisers has a nascent past. However, within a short period, it had virtually occupied the cultivation in a gargantuan way. Indian peasantry pursued cultivation based on compost and legume plants for time immemorial. Due to non-usage of fertilisers, the productivity was abysmally low, and it was not catered to the needs of the people. As per calculation, *"Organic manures contain low amounts of N.P.K. nutrients. Farmyard manures and compost contain 0.5 to 0.6 per cent K_2O while, potash fertilisers contain 60 per cent of K_2O. For example, to apply 60 kgs K_2O /Ha, you need to apply 10000 kgs. of Farm yard waste as compared to only 100 kgs of Potash."* (*Source:* International Potash Institute, Coordination India:www.ipipotash.org) at the same time it has warned "Actual recommendations depend on crop yield, crop variety, irrigation and soil".

Until the advent of the green revolution, the peasantry had no idea what so ever about the usage of chemical fertilisers. By this time, the Indian fields are inundated with the flow of fertilisers. No doubt, fertilisers were indispensable for the farming, but the judicious utilisation of fertilisers must have been the basis for cultivation. Unfortunately, this vital connection has missed out in the scenario and the plants and soil were suffering badly due to over usage of chemicals. Even, the users are facing serious threat to their own lives.

Green accounting for Indian states project categorically stated. *"Another serious problem of fertiliser usage is leakage/run-off into surface water, which has serious environmental consequences such as Eutrification (Nitrogen and Phosphorous over concentration due to fertiliser Run-off/ leaking). Eutrification leads to explosive growth of Algae, Oxygen depletion, death of fish, and loss of bio-diversity."* (*Source:* Estimating the value of agricultural crop and pastoral land in India: Page (1) further the report commented *"furthermore the contamination of ground water has serious health impacts because the majority of Indian population uses ground water, as a source of drinking water."*

Chemical fertiliser (hereinafter referred to as fertilisers) comprised the nutrients, which required to be supplemented based on the condition of the soil. India being a wide geographical area with so many types of soils and each soil was having its own unique characteristics. Unfortunately, the basic fact was failed to be considered for using fertilisers. Unlike doctors who do not prescribe one remedy for all the ailments, irrespective of the diseases of the soil one and only treatment with high doses was applied in the case of different soils resulting in the soil getting robbed. At any point of time, the field staffs did not try to educate the peasantry towards this direction. Quack doctors were playing a significant role in the health of the soil.

It is imperative to note that the usage of fertilisers is required for enhancement in productivity but at the same time indiscriminate usage of chemicals is also counter productive besides increased jeopardy in the situation. Fertilisers are required to be used essentially in a proper ratio failing which it can produce negative results. In respect of using DAP, there is a warning. It reads, *"DAP when applied as plant food, it temporarily increase the soil pH, but over a long term the treated ground becomes more acidic than before upon nitrification of the ammonium."* (*Source:* www.wikipedia.org)

The successive governments have been proclaiming about the soil testing centres and issuing of individual soil health cards. The ground level reality was narrating a quite contrary report. In the surveyed villages, peasantry in a unanimity told that they hadnot even heard about the distribution of soil health cards. The apex body of audit, Comptroller and Auditor General (hereinafter C and AG) conducted a survey about the soil health cards and as per the result of the survey, *"76 per cent proclaimed unawareness of the cards and only 21 per cent responded positively"*. In case of Andhra Pradesh, the report concluded *"Soil testing is necessary in order as certain the availability of primary and secondary nutrients in the soil so asto provide specific recommendations for the requirement of different fertilizers. However, out of the120.44 lakh of land holding, the Department of Agriculture was conducting soil tests for approximately 4.60 lakh (4 per cent only) landholding only. At this rate,it would take about 26 years to get all the land holdings tested"*. (Performance report on Fertilisers: C&AG: Page 21, Chapter 4).

Vijayakumar Gumma, Assistant Director of Andhra Pradesh state agriculture department who is working in this district explained the repercussions of the disorderly usage of fertilisers in this district saying, *"the peasantry was applying Potash and Phosphorus in less dosage and applying Nitrogen in higher doses. Instead of putting Nitrogen ratio as four, they were using at a ratio of eight. It resulted in the contamination of ground water resources. In fact, because of this higher usage, the productivity has not been increased but on the other hand, it caused stagnation in the production. Higher usage of these fertilisers was causing the extinction of microbes that are useful to crops. Due to higher dosage of Nitrates, cancer was becoming prevalent"*.

The working group of 11th five-year plan too confirmed this fact and asserted that the entire India showed this trend.

The peasant associations, without making any research on the ratio of usage and productivity, used to raise the emotions of the peasantry on the issue of subsidies. The associations should have strived to stimulate the peasantry about the judicious consumption and their right to know their soil health. However, the peasantry was forcibly caught in the web of chemicals due to these illogical subsidies. In view of such policies only, the peasantry did not bother about the capacity of the soil and was using these chemicals quite passionately. The association should change the agenda to push on these issues rather than the subsidies. Otherwise, their campaign would end with the serving of capital.

In fact, the policies did not educate the peasantry on the ratio of consumption of the fertilisers. The optimum ratio for the cropping of food crops was calculated as 4:2:1. However, the actual usage of these fertilisers in India showed 6.8:2.8:1. In fact, it is a national average but as seen from area wise studies, the ratio in the usage was abnormal in some areas. Due to all these, the over consumption of the fertilisers became common. Instead of making aware of these facts, agitations demanding subsidy on fertilisers would only defeat the sheer purpose of the usage but the peasantry was habituated of the usage because of these subsidies. Besides, these types of agitations constrained the peasantry to use the chemical even in the absence of such subsidies. It not only caused financial burden to the peasantry but was also becoming a threat to the soil and humankind.

Interestingly, government publicity was being aired in the televisions resulting in praise of the brilliance of the peasantry. The story of the advertisement reads, "A peasant comes to a fertiliser shop. Then the dealer gives big quantities of fertiliser to him in regular practice. The peasant tells him that he does not require such quantities since he knows the health of his soil. Then the dealer praises him in an exclamatory voice and gives the "sufficient" fertiliser".

The advertisement comes to interpret and proclaim not to apply fertilisers haphazardly but to conserve foreign exchange.

It indicated that the peasantry had so far used these fertilisers without heeding to the existing policies and wasted the foreign exchange unnecessarily. However, the successive policies were required to be enumerated to see the true picture.

Strategy of Successive Governments on Fertilisers

The economic survey for the year 1972-73 read, "*From all available indications there will be a considerable shortage of fertilisers in the world markets in the coming year, and in any case, prices are expected to further rise as a result of an increase in the oil prices. In these circumstances, it will be necessary to orient our agricultural production strategy in such a manner as to optimize yields from the use of the available quantity of fertilisers. This would entail among other things, the adoption of improved agronomic techniques, and other practices. Moreover, since now high yielding varieties are highly fertiliser intensive,the limited availability of fertilisers will necessitate other avenues of securing agricultural growth, especially those involving better managing locally available inputs, such as organic manures and supply of improved seeds of local varieties. In the long run coal based fertiliser plants may well provide the best means of reducing our dependence on oil-based fertilisers."* (*Source:* Economicsurvey 1972-73:www.finmin.nic.in: Emphasis added)

Back in 1972-73, the economic survey indicated that there was a need to develop local varieties in seeds but the earlier chapter indicated the actual happenings in that sector. Invariably the remaining inputs followed the same path for last 45 years.

Interestingly the economic survey 1975-76 showed a volte-face in the declared aim of 1972-73. The economic survey 1975-76 in its initial words proclaimed, *"There is also clear evidence that the initial impetus of the green revolution seems to have been exhausted"* but the same survey treated the disease in the same way. It read, *"The new agricultural strategy places heavy reliance on the use of chemical fertilisers. In this context the decline in the fertiliser consumption –from 28 lakh tonnes in 1973-74 to 26 lakh tonnes in 1794-75 is a matter of concern. Any sharp decline in the use of P&K can affect soil fertility and also the efficacy of use of Nitrogen, over time. In order to boost the consumption, government has twice within a period of five months, reduced the prices of fertilisers. However, it appears that total consumption in 1975-76 may not be much higher than the figure of 28 lakh tonnes reached in 1973-74. This serves to emphasise the need for proper identification of factors affecting fertiliser use so as to devise suitable promotional measures. At the same time, due emphasis has to be placed on the use of organic fertilisers in suitable combination with chemical fertilisers."* (*Source:* www.finmin.nic.in) (Emphasis added)

Both the surveys declared the targets in contradiction. The coal-based plants were being transformed as naphtha, gas based plants. Measures for the development of local inputs were significantly neglected. The encouragement measures for the consumption of fertilisers lead the peasantry to flood their fields annually with 250 to 300 lakh metric tons of fertilisers. Whatever on paper, the consumption of organic fertilisers had almost disappeared. However, the advertisement threw the blame of widespread usage on the Indian peasantry and trying to teach them about conserving the foreign exchange.

This Table 1 indicates the trends in fertiliser consumption all over India. As per the wishes of the policy makers, the consumption of fertilisers was touching new heights every year. As per the economic survey of 1972-73, the consumption of fertilisers in the year 1967-68 was 17.69 Lakh tonnes. In the year1970-71, it reached 21.77 lakh tonnes. Even the post-liberalised tenure also

Table 1. Consumption of Fertilisers in India

Year	*Fertiliser Usage (in lakh tonnes)*
1970-71	21.77
1980-81	55.15
1990-91	125.46
2000-01	167.02
2005-06	203.4
2006-07	216.51
2007-08	225.7
2008-09	249.09
2009-10	264.86
2010-11	281.22

Source: Compiled from the annual report of Department of fertilisers and State of India's agriculture 2010-11: GOI.

did not deter the rampant usage. In the initial years of post-liberalised regime, the usage was a mere 125.46 lakhs tons. By the turn of 20 years then, it reached a whopping 281.22 lakh metric tons thereby registering a net increase of 155.76 lakh MT. The percentage of growth was recorded at 124.51. The spiralling price besides regulation of subsidy regime too were not in a position to stop this process. The peasantry was accustomed to using these fertilisers and the *"promotional measures"* received much success in a span of forty years.

The consumption of fertilisers was uneven. The economic survey 1979-80 also noted this fact that, *"There are wide differences in per hectare consumption in different states ranging from 2.4 kgs. in Assam to 94.47 kgs in Punjab, with the average for the country being about 30 kgs nutrient in 1979-80, the fertiliser consumption continued to be concentrated in about sixty districts in the state; Punjab, Haryana, Tamil Nadu, Uttar Pradesh, Andhra Pradesh, West Bengal, Gujarat, Maharashtra, Karnataka and Rajasthan accounting for over 50 per cent of total consumption in 1975-76".*

However, the consumption drastically increased over a period of 30 years. C & AG report revealed that the consumption statistics in its performance report. It reads, *"Fertiliser consumption has gone up substantially from 317 lakh MT over the 11 year period and from 1998-99 to 2008-09. However, the pattern of fertiliser consumption (per hectare of gross cropped area) across different states was highly skewed. States like Andhra Pradesh, Punjab, Haryana, and Bihar accounted for high consumption rate of 240,221,202, and 179 kgs per hectare respectively, while the states like Madhya Pradesh, Orissa, Assam, and Jharkhand have a very low consumption rates of 71,62,62, and 56 kgs respectively.* (Performance report on fertilisers: C & AG: Page 21, and 41: Chapter 5)

Table 2. Fertiliser Consumption *vis-à-vis* Foodgrain Production

	2002-03	*2003-04*	*2004-05*	*2005-06*	*2006-07*	*2007-08*	*2008-09*	*2009-10*
Food grain production (in Million tonnes	1747.8	2131.9	1983.6	2085	2172.8	2307.8	2344.7	2182
Fertiliser usage (in million tonnes)	16.094	16.79	18.39	20.34	21.65	22.57	24.9	26.08
Ratio of food grain production to fertiliser usage	108.60	126.97	107.86	102.51	100.36	102.25	94.16	83.67

Source: Indian fertiliser scenario: Department of Fertilisers: GOI.

The agriculture strategy of 1972-73 proclaimed about the consumption of local inputs but the revised strategy only worked in the country. Back in 1975-76, government concluded that the initial impetus of Green revolution had evaporated. However all these years, the green revolution operation alone was continuing due to which, the fields were filled with HYV seeds. Fertilisers and pesticides like Siamese twins followed these seeds and inundated Indian fields.

Consumption vs. Production

India occupies second place in the consumption of fertilisers. Policies always linked the consumption with the productivity. In other words, it was propagated that enhancement of productivity is necessitating the higher dosage of fertilisers. However, as seen from the government data, even these arguments also lost its ground.

The Table 2 indicates the connection between those two factors. As seen from the Table the ratio between those two factors is deteriorating.

In 2002-03, for every kilogram of fertilisers, 108.60 kilograms of food grains was being produced. By the turn of 2009-10, it fell to 83.67 kilograms. The working group on fertilisers for the twelfth five-year plan commented that the soil was not responding to the fertilisers. As per their report, once the nature of responding had a ratio of 1:10, which later fell to 1:6.5.

The crop report of 1957-58 gave the figures of consumption for that year reading, *"The distribution of fertilisers also actively popularised with the distribution of 88,189 tons of Ammonium sulphate, 7,676 tons of Urea, 1,172 tons of Ammonium Nitrate, 2,310 tons of Super phosphate and 8,594 tons of other fertilisers to ryots"(ryots mean Peasantry)* (*Source:* Crop report 1957-58, Page 45 and 46: GOAP)

In all, the total fertiliser consumption in 1957-58 was 1,08,001 tonnes for the entire state. However, as per the information provided by the Department of Agriculture, in the district of Srikakulam for 2010-11 season, the usages reached 1,51,607 tons. It means that, usage of a single district surpassed the state usage over a span of 54 years.

As per the districtdata, "the peasantry used 1,51,607 tonnes for 5,15,300 hectares. The average consumption in the district was 294 kgs. Inter-Mandal variations were also alarming. Even the tribal dominated Mandals were also using these fertilisers at alarming level. In Bhamini Mandal, the average consumption was 1012 kgs. In fact, it was a tribal dominated Mandal and considered one of the backward Mandals in the district. The settlers have taken large chunks of land and making commercial agriculture in this Mandal. The alarming level of consumption had its roots in that mode of operation. Another tribal-dominated Mandal, Gummalakshmipuram was also reaching the heights. In that Mandal too, the average crossed 200 kgs." (*Source: The Department of Agriculture's answer to the RTI question*)

Fertiliser Companies and Drain of Public and Peasantry's Wealth

The promise of local varieties of seed did not come true. Hence, the people used the available HYV seeds in limited quantities. These seeds have thirst of chemicals. Hence, like a chain reaction, the Indian peasantry tied up with these companies.

Initially, highly subsidised fertilisers were supplied. As per Economic survey 1979-80, *"The rapid increase in fertiliser consumption in the recent years were facilitated by downward revisions effecting the fertiliser prices during 1975-76 and by maintaining them at the reduced level, and thereafter, despite appreciable increase in their cost of production and imports. This appreciable increase in fertiliser consumption had, however, led to an increase the burden of subsidy on the one hand and higher import bill on the other. In view of the recent increase in the feed stock it became increasingly difficult to maintain the supply price at the existing low level."*

This Para indicates the future besides many facts to reveal. The usage of fertilizer was increasing tremendously only because of low pricing of the commodity (Read it as "the peasantry has been habituated") with difficulty to maintain the present price structure. (Read it as "even the increase of the price structure cannot change the pace of usage").

The same was proved from the data of Table 1. De-regulation and drastic reduction in the subsidy bill could not prevent the usage of fertilisers. Considering the inelasticity of the land and the increasing trend of current fallows and conversion of land to the non-agricultural purpose, the quantum of usage was becoming callous besides posing a threat to humankind.

Drain of Wealth

The private capital, whether national or international, profited enough from the pockets of Indian peasantry. At every point, it was imperative to recognise a fact that 82 per cent of the peasantry were small players in this uneven play. The flow was two pronged. One was in the shape of subsidies the public money was transferring to the pockets of industrialists, which is an indirect transfer,and the other was direct flow from the pocket of peasantry. The drain in the indirect transfer could be seen from the official data.

As seen from the share of Indian public sector, the subsidy bill was dwindling swiftly to give way to the Indian and foreign private capital. During the year 2005-06, the subsidy amount remitted to public and co-operative sector was Rs. 7827.21 crores whereas the Indian private capital earned a subsidy of Rs. 7241.19 crores. In a span of five years, the situation had just reversed. In the year 2009-10, the duo (public and co-operative) earned a subsidy of Rs. 24,216.56 crores whereas the private capital garnered an amount of Rs. 31,691.91 crores. The sector-wise research indicated that the co-operative sector was earning more subsidy than its counterpart the public sector was. It also indicated that the private capital was earning money in the form of dividends in that sector.

As a whole, the role of foreign capital was also increasing. As seen from this table, the subsidy amount in concrete terms increased from Rs. 4237.87

Table 3. Subsidy Amounts Given to Fertiliser Companies (Rupees in Crores)

Year	*Subsidy to Indian Companies*	*Subsidy to Foreign Companies*	*Total Subsidy in Crores*	*Subsidy to PSU*	*Subsidy to Cooperative*	*Subsidy to Indian Private Companies*	*Share of India*	*Share of Foreign*
2005-06	15151.77	4237.87	19389.64	4493.69	3333.52	7241.19	78.14	21.86
2006-07	19298.54	8721.01	28019.55	6377.652	4519.58	7300	68.88	31.12
2007-08	26784.17	16534.99	43319.16	8993.4	7043.64	5314.64	61.83	38.17
2008-09	53925.84	45568.87	99494.71	11989.25	14284.06	14290.74	54.20	45.80
2009-10	33580.25	30452.04	64032.29	11824.65	12391.91	31691.91	52.44	47.56
2010-11	28980.73	23860	52840.73				54.85	45.15

Source: Compiled from Indian fertiliser scenario 2010: Department of Fertilisers: GOI.

crores in 2005-06 to a mammoth Rs. 30,452.04 crores in 2009-10 but showed as lighter reduction in 2010-11. In percentage terms, it increased from 21.86 per cent to 45.15 in 2010-11.

Remittances of Peasantry Overwhelming Statistics

Interestingly, all the government surveys and audit reports were consistently speaking about the burden of subsidy. Right from 1979-80 economic survey to the current survey did not exclude in mentioning these figures. The C & AG, in its performance report, laid emphasis on the burden. Unfortunately, no official report spoke about the burden on the peasantry besides the environment cost of the country. Though there was non-availability of such figures on hand, there was a possibility of reckoning the figures for one of the recent years.

It was not out of context to mention that many changes occurred in sanctioning the subsidy. An intellectual *modus operandi* came into existence in April 2010 called Nutrient based Subsidy (hereinafter referred to as NBS). NBS was nothing but reducing the subsidy burden in an intellectual manner. The process of determining NBS was placed in the Annual Report, which read, "*An Inter-Ministerial Committee (IMC) was constituted with Secretary (Fertilizers) as Chairperson and Joint Secretary level representatives of Department of Agriculture and Cooperation (DAC), Department of Expenditure (DOE), Planning Commission and Department of Agricultural Research and Education (DARE). This Committee recommended per nutrient subsidy for 'N', 'P', 'K' and 'S' before the start of the financial year for decision by the Government (Department of Fertilisers).*" *(Annual report 2010-11, Page 36: Department of Fertilisers)*. An interesting thing was the peasantry had no education regarding using the required quantity of the fertiliser. In other words, the companies could sell the same quantity to the peasantry with the reduction in subsidy cost.

As per the available data, the following table indicates the burden on peasantry with regard to major fertilisers only. The list was not exhaustive. As

Table 4. Burden on Peasantry for the Year 2010-11

Product	*Consumption*	*MRP per MT*	*Total cost (in Crores)*
DAP	10870000	9950	10815.65
MAP	98000	9950	97.51
MOP	3932000	5055	1987.62
TSP	87000	8050	70.03
SSP	2651000	3200	848.32
NPK	9862000	9080	8954.69
UREA	28113000	4830	13578.57
Total			36352.41

Source: (1) MRP has taken from Annual report 2010-11 (2) Consumption figures taken from Fertiliser scenario: Dr. D.S. Yadav, FAI, New Delhi mfmc.nic.in.

per this calculation, the Indian peasantry was paying Rs. 36,352 crores to the capital-intensive companies. As per the NSE data, the top Ten-fertiliser companies were recording their sales to be Rs. 54,302 crores in a year.

Source of Fertilisers

The peasantry was looking for the source of fertilisers from capital-intensive industries whenthe imports too were on the increase at alarming level. The following table shows the trends in the origin of the fertilisers.

As seen from this table, the dependence on imported fertilisers was increasing. Predominantly fertilisers are of three elements namely Nitrogen (N), Phosphorus (P) and Potash (K). For a long time,-Indian peasantry was not required to wait for nitrogenous fertilisers imports from abroad. Later, it was changing and during the year 2003-04, there was no import of urea. However, in the year 2008-09, the imports recorded 56.67 lakh tons. The raw material requirements for phosphorus (P) based fertilisers were largely import-dependent. There were no potash reserves in India. Therefore, the entire potash based needs was import-dependent.

Table 5. Share of Different Sectors in Consumption(in lakh tons)

Year	*Indigenous*	*The Public Sector*	*Co-op*	*Private*	*Imports*
1990-91	90.45				31.14
2000-01	147.04				20.91
2005-06	155.75	32.536	39.93	83.28	52.53
2006-07	160.95	32.797	41.33	86.8	60.8
2007-08	147.07	30.48	40	76.59	75.83
2008-09	143.34	31.172	40.49	71.68	101.51
2009-10	162.21	33.461	45.98	82.81	91.47
2010-11	109.73	33.261	47.24	86.57	99.85

Source: Compiled from Annual reports of the department of fertilisers, State of Indian agriculture 2010-11 and performance audit on fertilisers by C and AG].

To put briefly, the Indian peasantry was made to depend on capital-intensive industries for their basic material, seeds and the fertiliser instead of the peasantry's need to go to traditional compost yards and stand in queue in the market to get the basic raw material.

Companies: Public and Private Capital

The first fertiliser company was commissioned during 1906. The green revolution necessitated the establishment of fertiliser plants. Naturally, the public money was transformed into a capital. As per the annual report 2010-11 of Department of Fertilisers "*Green revolution in the late sixties gave an impetus to the growth of the fertiliser industry in India and the seventies and eighties then witnessed a significant addition to the fertiliser production capacity.*" (Page :5, GOI, Ministry of Chemicals and fertilisers).

Table 6. Share of Different Managements in the Production

Nutrient	*2001-02 Actual*	*2002-03 Actual*	*2003-04 Actual*	*2004-05 Actual*	*2005-06 Actual*	*2006-07 Actual*	*2007-08 Actual*	*2008-09 Actual*	*2009-10 Actual*	*2010-11 Actual*
Nitrogen (N)										
Public Sector	2879.5	2854.1	3007.9	3051	2958.6	3046.7	2887	2925.2	3118.1	3088.1
Co-operative Sector	2691.8	2800.9	2797.3	2901.7	2958.3	3004.3	3031	3133	3404.3	3434.5
Private Sector	5196.7	4906.5	5130.5	5382.5	5437.6	5526.9	4982	4811.5	5379.6	5652.9
Total (Nitrogen):	10768	10561.5	10935.7	11335.2	11354.5	11577.9	10900	10869.7	11902	12175.5
Phosphate (P)										
Public Sector	479.4	307.4	353.3	266.3	294.9	232.7	161.4	191.7	227.7	237.5
Co-operative Sector	793.3	949.5	778.7	938.3	1035.8	1129.7	969.2	916.2	1194.1	1290.5
Private Sector	2587.3	2647.3	2668.4	2862.7	2890.6	3154.8	2676.7	2356.4	2901.1	3004.1
Total (Phosphate):	3860	3904.2	3800.4	4067.3	4221.3	4517.2	3807.3	3464.3	4322.9	4532.1
Grand Total:	14628	14465.7	14736.1	15402.5	15575.8	16095.1	14707.3	14334	16224.9	16707.6

Source: Annual report 2010-11 of Department of Fertilisers.
Note: figures in '000 tons.

The public sector units played a significant role until 1992. The same report told about this sector in a detailed manner, which read, "*The Fertilizer Corporation of India Limited (FCIL) has its units located at Sindri (Jharkhand), Gorakhpur (Uttar Pradesh), Ramagundam (Andhra Pradesh) and Talcher (Orissa). It also has an un-commissioned project at Korba (Chhattisgarh). Against the authorised share capital of the company of Rs. 800 crore, the paid up share capital is Rs. 750.92 crore as on 31.3.2010. The corporation was declared sick in November 1992 by the Board for Industrial and Financial Reconstruction (BIFR). In view of the continuing losses of the company stemming from technical and financial non-viability of operations, the Government decided to close down FCI in September 2002. Consequently, a voluntary separation scheme (VSS) was offered to all its 5712 employees.*

Madras Fertilisers Limited (MFL) was incorporated in December, 1966 as a Joint Venture. This company too was referred to Board for Industrial and Financial Reconstruction during 1992.

Hindustan Fertiliser Corporation Limited: The Company was referred to BIFR during the year 1992 and since then it is still under BIFR. The Govt. of India had decided to close down Barauni and Durgapur Units and Haldia Division along with other offices and establishments of the company in the year 2002. (*Ibid:* Page: 45 to 47)

As per this report, another public sector company "*Rashtriya Chemicals and Fertilisers Limited (shortly RCF),* "was in the process of disinvestment. As per the report, "the total disinvestment was of the order of 7.50 per cent."

As seen from the report, it was clear that many public sectorshavebeen closed and on the other hand, the same report indicated that the private sector was enhancing capacity of the production. Table 6 indicates the production trends of various sectors in India in the last decade.

As seen from the table, the nitrogen-based fertilisers were showing a little progress in the public sector. However, in the case of phosphate-based fertilisers, right from the beginning of the decade, the private and co-operative sectors were dominating the scene. There was a fall of 50 per cent in the production of phosphate-based fertilisers in the public sector when compared to 2000-01 production to that of 2010-2011. In fact, as mentioned earlier, there was no indigenous production in the case of potash based fertilisers.

Pesticides

The green revolution brought another threat to the fields in the name of pesticides. As per the opinion of some researchers, there was no usage of pesticides in India until 1970. However, some statistics revealed that there was usage of pesticides but in minimal magnitude in the pre-green revolution period. As per their version, during the year 1955-56, there was an average usage of 15 grams per hectare. In the first decade of the green revolution (1966-1976), the usage touched 90 grams per a hectare.

The usage of pesticides is directly proportional to the cropping pattern and traditional food crops while commercial crop Mesta did not require the pesticides. The peasantry used to attack the pest using traditional methods. Cow dung and Neem powder were the main ingredients in fighting the pests. Increasing trend of cotton cultivation and HYV in the foodgrain sector was driving the peasantry to the market for chemical pesticides.

Even the number of pests too has drastically increased after the "revolution". Scientist in their writing clarified that prior to implementing modern methods; there were only five types of pests, which used to attack food grain crops. The same had increased to fifty in the post-revolution era. In this district during the pre-modern period, there was no pest attack on sugarcane but later it was understood that there are at least six types of pests to attack the crop.

Andhra Pradesh occupied first place in the consumption of pesticides. This state had a share of 25 per cent of the total usage in the country. The usage recorded was 865 grams per hectare in Andhra Pradesh during 1976-77, but later, it was reduced to 674 grams in 1997-98.

In this district for a long time, people cultivated Mesta as a commercial crop and paddy and ragi as food crops. Sugarcane also has been one of the commercial crops. People used to cultivate leguminous plants in the summer to provide natural potential. However, the situation had subsequently changed. There were no summer crops. Cotton and plantations were replacing the traditional Mesta. The changing pattern was consistently demanding chemical pesticides.

In this district, HYV seed of paddy infested with a new pest in 1986 and the peasantry was forced to use pesticides extensively. The percentage of bio-pesticides and organic fertilisers had drastically reduced and this situation inevitably drove out the peasantry to the capital-intensive industrial products.

Currently, voluntary organisations and departments are trying to "educate" the peasantry for the usage of cow dung and Neem for killing the pests. Departments are used to writing on walls to encourage usage of cow dung. They were writing "Cow-dung- green gold". The same villagers were revealing that the walls were once filled with "grow more campaign". To succeed the campaign, only the peasantry was forced to use these fertilisers and pesticides. After listening to all these new campaigns, a peasant, Satyanarayana of Chukkavalasa village desperately questioned, "Can we get dung by this tractor?"

Not only the usage of chemicals but also the establishment of these hazardous industries was also damaging the soil. Nagarjuna Agri-chem. industry was producing chemicals. It is situated in Arinam Akkivalasa village of Etcherla Mandal. The management was leaving the effluents into the Tank of Budumuru village. The tank was being contaminated and it was not becoming useful for any purpose. Noticeably, it was a dry land village.

It is not only the case of Budumuru village. In whole of India, the chemical and pesticide industries were being established in a big way with even policy changes made for this. The facts were reflected in the Annual Report -2011-12 of the Department of Chemicals, which read, "*In the Chemical Sector, 100 per cent FDI is permissible. Manufacture of most chemical products inter-alia covering organic/inorganic, dyestuffs and pesticides was delicensed. Apart from chemical fertilisers; pesticides played an important role in the "Green Revolution" during the 1960s and 1970s. Indian exports of agro-chemicals have shown an impressive growth over the last five years. The key export destination markets are USA, U.K., France, Netherlands, Belgium, Spain, South Africa, Bangladesh, Malaysia and Singapore. India is one of the most dynamic generic pesticide manufacturers in the world with more than 60 technical grade pesticides being manufactured indigenously by 125 producers consisting of large and medium scale enterprises (including about 10 multinational companies) and more than 500 pesticide formulators spread over the country.*" (*Source:* Page 5: Annual report 2011-12)

In India, the usage had reached its peak during 1990-91 recorded at 95,000 tons. Subsequently it showed a decelerating trend. Indian Council of Agricultural Research (ICAR) in its report stated that there was no adverse trend in the production pattern because of the less usage.

In India, the pesticide companies are manufacturing 80,000 tons of pesticides annually. The chemical industry turnover is reaching higher levels day by day. As per the annual report 2011-12, "*The growth of petrochemicals and chemicals is projected at 12.6 per cent and 8 per cent respectively in 11th Five Year Plan. According to the United Nations Industrial Development Organisation (UNIDO), in terms of value added at constant 2000 prices, the Indian chemical Industry was the 6th largest in the world and 3rd largest in Asia in the year 2008. As per the latest available information from industry associations, the size of the Indian Chemical Industry in the year 2010 was US$ 108.4 Billion*" (*Ibid:* page: 4).

The native wisdom of the peasantry was not taken into consideration at any point of time while introducing these chemicals. However, again the intellectuals, groups of official and non-officials were blaming the peasantry for indiscriminate usage and directing them to depend on bio-productions. Here is another story. When there was no natural production of these products, industrial production dominated this produce and the peasantry was caught in another fresh round of the onslaught of these companies. In essence, the capital robbed the peasantry directly and indirectly by extracting all the money from their pockets.

10

Credit

Peasant of Chintalapeta of Amudalavalasa Mandal philosophically expressed, "Neither there is a peasant without land nor without debt." It is an all-time ardent saying since many economists and official reports have been confirming this element for the last 150 years. The famous Royal Commission on Agriculture drew the same conclusion. Unfortunately, the institutional credit was like a mirage for the Indian peasantry despite many recommendations. For a long time, the peasantry depended on the various moneylenders for their investment on agriculture.

The Famine Commission, 1880 noted this fact and it confirmed the current statement of the peasant. It reads, *"We have found no reason to believe that the agricultural population of India have at any known period of their history been generally free from debt, although individuals or classes may have fallen into deeper embarrassments under the British rule than was common under the Native dynasties which preceded it." (Extracts from the famine commission report, 1880: Agricultural indebtedness and its remedies: Being selections from official documents: Page: 20 compiled by: S.C. Ray:* www.archive.org*)*

The above Para indicates the dominant part of debt in the Indian cultivation. The increasing debt burden on the peasantry had paved way to the insurrections during the colonial period. Hence, the colonial rulers were compelled to elicit the reasons for this "law and order" problem and detected that the enormous debt burden on the heads of peasantry playing the vital role in it. Then the rulers thought of giving institutional credit to the toiled peasantry. However, the schemes have not been fulfilled even now.

As from the official statistics, during the year 1951, the percentage of institutional credit stood at seven per cent. The village moneylenders and the rich peasantry used to give credit at exorbitant interest rates to the peasantry. Thus, the combined ruled this district until the early 80s. The debt burden played a crucial role in land alienation. Many villagers narrated such occurrences during the survey a prominent example of which can be seen from Kuppili village of Etcherla Mandal.This village is rain-fed with groundnut being a staple crop. An ordinary groundnut trader used to provide loans at usurious rates of interest. He could grab almost 500 acres of land from the peasantry. This incidence had historical precedence in India. During the colonial Rule, this was a common prevalent all over India.

This debt had two faces. One is in the shape of Faayida. Faayida is a loan based on cash-for-grain method. In the off-season, the trader used to give money to the peasant. Against this cash payment, the peasantry had to pay interest in the shape of crop. The rate of interest was so exorbitant that the peasantry could not re-pay the principal. The crop was just sufficient only to repay the interest portion. Thus, the mounting debt burden robbed the peasantry, and they invariably lost their land amidst the money lender-rich peasantry combine.

Another modus operandi was prevalent in the countryside. A moneylender gave a loan, and he determined the final price of the product at his will during the season of giving loan. During the time of harvest, the peasantry had to sell the produce at the pre-determined price to the moneylender. A fine model for this operation could be visualised from the example of Karivalasa village of Garugubilli Mandal. "The money lender (by caste Vysya) used to provide loans on a pre-determined price. The price of a paddy bag of 80 kgs. was fixed at Rs. 80 in the year 1986. Even at the time of harvest, the minimum price of the bag was around Rs.120 and thus the money lender (locally Sahukar) used to make Rs. 40 as interest for Rs. 80 for a period of three months. In this village, barring four households, all were marginal and sub-marginal peasants. Hence, mostly the entire yield was forfeited for the repayment of debt only." In this village not only, the traditional moneylenders but also the rich peasant's family with newly found teaching profession used to perform this business. Both were rich with lands in this trade.

Interestingly, the migration of youth of the peasant caste of this village to the sweets business saved the peasantry from the clutches of moneylenders. A peasant P. Lakshman Rao commented on this "otherwise, this village would have been transformed as a village of cannibalism."

Institutional Credit in this District

The institutional credit had two spheres with two phases. The first phase continued until early 80s. In the first phase, the co-operative societies and the national banks played a role.

Farmers' Co-operative Societies

When asked about the credit facility from these societies, the majority of the peasantry told in one voice, "the credit is only for bigwigs". Only the rural rich peasantry had gained from these societies. This table indicates the role of societies in a particular period.

Table 1. Credit from Co-operative Societies

Year	*Societies*	*Members*	*Loan amount*	*Average Credit*
1971-72	875	1,25,300	61,88,000	53.75
1972-73	877	1,24,900	1,05,00,000	84.06
1973-74	877	1,72,000	65,50,000	38.08
1974-75	1332	2,76,404	2,76,40,500	100
1975-76	877	2,77,448	1,75,27,000	63.17

Source: District handbook, 1977.

As seen from the table, the role of societies in catering to the needs of the needy was insignificant. Besides, the field visits clarified that these loans were reaching the rich lobby rather than to the needy. The co-operative sector had a share of 62 per cent of the institutional credit. In other words, the share capital of the public money had played a role of transforming the local rich peasantry into a capitalist farmers group.

The banking sector was not within the easy reach of this district. As per the district handbook of statistics, there were only 83 banks in this district.

Hence, it was clarified from the material evidence that the broad masses had invariably depended on the mercy of rural squeezers. It was not an exclusive feature of this district. All India Debt and Investment Survey of NSSO revealed that the private loans had a share of 68.3 per cen tin the whole debt of the peasantry in 1971.

The establishment of rural banks, nationalisation of banks and the instructions of the banking apex body had changed this scenario to some extent. Above all, the migration helped the peasantry to meet these challenges in the credit sector. Later, it became a dominant feature in the country side.

Table 2. Asset Holding vs. Loan

Sl. No.	*Asset Holding Category (in thousand)*	*Share of Institutional Credit*	*Share of Non-Institutional Credit*	*Total*
1.	Less than 5	42	58	100
2.	5 to 10	43	57	100
3.	10 to 20	44	56	100
4.	20 to 30	68	32	100
5.	30 to 50	55	45	100
6.	50 to 70	53	47	100
7.	70 to 100	61	39	100
8.	100 to 150	61	39	100
9.	150 to 250	68	32	100
10.	250 and above	81	19	100
All classes		66	34	100

Source: Indebtedness of rural house holdings as on 30/06/1991: NSSO 48th round survey, Report Number 420, Page 25.

In fact, even in the public sector banks too, the share of big wigs was playing a major role with the marginal and small peasantry in not getting their genuine share. The official bank reports and the top brass of the banking sector were revealing this truth on many occasions. This table indicated the trends of the institutional credit.

NSSO conducted survey on rural indebtedness for every 10 years. The survey results relating to fifth survey indicated the position that prevailed during the early 90s whereby it was clear that the credit facility was directly proportional to the asset holding capacity of individuals. The average share of all holdings was 66 but as seen from the categories, eight categories were well below the average. Up to category five, the non-institutional credit was playing a major role. The affluent section was drawing 81 per cent of institutional credit. Another visible fact was that usually the non-institutional debt of the poor and medium peasantry suffered from measly conditions while the rich peasantry could get that credit on liberal terms.

Another research indicated that the accounts of marginal and small peasantry in the banking operations were dwindling. A report indicated, "*There are some disquieting features of lending to small borrowers. The number of 'small borrower accounts' in case of commercial banks has come down over time indicating shifting of their focus to large borrowers. The rate of growth in agricultural advances to small and marginal farmers (less than two ha) by scheduled commercial banks in the 1990s has come down as compared to other farm size categories due to which their share declined from 54 per cent in TE 1993 to 51 per cent in total agricultural credit in TE 2002.*" (*Source:* Agricultural cooperation, finance and business management: P.S. Badal, Reader, Benaras Hindu University: www.nsdl.niscair.res.in)

The apex bank gave a data on the share of various layers of the peasantry in the banking credit sector. The following table indicates those trends.

The trends were evident as observed in the table. The share of rich peasantry at any point was near and above 50 per cent. Whereas the combined

Table 3. Distribution of Institutional Agricultural Credit by SCBs to Farmers according to Size of Landholdings (in per cent)

Sl. No.	*Period*	*Up to 2.5 Acres*		*2.5 to 5 Acres*		*Above 5 Acres*	
		Accounts	*Credit Amount*	*Accounts*	*Credit Amount*	*Accounts*	*Credit Amount*
1.	TE 1982-83	51.12	27.31	23.99	19.35	24.91	53.29
2.	TE 1991-93	46.96	29.4	30.71	24.79	22.33	45.81
3.	TE 2001-02	39.79	25.5	30.44	25.61	29.77	48.9
4.	TE 2005-06	42.29	25.41	30.57	25.34	27.13	49.25

Source: Institutional credit to the agricultural sector in India: performance and determinants: Agricultural economics and research review: Vol. 23: July to December 2010: Anjani Kumara, K.M. Singh and Shradhajali Sinha: the writers compiled the data from RBI, report on currency and finance various issues.

share of marginal and small peasantry were in and around 50 per cent. The accounts of marginal peasantry had since declined from 51.12 to an alarming 39.79 per cent and showed a marginal increase again to 42.29 per cent. In other words, 72.86 per cent of account holders were satisfying with 50.75 per cent of the amount and on the other 27.13 per cent of account holders were taking 49.25 per cent of institutional credit. As in co-operative sector, the big wigs were enjoying the fruits of nationalisation.

All banks were proclaiming to re-schedule the credits to the peasantry. However, in the surveyed villages in this district, a peculiar *modus operandi* was unearthed. Some of the peasants were not in a position to repay the debt of the banks. Then a moneylender came to the rescue by paying the debt along with interest in the name of the peasant and immediately thereafter, the banks re-schedule the loan to the peasant. The moneylenders usually charged 24 per cent interest from the peasantry. The difference between the bank interest and the interest charged by the moneylenders was a gain to the moneylender. This system prevailed in many villages. In light of the above, the actual share of marginal and small peasantry in the institutional credit became questionable.

The declared aim of formation of rural banks was to cater to the needs of the rural peasantry. However, statistics indicated that these banks were also showing enthusiasm in collecting deposits rather than issuing loans. In the year 1980, these banks gathered Rs. 222 crores from the countryside and the same figure reached Rs. 56,295 crores by 2004. At the same time, the credit amount increased from Rs. 269 crores to Rs. 25, 038 crores thus indicating that the banking sector did not give even half the amount they gathered from the rural people. At the same time, they collected an interest amount of Rs. 5, 535 crores in 2004 itself. In other words, the deposits and the interest amount had become vast resource for urban capital.

Debt Burden on Indian Peasantry

Debt burden on Indian peasantry carried a long history. Volumes of documents in the colonial rule spoke about the debt burden. The rural entrepreneurship always started as well as ended with debt. In the colonial period, the economists tried to elicit the reasons for this chronic disease and they could find out many reasons but they could not find a solution to the evil. At the most, they could only give the magnitude of the debt burden and the plight of the peasantry.

Report of the Deccan Ryots Commission 1875 recorded that 1/3 of the Indian peasantry was in debt burden. The Famine Commission 1880 declared that 1/3 of the peasantry was caught in a debt trap and another 1/3 in debt. The same commission of 1901 indicated that eighty per cent of the peasantry was in debt. Even after independence, the situation was continuing unabatedly.

The 2005 survey revealed that 48.5 per cent of the Indian peasantry was facing debt burden.

In Andhra Pradesh, the indebted families had crossed 82 per cent, which was higher than the figure of the colonial period.

The NSSO conducted a survey on the debt burden and revealed startling facts about the same. The survey was conducted during the calendar year 2003 and as seen from which, it was clear that the Indian peasantry was almost caught in a debt trap. The NSSO summarised the data and revealed startling facts about the indebtedness of the farming community. The crux of the report reads, *"At all-India level, an estimated 60.4 per cent of rural households were farmer households, and of them 48.6 per cent were reported to be indebted. The incidence of indebtedness was highest in Andhra Pradesh (82.0 per cent), followed by Tamil Nadu (74.5 per cent), Punjab (65.4 per cent), Kerala (64.4 per cent), Karnataka (61.6 per cent) and Maharashtra (54.8 per cent). Moreover, Haryana, Rajasthan, Gujarat, Madhya Pradesh and West Bengal each had about 50 to 53 per cent farmer households indebted. States with very low proportion of indebted farmer households were Meghalaya, Arunachal Pradesh and Uttaranchal. In each of these states less than 10 per cent farmer households were indebted.*

In absolute terms, out of an estimated 43.4 million indebted farmer households, 6.9 million belonged to Uttar Pradesh, 4.9 million to Andhra Pradesh, 3.6 million to Maharashtra, 3.5 million to West Bengal and 3.2 million to Madhya Pradesh. More than half of the indebted farmer households belonged to these five states." (Situation assessment survey of farmers: indebtedness of farmers households: Report number 498 (59/33/1) Page 10)

The situation was demanding more institutional credit, but the real picture was showing another trend. A national seminar titled "the National Seminar on Productivity in Indian Agriculture" was held in Pune during the month of September 2011. Mr. K.C. Chakravarty, Deputy Governor of Reserve bank of India presented a paper in that seminar. He asserted, *"It has also been observed from available data that the share of total agricultural credit supplied through rural branches has seen a decline from 55.5 per cent in 1990 to 38.5 per cent in 2010. The contribution of urban and metropolitan branches to agricultural credit has increased from 14.9 per cent to 33.7 per cent during this period, indicating that credit disbursement is mainly through non-rural branches. The available data raises questions about the segments to which the credit is actually flowing and whether it is reaching the intended beneficiaries."*

As seen from the NSSO survey, 4.9 million households were caught in debt. The situation of this district was not an exception for this character. The debt burden was a common feature in the district. Irrespective of the facility, whether irrigated or otherwise, whether traditional crop or commercial crop, no peasant was excluded from this net.

In the rural debt, the share of friends and relatives was decreasing with only the commercial interests were gaining. This situation has deprived the peasantry leading them to depression. *"Studies have shown that mainly economic and in scattered cases, non-economic factors have been responsible for farmers suicide. Among economic factors, the failure of crop (mainly cotton) and failure of investment in bore wells are responsible for involvement of farmers in debt trap. Stagnant agricultural yields among Punjab farmers have been found to a cause of their stress. In the wake of limited access to institutional credit, the small farmers are forced to borrow from non-institutional sources. At times, they rotate credit from non-institutional to institutional sources and vice-versa leading to their exploitation by multiple agencies. There are a large number of factors, which operate simultaneously and cause unbearable distress to the farmer. The resource poor farmers in all the major states reporting suicides constitute the largest proportion of suicide victims. Thus it can be concluded that the farmers suicides were more common in states which are forerunner of commercial agriculture. They are Andhra Pradesh, Karnataka, Kerala, Maharashtra and Punjab. The resource poor farmers suicides indicate that there is breakdown of the community sense and social support mechanism in areas of highly commercialised and competitive agriculture.*" (P.S. Badal: *Ibid*; Page: 20)

Changing Credit Pattern in Srikakulam District

As discussed earlier, until the establishment of rural banks, usurious money lending was common in the district. Majority of the peasantry were roped in with moneylenders with economic exploitation being the order of the day. Even the debtors used to work free of cost or at reduced wages in the fields of these moneylenders. Low yield too played havoc in the life of the peasantry. Major portion of the harvest used to take over by these lenders. This type of situation prevailed in India even during colonial history. After seeing this practice, *Sir G. Wingate remarked, "the Ryot toils that another may rest, and sows that another may reap". (Source:* Agricultural indebtedness in India: compiled by S.C. Ray)

The fayida system, the cash to grain business, advance determination of the price of the harvest and exorbitant interest rates have been disappeared from the district. In the surveyed villages, the last two factors are still prevalent in tribal dominated villages.

As seen from the official reports, the rural banking sector did not take 100 per cent part in the sector. However, the banking sector acted as a deterrent to the ruthless exploitation in the countryside. An example in Lakshminarasupeta Mandal for this was the Visakha Grameena bank, a rural bank that was operating in this district since the early 80s with its new branch in Lakshminarasupeta from where the peasantry used to take loans. A moneylender lost almost his business because of this bank. Attada Appalanaidu, an employee of this branch, and a fiction writer of this area said "the money lender used take a malicious campaign on the bank. He used to inform the peasantry that the bank would forfeit the assets in the case of a default."

The early 90s saw a tremendous change in the countryside. The youth and the bankrupt peasantry, as in earlier days, did not stick to their isolated villages. Migration became a common factor in this district. In fact, these ranks and file have never seen such a wage rate in their villages. The general frugality of the peasantry fetched them with some surplus and they could use their money to invest in the cultivation. This flow of urban money also deterred the money lending business.

As seen from the earlier example, in Karivalasa village, the economic exploitation was stopped during the late 90s because of migration to urban trade. Another typical example was in Boddam village of Rajam Mandal about Nakka Appalanaidu, a retired village administrative officer (former Munsab) of this village remarked about this migration. He complained that the migration was affecting the country side in two ways. Due to this migration, the wage rate was increased. Shortage of labour was playing a vital role in this hike. The migrated marginal and small peasants used to manage their cultivation from urban areas. To complete the task in haste, they were hiking the rural wage rate, which was affecting the peasantry (read as rich peasantry). The late 80s and early 90s had seen another change in the rural lending. The progeny of peasant castes settled as teachers in their villages. With this section entering the scene, the traditional moneylenders faced a competition. The caste played a catalyst role in the business of these sections. The traditional Vysya community was gradually disappearing from the scene to pave the way only for the peasantry castes. The peasantry who was out of ambit of banking operations became consumers to these new sections.

Dalaipeta of Komarada Mandals stood as another typical example. The Dalits of this village had migrated due inevitable circumstances. (Reasons for this migration discussed in detail in the chapter "Dalits") Ganteda China Gourunaidu said, "Earlier Dalits used to take advance wages and they used to work as bonded labour in the village. However, the situation changed later. Majority of Dalits had migrated to Chennai and were earning money and lending to peasantry at a simple interest of 12 to 18 per cent per annum. The peasantry was conducting the agriculture with the financial aid of the Dalits."

As seen from the entire situation, the methods of the debt were changed. However, the debt burden continued. Peasant and debt were continuing as indivisible parts. The undeniable feature was ruthless exploitation on the peasantry was almost stopped. A simple interest and repayment in simple conditions replaced the archaic system of exploitation.

11

Market

Probably, the marketing sector has not changed much when compared with all other sectors in this district. In the traditional cropping pattern, the peasantry used to sell sugarcane directly to the manufacturer. It was mostly a contract farming wherein a direct relationship between the end user and the producer prevailed. Though the peasantry cultivated Mesta extensively, there was no direct relationship between the producer and consumer. The traders played the entire role in the transaction. In the case of food crops, initially the moneylender-cum-trader used to purchase the harvest.

Now the cropping pattern has seen what had already been discussed. Many changes occurred in the pattern with no significant change in the marketing pattern. Barring sugarcane, the peasantry had hardly any role in dealing with the ultimate consumers. Of late, casuarinas plants established a direct link.

Many changes took place with the traders. Vysya community played almost complete role in this sector until late 80s.The peasant castes also started their role as traders in a modestly during the late 80s. This eroded the foundation of Vysya community. Mean while, the peasant castes were playing a dominant role in the trading sector and Vysyas had almost vacated the villages (though too early to judge). At least the Vysya community lost its grip in this trading sector.

No trader paid the amount to the peasantry at the time of purchase. The traders sold the produce in the market and only then, they would remit to the peasantry. In some occasions, they used to evade the payment. In the countryside, once these were common plight but the awareness of the peasantry averted this. However, a recent example of such evasion is unearthed in Batuva village of G. Sigadam Mandal. A peasant of that village said "of late, maize was replacing the ground nut and the traders normally of the peasant caste (read as our caste) purchased the crop and were remitting the amount as usual over a month. During the last season, however, they did not pay the full amount and thus betrayed them".

This district has market yards. When asked the peasantry why they are not going to market yards all the villagers told in one voice "we do not go to market yards. They show n number of reasons for not taking the produce. The staff would not available. Even if they are available, they call us to wait for a day. We have to pay all this expenditure from our pocket. Hence we sell the produce to the traders only".

12

Rural Industry

The ancient agricultural system developed necessary rural industrial bases in the social evolution process. Unfortunately, in India, it was linked with the caste system, and it was fixed on those castes to conduct the profession indicated by birth. In other words, it was an extraordinary social contract, which was envisaged and made mandatory by way of legal jurisprudence. Manu, probably the first compiler/writer of the Hindu jurisprudence clearly wrote, *"To Brahmans he assigned teaching and studying (the Veda), sacrificing for their own benefit and for others, giving and accepting (of alms). The Kshatriya he commanded to protect the people, to bestow gifts, to offer sacrifices, to study (the Veda), and to abstain from attaching himself to sensual pleasures; The Vaisya to tend cattle, to bestow gifts, to offer sacrifices, to study (the Veda), to trade, to lend money, and to cultivate land. One occupation only the lord prescribed to the Sudra, to serve meekly even these (other) three castes."* (*Source:* Translation of Laws of Manu: Translated by: Buhler).

Manu told about the cultivation which reads. *"(Some) declare that agriculture is something excellent, (but) that means of subsistence is blamed by the virtuous; (for) the wooden (implement) with iron point injuries the earth and (the beings) living in the earth"*. (*Ibid:* page 201).

Manu tried to dictate the profession of an individual, but the dynamics had changed this process and the Brahmin himself had transformed several ways to earn his livelihood. Probably, the first transformation started with this community itself that they had reaped the benefit of modernity even in the beginning of the modern age. George Campbell, a civil servant in the colonial period wrote detailed description on the origin of caste and professions that was linked with the caste and the changing pattern in the stratified Indian caste system in more detail in his work. He categorically wrote the changing profession of a Brahmin. It reads, *"The most remarkable feature in their present position seems to be, that they are almost the only class which engages in all professions. Among the rural population, they cultivate largely: they are very numerous among the sepoys of our army: they are commonly found as bankers and traders among the mercantile class: they take all kind of service, and are even constantly met with as common labourers. They are priests astrologers, and cooks, wherever they can find employment as such—cooks, because a Hindoo who can afford only one servant keeps Brahmin to cook his meals."* (*Source:* Modern India: A sketch of the system of the civil government to which it is prefixed some account of the natives and native institutions: Page 41: George Campbell ESQ).

The caste-based professions laid solid foundation to the rural economic structure. The authorities wanted to continue the pattern intact. Therefore, they made the profession compulsory and wrote Acts and proviso for implementation of the code of conduct. They were required to extract surplus only to seize it by compelling besides applying various laws and procedures. Manu further told, *"But a Sudra, whether bought or unbought, he may compel to do servile work; for he was created by the Self-existent (Svayambhu) to be the slave of a Brahmana. A Sudra, though emancipated by his master, is not released from servitude; since that is innate in him, who can set him free from it?*

"(The king) should carefully compel Vaisya and Sudra to perform the work (prescribed) for them; for if these two (castes) swerved from their duties, they would throw this (whole) world into confusion." (*Source:* Translation of Laws of Manu: Page 145: Translated by: Buhler) (Emphasis added)

The last Para of the above quote made it clear that people could overthrow the system only by means of cracking the profession. They could accomplish freedom only through disowning their profession that originated since birth.

Brahmins, the ancient tribe (in the words of Campbell) wanted to enforce the professions of individuals and even prescribed the punishments for violation thereof. The same Brahmins had resorted to change their profession. In this process, they broke their chains. Thus, probably they were the paramount rule breakers.

Land was freehold with no ownership to any one and when occupations (rural industries) originated. However, they played their role in surplus production and amassing which by a few was stratified in theology and umpteen scriptures. Brahmins, weak by themselves, had to enthrone Kshatriyas, clan muscles and accept their supremacy over the state and the rule, to be content with their hold over religion and rituals, which needed no brown power, but a bit of mere intelligence. In this process, they had to denigrate their prolonged occupation of agriculture to second place and concede it to Vysyas. In short, the priestly class made the caste setup as a prerequisite for flourishing the rural based production.

Campbell noted about the caste in his work. It reads, "*The institution of castes is in fact, originally nothing more than a great system of very minute hereditary division of labour. Our ideas of it are too much derived from descriptions of caste as it existed in Menu's time, or as Menu thought, it ought to exist. The four great classes are no longer in existence, but the variety of caste is infinite. I have been said that every occupation and subdivision of an occupation forms a separate caste, and these again are subdivided."* (Modern India : Campbell: Page 68)

Campbell noted that the every remaining occupation was subservient to the agriculture. The peasantry used to denigrate the other occupations. *"But all the other inhabitants-carpenters, Blacksmiths, priests and the large class of labourers who do everything except actual agriculture, and are sometimes employed to assist in that—all these are classed as "Kameens"or inferiors. And receive an annual allowance of grain for their services. I am afraid that a Bramin's profession is not so profitable in the North as in the South, for I find in a particular description of a village of Delhi (Revenue selections, III, 401, to which I would refer for a very excellent account of these communities) that, while the Washerman receives twenty seers of grain per plough, the tailor fifteen, and the musician twenty, the Bramin has but three quarters of a Seer."* (Modern India… Page 90: Campbell).

Campbell completed his work in 1852. By that time itself, the peasant castes used to denigrate the other occupations. In fact, this treatment had also juridical precedence. Manu prescribed this menial treatment to some of the occupations. He wrote, "*A shepherd, a keeper of buffaloes, the husband of a remarried woman, and a carrier of dead bodies, (all these) must be carefully avoided."* (*Source:* Translation of Laws of Manu page 50: Translated by: Buhler)

In any civilisation, agriculture was started on a small scale. In due course of time, many occupations came into existence in support of agriculture. Indian agricultural sector was not an exception for this mode. However, in the initial period, the Brahmins lived on the cultivation; they estranged the profession and branded it as a profession of Vysya community. In fact, farming was nothing but an industry, which required many skilled professionals for flourishing of the same. However, the peasantry castes treated their cultivation of repute and at the same time, they followed the suit of brahminical thought. In this cultural transformation, they thought all the remaining castes and occupations were dependent on them. This concept invariably led to hegemony. The peasantry castes did not bother about the labour value of such occupations and treated them as semi-slaves in the countryside. The peasantry always thought about the wages and never even thought about the surplus value of the labour. They forgot that the cultivation was invariably dependent on many other professions. In fact, in India, the integration of cultivation and many other occupations lasts long.

Agricultural system survived on ground level co-operation from rural industries. Barika (one among dalits) to render slave-like-labour, carpenter and smith to make implements, weaver to make clothes, washer man, barber and chiefly dalits, who were primarily agricultural labour who served as security to produce and boundaries, potter to make utensils, headman for accounting, priest to fill the philosophical space, Brahmin to decide the days and time for various agricultural operations, etc., played their role in fortifying the feudal structure.The bonded child labour is the herd keepers. The shepherd used to give organic fertiliser to the fields. The Erukula caste used to make bamboo implements. The woman folk of Dalits were used to cleanse farmyards. In this way, the agriculture survived on the innumerable professions. In other words, all these acted as auxiliary industries for smooth functioning of the agricultural industry. Both the Brahmin and Kshatriya purposely concealed and neglected the imminent dependence of agriculture on these castes and occupations of labour. So did the peasant castes, as they became proprietors of land.

In the feudal regime, the upper caste Brahmin and Kshatriya made a stamp on all the professions, which included agriculture as menial. They behaved with the majority of people in detestable way. Their economic and social hegemony went unabated for centuries.

In the natural process, the peasant castes got rid of Kshatriyas, Brahmin, and Velama Doras, who till then, wielded enormous power. Persons of these three castes, being very few in number, left the countryside. That was a decisive victory of the peasant castes, the death knell to the brutal power and hegemony of those with no role in production and laid iron fist over the whole produce. Those with no role in production yet laid their iron fist over the whole produce and met with their waterloo.

King and priestly class structure were a reflection of feudal mode of production. The duo ruled the country ruthlessly and quelled the people belonging to major castes. However, once the universal suffrage entered the scene, the situation changed rapidly. In a democratic country, the majority opinion and acceptance was an essential condition. Naturally, peasantry castes started playing a vital role.

The best example for this transformation could be seen from a village. Piridi a village in Bobbili Mandal was dominated numerically by Koppulavelama peasant caste. However, the upper caste Velama Doras had financial upper hand and used to intimidate the peasantry. Now, the Velama Doras had almost migrated with the power having been transferred to majority peasant caste. When asked about the process of transformation, Kolli Krishnamurthy Naidu, former sarpanch of the village narrated the process of a peasant leader of their caste Kolli Kurminaidu contested general elections to the state assembly in 1972 when a Velama Dora of Bobbili town was another contender. Forty Velama caste families were residing in this village. When asked them to vote for the local candidate, they rejected the proposal and voted against the candidate and the candidate lost with a narrow margin, which infuriated the situation. Though, the Velama Doras were minority in the village, their economic dominance and the support of Zamindar of Bobbili made them egocentric. Thus, the election had acted as a tipping point. Peasant caste elders sat together and took a decision to social boycott the Velama Dora when they implemented the social boycott scrupulously. Because of this they could not even harvest their crop. At last, they came to compromise with the social hegemony on the peasantry castes came to an end.

Majority of the caste went to the extent of rejecting the constitutional right of Velama Doras and attained dignity. In this process, they were freed from the clutches of rural landlordism. An interesting story was the same peasant castes never recognised the concept of dignity of other backward communities leave alone the Dalits. They used this weapon on every other caste until recently. They chanted this mantra against carpenters, the Dalits. At that juncture, they did not even bother to look into their history.

By this time, the peasant castes dominated the legislature and parliament. Barring reserved seats, majority of the seats were in their hands. The issue was already discussed in the first chapter in detail. Though many castes had a status of the backward caste reservation, only these four castes could dominate the scene. Local bodies' elections were also not an exception for this process. Interestingly, many political parties spoke about their services to the backward classes in this region. The statement carried a complete validity though the entire development had gone to the credit of these four castes.

The plight of artisans and castes of servitude and Dalits had no boundaries. Due to space constraints, there was an issue to recount the entire examples. However, some examples should be seen.The peasantry continued to give the wage in the form of grain to these castes particularly to barbers, washer man, and carpenters. Traditionally, caste violence as a practice did not appear on smith community. However, economic exploitation was a common feature on them with no legitimate agitation to demand enhancement in their wage rate. The two communities almost led a semi-serf life in the countryside with no organisation struggling exclusively for them. Another unfortunate thing was that the Dalits have at least constitutional safe guards while these two castes did not have the same. Hence, the social and economic oppression continued for a long time. They were the couriers as well as watchmen at funerals, were required to clean all the mud of the villages, refrain from pursuing their profession at their will nor should they go to the houses of Dalits. They were the music party forall village functions at pittance.

A barber had to go from house to house to perform his profession a practice that prevailed in the countryside for long. In Korasavada village of Patapatnam Mandal, a barber was disgusted with his profession and wanted to establish a saloon in the village during late 80s. He lamented that initially nobody came to his shop and he used to sit idle the whole day. The village was famous for cloth trading. Subsequently, the business travellers and the people of other villages started coming to the saloon. Slowly the villagers too followed suit. Lately, there were many saloons in the village.

In Latchayyapeta village of Bobbili Mandal, a woman belonging to washer-man community told about existence of annual payment for 210 kgs of paddy with improper measurements though their demand for cash payment was accepted when they were getting Rs. 300 per hundred clothes. They were able to send their children to school and they were the last washer-man left in the village.

Penta Venkati, a youth of the washer-man community discontinued his studies after +2 and was pursuing the profession. He narrated a heart-rending episode on his profession stating existence of reservation under backward castes and could not get a job despite qualification, which forced him to this profession he got accustomed to the same though he had to experience painful moments. The peasantry used to give even the menstrual clothes for the washing purpose even which he could not reject.

However, there was an opposite voice heard in Kothuru colony of Vaddithandra Panchayat in Santabommali Mandal. Kalinga, rich peasant with an "empowered" voice did not complain about the washer-men's indifference in heeding to them nor were they doing their profession. Everybody wanted to leave the village, as they wanted only to wash the menstrual clothes since it was difficult to cleanse for their women.

The voice showed the true colours of the peasantry. A feeble caste in terms of their strength tried to request the majority for democratisation of the profession. However, the majority of the caste reminded them that it was their innate duty.

In fact, the peasant castes had a prolonged battle with the three upper castes before gaining control over them. The three upper castes legally had a control on the means of production from 1802 to 1948 in this district. Their control on the means of production was the basis for the oppression. Protracted legal battles and necessity of elections made a foundation for these majority peasant castes. In this process, the economic and social oppression on these castes abolished. In fact, the upper castes were minority in number and hence they fled from the villages.

The elimination of the upper caste hegemony was not sufficient to take the agrarian society to the higher stage. The feudal latifundium and the low productivity were the main obstacles in the upward mobilisation. Hence, the disintegration of the mammoth land holdings and invoking modern practices were prerequisite for the transformation. Hence, both these methods were infused.

As seen from the crop report of 1957-58 of Andhra Pradesh with the Economic surveys of the late 50s and early 60s, a reader could recognise the nascent beginning only towards this direction. Dialectically, the surplus produced lead to shattering the foundations of the very system of its origin, the feudal system of production, which required capital. Cheap capital, in the name of institutional credit through co-operative societies, land mortgage banks, co-operative banks and commercial banks started penetrating into this district during the 70s. Big farmers had access to this mainly because the credit was based on ownership records and because of their enhanced consciousness. Education facilitated information about government schemes, subsidies and technical knowhow. With little or almost no education, the poor and the marginalised stood gasping and hoping. Capital, call it institutional credit, brought with it the pesticides, fertilisers, subsidised seeds besides access to one of the most important natural resource the water. Those who had capital were able to draw large quantity of water until then a collective and common resource through oil motors and diesel engines were immensely benefitted. Availability of water not only enabled increase in productivity but also changed the crops and their pattern and increasing cultivation of commercial crops. While that was on one side, let us understand that capital essentially compounds inequalities, for the very nature and survival of capital lies in that. With more water and enough capital, big farmers needed better implements. Cheap capital, cheap labour, increased productivity, access to markets helped big farmers grow little stronger and their attention was drawn towards education. Backward classes reservation buttressed the desire and slowly a beginning was made to form new educated elite from among these peasant castes and this education later turned out to be social capital. This section, new generation of these peasant castes, armed with education journeyed to towns and cities, into the arena that was opening up job opportunities in industries, private sector, etc.

All these benefits reached the rich-peasantry (read it as once the large and moderate tenants) and they were established as a formidable class in the rural sector. In other words, these sections because of the technical reach, transformed as rural entrepreneurs. Above all, the ignorance of the rural masses, their hopeless conditions, their inability to bargain and above all the disunity among themselves led to supply of cheap labour to their business. In view of these dual benefits, the golden age prevailed in the agrarian sector for these affluent sections for twenty five to thirty years in the countryside.

Along with this, the education played a catalyst role in the development of peasant castes. The reservations that provided during the early 70s gave a giant leap to the people with lands. This aspect has already been discussed in detail under human resources chapter. The multiplied wealth made the rich peasantry forget the history and they had resorted to brutal economic oppression on their fellow caste people while economic and social oppression on Dalits and the castes of servitude.

As things continued this way, the same modernity gave social consciousness to the poor and downtrodden. They came to realise that all their labour became an instrument in gathering surplus value. They realised that with that surplus value, only the rural rich peasantry amassed wealth. However, there were no organised struggles in the rural areas to release them from the clutches. Their trails towards this direction always ended with social boycott, or with despair and hunger. The new transportation facilities drove them from the rural clutches and they were travelling to the urban centres.

An interesting feature to note was that due to the majority in their number, the peasant castes drove their oppressors from the countryside and thus was able to gain control over the production. However, this did not happen in the case of rural proletarian who succumbed to the brute force of the peasant castes. Hence, migration was the only solution that came to rescue from the clutches of rural oppression.

Later, the rural rich peasantry faced the heat. They were blaming the rural proletarian for leaving the villages. Their dreams were shattering. The cheap labour in the form of caste-based occupations forming a basis for their wealth was eroding. They were preaching that the golden era in the villages had destroyed. Increased addition of capital was replacing the labour in the countryside. Instead of blaming the capital, they were blaming the rural proletarian for the turn of their fortunes. Unfortunately, the intellectuals were also adding chorus to this voice. These sections were giving slogans for saving the occupation structure that was based on the archaic caste system.

Hitherto the upper caste strata of this society blamed the new productive forces (Read as peasant castes) for their role in dismantling age-old system that prevailed in India. The intellectuals and theoreticians preached for the continued Hindu Dharma in the countryside. However, the majority of the society correctly recognised the facts and rejected the out-dated philosophy. Then the same peasantry tried to preserve their dominance intact. The rich peasantry who turned as followers of Manu were blaming the rural proletarian for dismantling the village structure.

Many auxiliary industries and the agricultural industry have an inseparable relation. However, the feudal oppression and the capitalist penetration started weakening this link. In the colonial period itself, the capital tried to disintegrate this. Marx observed, "Over the entire surface, the British stream and science uprooted the union between agriculture and industry".

The capital had surpassed all the man-made geographical boundaries. In principle, capital and labour were peripatetic in nature. Capital attracted all the sources that were required for its thriving. It always created consumers for the new commodities. It was always trying for new markets. The hunt resulted in the disappearance of distinct characters of tribal hamlets, villages, town and cities. This process gave rise to new agitators and lovers of the old environment. They start agitations and write volumes for saving the old. They intentionally or unintentionally tried to embrace the customs and out-dated economic foundation. In this process, they resembled the once conservative writers and thinkers. Interestingly during some times, the intellectuals of the subdued layers were giving chorus to the "modern old song".

When American clergymen asked Gandhi about the inclusion of caste in Hindu religion, he replied, *"Hinduism does not believe in caste. I would obliterate it at once. But I believe in Varna dharma, which is the law of life. I believe that some people are born to teach and some to defend and some to engage in trade and agriculture and some to do manual labour, so much so that these occupations become hereditary. The law of Varnais nothing but the law of conservation of energy. Why should my son not be a scavenger if I am one?"* (*Source:* Teachings of Mahatma Gandhi: Page 70 Edited by: Jag Parvesh Chander: www.archive.org)

Even during the colonial period, there were conflicting views on the penetration of capital and the repercussions of the capital in the rural sector.

Gandhi wanted to establish village-based economy and even preached for the continuation of caste-based occupations. Dr. B.R. Ambedkar strongly condemned this and preached for dismantling the entire existing Hindu dharma.

The capital entered the remote rural areas in many forms and it almost dismantled the indivisible bond between agriculture and its auxiliary industries. It decidedly and decisively completed its mission as per its wishes. The age-old ruthless oppression and exploitation paved the way for its destruction. It is an inevitable process in the dynamics of development. The broad masses of different castes did not have any right on the basic means of production. The Hindu dharma rejected the right of ownership for broad masses. The feudal mode of production treated these masses as semi-serfs and thrived on its labour. The people who correctly recognised this fact, in inevitable circumstances left the village in search of livelihood. The occupation, which is determined by caste, is a barbaric feature. Progressive forces and genuine supporters of the rural proletarian should have accepted this process. In fact, the genuine forces had to fight hard to remove this barbaric feature from the countryside. The migration and their resistance in the villages paved the way for destruction of the hegemony of rural rich peasantry. Hence, these classes were crying loudly and trying to turn the clock back. In the human history, every oppressing class tried to do this during the time of dissolution of their power but proved futile. There was no golden age in the history. The preaching about the golden age was proved wrong.

In general, the çaste system was a manifestation of feudal system aided by religion, the destruction of which had to be not merely accepted but to be helped out as well. Continuation of economic system based on caste system, i.e., rural industries, was only to support the rural regressive forces. Any attempt to maintain this arrangement was nothing but an attempt to revive the callous exploitation and oppression in the countryside. It continued until capital started its penetration. Survival and progress of rural economy depended on its linkage with urban areas. In other words, the villages that appear to be separate places were to have been seen and understood as extensions of urban areas.The capital needed freedmen to work at the behest of capital.

Marx delved at length the entry of British capital and destruction of villages. Many a sad tone would raise. Elegy is written. Melic pathos sung. However, it is certain and necessary. He only wondered if the capital shatters that feudal foundation a clean and fully. In the context of destruction of linkage between handlooms and rural production system, hewrote, *"Now, sickening as it must be to human feeling to witness those myriads of industrious patriarchal and inoffensive social organisations disorganised and dissolved into their units, thrown into a sea of woes, and their individual members losing at the same time their ancient form of civilisation, and their hereditary means of subsistence, we must not forget that these idyllic village communities, in offensive though they may appear, had always been the solid foundation of Oriental despotism, that they restrained the human mind within the smallest possible compass, making it the unresisting tool of superstition, enslaving it beneath traditional rules, depriving it of all grandeur and historical energies. We must not forget the barbarian egotism which, concentrating on some miserable patch of land, had quietly witnessed the ruin of empires, the perpetration of unspeakable cruelties, the massacre of the population of large towns, with no other consideration bestowed upon them than on natural events, itself the helpless prey of any aggressor who deigned to notice it at all. We must not forget that this undignified, stagnatory, and vegetative life, that this passive sort of existence evoked on the other part, in contradistinction, wild, aimless, unbounded forces of destruction and rendered murder itself a religious rite in Hindostan. We must not forget that these little communities were contaminated by distinctions of caste and by slavery, that they subjugated man to external circumstances instead of elevating man the sovereign of circumstances, that they transformed a self-developing social state into never changing natural destiny, and thus brought about a brutalising worship of nature, exhibiting its degradation in the fact that man, the sovereign of nature, fell down on his knees in adoration of Hanuman, the monkey, and Sabbala, the cow.*"(Marx on India: page: 16)

The caste based occupation system was an axis to the feudal mode of production as an unparalleled social contract in the Indian context. The burden of inhumanity was largely borne by the subdued castes. Capital was the only accurate medicine to the malady. Capital cannot exist without destructing the feudal base. At the same time, it clears the feudal set-up as per the needs of it. Marx with a clear vision wrote that capital alone could destroy this stinky, parasite and feudal system in any country. Capital almost completed this task in the countryside. It does not mean that the feudalism has totally disappeared. Marx commented on this dual character, which reads, *"In all other spheres, we, like the rest of Continental Western Europe, suffer not only from the development of capitalist production, but also from the incompleteness of that development. Alongside the modern evils, a whole series of inherited evils oppress us, arising from the passive survival of antiquated modes of production, with their inevitable train of social and political anachronisms. We suffer not only from the living but from the dead."* (Preface to the First German Edition: Marx, 1867).

This is a relevant fact even to India where capital works as a remedy to the evils of feudalism. However, the Feudalism cannot be a remedial measure to the evils of capitalism. By observing the evils of capital, some are dreaming about the feudal mode of production, which is against the dynamics. These types of remedial measures represent only regressive and harmful to the broad masses that are bonded to their profession involuntarily. In other words, they will be proved as modern Manus.

PART–II

13

Forest and Adivasis

Human society has its genesis in the forests. The primitive man started his life in forests. Food gathering and hunting were the first occupations for the human beings. Now, the migration is rampant in villages. It did not mean that the entire villages are abandoned. In the same way, a part of the humankind stayed back in forests. In fact, even in the advanced countries too, the forest dwelling and out-dated mode of production survived. Morrison quoted from, "The Distribution of Products' Ed. Atkinson stated about such conditions in England read in, "*These primitive conditions can even now be observed in the mountain sections of the Southern States.*" (Economic Transition in India: Theodore Morison: Page15 www.archieves.org)

Capitalists thought that every resource on the planet was created for its consumption. To cater to its needs, the capitalist destructed the natural resources rapaciously. Even the most essential resources like forests, land and water were not exception for this obliteration. The same capitalists in a classic way talked loudly about saving the resources. It censured others for this destruction. The propaganda methods of the capitalists mesmerised the people. People who were not based directly on the sources easily believed this propaganda and gave a voice to it. In fact, the forest dwellers (hereinafter called Adivasis) could not exist without the support of the forests. Forests are the life and blood for them. Their survival is closely linked with that natural resource. Considering this fact, capitalists tried to fix them as destructors and conducted vicious campaign against them. Capitalists knew well that in presence of Adivasis, it was a difficult task to grab the forest wealth easily. Hence, the propaganda was a far-sighted strategy only to acquire the resources for its consumption. The main task of the propaganda was only for "manufacturing consent".

The British capitalists had a notorious name for the destruction of forests. However, they got a "pious" idea of saving Indian forest tracts. Hence, with a pen stroke, they nationalised forests during their rule and declined the natural rights of the Adivasis. The policy stated its prime aim, which read, *"Forests which are the reservoirs of valuable timbers should be managed on commercial lines as a source of revenue to the States".*

The colonial rulers had seen the forests only to acquire wealth for their commercial interests and they had implemented draconian onslaught on the Adivasis. The intimidation had paved the way for innumerable revolts across India. The stamp of destructors has still not been removed even now. The independent rulers proclaimed that relation between Adivasis and the forest was symbiotic. However, anthropologists and of late environmentalists were criticising the successive governments for not framing the pro-Adivasi policies.

The first forest policy after independence was formulated in1952. Debar Commission criticised the government for non-recognition of symbiotic relationship of Adivasis and forests. In fact, the government had appointed this commission to enumerate the condition of Adivasis during 1961. The 1952 Forest policy used a term "accidental" for the forest dwellers and the people who were living adjacent to the forests. The term accidental was itself against to human evolution theory. In fact, human existence started from forests itself.

The Expert committee appointed by the Planning Commission commented on the plight of Adivasis in its report which read, "As the Indian states were merged into the Union and their forests merging into the reserved forests with no modicum of decency of rule of law was being followed, traditional rights were neither respected nor recorded, age old arrangements were dismissed, the tribal forest dweller became a timber thief and an encroacher, a criminal in his own home." (*Source:* Report of the expert group on prevention of alienation of tribal land and its restoration: Page 75)

Lal Bahadur Shastri National Academy started a *Centre for Sustainable Development* during 1994. It conducted a three-day workshop on forest policies and its implications during the month of July, 1994. Sri N.C. Saxena, the Director of the academy reviewed the policies in detail and commented, *"Twenty three per cent of India's geographical area has been declared as forest land and is mostly under the control of the government. For almost a century and until 1988, the policy was to use these lands for commercial purposes. Man-made plantations of industrial species were encouraged on forestlands, often by clear felling of mixed forests. Even after India became independent in 1947, this policy continued. This policy led to deforestation, which increased rural poverty and unemployment on one hand, and social unrest and conflict over rights on the other."* (Forest, People and profit net equations for sustainability: Dr. N.C. Saxena)

Even the Indira Gandhi National Forest Academy also stated, "The main thrust of managing forests for production of timber products as in the British period continued even after the reconstitution of IFS in 1966" (*Source:* www.ignfa.gov.in)

In essence, the existence of forests has vital link with the Adivasis existence, which were mutually dependent. All these policies had forgotten this fact and tried to save the forests from the Adivasis in view of which, neither the forest nor the lives of the Adivasis flourished. Debar Commission noted with pain that the national forest policy did not frame to meet the interests of Adivasis and it recommended the policy makers for redress. Unfortunately, the National Commission on Agriculture, 1976 made stringent recommendations and it almost rejected the existence of Adivasis. The commission in its voluminous report allotted IX section to discuss the issues of forest. It commented, *"The Production of Industrial wood have to be raisen d'etre for the existence of forests. Actually it is in this value that many other values that have been claimed or stressed for forests so far can be absorbed."* (National Commission on Agriculture,1976)

This commission categorised the forests in three type and they are, (a) protected forests, (b) production forests and (c) social forests (National Commission on Agriculture, 1976: Forestry; page 37).

The commission made punitive comments on the Adivasis. It read, *"Free supply of forest produce to the rural population and their rights and privileges has brought destruction to the forests and so it is necessary to reverse the process. The rural people have not contributed much towards the maintenance or regeneration of the forests. Having over-exploited the resources they cannot in all fairness expect that somebody else will take the trouble of providing them with forest produce free of charge"*.

National Commission on Agriculture is not an exclusive commission for forest related issues. It made many comments on the existing Adivasis and forests and gave many instructions for the better management of forests. All these instructions were implemented without any delay. In fact, the commission submitted its final report in January1976. Because of its recommendation, the subject of forests was transferred from state list to concurrent list.

In view of its recommendation only, many changes took place in production and sale pattern of forest produce. In the words of Andhra Pradesh Forest Corporation, *"The National Commission on Agriculture (N.C.A.) had suggested setting up of Forest Development Corporations in every state, which would be able to raise institutional finance for raising man-made forests so as to meet the domestic and industrial needs of forest produce, reclosed the degraded forest areas and bring them under productive use. Pursuant to the recommendations of N.C.A., the Andhra Pradesh Forest Development Corporation Limited (APFDC) was established on 16th June, 1975."* (*Source:* www.apfdc.nic.in)

Interestingly, even before the submission of the final report, the corporation was established on 16th June 1975. As per the recommendations laid by the commission, the corporation had defined its functions and goals which read, *"To raise industrial plantations like Eucalyptus, Bamboo, etc., to meet the raw material requirement of the wood based industries in the state.* [*Source:* www.apfdc.aptc.gov.in]

1988-forest policy had redefined its target, and it was recommended for man-made plantations in the private lands. However, the same old pattern was continuing in the state.

Table 1. Production and Revenue Earned through Sales of Eucalyptus

Sl. No.	*Year*	*Yielding of Pulp-wood (in tons)*	*Revenue Earned (in Lakhs)*	*Price per Metric ton (in Rupees)*
1.	2007-08	1,15,820	2,096.34	1810
2.	2008-09	59,747	1847.16	3099
3.	2009-10	31,333	822.22	2641
4.	2010-11	1,59,426	505.40	307
5.	2011-12	1,92,602	548.90	285

Source: www.apfdc.aptc.gov.in.

As decided in 1976, the forest corporation constructed man-made plantations in 83,669.50 hectares. Eucalyptus was planted in 56,341.96 hectares of forestland. Eucalyptus occupied 67.33 per cent of the total planted area. Adivasis could not get any minor forest produce from this plantation. Coffee was categorised in non-forest crop. However, it occupied 4.01 lakh hectares.

The corporation disclosed the revenue realisation from these man-made plantations in its official website, which are tabulated here.

As seen from this table, the corporation earned total revenue of Rs. 58 croresover a period of five years. In the first year, it almost earned Rs. 21 crores, and it dropped to Rs. 5.5 crores in 2011-12.The yield during that year was 1, 15,820 tonnes whereas the yield increased to 1,92,602 tonnes. It recorded a net increase of 76,782 tons. However, the decrease in revenue was Rs. 15.48 crores. The percentage of increase in the productionwas recorded as 66.3 whereas the percentage of decrease in revenue was recorded as 73.9.The main raw material for the paper industry is Eucalyptus. There was no significant competition in the market for the pulpwood. Hence, there was every possibility of a buyer's market for this produce. It was glaring from the data that the cartel of paper industrial lobby had plundered the forest wealth.

As seen from the data, the price of the pulpwood reached its peak during 2008-09. In that year, the price of the industrial input was priced at Rs. 3,099 but the same price fell sharply to Rs. 285 in the year, 2011-12. The net fall in the price was Rs. 2,814. In percentage terms, the fall was 90.80 when the national commission put the blame on Adivasis for not making profit on forests. It recommended the government to link the forestry to the commercial interests to enable the sustainable development of forests. However, in real terms, at the cost of livelihood of Adivasis, the handful industrialists reaped the benefits with the plantations being made with the hard-earned public money. One billion people were paying taxes for the welfare of broad masses. Unfortunately, some of that money was utilised to manufacture raw material to the industries. Those industrialists plundered the forest wealth with the bare minimum cost.

The forest policy 1988 stated, "*As far as possible, a forest-based industry should raise the raw material needed for meeting its own requirements, preferably by establishment of a direct relationship between the factory and*

Table 2. Estimated Plantations

Species (in ha)	*2012-13*	*2013-14*	*2014-15*	*2015-16*	*2016-17*
Eucalyptus (Clonal)	4500	3500	3000	3000	2000
Bamboo	100	100	200	200	200
Teak	10	100	100	100	100
Total:	4610	3700	3300	3300	2300

Source: www.apfdc.aptc.gov.in.

the individuals who can grow the raw material by supporting the individuals with inputs including credit, constant technical advice and finally harvesting and transport services." (*Source:* www.moef.nic.in)

This policy proclamation was twenty-five years old. Even after thirty years of the policy directive, the state forest development corporation was still planning to plant Eucalyptus to cater to the needs of industrial lobby. The on-going details of the plantation could be seen from the data of the Corporation.

APFDC had chalked out a five-year plan for planting industrial raw material. It planned to plant Eucalyptus in 17,000 hectares during the ensuing coming five years. In other words, the Adivasis lost their minimum livelihood in that area. The 1988 policy spoke about the welfare of Adivasis in volumes, but in practice, the corporation did not even bother to heed it.

It is not only the case of pulpwood the corporation had sold not only the pulpwood at cheaper rates to the industrial lobby rather they sold coffee, cashew, bamboo and pepper at throwaway prices. Every year showed deceleration in the price. They sold cashew for Rs. 1, 02,417 per metric ton in 2007-08. The price of the same fell to Rs. 67,066 in 2011-12.The net decrease in the price was Rs. 35,351. In percentage term, the decrease was 34.52. In case of coffee, the percentage of decrease was 12.4. On one hand, the food inflation is spiralling every day. At the same time, the raw material cost of the final products was showing a steep decrease. Both ways, the people were becoming bankrupt. On one hand, with the public money, the industrial lobby was procuring the raw material, and on the other hand, they were selling the final products at an exorbitant price. In other words, people were paying to the lobby indirectly through taxation; they were also paying directly to the industrialist from their pockets through the purchase of food items.

Even the policy framework was unable to stop this plunder. This was not only in case of Andhra Pradesh. The national scenario was also showing the same trend. The expert committee of the Planning Commission gave the data relating to Odisha state. It is reproduced as hereunder.

The expert committee questioned the legality of the contract in the light of 1988 policy. It reads, "*The present arrangement in Orissa not only revives the old contractor system, but is even worse, as at least in the older system there was some transparency and fair plays only the highest bidder could become*

Table 3. Sale of Bamboo to Different Consumers

To Industry	33,60,000 pieces (Roughly at 15 paisa a piece)
Through open auction	27,275 pieces (rupees 10 to 13 a piece)
Sent to other divisions	2,892 pieces
Local sale to cultivators (Tenants)	350 pieces (Rupees 4.30 per piece)
Sale to artisans	Nil

Source: Leasing of degraded Forestlands: page: 27 working group of the planning commission: www.planningcommission.nic.in.

contractors. The order appointing industry as 'raw material procurer' goes to the extent of stating that 'other terms and conditions may be settled in consultation with the industry.' This must be the only case in government where lessees are appointed first and then are left free to lay down their own terms! Probity demands that one advertises and gets the offer of terms from the lessees, before deciding who should get the lease. Therefore, Forest leases in favour of private parties in Orissa are against the Forest Conservation Act. As the permission of the GOI has not been taken for the assignment of bamboo forests to industry, the entire arrangement was unlawful. Officers are taking grave risk of prosecution in being a party to such illegal arrangements". (Emphasis added)

The chairman of the above committee, N.C. Saxena in his paper commented on this with anguish, which read, "*There is no system by which artisans and the landless can get bamboo even at a price, and are thus forced to resort to illegal harvesting. A scheme for artisans should be to a cooperative society for bamboo that had remained a non-starter in Orissa.* (Livelihood Diversification and Non-Timber Forest Products in Orissa: Wider Lessons on the Scope for Policy Change: N.C. Saxena).

This plunder was going unabated for long. Indian forest wealth was being given to industrial lobby at highly subsidised rates. The industrialists were not even bothered to set-off the subsidy in determining the price of the final product. Food and Agricultural Organisation (FAO), has commented about this policy and it reads, "*While in the past, government policies have stimulated growth of forest based industries, supply of raw materials to industry, at below market prices, has resulted in the transfer of resources from government to private industries. It has also encouraged waste and forest degradation. Low raw material prices have also not encouraged private producers to plant for industrial uses. The pressure to meet raw material needs to industry has often led to replacement of natural forests by monoculture plantations, thus alienating local communities depending upon multiple products generated by mixed forests.*(*Source:* Asia-Pacific forestry sector outlook study: working paper series, working paper no: apfsos/wp/26:in-depth country study – India: page 45: M.F. Ahmed, former inspector general of forests).

The policy envisaged in 1988, at least on paper, recognised the need of community based development and tried to follow the joint forest management policy in principle. It had a World Bank directive too. World Bank strongly criticised the forest policies of Indian government and colonial governments. In the line of the implementation of the 1988 forest policy, the stage was set for community based forestry projects and social forestry projects. The World Bank extends loans for this purpose. In Andhra Pradesh, it sanctioned two such projects. In the words of World Bank, *"The project will be implemented in 14 of the poorest districts of Andhra Pradesh, and will cover 3.86 million hectares of forest land. It follows the first AP Forestry Project (1994-2000) which was successful in bringing 0.85 million hectares of forests under the joint management of the State forest department and forest communities. The 14 districts to be covered in this new project are Adilabad, Nizamabad, Mahabubnagar, Medak, Khammam, Warangal, Karimnagar, East Godavari, Visakhapatnam, Vizianagaram, Srikakulam, Chittoor, Cuddapah and Nellore."* (Document of the world Bank: Report Number: 24184-N, June 19, 2002).

The micro level survey on this project has made remarked, *"In Chapariguda Village, Srikakulam District, for example, one RAP implementation under which an NGO had allegedly unjustly collected money from 18 Sávara families promising them that through such payment, they would get benefits under the RAP scheme.The villagers have not seen the NGO staff person for 11 months and have no information since then about whether or not their village has been included in the compensation scheme by the Andhra Pradesh Forest Department (APFD)."* (*Source:* India: World Bank project goes from bad to worse: prepared jointly by "Samata" a voluntary organisation and "forest people programme" based in U.K).

In fact, in these projects too, the plantations that were useful to industrial needs planted. People's need-based plantations were ignored. At the most, the Adivasis were used for planting the plantations as wageworkers. In other words, the policy supplied a reliable wage labour along with the industrial wood to the industrial lobby.

In 1980, the government passed an Act for the preservation of forests by incorporating stringent measures in that act. However, the diversion of forest land was being ignored unabatedly. The forest and wild life statistics, 2004 showed that there was no constraint on this diversion. During the year 1980, the forest land diversion was nil. During1980-2004, in a span of twenty-four years, the total land diverted to other needs was 9,54,839 hectares. At the same time, during 1947 -1979, in a span of 32 years, the diverted land was 43, 28, 000 hectares.

To put into brief, for a period of 94 years from 1894 to 1988, the successive rulers had considered Adivasis as the destructors of the forests. They believed the forests as suppliers of industrial raw material. In this process, many violent and non-violent agitations erupted in the green belt. Due to these agitations, green belt turned red with the blood of the sons of the forests. To enumerate the reasons for the unrest, the successive governments appointed number of commissions. They produced voluminous reports and recommended for better measures for the welfare of Adivasis. Except 1952 policy and National Commission on Agricultural, 1976 the remaining all have tried their best to give a positive solution to the plight of Adivasis. However, it appeared that no such recommendations yielded any result.

Forests in Srikakulam

The natural beauty was described in Vizagapatam district manual. It read, *"The chain of Ghauts, which extended in a line parallel to the sea coast from Mahanadi River to Godavari, is carried through this district. The higher peaks of this range reach an elevation of more than 5,000 feet above the sea: the eastern and western slopes are clothed with tall tree jungles, while the bamboo grows luxuriantly in the valleys."* (*Source:* A manual of the Vizagapatam District in Madras presidency: page: 2: D.F. Carmichael, M.C.S, Collector, Ganjam District)

In Telugu films the villain always warns the honest officer to make a transfer to forests of Srikakulam district. The situation had a reality until the advent of the colonial rule. In fact, the then Vizagapatam district had a dense forest and mountains. It is the heart of rich biodiversity. However, all those were a past glory. The forest cover had almost disappeared.

The Gazetteer of Srikakulam district reads, "The land in the plains, embedded with water ponds and engrossed with rivers and perennial streams, bearing veritable trees either in single or in clumps here and there, leads one to believe that they once bore extensive forest. With the advancement of civilisation and increase in the population, these were increasingly subjected to clearance. On the other hand, clearance of forests was encouraged for bringing the area into cultivation and establishing towns and villages with communication facilities. Large scale devastation of forest areas appeared to have been started with the laying of Madras-Calcutta railway line during A.D.1860-70 and of Vizianagaram Railway line during 1930-33." (Andhra Pradesh district gazetteer, Srikakulam: page: 11 Dr. N. Rameshan I.A.S.).

This was the beginning of the end of forests regime in Srikakulam district. The forest cover was dwindling day by day in this district. The data from the district handbooks disclosed this fact.

As seen from this table, in the year 1977, the entire area of the forest was recorded as 9, 09,959 acres and the percentage of forest was 37.27. By 1990, it is decreased to 3,58,817.04 acres which registered, a net decrease of 5,45,132 acres. The percentage of reduction in a period of 13 years is 59.90. Again in a span of twenty years, in 2010 the area under the forest is increased marginally to 4,00,330.60 acres. The overall increase show in the area is 41,513.20 acres. The percentage of increase is 11.56 only.

Table 4. Forest Cover in Srikakulam District (in Acres)

Year	*Total Geographical Area*	*Forest*	*Barren and un-cultivated land*	*Percentage of Forest Land*	*Percentage of Barren and un-cultivated Land*
1977	2425366	9,03,959.0	846126.8	37.27	34.88
1990	2425366	3,58,817.4	280887.7	14.79	11.58
2010	2425366	4,00,330.6	244612.6	16.50	10.08

Source: Compiled from various district handbooks.

Forest survey of India used to publish a survey report for every two years. It noted about the state of forests in present Srikakulam district in a tabular form. As per the data of the table, *"There is no dense forest area in this district. Moderate dense forest area is extended in 108 square kilometres. Open forest area is extended in 508 Square kilometres."* [*Source:* India state of forests report 2011 page: 93]

Record of Forest Right: Land to Adivasis

Shri A.K. Chugh, Secretary (Tribal Affairs) stated *"However, high rate of rejection of claims and very low receipt of community claims were matters of serious concerns"*. He also reminded the participants, *"the State/UT Governments now need to concentrate on convergence of developmental programmes/schemes for raising the income levels of the title holders to bring about visible improvement in their quality of life."* (*Source:* Minutes of the meeting of State secretaries/commissioners of Tribal welfare dated 07/04/2011 New Delhi).

The government brought an Act to confer rights on the forest lands to those Adivasis who occupied before 1980. In other words, the activity made after that base year was invalid, and the government would not consider conferring the titles. "In this district, department received 27,584 applications for regularisation. The department, for various reasons, rejected 3,556 applications involving 9,971.07 acres. At the same time, the department conferred titles in 24,028 cases with land involving 54, 744.95 acres." [*Source:* reply to the question under RTI Act]

Reservations to Scheduled Tribes

After the proclamation of British forest policy 1894, Adivasis lost their rights. Unrest prevailed in the tribal tracts and the British were forced to take some welfare measures. In the 1935 Act, they provided some constitutional safeguards to this vulnerable section. During the post-independence too, the constitution guaranteed the reservations and welfare measures.

"The term 'Scheduled Tribes first appeared in the Constitution of India. Article 366 (25) defined scheduled tribes as "such tribes or tribal communities or parts of or groups within such tribes or tribal communities as are deemed under Article 342 to be Scheduled Tribes for the purposes of this constitution." (*Source:* tribal.nic.in: Ministry of Tribals)

However, the constitution did not give the definition to add a group into the list. Broadly, it took some measures to recognise a group as scheduled tribe. It reads, *"The criterion followed for specification of a community, as scheduled tribes are the indications of primitive traits, distinctive culture, geographical isolation, shyness of contact with the community at large besides backwardness. This criterion is not spelt out in the Constitution but has become well established. It subsumes the definitions contained in 1931 census, the reports of first Backward Classes Commission 1955, the Advisory Committee (Kalelkar), on Revision of SC/ST lists (Lokur Committee)"* (*Source:* tribal.nic.in: Ministry of tribals).

Based on these characteristics, the then Madras presidency recognised forty tribes as Scheduled Tribes.The then Hyderabad State recognised nine tribes as scheduled tribes. After the formation of Andhra Pradesh state on a linguistic basis, an amendment to scheduled tribes recognised 23 tribes as scheduled tribes in the entire state. It recognised three tribes on the basis of their residence. In the year 1976, with an amendment, the government added seven more tribes into the list. Again, the two more tribes were added to the list in 2002. Hence, the total recognised scheduled tribes in the state stood at 35.

Demography: 35 recognised Scheduled Tribes are living in Andhra Pradesh. The population of Adivasis was steadily rising. The changing pattern in the population in the last four censuses can be seen from the Table.

As seen from the Table, the Adivasi population was almost doubled during 1971-81. In the year 1977, seven categories of Adivasis were included in Schedule Tribes list, this being one of the reasons for the increase in the population. However, the major reason for the swelling of Adivasi population has its origin in the inclusion of Lambadas/sugaliin the list in 1956. They had no reservation in adjacent states. Hence, these people migrated to this state in a big way. The changing pattern in the population of Lambadascanbe seen from this Table.

Table 5. Changing Pattern of Adivasi Population in Andhra Pradesh

Sl. No.	*Year of the Census*	*Total Population*	*Adivasi (S.T) Population*	*Percent-age of Adivasis*
1.	1971	4,35,20,708	16,57,657	3.81
2.	1981	5,35,49,673	31,71,001	5.93
3.	1991	6,65,08,008	41,99,481	6.31
4.	2001	7,62,10,007	50,24,104	6.59
5.	2011	8,45,65,533	59,18,073	7.00

Source: Primary census abstracts.

Table 6 shows the alarming rate of increase in the Lambadi population. In the year 1961, their population was below one lakh, but the population numbers reached almost 21 lakhs during 2001. When compared with 1961, the net increase in their population was 19,81,773. The percentage of increase in their population was 2060.01. Lately, in Andhra Pradesh, the remaining tribes were fighting against this influx since Lambadas enjoyed the major portion of the reservations.

Table 6. Changing Pattern Lambada Population in Andhra Pradesh

Sl. No.	*Census year*	*Population of Lambadas/Sugali*	*Percentage of Increase*
1.	1961	96,174	
2.	1971	1,32,646	37.92
3.	1981	11,58,342	772.38
4.	1991	16,41,897	41.74
5.	2001	20,77,947	26.55

Source: Basic statistics: www.aptribes.nic.in.

Adivasi Population in Srikakulam District

Though there were 35 tribes in this state, three tribes were prominent in number in this district. They are Savara, Jatapu, and Kondadoras. Apart from these, Gadaba, Mali, Mannedoras, and Mookadora were also living in this district in a small number. The government had recognised some tribes as primitive tribes. In this district, Sávara and Gadaba were classified as primitive tribal groups. To examine the actual trends of Adivasi population, there was a need to examine the changing pattern in the combined Srikakulam district (before the division of the district), present Srikakulam district and the carved out area of the combined district.

Prior to the division of this district, Adivasi population was concentrated in Parvatipuram, Saluru, Patapatnam and Palkonda Taluks. In this division, the first two taluks were transferred to Vizianagaram district. In the Srikakulam district, the Adivasi population was 2,12,459 during the year 1971. This population showed an increasing trend reaching 3,71,884 in 2011 census. In percentage terms, it was increased from 8.20 per cent to 9.64 per cent.

Table 7. Adivasi Population in Srikakulam District

Sl. No.	*Year*	*Srikakulam District Population*	*ST Population*	*Percentage of ST*
1.	1971	2589991	212459	8.20
2.	1981	2875570	240937	8.38
3.	1991	3372390	298302	8.85
4.	2001	3658846	340776	9.31
5.	2011	3859235	372227	9.64

Source: Primary census abstracts.

Table 8. Adivasi Population in Present Srikakulam District

Sl. No.	Year	Total Population in Present Srikakulam	Adivasi Population in Present Srikakulam	Percentage of Adivasi Population
1.	1971	1536873	93086	6.06
2.	1981	1959510	105142	5.37
3.	1991	2317915	134067	5.78
4.	2001	2537593	151249	5.96
5.	2011	2703114	166118	6.14

Source: Primary census abstracts.

The trend in the population of present Srikakulam, showed that after this division, the Adivasi population had little share in this district. During 1971, the population of Adivasis was 93,086. It increased to 1,66,118 in 2011 census. In the percentage terms, the share of Adivasis fell from 6.06 in 1971 to 5.96 in 2001 census and increased to 6.14 per cent in 2011 census.

Table 9. Adivasi Population in the Carved Out Area (Presently in Vizianagaram District)

	Year	Total Population Carved out Area	Adivasi Population in Carved out Area	Percentage of Adivasi Population
1.	1971	1053118	119373	11.34
2.	1981	916218	135795	14.82
3.	1991	1040816	164235	15.78
4.	2001	1121253	189527	16.90
5.	2011	1156121	206109	17.82

Source: Primary census abstracts.

In the *carved out area,* the Adivasi population was 1,19,373 in the year 1971. This was increased to 1,89,527 in the year 2001 census. The share of Adivasis in that area was 11.34 in the year 1971. In 2011 census, the share of Adivasis had gone up to 17.82.

Due to constant revolts in the colonial period, the British government had declared some area in this district as partially excluded area. Adivasis had protective rights in that area. The arrangement is continuing and those areas are now called Scheduled areas. In this area, at least the Adivasi people had constitutional rights and they have the possibility to fight against the violations.

Trends of the Adivasi Population

In the present Srikakulam district, the Adivasi population is concentrated in seven Mandals namely Saravakota, Meliaputti, Seetampeta, Bhamini, Kothuru, Kanchili and Mandasa. The population of Adivasis as per 2011 census was 1,10,415 in these Mandals. In percentage terms, it was 66.47. In other words, 66.47 per cent of Adivasis are dwelling in seven Mandals and remaining 33.53 are scattered in thirty-one Mandals. When compared with the present district population to population of Adivasis of the Mandals, Seetampeta Mandal had 1.88 per cent. However, no other Mandal had a competing figure of Adivasis when compared with the present Srikakulam district.

In Seetampeta Mandal, the tribals had a share of 90.87 per cent in the population of the Mandal. Meliaputti followed this Mandal with a percentage of 28.27.

In Gummalakshmipuram Mandal, the tribals had a share of 86.69 per cent in the population of the Mandal. Kurupam followed with a percentage of 71.98. In Saluru, Pachipenta, Komarada Mandals, Adivasi's share was in the slab of 25 per cent to 50 per cent. In Jiyyammavalasa, Makkuva Mandals, Adivasi's share was in the slab of 20 per cent to 25 per cent.

In the present Vizianagaram district the total Adivasi population is 2,35,556. The carved out area consists of 2,05,566. Thus, the carved out area has 87.31 per cent of adivasi population in the present Vizianagaram district. G.L. Puram, Kurupam and Saluru have 1.85,1.48, and 1.43 per cent of share in the total population of the district respectively.

As seen from this data, it was clear that the Adivasi population was concentrated in the carved out areas of the Srikakulam District.

Adivasis and the Land

Forest is the indispensable resource of the Adivasis and the following resource for their livelihood is land. As the policies almost deprived them of using forests, the pressure on the land had increased tremendously in the Adivasi areas. An important thing to note was that major area in their dwelling places was under the control of the government in the name of reserved forest area. In other words, state was the biggest landowner in those areas. Usufructuary rights were denied on that land. Land alienation was a general feature in the Adivasi areas. Even the protected areas were also not an exemption to this. There are Acts in vogue, which is intended to curb the alienation, but it is continuing unabated in the tribal tracts.

In fact, Adivasis had not recognised the need of legal titles on the land. They thought that the cultivation of the land itself was a right on the land. They were even unaware of the man-made Acts. In the modern interpretation, illiteracy in terms of the social process, the absence of formal individual property rights was the dual reasons for their passive attitude for recording their rights over the land. Taking the cue, the people from plain areas could create "papers" on the land and large chunks of land alienated legally.

Even in some areas, the titles on the land had not given any protection to their rights. In many ways, the land grabbers grabbed the land from Adivasis. As seen from many survey and reports, the land alienation is continuous in nature.

The government of Andhra Pradesh expressed deep concern on this issue in the budget speech of 1971-72. It thought of remedial measures for this. It read, *"Another notable feature is the effective implementation of the protective legislation for the Scheduled areas. Various protective measures including the Land Transfer Regulation which prohibits the alienation of land to non-tribals; the enactment of similar protective legislation for Scheduled Tribes outside the Scheduled areas as recommended by the Debar Commission is under the active consideration of the Government".* (*Source:* the budget speech of 1971-72)

This commitment was forty years old. However, many agitations and government reports could not bring that promise into reality.

During 1959-70, this district encountered severe agitations in the tribal tracts. During 1959-67, the movement broadly went off peacefully though there were some provocative actions from the local landlords and revenue machinery. This movement stressed the contents of the budget speech only. The movement demanded the implementation of the Acts in existence and for inclusion of all the tribals dominated into the Vth schedule. However, violence erupted in the movement, and this tribal heartland was wetted with their warm blood once again.

In fact, the budget speech spoke about for various safety provisions. It reads, *"The Debt Relief Regulation under which the existing debts have been scaled down to the level of the principal; extinguishing the interest element altogether and providing for a moratorium of two years on the repayment of the scaled down debts; the abolition of the Muttadari system; the regulation of money lending in tribal areas, etc., have been implemented with a special emphasis, with the assistance of staff exclusively charged with this task. The amendment to the Land Transfer Regulation to permit the mortgage of the lands in favour of Cooperative Societies and Commercial Banks is awaiting the approval of the President."* (Budget speech 1971-72).

In fact, such Acts already exist on the papers implementation was pending due to which, the tribal land alienation was becoming a regular feature in the protected and non-protected areas.

Land Alienation in Scheduled Areas

Two Integrated Tribal Development Agencies (shortly I.T.D.A.) are functioning in this district with one having its headquarter at Parvatipuram, and the other at Seetampeta. The Table indicates the extent of Tribal area and

Table 10. Scheduled Villages in the Tribal Tracts

Sl. No.	*ITDA*	*Area in sq.kms.*	*No. of Scheduled Villages*	*No. of Non-Scheduled Villages*	*Total Villages*
1.	Seetampeta	1289.32	108	240	348
2.	Parvatipuram	1740.98	302	181	483

Source: Basic statistics: www.aptribes.nic.in

the Adivasis dwelling in this area and the area covered under protected legislation.

In the I.T.D.A. Seetampeta, there were 348 total Adivasi villages. Out of those, only 108 villages were covered under this Act. These villages were spread under Seetampeta Mandal. No other Mandal was covered under the Acts. In population terms, in the *present Srikakulam district* out of 1,51,249 Adivasis, only 33,935 persons were under the umbrella of protective legislation. Remaining 1,17, 314 persons were out of the ambit. Hence, the applicable population was in percentage terms stood at 22.43. 3/4th of the Adivasi population succumbed to the pressure of outsiders.

In the I.T.D.A. Parvatipuram, there were total of 483 Adivasi villages. Out of those, only 181 villages were covered under these Acts. These villages were spread across six Mandals. In population terms, in the *carved out area of Srikakulam district,* out of 1,89,527 Adivasis, only 88,828 persons were under the umbrella of protective legislation. Remaining 1,00,699 persons were out of the ambit. Hence, the applicable population in percentage terms stood at 46.86. More than half of the Adivasi population succumbed to the pressure of outsiders.

This situation led to the alienation of land in tribal tracts in general and particular in non-scheduled areas. The ground level study and the official reports also disclosed this fact.

The Government of Andhra Pradesh released strategy paper namely "Strategy Paper on Welfare of Scheduled Caste and Scheduled Tribe Population" in 2003. The paper indicated the land alienation and restoration particulars of the land. It reads, "*69,119 cases have been booked covering an extent of 3,40,491 acres of land. Out of 59,849 cases, which were disposed of, 27,461 cases went in favour of tribals restoring 94,823 acres of land to the tribal.*

The tribal protection Acts are age old. The first such Act was passed during 1917. During the year 1959, another Act was proclaimed for safeguarding the Adivasi lands. One more amendment had come to give some more security in 1970 to this Act. Despite all these Acts, the alienation wás unabated. As seen from the above cases, still 2 45,668 acres were in the hands of non-tribals. In other words, 72.15 per cent of tribal land was in the hands of non-tribals. It is the case of scheduled areas. As seen from this data, out of 59,849 cases, only 27,461 cases were being settled in favour of Adivasis. It meant that only 45 per cent cases went in favour of Adivasis; in other words, 55 per cent of cases went in favour of Non-tribals. Even the ratio figures indicated that the non–tribal could establish legal rights on 1,10,469 acres. The paper indicated only the figure of the cases but not gave the figure of the land particulars that went in favour of non-tribals. This situation clearly indicated that in the non-scheduled areas, it was just impossible to keep the land in the hands of Adivasis.

In Srikakulam district too, the alienation went unabated even in the protected areas. The table indicates the official data on the land alienation. As per the RTI Act, the officials of I.T.D. A. have supplied this information.

Table 11. Land Alienation in Srikakulam Scheduled Areas

Sl. No.	*ITDA*	*Cases Booked*	*Total Land Involved (in Acres)*	*Cases Settled in Favour of Tribes*	*Land Involved*	*Land Handed Over in Cases*	*Land Handed Over*
1.	Seetampeta	462	1100.93	302	564.5	252	529.27
2.	Parvatipuram	1370	7551.23	984	5685.67	850	5498.05

Source: Reply under RTI Act.

This table also supports the state data. In Seetampeta ITDA area, the total land in controversy was 1100.93 acres. Out of these, only 564.50 acres had gone in favour of Adivasis. Even in that case too, 529.27 acres were restored. In other words, while the pendency was almost zero, the remaining land of 536.43 acres was officially legalised in favour of non-tribal.

In the Parvatipuram ITDA area, the total land in dispute was 7551.23 acres. Out of these, only 5685.67 acres went in favour of Adivasis. Even in that case too, 5498.05 acres were restored. Since, the pendency was almost zero, the remaining land of 1865.56 acres were officially legalised in favour of non-tribal.

Field Level Observations

In the surveyed villages, eight villages were Scheduled villages and 35 villages Non-scheduled villages. Mostly no village was an exception for the land alienation. There was a scope to enumerate some of the examples here.

These eight villages were spread across Gummalakshmipuram and Kurupam Mandals. Out of these eight villages - Lankajodu, Valasaballeru are in Kurupam Mandal and Pedakharja is in Gummalakshmipuram Mandal. These three villages played a crucial role in Srikakulam Tribal revolt where by mostly, the entire population of these villages was imprisoned. The major source of their participation had its roots in the land alienation and oppression of the landlord-trader combine.

In the words of Arika Gumpaswamy, a Jatapu and leader of tribal movement, "Though these villages are in the purview of scheduled areas, almost our total lands were alienated. All our land were alienated to four Sondi (by profession these are liquor traders) families. We conducted peaceful agitations for a long period. It had been turned violent because of the landlords. Most of the villagers were in prison for a long period. In this course, the landlords fled from the village. Our association took over all the land and we carried out the cultivation in a co-operative way. Later the state leaders Tarimela Nagireddy and D. Venkateswara Rao directed us to distribute the lands among the families. We carried out the same and even later, we kept our lands with us. After that distribution, we are conducting individual farming".

Pedakharja has a different example. In the words of Raguramulu, a serious participant of the revolt "we lost all our lands to the traders. While all the villagers were in prison, the government officers surveyed all the lands and distributed the land equally to all the families. Now we are cultivating it".

These two villages are splendid examples for land alienation and restoration of the lands. Whereas in the non-scheduled villages most of the land had gone out of the hands of the tribals, and there was no legal opportunity for the restoration of the land. In the absence of legal rights, in one of the villages, Adivasis fought for the land rights and the land is under their possession.

Bobbili is one of the advanced towns in the district. In and around 10 kilometres to this town, there are six non-scheduled tribal villages while even now there is no access to these villages. One has to go on foot to these villages. Bobbili town is well connected to the world with railway lines and roads well connected to other areas, near and far. However, the inaccessibility too has not prevented the land alienation with almost all the lands in these villages alienated.

Chitrakotaboddavalas is a Panchayat in Bobbili Mandal. This village has six Adivasi hamlets which are Nimmalapadu, Chellivalsa, Koyyakundavalasa, Simidiguddivalasa, Kothavalasa and Keshivalasa. In the first two villages, Adivasis had lands though they were alienated of late. Adivasis of Nimmalapadu sold their lands to the peasantry of Butchempeta village long back and now they sold their lands to the Kamma settlers, who belong to Krishna and Godavari districts. Now they have leased out the lands to Adivasis.

A former member of the legislative assembly bought the lands of Chellivalsa village, and now there are mango groves in those lands.

There was an interesting incident about the land alienation in Madavalasa village. As per the villagers, "they had 100 acres of land. This is a hamlet of Kesali village. Their lands were alienated long ago to Gopalasetti Sriramulu, Dharmarao and Venkataswamy traders of Kesali village. In the early 70s, the then collector, B.N. Yugandhar visited this village, asked the villagers to occupy the lands, and promised them of restoring the lands. The Adivasis told Sri Yugandhar about the principles of honesty and rejected the offer. Sri Yugandhar, in a woebegone voice told them that even the god could not save them and returned. However, till recently, they were the tenants of the land. To conduct the cultivation they took loans from the same landowner and they used to give the wholecrop in repayment of the loan."

In other words, without any expenditure, almost for the last 60 years, the traders expropriated the labour of these Adivasis. The salvation for these Adivasis came in the shape of Peddagedda reservoir. The government built a reservoir at Madavalasa with all these lands getting inundated. Hence, they vacated the villages and settled in the newly built village. Thus, the cultivation and the bonded labour came to an end. Interestingly, many political parties prominently left organised agitations for enhancement of compensation for the lands. The government had given one lakh and above to these fields. Hence, the squeezers could takealmost Rs. one crore because of this and even a single rupee did not reach these Adivasis. Another interesting feature was that some procured land was still useful to carry out cultivation. The Adivasis of Kodikallavalasa were trying to cultivate the land since those lands belonged to Government and they had the right to use the Government land for their livelihood purpose. However, all parties including the Left withdrew from the scene with nobody willing to raise a voice to the Adivasis even for their genuine purpose.

Kurukuti is a village in Saluru Mandal. As per the Adivasis of the village, "all the land belonged to hill zamindars of the village. A Kshatriya of Godavari district settled in the village, used the innocence of the Hill zamindar and occupied all the lands. Communist Party of India (C.P.I.) staged a prolonged agitation on this, and they could occupy the lands. Now the Adivasis are cultivating the lands. In this process, the non-tribals also participated, and the Party had given lands to the non-tribals".

Dabaru is a village in Meliaputti Mandal wherein the Adivasis belonged to Sávara tribe with all the lands belonging to a Kalinga landlord. His name was Sampatirao Yogeswar Rao. He did the cultivation under his control for some time. After that, the Adivaṣi cultivated the land under tenancy. As usual, the crop was forfeited every year as interest on the loan. Later, he sold all the land to the peasantry of nearby villages. Under the assignment Act, the government distributed 0.90 acres to 29 Adivasi families, but cultivable land was only 0.37 acres in 0.90 acres. In this process, neither the tenancy Acts nor the land reform Acts could serve the purpose.

Tumukonda Ramchandrapuram is another village in the same Mandal where "the government distributed two acres each to the Adivasi families in 1975. However, the land was mountainous and hence it was not possible to cultivate. Again, the government allotted one acre each. We are cultivating the land even now. In a fire accident, all the land titles were burnt and despite many efforts, the government was not issuing duplicate titles. Hence, the land development schemes and the institutional credit were not available to us."

Land alienation was a common factor in every non-scheduled village.

Land Holding Pattern of Adivasis in the District

In the year 1987, as seen from this table, 40,905 land holding families had land. They possessed 1,10,432.20 acres. In the year 2005, this number increased to 62,311, and the land possessed was 1,34,614.10 acres. The increase in the land holding families were 21,406 whereas the increase in the land was 24,181.90 acres. It clearly implied that fragmentation was instrumental in the increase of land holding families rather than re-distribution of lands.

As analysed category wise, in the year 1987, marginal and small landholders had a total of 35,893 in number. In percentage terms, they were 87.74. The land under their possession was 52.78. Hence, it was clear that 87 per cent of the land holding families have survived on 53 per cent of the land.

By 2005, marginal and small landholders were 56,680 in number. In percentage terms, they were 90.96.In percentage terms; the land under their

Table 12. Land Holding Pattern of Tribes in Srikakulam District

Year	Marginal (<2.46 acres		Small (2.47 - 4.92 acres)		Semi Medium (4.93-9.87 acres)		Medium (9.88 - 24.7 acres)		Large (> 24.71 acres)		Total all Classes	
	No	Area	No	Area	No	Area	No	Area	No	Area	No	Area
1987	28340	31483	7553	26813.6	4451	40172.2	387	5527.91	174	6435.44	40905	110432.15
1990	38338	41387.9	10255	35019.7	5788	36618.9	376	5087.26	139	4809.67	54896	122923.43
2001	41150	43256.6	11002	36915.7	4498	29207.6	1292	18053.2	98	3596.52	58040	131029.62
2005	44476	47559.9	12204	41244.12	3154	22363.1	2407	21198.81	70	2248.12	62311	134614.1
2011	52116	99927.6	13580	77166.85	4833	46737.9	1086	20404.67	66	2999.87	71951	247237.00

Source: District handbook of statistics and agcensus.nic.in.

Table 13. Land Holding Pattern in Carved out Area

Year	Marginal (<2.46 acres)		Small (2.47 - 4.92 acres)		Semi Medium (4.93-9.87 acres)		Medium (9.88 - 24.7 acres)		Large (> 24.71 acres)		Total all Classes	
	No	Area	No	Area	No	Area	No	Area	No	Area	No	Area
1990	18356	21625	5910	20431			4082	35556	111	3796	28459	81408
2001	20218	21756.24	6194	20907.54	2933	19296.24	1018	14213.18	70	2297.64	30,433	78470.8
2005	22151	24269.84	6920	23601.29	2885	18882.89	831	11318.73	57	1818.92	32844	79891.7
2011	24492	27278.2	7461	25219.92	3131	20516.4	771	10280.34	46	148092	35901	84775.78

Source: District handbooks and agcensus.nic.in.

possession was 65.96. Hence, it was clear that 90.96 per cent of the land holding families were surviving on 65.96 per cent of the land.

Even the National Commission of Agriculture 1976 stated "if even two Ha per family which may turn out to be uneconomic in the hilly terrain". In light of the above, 90.96 per cent of Adivasis were dwelling on uneconomic land holdings. In Parvatipuram Revenue Division, the government assigned 26,437.91 acres of land to Adivasis from 1969 to date. The Planning Commission reports, independent research reports and the current ground level study confirm that the assigned lands were not worth enough to cultivate. Under the ROFR Act, the government conferred the titles on the occupied lands of Adivasis. In other words, the land already in possession was legalised but as statistics revealed, the Land was not increased.

Landholding Structure in Carved out Area

As seen from the population terms, the carved out area has more Adivasi population than the present geographic part of Srikakulam district. Comparatively it has more protected area. The changing pattern of land holding pattern is depicted in a tabular form.

In the year 1990, as seen from this table, 28,459 landholding families had land admeasuring 81,438 acres. In the year 2005, their number increased to 32,844, and the land held was 79,891.70 acres. The increase in the landholding families were 4,385 whereas the decrease in the land was 1,546.30 acres. It clearly implied that fragmentation was instrumental in increasing landholding families rather than re-distribution of lands.

As analysed category wise, in the year 1990, marginal and small landholders had a total of 24,266 in number. In percentage terms, they were 85.26. The land under their possession was 51.64. Hence, it was clear that 85 per cent of the land holding families were surviving on 51.64 per cent of the land.

By 2005, the marginal and small landholders had 29,071 in number. In percentage terms, they were 88.51.The land under their possession was 59.92 Hence it was clear that 88.51 per cent of the land holding families were surviving on 59.92 per cent of the land.

By the turn of 2011, the marginal and small peasants further increased to 31,953. Out of this, marginal peasantry stood at 24,492 and constituted 68 per cent of the whole of the peasantry and small peasantry stood at 20.7. In other words, 88.7 per cent of peasantry is getting their "livelihood" on 61 per cent of land. It is very painful to note that 68 per cent of marginal peasantry is eking their livelihood on a mere 32.17 per cent of land.

Micro-level Analysis of Land-holding Pattern in two Mandals of Present Srikakulam District

In the present Srikakulam district, only Seetampeta Mandal has a protected area. Hence, it is appropriate to observe the landholding pattern of Adivasis of this Mandal. As already said, 108 villages were under the cover of protective legislation. Before analysing the landholding pattern, the pattern of Adivasi population can be seen from this table.

Table 14. Trends of ST Population of Seetampeta Mandal

Census Year	*Adivasi Population*	*Total Population*	*Percentage of Tribal Population*
1981	29098	32080	90.70
1991	40189	44883	89.54
2001	45741	52282	87.49
2011	50747	55848	90.87

Source: Compiled from Primary census abstracts.

As seen from this table it was clear that this Mandal belonged to Adivasis. In 1981 census, the Adivasi population was 29,098 and it went up to 45,741 in 2001 census. However, in percentage terms there was a drop from 90.70 per cent in 1981 to 87.49 per cent in 2001 census. However, the current census has shown that the Percentage of Adivasis is increased to 90.87.

As seen from this data in the year 1991, total landholdings stood at 9,421 and those are dropped to 9,076 in 2005, and further those are increased to 14,502 in 2011. The land also scaled down during 1991-2005, and it recorded a growth in 2011. However in this Mandal too, the marginal and small landholdings occupied a lion's share - 88.43 per cent in 1991 *vis-a-vis* 91.82 in 2011. Here is another interesting thing can be observed from the net sown trends of this Mandal.

Table 15: Landholding Pattern in Seetampeta Mandal

Year	*Holdings*	*Acres*	*Percentage of Marginal*	*Percentage of Small*
1991	9421	20894.88	71.27	17.16
2001	9030	20344.2	69.76	19.68
2005	9076	19962.45	70.15	19.73
2011	14502	32221.21	69.61	22.21

Source: Compiled from District Handbooks, agcensus.nic.in and Reply to RTI.

Table 16. Trends in Net Sown Area of Seetampeta Mandal

Year	*Land with Tribals*	*Net Sown Area in Mandal*	*Percentage of Net sown Area*	*Estimated Land that is Sown by Tribes in Seetampeta Mandal*
1991	20894.88	18988	25.3	5286.40
2001	20344.2	21101.88	28.3	5757.41
2005	19962.45	21374.94	28.7	5729.22
2011	32221.21	17160.96	23	7410.88

Source: Compiled from District handbooks.

As seen from this Table, the net sown area was drastically decreased from 21,374.94 acres to 17,160.96 Acres during 2011. At the same time, the land under Adivasis had increased from 19,962.45 acres to 32,221.21 acres. This Mandal registered a net sown area at 23 per cent only. If the same percentage was applied to Adivasi landholdings, they could cultivate only 7,410.88 acres. In other words, though they possessed land, the efforts to bring the terrain under cultivation were not successful. At the same time, it must be noted that only because of the protective legislation; at least they could retain the land though it was not useful for cultivation.

Table 17. Trends of Adivasi Population in Meliaputti Mandal

Census Year	*Adivasi Population*	*Total Population*	*Percentage of Tribal Population*
1981	9464	44109	21.46
1991	12155	48990	24.81
2001	13435	50490	26.61
2011	14908	52737	28.27

Source: Compiled from Primary census abstracts.

The pessimistic statement about retaining the land was proved when the trends were observed from Meliaputti Mandal, which had second largest Adivasi population in the Srikakulam after Seetampeta.

In 1981 census, theÅdivasi population was 9,464, which were increased to 13,435 in 2001 census. In percentage terms, the increase raised from 21.46 per cent in 1981 to 26.61 per cent in 2001 census. The current round of Census has shown that the percentage of population is increased to 28.27. Though 1/4th of the population was Adivasis and considerable arêas were Adivasi-dominated, not a single village was declared a scheduled area. Hence, the Adivasis were losing their foothold on the land as visible from the table.

Table 18. Landholding Pattern in Meliaputti Mandal

Year	*Land Holdings*	*Acres*	*Percentage of Marginal*	*Percentage of Small*	*Percentage of Other Land Holdings*
1991	3366	5058.96	82.71	12.54	4.75
2001	3153	4966.74	82.52	13.26	4.22
2005	3410	5295.52	82.55	13.72	3.72
2011	3061	4848.23	82.26	13.62	4.12

Source: Compiled from District Handbooks, agcensus.nic.in and Reply to RTI.

As seen from this data, during the year 1991, the total landholdings stood at 3,366, which were dropped, to 3,061 in 2011. All these census rounds were consistently showing a decreasing trend in the holdings. The land too scaled

Table 19. Trends in Net Sown Area of Meliaputti Mandal

Year	*Land with tribes*	*Total land available for cultivation*	*Net sown area*	*Percentage of net sown area*	*Estimated land that is sown by tribes*
1991	5058.96	22115.91	18688	31.56	1596.53
2001	4966.74	21404.46	17377.4	29.35	1457.50
2005	5295.52	21501	15485.7	26.15	1384.82
2011	4848.23	20998.11	13758.78	23.23	1126.24

Source: Compiled from district Handbooks.

down during all these years. During 2005 and 2011, the net alienation of the land was 447.29 acres. In this Mandal too, the marginal and small land holdings accounted for a lion's share at 95.25 per cent in 1991, which further went up to 95.88 in 2011.

As seen from this table, the net sown area had drastically decreased from 18,688 acres to 13,758.78 acres in 2011. At the same time, the land under Adivasis had decreased. This Mandal registered a net sown area at 23.23 per cent only. In fact, the net sown area was also showing a continuous declining trend. During the year 1991, the percentage of net sown area was shown as 31.56. If the same percentage was applied to Adivasi landholdings, they could have cultivated only 1596.53 acres in 1991. In 2011, they could cultivate only 1126.24 acres. In fact, the land under their possession was meagre. Even, that land also had not been cultivated mainly because of crunch in the water sources. In a meagre 1,848 acres, they could cultivate an estimated 1126.24 acres.

In fact, the estimations may be incorrect since generally, the land under the possession of Adivasis was hilly tracts. In real terms, the cultivation figures may be lower.

Micro-level Analysis of Landholding Pattern in two Mandals of Carved out Area

Unlike Seetampeta Mandal, the entire Gummalakshmipuram Mandal barring three villages was a scheduled area. As per 2001 census, the population of these three villages was 3,299.

As seen from this data in the year1987, total land holdings stood at 4,844 and those are increased to 7,145 in 2005. The land also increased during 1987-1991, and it is recorded an increase of 2,275 acres. Again, there was a decrease in land during 1991-2001. The net decrease was 216.72 acres. In fact, officially there is a possibility of land alienation in the three village panchyats only. It appears from these statistics in those villages only this much of land was alienated. Again, the land is increased from 19109.28 to 19,397 acres during 2001-05 thus the net increase was 287.72 acre. In actual terms when compare with 1991 the net increase in the land is only 71 acres. However, in this Mandal also the marginal and small land holdings occupied lion's share. Those were

Table 20. Landholding Pattern in Gummalakshmipuram Mandal

Year	*Holdings*	*Acres*	*Percentage of Marginal*	*Percentage of Small*	*Percentage of Others*	*Net Sown Area*	*Percentage of Net Sown Area*
1986-87	4844	7051.41	59.85	19.30	20.85	7236.00	41.28
1991	6191	19326	61.33	20.71	17.96	16870.68	85.06
2001	6800	9109.28	63.81	19.66	16.53	17849.76	90.56
2005	7145	19397	63.69	21.32	14.98	17849.76	90.05

Source: District handbooks and agcensus.nic.in

79.15 per cent in 1991 and further increased to 85.01 in 2011. Even this Adivasi Mandal was not an exception for uneven landholding pattern. Idealists dreamed that the inequalities in the landholding pattern did not prevail in the forest or Adivasi Mandals. However, here too, the inequalities prevailed on a large scale. As seen from the 2005 census data, 85.01 per cent of marginal and small peasants were contented with 51.82 per cent of the total land. The large landholders were 0.32 per cent. They had 3.55 per cent of land with them. Here too, the medium and semi-medium peasants were playing a dominant role as in the plains in percentage terms standing at 14.66, but they were controlling 44.62 per cent of the land.

Landholding Pattern in Saluru Mandal

Saluru was also one of the Mandals that consisted of a sizeable Adivasi population. As per 2001 census, it had a share of 30.12 per cent in the total population. As per the official report, there were 68 Adivasi villages in this Mandal. Out of these, 24 villages were in the ambit of Scheduled area and the remaining 44 villages are out of the ambit. In population terms, 20,456 people are living without any protective legislation. This situation naturally led to rampant land alienation in this Mandal.

As seen from this data in the year 1987 total land holdings stood at 2,957 and those are increased to 4029 in 19911. The land also increased during 1987-1991, and it is recorded an increase of 1,738.67 acres. Again, there was a decrease in land during 1991-2001. The net decrease was 1,110.84 acres. Again, the land is decreased from 10,445.16to 4,740.17 acres during 2001-05.Thus, the net decrease was 5701.16 acre. It is pertinent to note that considerable influx of rich peasants from Godavari and Krishna District has been started in early 90s., in a span of 15 years the Adivasis lost 6816.83 acres of land to others.

Table 21. Landholding Pattern in Saluru Mandal

Year	*Holdings*	*Acres*	*Percentage of Marginal*	*Percentage of small*	*Percentage of Other Holdings*
1986-87	2957	9818.33	55.94	26.21	17.86
1991	4029	11557	60.76	25.42	13.82
2001	4410	10445.16	66.80	23.31	9.89
2005	1883	4740.47	63.94	22.94	13.12

Source: District handbooks and agcensus.nic.in.

However, in this Mandal too, the marginal and small landholdings occupied a lion's share at 82.15 per cent in 1987 which went up to 86.88 in 2005. The data indicates that the share of marginal peasants had come down to 63.94 per cent from 66.80 per cent of 2001 indicating that 2 .86 per cent of marginal peasants altogether lost their foothold on the land.

As seen from this, though the Adivasis had land in their hands in the scheduled areas, the land was not being used for the intended purpose due water starvation and the land was becoming fallow. On the other hand, the Adivasis were losing their land continuously in the non-scheduled areas.

Adivasis Methods of Cultivation- Forest Produce

In the surveyed villages, the unevenness in the methods of cultivation prevailed. In Haddubangi village of Seetampeta Mandal, the tractor had almost replaced the ploughing operation. Adivasis on custom hiring brought tractors from Kothuru and Seetampeta to conduct the cultivation. At the same time, primitive implements Kanka and Jiggi are also on the work spot.

Adivasis are using these primitive implements in the Podu (shifting cultivation). In Podu land, the Adivasis used Kanka for ploughing. Kanka was a four feet stick with five to six nails at one end. Adivasis used to plough the land with this implement and sow various types of seeds at a time. The entire crop of all these seeds could not exceed 400 kilograms. This is not even sufficient to their needs. Hence, the marketable surplus did not arise in this cultivation.

To give water to land, the government constructed check dams across the streams with the help of International fund for agricultural development (IFAD). "In the ITDA area of Parvatipuram, the government built 18 check dams across various streams and spent Rs.1.08 crores during 1990-2000. It intended to provide water to 2,261 acres, which was beneficial to 973 Adivasi peasants. However, only two check dams are functioning." (*Source:* reply to RTI question from ITDA, Parvatipuram)

Part of the IFAD programme was availed in government-encouraged cashew plantations in the tribal tracts. In the initial days, the Adivasi supportive organisations discouraged these plantations on the pretext that it would create food scarcity to the Adivasis. However, Adivasis preferred these plantations, and now they became a source of income to Adivasis during lean season. As mentioned by Adivasis, the Girijan Co-operative Corporation is not purchasing the cashew due to which, the private traders are exploiting Adivasis in the trade.

The primary forest produce in this district included hill brooms, tamarind, soap nuts, Mahwah flower, etc., in the forest and they used to sell it to the traders. Traders used to exploit Adivasis rampantly. The government of Andhra Pradesh on the recommendation of Palaniappan Committee established a co-operative corporation in 1956. Now it is called Girijana Co-operative Corporation (hereinafter called GCC) with head quarters office in Visakhapatnam.

GCC proclaimed its aims in their official website, which read, *"To protect them from exploitative middlemen, petty traders had establish a mutually beneficial relationship between them and rest of the world."* (www. apgirijan. com).

Unfortunately, right from its inception, the GCC could not get fame in the Adivasi areas. Wayback in early 60s, Adivasis complained about the fixing of price with wrong measurements. Some argued that the GCC was acting as a monopoly trader and it removed the difficulties of traders rather than Adivasis. During the Srikakulam prolonged agitations, many wrote field level survey reports on the mal-functioning of GCC. By showing this, some are arguing for the abolition of GCC and some are arguing for curtailing the powers of GCC. In fact, it is an unfavourable argument as it is against the Adivasis. Even the World Bank in its paper wrote about this monopoly nature. It read, *"The AP Scheduled Areas Minor Forest Produce (Regulation of Trade) Regulation of 1979 created a state monopoly for trading certain minor forest produce (MFP or NTFP) under which GOAP appointed the Girijan Cooperative Corporation Ltd. (GCC) as an agent for the purpose of purchase of, and trade in, any MFP on behalf of the State Government. This Regulation restricts sale, purchase, curing or processing, collection, storage and transport of the MFP covered under the regulation, by any person other than GCC in scheduled areas. This means processing and value addition by the tribal community is not permitted. GOAP is to review the above regulation and has agreed to relax its provisions."* (*Source:* Document of the World Bank: Report No: 24184-IN: Project appraisal document on a proposed credit in the amount of sdr 85.5 million (US $108 million equivalent to India for the Andhra Pradesh community forest management project June 19, 2002)

The departmental manual also spoke about this and it had expressed intentions to liberalise the GCC in the marketing activity. *"Presently GCC is exercising monopoly control over the collection of certain items from tribals pertaining to Minor Forest Produce such as Tamarind, Gum, Brooms, etc., while fixing these items price unilaterally. In this system, the tribals are at receiving end and have to sell their MFP to GCC only and not allowed to sell to others who may offer better price. Therefore, GCC's role maybe limited to offer minimum support price to such items only and freedom may be given to the tribals to fetch price for their products."* (Tribal welfare department, Departmental Manual: Page 64-65).

In fact, these arguments are detrimental to Adivasis and as told by GCC itself, they are becoming the soft target for the exploitation. As mentioned earlier in the cashew trade, the Adivasis are already bearing the burden of exploitation. The recommendations and proposals must be directed towards strengthening the organisation rather than closing it.

As seen from the Adivasi villages, unevenness in the landholding pattern had prevailed. This unevenness is common in the ownership of tamarind trees. Many Adivasis could not exercise any right on these trees. Tamarind is one of the major revenue-earning sources for Adivasis. In the absence of such rights, those people used to go to remote areas to collect minor forest produce to earna livelihood.

Adivasis used to sell firewood. In technical terms, they are called head loaders. In the surveyed villages, it is also one of the sources to earn a livelihood. In the tribal hamlets of Bobbili Mandal, the Adivasi women and men used to carry the head loads to Bobbili town on foot with the firewood. For one load of wood, a woman used to get Rs. 30 and a man Rs. 60. After deducting the auto fare, they could retain Rs. 22 and Rs. 52 respectively. On an average, they could come to town 10 times a month. By this way, in a month, a woman is earning Rs. 220 and a man Rs. 520 only. These examples prevailed all over the tribal tracts.

Occupational Structure of Adivasis

As discussed, the Adivasis earn their livelihood on forest resources, as cultivators and agrarian labour. The occupational pattern as per census records can be seen from this data.

Table 22. Occupational Pattern in Present Srikakulam District

Census Year	*Population*	*Cultivators*	*Agrarian Labour*
1981	1,05,156	19,652	32,907
1991	1,34,057	16,814	41,342
2001	1,51,249	14,775	32,804
2011	1,66,118	6,988	42,330

Source: www.aptribes.nic.in.

As seen from the table, it is clear that there was a steep decrease in the number of cultivators. During 1981-1991, the decrease in number was 2,838, and in percentage terms, it was 14.44. During 1991-2001, the decrease in number was 2,039, and in percentage terms, it was 12.12. During 2001-2011, the number is further shown a decrease of 7787. In the current decade itself 53 per cent of Adivasi cultivators lost their age old profession. After repeated promises of enhancement of land ownership among the Adivasis, in a span of thirty years 64.44 per cent of Adivasis left their lands.

Table 23. Occupational Pattern in Parvatipuram ITDA Area (carved out part)

Census Year	*Population*	*Cultivators*	*Agrarian labour*
1981	1,35,637	30,197	34,859
1991	1,67,695	35,001	25,215
2001	1,89,527	31,302	51,291
2011	2,06,109	12,217	66,636

Source: www.aptribes.nic.in.

As seen from the table, that there was an increase in the number of agrarian labour during 1981-1991, while the decrease in number was 8,435 and in percentage terms, it was 25.63. During 1991-2001, the increase in number was 8,538, and in percentage terms, it was 20.65. During 2001-2011, it shows an increase in the agrarian labour to the tune of 9256. In the initial stage, it appeared that the stripped cultivators had joined the crowd of agrarian labour. As seen from the 2001 census, the number had touched it's lowest. It showed that along with the traditional agricultural labour and new recruits were leaving their residence only to join urban of proletariat. However, the current census has shown a marginal increase in the agrarian labour.

As seen from the table, it showed different trends though there were some protected areas. During 1981-1991, the increase in number was 4,804, and in percentage terms, it was 15.90. During 1991-2001, the decrease in number was 3,699 and in percentage terms, it was 10.56. The current decade is revealing staggering facts about the occupational structure. In the current decade, even in the protected area the decrease in the cultivators is recorded as 19,805 and 60 per cent of Adivasis stripped out from their ancient profession. On the other hand ironically the agricultural census 2010 revealed that the land under the Adivasi category has been increased. It shows a net increase of land to the tune of 4,844 acres.

As seen from the table, there was a reduction in the number of agricultural labour during 1981-1991 at 8,435and in percentage terms, it was 27.66. During 1991-2001, the increase in number was stupendous reaching a whopping 66,636. The net increase recorded was 41,421, and 164 per cent of increase has been recorded in this category in two decades of globalisation.

These circumstances reveal that the Adivasis had lost their base in the forest as well on land. Hence, the migration was necessitated to earn the livelihood.

Indebtedness among Adivasis

Though the Adivasis had land, in the hill tracts, the cultivation was primitive in nature. Since they did not have proper titles, majority of Adivasis could not get Bank loans. Hence, they were invariably depending on private moneylenders. The debt burden was considerable on Adivasis. The interest rates were still exorbitant in the tribal tracts and due to this debt burden; the Adivasis were losing their foothold on the land whereas in Scheduled areas, the Adivasis could keep their lands because of the protective measures.

As seen from the surveyed villages, the private traders made advances in the shape of credit to the Adivasi on strict conditions that the price was determined at the will of traders with cashew to be sold to that trade only. Since, GCC was not in the scene, the traders had a final say in this transaction. As per the Sávara tribe of Panasaguda village of Seetampeta Mandal, "*we have to sell the cashew to the trader only. The rate of interest is 60 per cent per annum. Suppose if the market price is Rs. 100 we have to sell at Rs. 80 to the trader.*"

Vennelavalasa is a solitary Adivasi village in Sarubujjili Mandal. As per the villagers, "*we usually receive loans from the traders. In one season, we took loans from the bank. In that particular year, due to drought, we could not repay the money. The officers lodged a police complaint, and we were taken to custody. Then the trader came to rescue by giving credit at 24 per cent interest".*

In fact, Reserve Bank was issuing guidelines to the banks regarding agricultural loans through many circulars. However, the same were not being implemented in Adivasi areas. The words of Vennelavalasa people spoke, "*we have not seen any difference between the bank and a private trader*".

As told earlier, Pedakharja village as a whole lost their lands and the government restored their right on the land after the revolt. In fact, the indebtedness was the only cause for the land alienation in those days. In the words of Adivasis of that village, "*in those days the traders grabbed our lands. After a prolonged struggle, we could get our lands back. In fact, the traders were exhibiting more insight when compared with the past. Nowadays, they are not grabbing our lands. However, with the harsh interest rates, almost all the produce is going into their hands without any pain. They do not give market price to our products. We have to sell the produce at the pre-determined price. We have to sell the paddy at Rs. 250 per a quintal, and we have to sell cashew at Rs. 20 per kilogram. This economic plunder made us strive in our fields only to enrich the traders.*"

Valasaballeru also participated in the revolt and even later one or other revolutionary organisation was working in this village. This village not an exception to the debt cycle, "*GCC was giving some loans to us. However, for non-agricultural purposes and the agricultural purposes too, there was a constant need of money. Hence, it was inevitable to take loans from private moneylenders. The interest payments were in cash. We have to sell the produce to the same trader at the price of his will. He took cashew at Rs. 25 a kilogram and paddy at Rs. 300 per quintal.*"

These happenings were only a tip of the iceberg. In all the surveyed villages, the same debt cycle was in operation. The Acts relating to the money lending regulation have no locus stand in these areas though those are intended to applicable in the Adivasi areas. In one word, the Adivasis livelihood depended on the mountains, and they gained control on every mountain of the tracts. They only fear about the mountain of debt.

Migration

Mankind always tried either to travel for its survival or to exploit the sources of the weaker sections. In this district, Adivasis are migrating in search of livelihood. The landlessness, the land alienation, debt burden, the primitive mode of production and stringent forest policies made them to migrate to earn a livelihood.

Until 1959, the Adivasis had no connectivity with the world. The Adivasi associations under the banner of the then Communist Party of India (CPI) started their work here and tried to educate them. In this process, they used to make rallies, processions, and picketing at the government offices at various places. This was the first link for them with the world. In this process, they were sent to local to central prisons situated in Parvatipuram and Visakhapatnam. In the words of an old aged Adivasi "*after our release from jail we went to see the sea in Visakhapatnam. We astonished to see such a large tank.*"

However, later, the Adivasis was travelling towards various places across India in search of work. A considerable portion of Adivasis is on the path of migration. The exodus of Adivasis has no limits to the villages adjacent to roads. Even the remote villages were not an exception to the exodus. An Adivasi of Burujola village of Bhamini described this exodus "*it is just like going to a shandi (weekly market).*"

Examples of Migration

At Burujola, there are 70 Adivasi families. They belong to Sávara tribe. Government distributed each an acre for five families, 0.50 acres each to 40 families and 0.30 acres each 25 families. Alongwith this, the Adivasis used to make Podu. Because of the wild bores, they left the Podu and continued their cultivation in their land. The government conducted numerous surveys to give irrigation, but nothing came in practice. As usual, these villagers were also told about the possibility of getting irrigated water. Hence, drought was a common factor here. The debt burden and lack of opportunity to conduct the cultivation drove them to town and cities across India. Almost one person of every family was on migration going to Chennai, Poluru, Bangalore, Mysore and Hyderabad.

Loharjola village is in this Mandal with 50 Jatapu and 20 Sávara families being the natives. During the tribal uprising, they occupied some land but the government did not confer titles thereon. Government also did not distribute any land to them. The village was a rain-fed where out of 70 families, 56 families were on migration to Chennai and Bangalore. The cities were also not an exception for cheating in the case of this ignorant Adivasis. In Chennai, they worked under a sub-contractor of L and T Company. The company paid the entire amount to the contractor, but the contractor evaded the payment to these Adivasis.

Atchanapuram, a village in Meliaputti Mandal was once under the control of the Zamindar of Parlakhemundi. At that time, it was a thick forest. Of late, Sávara tribe of this village brought some land into cultivation. Once the yield was so low that they could get only two bags of paddy an acre. Later, they could improve the yield to 10 bags though it was insufficient to cater to the needs. Hence, 15 persons of this village had migrated.

Tikkabai, a scheduled roadside village in Kurupam Mandal was accessible to government schemes. Even then, the migration was rampant here. Kamma-rich peasantry bought/leased large chunks of land around this village. Later, all the Adivasis were working in these fields. Since they were reliable besides cheap labour, the rich peasantry used to send tractors for them to commute to the work place.

Masenuputtuga, a village in Burja Mandal sent 15 families including women on migration to Chennai. They used to visit the village twice in a year. As mentioned earlier, the Adivasis of Kurukuti village could get land after a prolonged struggle. However, this village too was not an exception for the migration. Temporary migration was a common factor in this village and 30 families migrated permanently to Chennai with the migration starting 10 years ago.

During the thirties, a poet Sri Sri wrote his magnum opus Mahaprasthanam in Telugu. In that volume, he depicted a youth life who wanted to migrate in search of lively hood. In that poem, the youth ultimately perished in that task and the poet symbolically depicted the grief of his mother. However, the situation was just a reverse in this district. The parents migrated leaving their children with their old-aged parents. These circumstances also lead to pathetic incidences. A recent news item described such a pathetic incident that happened in Bhamini Mandal. "Bhouri Upendra Kumar was a student of VII standard. His parents left for Chennai in search of livelihood. He along with his elder sister was with their grant parents. The boy was attacked with fever, and when the grandparents tried to take him to hospital, the boy expired." (*Source:* Eenadu. Srikakulam tabloid)

Even the development process was also a main reason for their migration all over India. The Prime Minister appointed a committee to look into the land related matters and the committee submitted a report titled "Report of the committee on state agrarian relations and the unfinished task of land reforms." As per the report *"Nowhere is the distress more evident than in the tribal areas, particularly those falling within the Schedule V. The tribal people have been the biggest victims of displacement due to development projects. Though constituting only nine per cent of the country's population, the tribal communities have contributed more than 40 per cent to the total land acquired so far. The Parliament has legislated the most radical of its Acts in the form of Panchayat (Extension to the Scheduled Areas) Act, 1996, applicable to nine States. All these States under Schedule V had stringent laws protecting the corpus of tribal lands which, however, continued to be subjected to a steady erosion".* (*Source:* Report of the committee on state agrarian relations and the unfinished task of land reforms page 8)

Further, the same report mentioned, *"Massive transfers of agricultural and forest land for industrial, mining and in the name of development or infrastructural projects have created rural unrest and distress migration in those areas. Findings indicate that about 7,50,000 acres of land has been transferred for mining and another 250,000 acres for industrial purposes during last two decades [Centre for Science and Environment]."*

The same story was repeating in this district too. Because of the Vamshadhara Phase II reservoir, the Adivasis of four villages had lost their place of existence and migrated. Due to the Peddagedda reservoir five, Adivasi villages were vacated and the villagers were placed in fishing occupation in that reservoir.

In fact, the government expected to stop migration by way of giving assured work through joint forest management (JFM) and community forest management (CFM). These schemes were started in 2002 and completed in

2010. The government spent Rs. 480 crores on this project with the aid. However, the assessment report of World Bank told that it did not check the migration completely. However, it arrested the migration to the extent of 37 per cent.

Table 24. Comparison of S.T. Literacy Rate at National Level

Census Year	*General*			*STs*		
	Male	*Female*	*Total*	*Male*	*Female*	*Total*
1971	45.96	21.97	34.45	17.63	4.85	11.3
1981	56.38	29.76	43.57	24.52	8.04	16.35
1991	64.13	39.29	52.21	40.65	18.19	29.6
2001	75.26	53.67	64.84	59.17	34.76	47.1
2011	80.89	64.64	72.99			

Source: Compiled from Census reports and National S.C. Commission reports.

Education and Employment

In this district, prior to 1970, private-aided schools were established in the tribal tracts.Usually Patnaiks were the managers of those schools. Though they took government funds to run the schools, the schools miserably failed to impart education to the Adivasis. During 1960-70, the Adivasi union tried to educate the Adivasis. There is a need to compare the literacy levels of Adivasis in National, State and District level all along these forty years as per the official data.

Table 25. Comparison of ST Literacy Rate at the State Level

Year	*General*			*STs*		
	Male	*Female*	*Total*	*Male*	*Female*	*Total*
1971	33.18	15.75	24.57	8.47	2.12	5.34
1981	24.59	20.39	29.94	12.02	3.46	7.82
1991	55.13	32.72	44.09	25.25	8.68	17.16
2001	70.32	50.43	60.47	47.66	26.11	37.04
2011						

Source: Census reports.

As seen from the table, until 1981, the literacy rate stood just at 16.35 with the femaleliteracy not even touching two-digit figure even after 34 years of independence. In 2001, the literacy rate had reached 47.1 per cent.

As seen from the table, the state of literacy in Andhra Pradesh is poor even in the general population. This situation was worse in the case of Adivasis. At any point of time, this state did not achieve the national average. Even the 2011 census revealed the state not to be progressing well. It got 31st place in India in the literacy. The Adivasis position also reflected the same trends. Up to 1981, the literacy rate in Adivasis stood at 7.82. Even in 1991, it did not even reach 20 per cent.

Table 26. Comparison of S.T. Literacy Rate at District Level

Sl. No.	*Year*	*Literates in ST*		*Literacy percentage of ST as per official statistics*			*Literacy percentage of ST compared with district literates*			*General*		
		Male	*Female*	*Male*	*Female*	*Total*	*Male*	*Female*	*Total*	*Male*	*Female*	*Total*
1.	1971	6526	1114	6.11	1.05	3.60	1.84	0.89	1.59	31.33	11.11	21.08
2.	1981	15616	5240	12.91	4.37	8.66	3.44	2.88	3.28	34.89	13.98	24.32
3.	1991	30053	7911	20.13	5.31	12.73	4.53	2.47	3.86	42.59	21.06	31.76
4.	2001	68847	40650	56.54	33.57	45.14	6.70	6.06	6.44	58.70	38.09	48.33
5.	2011											

Source: District handbooks.

Magic in the Statistics

A puzzling fact in these statistics was the literacy rate of Adivasis calculated on the basis of their population. Hence, it appeared that literacy was increasing in a good way. The formula of statisticians is like this.

$$\frac{\text{Literates in Adivasis}}{\text{Total Adivasi population}} \times 100$$

However, the comparison between Adivasi literates and total literates were showing startling facts about these official figures due to the formulas taking this. The following table reveals both the figures.

$$\frac{\text{Literates in Adivasis}}{\text{Total literates in the district}} \times 100$$

As seen from this data, the Adivasi literacy continued slowly until 1991. Surprisingly, it took a major leap in 2001 census reaching from mere 12.73 per cent to a whopping 45.14 per cent, which appeared to be unrealistic. Since it is official statistic, there is a need to stick on this data.

If the second formula was applied to the data for every 100 literates, Adivasis literates were only 1.59 in 1971. The figure reached only to 6.44 in 2001. In other words for every 100 literate men of the district, only 6.70 Adivasi males were literates. In the case of women, only 6.06 were literates.

Level of Education

The Ministry of Tribal Affairs, India came with a compendium on the state of Adivasis in 2010 providing abundant information. As seen from that compendium, the state of dropout was visible during 2007 as reproduced hereunder.

The ministry commented on these dropout rates, which was self-explanatory reading, *"The overall picture of Dropout rates for All India depicts that it has been steadily declining from 1990-91to 2007-08 for both boys and girls from class I to X. However, dropout rates are considerable lower in the Classes I - V than the higher classes (I to X). This indicates that the dropout rates are alarmingly higher in the higher classes. Analysis of data of Census 2001, on a percentage of STs by gender across different levels of education shows a gradual decline, starting from 'Below Primary' classes to 'Graduate and above'. The decline in the percentage of STs by gender is almost similar and uniform in both rural and urban areas."* (*Source:* Statistical profile of scheduled tribes 2010: ministry of tribal affairs)

The same ministry gave the particulars about the level of education of Adivasis, which showed abysmal performance. It can be seen in the following table.

This table clearly indicated the level of education in the higher education sector running in fractions. This was the state of literacy and education of Adivasis even at national level. The micro level analysis also provided this data.

Employment of Adivasis:

The national statistics indicated that the representation of Adivasis in Group A and group B posts was nominal. In the total employment sector, they were representing only 6.43 per cent.

Table 27. Employment Pattern of Adivasis in Surveyed Villages.

Sl. No.	Gender	Total house holds	State Govt.	Central Govt.	Teachers	The Public Sector	Police	Defence	Home Guard	Anganwadi	Health Worker
1.	Male	1991	9	3	33	8	8	1	1	0	0
2.	Female	1991	0	0	3	0	0	0	0	1	3
	Total	1991	9	3	36	8	8	1	1	1	3

This table indicates the employment pattern of Adivasis in the surveyed villages. In the total of 48 villages surveyed, 569 families belonged to savara, 689 families to jatapu, 523 families to Kondadora,10 families to Kondakammari, 80 families to Mookadora, 83 families to Mannedora, 4 families to Mali and 33 families to Gadaba.

Out of these 48 villages, there was no single employee in any of the 34 villages.70 employees emerged from remaining 14 villages. Pedakharja, Lankajodu, Valasaballeru have sizeable representation in the employment. 15 from Pedakharja, 4 from Valasaballeru and 12 from Lankajodu wererepresenting the total employees. Almost these three villages had 44.2 per cent share in the employment.

As seen from the table, majority employees were teachers. In the year 1988-89, the government recruited Adivasi youth as teachers with a qualification of secondary school certificate or with intermediate. Subsequently, the government imparted teacher training to them and hence, they could become teachers. Out of the seventy employees, only seven were females.

As seen from the villages, though the literacy level was poor, even the educated persons were not getting the assured employment. Many rural Adivasi youth remained unemployed.

I am compelled to share an experience with the readers. As a part of the survey, when I visited Panasaguda village, a girl came across and told that she passed X class in the first division. Lack of financial support did not allow her to continue her further studies. In other words, she has also in the 83.61 per cent of dropouts. When asked about her future course of action, she replied that she is waiting for the job card and stated that the minimum age to get the card is 18 years. Since she is16 years, she has to wait for two more years to get the job card. I presumed that the government was issuing job cards to Adivasi youth. I asked her the department the cards were pertaining to. She replied that

Table 28. Dropout Rate of S.T. Students as on 30th September 2007

	Class I –V			*Class V-X*			*Class I -X*		
	Boys	*Girls*	*Total*	*Boys*	*Girls*	*Total*	*Boys*	*Girls*	*Total*
All India	32.04	32.45	32.2	63.54	63.13	63.36	75.83	77.38	76.4
Andhra Pradesh	43.56	49.07	46.3	70.19	74.73	72.4	81.08	83.61	82.3

Source: Statistical profile of Scheduled tribes 2010: Ministry of Tribal affairs.

Table 29. Percentage of Education Level by Sex for Scheduled Tribes

	Higher Secondary/Intermediate			*Non-technical Diploma*			*Technical Diploma with a Certificate*			*Graduate and Above*		
	Person	*Male*	*Female*	*Person*	*Male*	*Female*	*Person*	*Male*	*Female*	*Person*	*Male*	*Female*
Total	1.46	1.03	0.43	0.01	0.01	0	0.12	0.09	0.02	0.9	0.68	0.23
Rural	1.05	0.78	0.43	0	0	0	0.08	0.06	0.02	0.55	0.44	0.11
Urban	0.04	0.25	0.43	0	0	0	0.04	0.03	0.01	0.35	0.24	0.12

Source: Statistical profile of Scheduled tribes 2010: Ministry of Tribal affairs.

it is Mahatma Gandhi National Rural Employment Guarantee Scheme. The reply had sent shockwaves in me.

With a rich experience, the Hon'ble Minister of Tribal Affairs and Panchayat Raj, Shri V. Kishore Chandra Deo commented on the state of affairs with a deep concern. It read *"Scheduled Tribe community constitute more than eight per cent of our national population and are still waiting to receive the benefits of freedom even after a lapse of more than sixty years since we achieved independence."* (*Source:* Conference of governors speech of *Hon'ble Minister of Tribal Affairs and Panchayati Raj, Shri V. Kishore Chandra Deo* (30th October, 2011. Ashoka Hall, Rastrapati Bhavan)

14

Dalits

Even during the colonial period, the dalits conducted many agitations against the social and economic oppression. Dr. B.R. Ambedkar took a leading role in these struggles and fought for the cause of dalits. Because of these, colonial rulers made some corrective steps to improve the condition of dalits. At that time, they were called depressed classes. In the 1935 Act, the colonial rulers provided reservations to these classes. After independence, these sections were called scheduled castes (hereinafter called dalits). As per the proceedings, the respective state governments had to recognise the scheduled castes to provide reservation. Andhra Pradesh officially recognised 59 castes as scheduled castes. In Srikakulam district, the leading scheduled castes are Mala, Madiga, Relli and Pydi.

Demography: The following table indicates the population of dalits in Srikakulam district.

As seen from the table, the dalits occupied a share of 9.11 per cent in 1971which slightly rose to 9.89 during 1991 and it fell to 9.62 per cent during

Table 1. Changing Pattern in Dalit Population in Srikakulam District

Sl. No.	*Year*	*Total Population*	*SC Population*	*Percentage of Dalits*	*Growth Rate in Dalit Population*	*Growth Rate in Total Population*
1.	1971	2589991	235919	9.11		13.7
2.	1981	2875728	275769	9.59	16.89	11.03
3.	1991	3358731	332267	9.89	20.49	16.80
4.	2001	3658846	351967	9.62	5.93	8.94
5.	2011	3859295	383493	9.94		5.80

Source: Primary census abstracts.

2001 census. The current Census has shown the slightest increase of percentage of dalits. It is recorded as 9.94 per cent.

The changing pattern of dalit population in the present Srikakulam district can be seen in this Table.

Table 2. Changing Pattern in Dalit Population in Present Srikakulam District

Sl. No	*Year*	*Total Population*	*SC Population*	*Percentage of Dalits*
1.	1981	1959352	179775	9.18
2.	1991	2317915	216676	9.35
3.	2001	2537593	229609	9.05
3.	2011	2703114	255664	9.45

Source: Handbooks of statistics.

The present Srikakulam Dalit population indicates many trends in its pattern. During 1981-91, the percentage of Dalit population increased from 9.18 to 9.35. By 2001, it had even dropped to 9.05 per cent. It showed a decrease even to their share during 1981. In concrete terms, the increase in the population during 1981-1991 was 29,901 whereas in the following decade, the increase was mere 12,933. The growth of the general population rate of this district during 1991-2001 was 8.93 whereas for Dalits, it was 0.13.the current 2011 Census has shown the percentage of Dalits as 9.45.

Table 3. Changing Pattern in Dalit Population in Carved out Area of Srikakulam District

Sl. No.	*Year*	*Total Population*	*SC Population*	*Percentage of Dalits*
1.	1981	916376	95994	10.48
2.	1991	1040816	115591	11.11
3.	2001	1121253	122358	10.91
4.	2011	1156181	127829	11.05

Source: District Handbooks of Vizianagaram district.

As seen from the table, the dalits occupied a share of 10.48 per cent in 1981which slightly raised to 11.11 in 1991 and it dropped to 10.91 per cent during 2001 census. In concrete terms, the increase during 1991-2001 was 6,767, but in the previous decade, it was 19,597. The current Census show an increase of a mere 5471 in number. The percentage of Dalits stood at 11.05 only.

Hence, it appeared that the population of Dalits was leaving the district in search of livelihood.

Means of Production-Land

As Karl Marx told, *"the property in the soil is the original source of all the wealth, and has become the great problem upon the solution of which lies the future of working class."* (*Source:* The Nationalisation of the land: Karl Marx)

In the case of Indian population, various castes contribute labour to create the wealth, but the history proves that the Dalits in Toto are proletarian. Dr. Ambedkar told, *"An untouchable must not own and cultivate land and lead an independent life. For his livelihood, he must depend upon stale remnants of food left over by the Hindu households and upon meat of cattle that die in the village. These remnants of food he must collect from door to door. For, he must go on his begging round every evening."* (*Source:* Essays on untouchables and Untouchability: Social www.ambedkar.org)

Dr. Ambedkar categorically stated that there was no right to Dalits to have a land to get a respectful livelihood. After independence, during 1955, Daniel Thorner made an extensive survey in Indian villages on the subject of Agrarian structure in the wake of abolition of intermediaries. He delivered five lectures in Delhi University on this subject, and he concluded, "*the rare Chamar, Mahar, Panchama or other untouchable who prospects economically and attempts to secure a foothold for his family buying land may find insurmountable obstacles in the way of purchasing"* (The agrarian prospect in India: Page 11: Daniel Thorner).

Daniel Thorner used the words land reforms to indicate the abolition of intermediaries. In this process, he studied all the Acts and concluded that the concept land tiller was become a farce.

In fact, the elimination of intermediaries created rich peasantry in the place of intermediaries. It resulted in the rural unrest and the successive governments invariably spoke about land reforms.

On one, hand, the primary right of earning a livelihood respectfully was rejected and on the other, the social oppression on Dalits went unabated. In other words, economic and social oppressions are implemented along the countryside in India. Hence, propaganda erupted about the allotment of lands for these sections.

Not Only the Temples but also the Endowment Lands

Dalits have no right to enter the temples. To gain access to the temples, they fought with the savarna castes even later. They were successful because of their rightful demand and because of the constitutional safeguards. However, they could not gain access to endowment lands.

Brahmin priestly class had a right on these lands. At that time, peasant caste people were recorded as tenants and in real terms, the Dalits were labouring on these lands. After the abolition Acts, the Brahmin caste almost were vacated the countryside and the landhad gone in favour of peasant castes. The Dalits could not get even a bit of land.

There are a number of examples in the villages surveyed for this process. To enumerate, certain examples were taken into consideration.

Ajjada is a village in Balijipeta Mandal. Traditionally it was a Brahmin Inamdari village. The Brahmins gambled with the zamindar of Bobbili and lost 450 acres in that play. The zamindar rejected to take the land with a devotion to Brahmins and asked them to maintain the lands. They did not agree to that proposal. Hence, the zamindar gave those lands to their god Venugopalaswamy and made them as trustees. After the abolition of Inamdaris, they lost economic and social control in the village and the rich peasantry of Koppulavelama caste occupied those lands. Later they did not even pay the nominal rent to the exchequer. In this process, the peasantry even started selling and distributing those lands among them. In all these process, the Dalits of that the village could not get even a square meter of land.

After prolonged agitations and legal battles, the Dalits of Seebillipeddavalasa and Kitchada villages could get these lands. The expert committee of the planning commission recommended 22 years back, "*Where lands with religious and charitable institutions are leased out, at least, 50 per cent should be earmarked for Scheduled Castes agricultural labour on mutually fair terms." (Quoted in National S.C. Commission report 1994-95)* The Finance Minister of Andhra Pradesh in 1971- 72 budget speech told *"Certain other measures such as leasing out of lands of various institutions to the landless poor on a preferential basis....."* (*Source:* Andhra Pradesh Budget speech 1971-72)

However, neither the recommendation nor the promise of the minister saw the light in this district.

Endowment Lands in this District

As per the Endowment Department, in this district, 22,649.56 acres, 190 shops and establishments were under the "control" of the department. As seen from the information and the field survey, it was clear that the Dalit almost lost their say on these assets. In the present Srikakulam district, the land under the department was 11,201 acres, and as per the information, 116 Dalit families were tilling a meagre portion of land. The officers told that the lands were being auctioned. It was clear that Dalits could not remit such amounts in the auction and hence they could not get any right to cultivation on these lands.

The deputy commissioner of endowment in an interview to the press told, "In North Andhra, 55,000 acres of land were under the name of the department and out of these, 8,000 acres were occupied." (*Source:* Eenadu, Srikakulam district tabloid dated 10/5/2012). Undoubtedly, the Dalits did not occupy these lands.

Implementation of Land Reforms

The Government of Andhra Pradesh, in its budget speech, proclaimed, *"No scheme of welfare for the Scheduled Castes or Scheduled Tribes can be considered adequate in the present socio-economic situation, unless it is based on a definite programme of distribution of Government lands and the redistribution of the surplus lands taken over under the Land Legislations."* (*Source:* Andhra Pradesh Budget speech 1971-72).

The land distribution statistics always had uncertain data and despite providing numerous data understanding of the statistics proved difficult. There were so many calculations on this distribution in the above said budget speech.

In the second page of the budget speech, it read, "*The House is aware of the crash land assignment programme, under which more than a million acres have been distributed since November, 1969.*"

The following pages of the same budget speech read, "*Under the programme of assignment of land, more than 24 lakh acres of land have been distributed to the landless poor including Harijan and Girijans. In order to make additional lands available, de-reservation of forest was also taken up recently releasing 1.28 lakh acres for distribution*" (*Source:* Andhra Pradesh Budget speech 1971-72)

In the 1974-75 budget speech, the government said, *"Government have undertaken a fresh assessment of the availability of Banjar lands in various districts and have decided to embark upon a crash programme for the assignment of such lands by appointing special staff, wherever necessary"*. (*Source:* Andhra Pradesh Budget speech 1974-75).

In the 1976-77 budget speech, the governmentsaid, *"The Hon'ble Members are aware of the substantial public investments that have been programmed for the welfare of the weaker sections in the recent past. This year, however, we have taken far-reaching steps in terms of a Legislative and Institutional package of measures for bringing about radical changes in the rural sector in favour of the weaker sections. These include tackling of the primary problem of land ownership through implementation of land reforms as well as distribution of Government land"* (*Source:* Andhra Pradesh Budget speech 1976-77). (Emphasis added)

All the budget speeches of that decade spoke volumes about these judicious re-distribution and distribution of wasteland. However, from 1980 onwards, these words also had disappeared from the budget speeches. During late 90s, the government declared that the development of Dalits was linked with education. The focus now shifted from the land to education.

The government introduced Land Ceiling Act in 1961. The data relating to the Act was incorporated in the Gazetteer of this District which read *"over 2000 declarations were filed in the district under the appropriate sections of the Act and an extent of 235 hectares declared surplus."* (*Source:* Srikakulam District Gazetteer: page 131).

It appeared that there was no need to discuss further on this Act as far as this district was concerned. The national scene too reflected the same and the sub-group on land related issues of 11th five year plan commented, *"In fact, the ceiling laws of phase I remained, both theoretically and practically, a nebulous item in the scheme of agrarian reforms"*. (page:118)

State of Land Reforms in Andhra Pradesh

The government spoke about the second round of land reforms in its budget speech 1976-77. It reads, "*Hon'ble Members are aware; the Government have taken up the implementation of land reforms in a determined and vigorous manner. About 4.50 lakh declarations have been received. To enquire into the declarations and to determine surplus land in each case, 70 Land Reforms Tribunals have been set up all over the State, 311 Special Deputy Tehasildars have been trained and put on the job for verification of the declarations received. Over 2.15 lakh declarations have been verified by the Special Revenue staff and the Tribunals have disposed of 84,871 cases, of which about 4,000 are surplus cases, the surplus land declared being 70,329 acres. The implementation of the Act is thus in full swing and it is expected that about 10 lakh acres of land would be rendered surplus under the Act."* (*Source:* Andhra Pradesh Budget speech 1976-77).

As per these statistics, by that year, 70,329 acres were available for distribution. Government committed to distribute half the lands to Dalit and Adivasis. Even in these terms, 50 per cent was worked out to 35,164.50 acres. Even the Dalits got 50 per cent of share in this land to the extent of 17,582.50 acres.

As per the 1971 census, the total rural Dalit population was 50,92,130. The family size was roughly 5. In that way, the rural Dalit households numbered 10,18,426. It was easy to assume the extent of land that could cater to the needs of the needy.

The same budget speeches had proclaimed on the implementation part of the land reforms. It read, *"Successive Governments have launched programme of distribution of Government land to landless poor. In a number of cases lands assigned have not been delivered to the assignees. The land possession fortnight was therefore observed from 1st June to give necessary impetus to the programme of giving physical possession to the beneficiaries who were assigned lands either from the surplus land available under the Ceiling Act or the Government waste land."* (*Source:* Andhra Pradesh Budget speech 1978-79).

Subsequently, the land distribution particulars under this Land Reforms Act in this state were "a total land to the tune of 5,85,670 acres had been distributed. It was distributed among 4, 58,271 beneficiaries. Among them, Dalit beneficiaries were 1, 88,806 who got land to the tune of 2, 32,215 acres. Among them, the Adivasi beneficiaries were 74,322 who got land to the tune of 1,19,992.47 acres. Among them, the backward caste and other beneficiaries were 1,95,863. They got land to the tune of 2, 33, 456.60 acres. (*Source:* Paper on land revenue administration-a historical outlook: Shri C. Umamaheswara Rao, I.A.S., Commissioner, AMR-APARD)

Subsequently, the land distribution particulars under this Land Reforms Act in this district were, *"a total land to the tune of 11,388.68 acres had been distributed among 18,491 beneficiaries out of which the Dalit beneficiaries were 6,833 who got land to the tune of 4,379.64 acres. Among them, Adivasi beneficiaries were 2,933 who got land to the tune of 2,643.28 acres, backward caste and other beneficiaries were 8,615 getting land to the tune of 4,365.76 acres."* (*Source:* Paper on land revenue administration—a historical outlook: Shri C. Umamaheswara Rao, I.A.S, Commissioner, AMR-APARD). In the villages surveyed, the particulars of land distribution are given hereunder in a tabular form.

Table 4. Land Distribution under Land Ceiling and Assignment Act in the Surveyed Village

Land reforms						*Assigned land*					
SC	*Land*	*ST*	*Land*	*BC*	*Land*	*SC*	*Land*	*ST*	*Land*	*BC*	*Land*
296	100.28	166	337	468	189.7	1411	1409.3	1285	2976	2330	1656.1

Source: Reply to RTI question from the Mandals, (Land in Acres).

Regarding national figures again, there was a need to study the above Planning Commission sub-group report as per which. "*As on 30-06-2006, the total land declared surplus in the entire country is 68.61 lakh acres, out of which about 60.15 lakh acres have been taken possession of and 49.87 lakh acres have been distributed to 53.98 lakh beneficiaries of whom 38.94 per cent belong to Scheduled Castes and 15.87 per cent belong to Scheduled Tribes. An area of 8.56 lakh acres has been involved in litigation.* (Report of Sub-group on Land related matters: Page 118).

By citing these statistics, the report commented in an indictment voice. *"In total terms, in most part of Indian agriculture, the maximum potential addition to the net operated area with marginal/small farms through the process of land ceiling has been ridiculously small. Secondly, out of whatever small 'area declared surplus' was notified in each state, a fairly high proportion has not been available for distribution."*(*Ibid:* page 119).

Further, the Ministry of Rural Development stated that the majority of the lands under ceiling were entangled in legal disputes. In this category, Andhra Pradesh occupied the first place. As per its calculation, 2.05 lakhs acres of land were under the legal dispute in this state. The Ministry of Rural Development, in the path of implementing 20 point formula, fixed a target of 5,98,563 acres for distribution by 1993-94. However, at the national level, the distribution was restricted to 70,887 acres. The nation achieved only 12 per cent of the target. The report told that Andhra Pradesh state fared a poor performance in this target. While the target fixed was 1,22,810 acres, the distributed land was only 25,139 acres.

In the year 2007-08, the Andhra Pradesh government reviewed the situation on the land reforms and concluded, *"History tells us that since ages, inequitable distribution of land has been the root cause of all the social maladies. But the remedial measures taken to root out this scourge have not succeeded to the expected level."* (*Source:* Andhra Pradesh budget speech, 2007-08).

Apart from these ceiling laws, the governments intended to distribute government wastelands to the Dalits, Adivasis and the landless poor. Government named this project as an assignment of government land which was introduced in 1969. The distribution particulars are as follows.

"Total land to the tune of 48,30,712.21 Acres were distributed under this assignment of government lands Act. It was distributed among 33,79,699 beneficiaries among whom, the Dalit beneficiaries were 7,48,217 who got land to the tune of 10,15,424.74 acres, Adivasi beneficiaries were 9, 24,031 who got land to the tune of 12,77,100.85 acres. Among them, backward caste beneficiaries were 7,39,208 who got land to the tune of 9,45,167.28 Acres." (*Source:* Paper on land revenue administration—a historical outlook: Shri C. Umamaheswara Rao, I.A.S, Commissioner, AMR-APARD)

Later, the land distribution particulars under this assignment of government lands Actin this district are "Total land to the tune of 1,27,365.05 acres had been distributed among 1,32,254 beneficiaries among whom Dalit beneficiaries were 28,488 who got land to the tune of 26,583.60 acres. Among them, Adivasi beneficiaries were 43,817 who got land to the tune of 47,597.25 acres, backward caste beneficiaries were 32,861 who got land to the tune of 23,247.02 Acres." (*Source:* Paper on land revenue administration—a historical outlook Shri C. Umamaheswara Rao, I.A.S, Commissioner, AMR-APARD).

The distributed lands were worthless in nature as they were rocky and filled with shrubs. The Dalits traditionally had no where withal to cultivate the land. In many occasion, the Dalits tried to bring loans and strive hard to get the good soil. However, as part of this credit, either they had to forfeit the crop or they had to sell the land. Moreover, during 1970-80, the Dalits had no other occupation except the agrarian labour. Their wage was not even enough to feed them. In these circumstances, either they had left the lands barren or they had sold the lands. The peasantry castes who grabbed these lands used to mock at Dalits and comment, "Can the Dalits keep their lands? They are too lazy to do field work."

In fact, the peasantry castes amassed the wealth on the labour of these Dalits. They conveniently forgot this fact while making these rude remarks on Dalits.

In fact, in the villages surveyed, majority of lands were alienated from Dalits. These programmes were worked as indirect distribution of government land to rural rich peasantry. The Agricultural Minister of Andhra Pradesh, Hon'ble Raghuveera Reddy declared, *"so far in Andhra Pradesh, the government distributed 46 Lakhs acres to the landless. Almost 1/10th of the land, i.e., 4.35 lakhs of Acres were alienated. Some lands were sold by beneficiaries while some are grabbed. So far, the government had taken over 2.88 lakhs Acres."* (*Source:* Andhra Jyothy daily, dated 01/01/2013).

Occupational Pattern of Dalits

Even at the national level, the percentage of Dalit cultivators was decreasing. As per the data of the National Scheduled Commission 2004-05, in the year 1961, the percentage of cultivators among Dalits was 37.76, which dropped to 27.87 during 1971. It showed an increase in 1981 and recorded 28.17. Further, it slipped down to 25.44 per cent, recording as 22.08 per cent in 2001. Thus, it was understood that the judicial redistribution of land to landless specifically to Dalits was not successful. The statistics revealed that the Dalits were losing their nominal base on land. As per the national reports, at all India level, 12.26 per cent of Dalits is landless whereas in Andhra Pradesh, the percentage is 13.88.

Table 5. Landholding Pattern among Dalits in Srikakulam District

(Area in Acres)

Year	Marginal (<2.46 acres)		Small (2.47 - 4.92 acres)		Semi Medium (4.93-9.87 acres)		Medium (9.88 - 24.7 acres)		Large (> 24.71 acres)		Total all Classes	
	No	Area	No	Area	No	Area	No	Area	No	Area	No	Area
1987	35188	30970.99	3432	10922.37	661	4392.38	34	415.02	3	78.15	39318	46778.91
1990	35995	28720.37	2928	9790	791	5368.11	58	765.16	9	251.7	39781	44895.34
2001	36508	23924.46	3531	11643	1023	5888.89	305	2815.4	0	0	41367	44271.71
2005	36256	30074.09	3358	11038.88	125	1554.48	884	5495.6	0	0	40623	48163.06
2011	36480	29051.4	2845	9220.08	550	3419.4	104	1355.46	0	0	40339	43046.34

Source: District Handbooks and agcensus.nic.in

Table 6. Cultivators Among Dalits

Sl. No	Census Year	Dalit Main Workers	Dalit Cultivators	Percentage of Dalit Cultivators to Dalit main Workers
1.	1981	135597	21587	15.92
2.	1991	150959	15537	10.29
3.	2001	117993	9058	7.68
4.	2011	136606	4723	3.47

Source: Primary census abstracts.

As seen from this table 5, there was no considerable increase in the quantum of land. In the year 1987, total land rested with Dalits was 46,778.91 acres out of which majority holdings were marginal and small. In the year 1987, these holdings stood at 98.22 per cent. By 2005, the total holdings went up to 40,623, with the land resting with them was 48,163.06 acres. In the current decade even the land was alienated from the Dalits. They lost 5,116 acres of land to others. The share of marginal and small peasants stood at 97.48 per cent. In fact, this table shows medium land holdings as 884. However, in the surveyed villages, not even a single medium sized land holding rested with Dalits.

The pattern of cultivators among Dalits was to be examined. The table 6 indicates the changing pattern. This table reflects the national trends. In the census year 1881, there were 21,587 cultivators in Dalits and it had a share of 15.92 per cent of Dalit main workers. In 1991 census, it dropped to 15,537 cultivators. The overall decrease was 6,050 and the percentage in decline was 28.02. During 1991-2001, the actual cultivators were a mere 9,058. The net decrease in the number was 6,479, a whooping 41.70. Over a span of 20 years, the net decrease in the Dalit cultivators was by 58.03 per cent to 12,529. In 2011, the number of cultivators further dropped to 4,723. Thus a net decrease in the current decade recorded as 4,335. In percentage terms it is recorded as 47.85. In a span of 30 years after repeating promises for land distribution, the Dalits are consistently loosing their profession as cultivators. In a span of 30 years the net decrease is 16,864 and in percentage terms it is recorded as 78.12. It is clear that more than per cent of the erstwhile Dalits peasantry turned as proletarian.

It showed the reality of the land ownership among Dalits. In other words, the land holding pattern during the year 2011 was 40,339 with the number of cultivators being 4723. It can be construed that either the Dalits gave their piece of land to the lease or they made the land as current fallow.

The survey results across the district showed a forlorn figure in the ownership on land. The research on Dalits covering 56 Mandals/Tehsils across the Srikakulam district revealed the facts regarding the land holding pattern among Dalits to be excruciating. In the surveyed 120 villages that were surveyed, Dalits resided in 78 villages' with 4,855 Dalit families. Out of them, 3,462 families belonged to Mala sub-caste, 892 families to Madiga Sub-caste, 290 families to Pydi sub-caste and 67 families to Relli Sub-caste.

Out of 4,855 families, only 67 families have G. Ryti titles meaning that only 1.3 per cent of Dalits were initially owning land. In the wake of land reforms, assignment of lands and occupying of tank beds made Dalits the "Land owners". As such, in 39 villages, 1063 families could acquire lands to the extent of 679.67 acres. The data derived the percentage of landless people in the surveyed villages stood at 76.72.All the Dalits were marginal and sub-marginal peasants.The abolition of intermediaries could not provide a parcel of land to these deprived sections. Barring one village, in all other villages, the Dalits could not get the benefits of abolition. In the villages surveyed, only in Adavaram village, two Dalit families could get four acres each.

In majority of the villages, the Dalits lost their lands to the rich peasantry of their villages. In one village (on the plea of anonymity) on record, 95 acres were distributed but all the lands were rested with the rich peasantry. Though they had a patch of land, as in Thorner's words, they faced insurmountable difficulties in their cultivation. They ranged from obstruction of cultivation to annihilation of Dalits. No village was an exception to these attacks. However, the space constraint restricted to recount all the examples. Every incident revealed the brutal nature of the rich peasantry that was even disheartening to hear.

As already said, influential sections of these four peasant castes replaced the three upper castes because of the elimination of intermediaries. The Brahmin community had almost been vacated from the villages. The upper castes only had economically powerful numerically less in the villages. The influential sections of these peasant castes had an additional weapon specifically the caste. In the absence of class consolidation, these sections raised the sentiments and kept the innumerable number of people with them. These sections were being used as an unpaid army along the countryside to these rich peasantry sections.

Gopannavalasa is a village in Merakamudidam Mandal where the Government distributed 6.76 acres of land to Dalits with Toorpukapu being the major peasant caste here. Toorpukapus objected this assignment on the plea that those were tank-bed. Revenue administration surveyed the lands and certified that those were not tank-bed.Toorpukapus pleaded that the land allotted to the Dalits receives the rain water first and from there the water would be channelled to other tanks.

Dalits started cultivation in those lands. Meanwhile, the peasantry alleged that the Dalits were trying to occupy the tanks. This led to legal disputes and both the parties took to litigation. On one hand, while the legal proceedings were on, on the other hand, two Dalit leaders were murdered. In fact, the Dalits agitated many times across the District, and criminal cases were booked against the peasantry. The session's court sentenced all the accused but were freed by high court. While the murders were true, the murderers were unknown forever. The proverbial expression "*dead men tell no tales*" was again proved in this incident.

Tolapi is a village in Ponduru Mandal where Kalinga caste is the major peasant caste. Government allotted 0.15 acres each to 39 Dalit families during the mid-70s where the Dalits tried to cultivate the land. Kalinga obstructed this and attempted to prevent those cultivations. In every harvest season, they used to drive their cattle for destructing the crop. Finally, they stopped their cultivation.

Konuru is a village in Garividi Mandal where Kshatriya family owned almost 90 per cent of the agricultural land. The family imposed ruthless economic and social oppression on the entire population of the village. The abolition of intermediaries conferred a massive land to that Kshatriya family. To evade the land ceiling Acts, the family even created titles on their attached lanbour. Majji Tammanna, an attached labour, came to know of this fact and tried to protest this action. The majority peasant caste Toorpukapu too faced the social oppression. Hence, some of the families of this caste supported the cause of Tammanna. By that time, the district scenario had changed considerably and significant economic and political powers were transferred to the peasant castes. Gorle Sriramulunaidu of that taluk (before the creation of Mandals, the village was in native taluk of Gorle Sriramulunaidu namely Cheepurupalli) was emerged as a crown-less king in the district. When the kapus met him, he told them to assault the Kshatriyas physically and reminded them about Kapu pride. One day as usual, the Kshatriya family had called the kapu peasantry in a filthy language and used abusive language on the whole caste. Since they already obtained assurance from Gorle Sriramulunaidu, the kapu caste people attacked physically on them. With this incident, they stopped the practice on Kapus. However, Tammanna continued to agitate for the land with kapus withdrawing from the same. The issue went to district revenue machinery. Dalit families met the collector.

Since the collector was on camp, with their entire families they stayed all night in the headquarters waiting to meet him. Meanwhile, Shodhana, a voluntary organisation based in Cheepurupalli supported the agitation. They reminded the Kshatriyas about the constitutional safeguards provided to Dalits and warned the family with dire consequences. The changed political scenario during the early 80s also came in relief. Finally, Tammanna got rights on the land. However, the remaining Dalit families could not dare to cultivate the lands, which were on their names legally. Tammanna warned them that he would take the lands. Then the Dalits took possession and for a long time, they were cultivating the lands. Despite this, the entire family still owned almost three-fourth of the village land. They could keep their land intact, but they could not conduct the archaic feudal exploitation on the village. Now they planted mango groves in the majority portion of land because of the non-availability of cheap labour.

Boddam is a village in Rajam Mandal. Polinativelama is the major peasant caste here. During the late 70s, the government distributed 40 acres to 60 Dalitfamilies who tried to cultivate the lands. The peasant caste people obstructed the cultivation and attacked the Dalits physically. The Dalits lodged a complaint in the police station at Rajam. Incidentally, the sub-inspector of police belonged to Dalit. He immediately responded and booked the case. Nothing happened and the lands remained uncultivated for long.

Dalaipeta is a village in Komarada Mandal. Despite the best efforts of two Dalit I.A.S officers, the Dalits could not cultivate in the village. The Dalits occupied the lands under the banner of the then undivided Communist Party of India (CPI) during the early 60s. Actually, this land belonged to the Hill zamindar of Kurupam. The government had not conferred any title on the land. Since it is rain fed, they could not cultivate the land profitably. During the late 70s, Shri B. Danam, the then District collector tried to provide irrigation facility to the lands by planning to build a reservoir in Madalangi village only to Channalise the water from Gummadigedda, a regular stream from the hill tracts. The villagers of Madalangi objected this plan on the pretext of inundation of the lands of their village. The villagers went to the court and the judgment came favouring the villagers. Hence, the proposed project was stopped. Again during the early 90s, the then collector (by that time, this area was transferred to Vizianagaram District) Shri Radha tried to provide irrigation and sanctioned lift irrigation scheme and the water was planned to be drawn from the river Nagavali. The Dalits had to manage with the system properly. For two years with a unity, all the Dalits managed the system well and they could reap the benefit. Naturally, their effort worried the peasantry and they planned to end the cooperation among Dalits and the general election of 1994 enable them to succeed in the ploy. The consensus among Dalits had been disrupted and hence they could not perform the lift irrigation system besides the lands becoming barren. Later, 90 per cent of the Dalit families migrated to Chennai.

Ponugutivalasais a village adjacent to Rajam, a Mandal headquarter. This village was under the jurisdiction of Santakaviti Mandal. In the post 90s, Rajam turned as an industrial town under the aegis of the world famous GMR group. In Ponugutivalasa village, the government distributed the lands to Dalit families during the early 70s. It was also a rain fed village and the land could not fetch the livelihood for them. To get rid of the debt burden, they sold the lands. A son of a rich peasant became a doctor during late 60s, and he emerged as a district officer in the health department. He bought majority of lands in the village. In this way, the Dalits also sold their lands at throw away price. Due to industrialisation, the land rates spiralled and it was too difficult to buy a square yard there. To sum up, the rich peasant turned-bureaucrat benefitted a lot.

Though it was peculiar to hear, in some villages, the government schemes had made the Dalits leave their lands. Some examples were required to know the facts.

Sirusuvada is a village in Kothuru Mandal where the Government allotted barren lands to 50 Dalit families who with all efforts made the lands cultivable. The government took over some land to build houses for the backward classes. Some land was acquired to build a flood channel to Vamshadhara Phase II reservoir.

Annavaramis a village in Palakonda Mandal where Government allotted river poramboku lands to the Dalit families who brought the lands under cultivation.They put bore well connection to the fields, planted cashew and mango groves in those lands, and reaped the benefits. In the year 1990, floods came in the river Nagavali and the village faced the problem of inundation. The government built a retaining wall to the river Nagavali. In that process, all the lands of Dalits fell into the river and became impossible to cultivate.

Gochekka was a village in Parvatipuram Mandal. As mentioned earlier, the Mandal was 100 per cent rain fed. Not only in Gochekka but in many villages of this Mandal too, the villagers had lost their lands to capitalist farmers. The capitalist farmers include the professionals of the peasant castes and settlers from other districts. It was one of the strange examples of the land alienation. The Dalits had sold the government assigned lands to pay the debt that caused by another government scheme. One government purchased the land from a Kamma settler through scheduled caste corporation and distributed two acres each in which cashew plantations were put. The Dalits were benefitted from the distribution. After 2009 elections, the government sanctioned houses under the housing scheme to Dalits. The housing scheme was named after the late Prime Minister Indira Gandhi. In local dialect, it was called "Indiramma Illu". The amount sanctioned under the scheme was insufficient to complete the construction and hence they took loans. By the time of completing the houses, the mounting debt burden made them sell the lands to another Kshatriya settled farmer.

Even the National Commission on Scheduled Castes recorded this feature. It quoted the report of Expert Committee of VIII Five-year plan, whichread, "*Allottees of ceiling surplus or government land are generally victims of harassment by dispossession, obstruction to cultivation, etc. Invariably in such cases, the administration should defend the Scheduled caste assignee particularly by getting them added as necessary parties in the litigation, etc., and protecting the land with Scheduled Castes is essential. Very often the others try to trap the Scheduled Castes people by making them borrow money on usurious interest mortgaging the land with them. The conditions of allotment and the debt relief provisions should be strictly enforced to.*" (*Source:* National S.C. Commission report, 1994-95)

The list was endless. However, the National Commissions recommendations could not protect the lands of the Dalits in the surveyed villages.

Attached Labour-Replica of Semi-serf Life

There was no alternative to rural Dalits except the labour on the land since there were mostly no rights of ownership on the lands for these sections. Since the agrarian labour was seasonal in nature, the Dalits preferred the attached labour (in the local dialect Telugu, it is called Kambari/Paleru) to earn their livelihood. In the district, many landless people of different castes worked as attached labour in this district, but most Dalits were attached labour.

Rakesh Basant made a detailed study on the attached labour during the early 80s. It read, "*In so far as the socially and economically handicapped scheduled castes, scheduled tribes and other backward castes acquiring the bulk of the attached labour contracts, and their employers are large farmers the latter may be in a position to pay them lower wage rates and/or depress the effective wage rates for this category of workers by extracting longer hours or more arduous work."* (Attached and casual labour wage rates: Rakesh Basant: Economic and political weekly, 3rd March, 1984 page: 393)

Further, he added, *"The employment of attached labour could, however, adversely affect the wages of the casual workers by reducing their bargaining power. The already weak bargaining power of wage labour can be further eroded when they get divided into those having security of employment and those without".* (Attached and casual labour wage rates: Rakesh Basant: Economic and political weekly, 3rd March,1984 page: 393)

The wages of the attached labour were extremely miserable. They were not even sufficient to cater to their minimum needs. There was no time schedule to work. Normally, the work started at 4 am and ended at 8 pm.

During the early 70s, the wage was paid in the form of grain, which during those years was 180 kilograms of grain. The measurements were also faulty. The peasantry used to give inferior quality food for three times. Rich peasants used to give 0.05 or 0.10 acres to the attached labour and the yield on the land were used to be given to that attached labour. The Dalits, who were always starved, used to keep their children in the house of rich peasantry as child labour. These children used to work as cattle keepers. They used to work in the houses of rich peasantry from the age of seven years. The term was nothing but an apprenticeship for the future full-time attached labour to the progeny of Dalit attached labour. The wives of the attached labour used to work in the house as a house cleaner and in farmyard only to get a pickle at the end of the day. To put briefly, the total family of the attached labour were bonded to the rich peasantry only to get a "permanent" job with a minimum guarantee of semi–starvation.

During 1960-67, the then Communist Party of India and Communist party of India Marxist, CPI (M) tried to organise the attached labour in this district. Their influence was limited to small places in the plain areas and to considerable areas in tribal tracts.

After that period, mostly there was no agitation supporting this attached labour. The economic and social oppression had no limits in the country side. Almost it went unbridled. No organisation, which ever theory it embraced, came to organise them. In the villages surveyed, barring one tribal village, nobody had reported such struggles. In fact, the attached labour they were unable to recognise their state of affairs.

When asked them the reason for making such a menial profession, a former attached labour aged about 80 years in Kanugulavalasa village told in an awful feeling "Hunger! We were famished. Even we had dreams about taking food. When we were going along the riverside, there were sand dunes. We always used to dream if these sand dunes could transform as heap of rice to enable us to eat in a voraciously."

The ushering of capitalist relations in the shape of transport, communication, education and electricity, etc., had paved the way for freeing these semi-serfs from the clutches of rich peasantry. The alternate employment opportunities that followed with the self-consciousness liberated them from the iron fist of that laborious work. The retreat slowly started during the late 80s in this district, and it reached its peak during the late 90s. By the turn of 21st century, almost the profession had disappeared from the countryside. In fact, it was a decisive victory of the new opportunities on the out-dated relations.

However, the hearts of the medium and rich peasantry were crammed with anguish due to disappearance of this profession. When asked about the reasons particularly for such disappearance of the profession and on the changing labour relations in the countryside, octogenarian peasant caste women in Dalaipeta village replied outrageously "*over! The good olden days had gone. Nowadays, these Dalits are not even listening to us. Earlier, we used to compel the Dalits from their huts by 4 am in case of their absence, used to tie them to pillars and whisk them with whips*". This statement represented the opinion of rural affluent sections. In the villages surveyed, only in one village, an organisation tried to organise the attached labour. Duggeru is a tribal hamlet in Makkuva Mandal. In this village, the association of peasants, labourers and poor people (in Telugu Rytu coolie pedala sangham, Andhra Pradesh) organised Adivasis and Dalits for seeking a hike in the wages of attached labour and achieved a partial success. However, by that time, the profession as a whole waned out in the remaining broad plain areas.

Dalits as Agrarian Labour

After the previously mentioned profession, the other alternative to the Dalits in the district was agrarian labour. Official Data is indicating that the army of agrarianlabour is swelling day by day. Thousands and lakhs of the peasantry is losing their foothold on their patch of land and adding to the army of rural proletarian. From the beginning, the Dalits who had no right on the land had to work on land either as attached labour or as daily wage earner. Until the early 90s, almost the entire population who had no chance to earn the livelihood as an owner, had to work as agrarian labour since the migration was almost unknown to them. Added to this, the opportunities also appeared to be bleak during that period prior to early 90s.

National figures indicated that the percentage of Dalit coolies was increasing. In 1961, their percentage was recorded as 34.48, and it went up to 52.23 per cent in 2001 census.

Table 7. Agrarian Labour among Dalits in the District

Sl. No.	*Census Year*	*Dalit Main Workers*	*SC Agl Labour*	*Percentage of Dalit Agl. Labour to Dalit main Workers*
1.	1971		97740	
2.	1981	135597	94594	69.76
3.	1991	150959	113213	75.00
4.	2001	117993	82238	69.70
5.	2011	136066	67900	49.90

Source: Primary census abstracts.

As seen from this table in the year 1981, the percentage of Dalit agrarian proletariat among Dalit main workers was recorded as 69.76. This was escalated to 75 per cent in 1991, which had further dropped to 69.70 per cent during 2001. In concrete terms too, it drastically dropped during the 2001 census. In concrete term, it had increased during 1981-91to 18,519 with the percentage increase as 19.68. The agrarian proletariat had drastically decreased during 1991-2001 to 30,975 with the percentage decline as 27.35. In the current decade the decrease in the agrarian labour recorded as 14, 338 and in percentage terms it is 17.43. In a span of 20 years of "globalisation" the Dalit agrarian labour dwindled in absolute number 45, 313. Nearly half lakh people vacated the age old profession.

The data revealed interesting information that even the main workers were also showing a decreasing trend. Dalit had to earn their livelihood as workers only. Then where the Dalits were going and where were they earning their livelihood? It was clear that the Dalits were leaving the villages to avoid the obnoxious circumstances that haunted them in the footsteps of Manu.

During the Census year 1971, the total agrarian labour in this district was 4,13,538. During the same year, the Dalit agrarian labour was 97,740 with percentage wise Dalit agrarian labour to be 23.63. Almost every one Dalit person out of 4 persons was an agrarian labour. The situation changed drastically by 2001 census. By 2001, the agrarian labour was almost doubled reaching 8,20,197. The net increase in the agrarian labour was 4,06,659 with the percentage increase as 98.33. Since the crowd was swelling with other social groups, and the percentage of migration of Dalit labour over agrarian labour as a whole is decreased to 18 per cent during 1991 and 10.03 per cent.

Hence, the data indicated that the Dalits were leaving the land as a cultivator and workforce.

In general, the agrarian labour and particularly the Dalits had strived hard to earn their livelihood from the wages in the agrarian sector. Their income was too meagre to meet both the ends.

The wage rate was determined at the mercy of the rich peasantry of the villages. As already said, the influential sections of the four peasant castes had enjoyed considerably for almost 30-35 years in the countryside. The cheap labour earned profits in the agricultural sector for them. The sordid lifestyle could not grab much money from them. They could turn this profit as a rural capital and at the same time their savings exported the capital to the urban sector. Their usurious interest rates worked as a powerful implement in amassing the rural wealth from the hapless rural proletarian. Even the minimum wage Acts were not being implemented there. There was no sufficient machinery to implement these Acts along the countryside. The rural proletarian was not in a position to know anything about these Acts. The rural labour enquiry 1974-75 confirmed this fact and remarked, *"Only about two per cent of agricultural workers were even aware of the Minimum Wages Act, and the wages fixed under these Acts for their respective regions."* (Quoted in Economic and political weekly, June 14-21, 1980 page 1045).

Profit in a business is nothing but extraction of surplus value. This surplus value had reached the entrepreneurs of the countryside in the form of attached labour and in the form of cheap agrarian labour. Along with this, the highly subsidised inputs reached the destination, which was invariably the house of rich peasantry. In other words, the crores of money that gathered through taxation had reached the houses of rich peasantry and the urban input manufacturers. All these methods seemed to strengthen the rural rich peasantry. However, in real terms, not every rich peasant could be turned as an urban entrepreneur. They invariably either spent the surplus money or saved them. Nevertheless, the expropriated rural wealth reaches the urban to strengthen the urban entrepreneurs.

In the initial phase, the urban capital grabs the progeny of rich peasantry as their intellectual base and settles them as high-paid wage earners. The rural proletarian procreated the urban proletarian. The first process made the rich peasantry happy and the other made them unpleasant. The second process made them reduce their profit in the shape of surplus value. The second process weakened the process of exploitation and social oppression along the countryside.

Ignorance, Illiteracy, aloofness and scattered workforce in 6,00,000 and above villages made them disunited. No political organisation irrespective of their ideology came to rescue them from this drudgery. In the absence of class-consciousness, the rich peasantry used the caste sentiment as a formidable weapon in arresting the wage rate. In the villages surveyed during 1970-2011, no united struggles for the cause of rural proletarian took place in this district. There were no unions for them. The rural labour enquiry of 1974-75 confirmed this fact and remarked "only 1 per cent of agricultural labourers were members of any organisation or union of farm labourers." (Quoted in Economic and political weekly, June 14-21, 1980 page 1045).

The national situation also revealed the same scenario. Duringthe early 70s, the average daily wage rate in the countryside was only Rs. 2.70 Rs. 10.41 during 1984-85. Even the policy makers of the minimum wage Acts were of the opinion that the circumstances were not conducive to fix a reasonable wage rate in the countryside. "Economic and Political Weekly" quoted the remarks of the Andhra Pradesh minimum wage committee members reading, *"the national income was low and therefore any wage fixation on ethical grounds would adversely affect the state of the economy and retard agricultural production itself"*. Further, the same article carried the Gujarat state minimum wage committee remarks which read, *"The capacity of agriculture to pay a minimum wage and the needs of workers were illusory concepts"*. The committee recommended a wage rate "which would not be burdensome to agriculture". (*Source:* Sham of minimum wages: Economic and Political Weekly, June 14-21, 1980 page 1044).

Professor Late G. Parthasarathy made a comprehensive research on the stagnation of real wages and concluded, *"Despite considerable rise in money wages, real wages of agriculture labour in Andhra Pradesh are marked by stagnation. There is no association between trends in real wages and per capita (rural) agricultural production. The picture of stagnation at the state level applies also to mostly all districts. A note worthy aspect of the data is the negative, though not statistically significant, trend in real wages for a relatively well developed district such as West Godavari which is known to have experienced significant changes in technology"* (Real wages of agricultural labour in Andhra Pradesh: two decades of stagnation: EPW July 31,1982 pages 1248: G.Parthasarathy).

This research indicated that the development in the productivity of the agriculture could not lead to automatic enhancement of wage rate in the rural proletarian. As seen from the research report of G. Parthasarathy, West Godavari was the finest example of the expropriation of rural surplus value.

In fact, along with the caste sentiment, there was also a class collaboration, which prevailed in this district. The small and marginal peasantry too had to use wage labour to some extent. The surplus extraction of these ordinary people was also not in small number. Hence, these sections also give voice to rich peasantry in curbing the voice of rural proletarian. In fact, in some villages, the agrarianlabour had their groups on caste basis. Of late, it is vanishing. In the villages surveyed, Piridi of Bobbili Mandal was a splendid example for this wherein the agrarian labour of peasant castes formed a group with Dalits forming a separate group, which was continuing for a long period though the groups are not functioning of late. A rich peasant Balaga Rama Rao of Piridi Village complained about the enhancement of wages and commented, "Even the marginal peasants and sub-marginal peasants of our peasant caste were demanding higher wage. They do not have any caste sentiments but are giving voice to proletarian. Since they possessed a patch of land, their earnings on the wage were better than their earnings on the cultivation." Probably it was indicating the sharpening contradiction between the rural proletarian and the rural rich peasantry.

Though the rich peasantry was complaining about the hike in the wage rates, it appeared that the real wage growth was nominal.The main reason for the stagnation lied in the disunity among the vastly scattered masses.The rural agricultural sector was feminising day by day. The men of the villages were moving to better places with earning potential. Even later, a female was getting half the wage rate of her counterpart. This situation was leading to earn profits for the settlers who were making cotton cultivation on a large scale. However, women are self-contending with this paltry wage on the pretext that the workdays were increased. Thus, it showed the miserable state of wages in the rural sector.

Mechanisation and migration were the two reasons for the increase in the wages at least in numbers. Rich peasantry had discovered a method to deter the hike in the wage rates. In any village, whenever any rural proletarian requested for a hike, the rich peasants threatened them from introducing machinery. Gradually, these methods annoyed the agrarian labour and thus started withdrawing from the scene as soon as they had opportunities. The withdrawal of agrarian brought some demand to the rural proletarian in the countryside and the nominal wages were increased.

With the inevitable increase in the wage rate, the rural rich peasantry transformed themselves towards less labour intensive crops like oil palm and plantations. The rural sector was traversing in a mutual adjustment process.

Social Oppression and Attacks on Dalits

As seen from the historical backdrop, the upper caste Brahmin, Kshatriya and Velama Dora had unleashed economic and social oppression on the peasant castes ruthlessly. During that period (time immemorial to late 60s), their oppression had no bounds. It was clear from the earlier Brahmin Inamdari villages that their oppression was mainly carried out on peasant castes. Since the upper castes had a large cushion, the Dalits appeared to be free from the bite of these upper castes. As revealed by Dalit sections of these Inamdari villages, they were not even allowed to go even to the streets of Brahmin dwellings and they did not even touch them. Putting briefly, the Brahmins ostracized the Dalits and it had put strong agony in the minds of Dalits but it appeared that the Brahmins did not instigate physical attacks on them.

The peasant castes who acquired economic power from these upper castes, had also acquired the mantle of brahminical order. They re-enacted the drama of social oppression on the Dalits, artisans, and castes of servitude. The attacks were not limited to untouchability; rather those were converted as physical attacks, sexual exploitation, social boycotts, rejecting their right of work besides extraction of surplus value. No village was an exception for the despicable practices. In the villages surveyed, there mains of the shadows of the social and economic oppression still existed. No village is an exception for such atrocious deeds. The Dalits had reached a position to accept it as a common feature till the early 90s.

In every village, a twin theory was being practiced. In any village, if Dalits asked for meagre hikes in the wage rate, they used to lose the right to work. Soon thereafter, the peasant castes ordered for a social boycott. The barber and washermen do not go to their houses on fearing the atrocity. Still in many villages, the Dalits were struggling to enter the temples. Normally, the peasant castes were using brute forces to utilise and grab the common property resources of the village. Above all, the attacks on the Dalits were directly proportional to their assertiveness of their rights.

Regarding physical assaults on these Dalits, no peasant caste had an exception. In fact, all these Sudra castes were identified as backward classes. In seven to eight Mandals of this district, Kalinga caste was a dominant peasant caste that was in the list of backward classes. Andhra Pradesh government categorised backward classes in to four categories as A, B, C, D groups. The order was in ascending order of their social position. 'A' category is considered the most backward. Kalinga was placed in "A" category, along with them, the barbers and washer men in such castes of servitude were grouped in the category. In fact, this caste was a closely knitted caste and they had no exception in conducting such attacks on those deprived castes. They had their own priests in their caste and the only peasant caste in North Andhra wear the sacred thread.

As per the list of reservation order, they are just one-step ahead of Dalits. In this district, this is one of the castes, which had a strong economic and political base. They used to follow and implement the brahminical social order. Tolapi, a village in Ponduru Mandal was a fine example for their atrocious behaviour on Dalits. During the year 2001, the then TDP government used to carry "Janmabhoomi" (Mother land) programme in the state. The intention of conducting this programme was to send the officers to the village to know the problems encountered by the public. In that meeting, the Dalits complained to the officers on practicing untouchability. Kalingas, who came to know about the complaint, rallied all the castes of those villages and attacked the Dalits on 15th July 2001. They beat, carried out arson and rummaged their huts. The helpless Dalits started fleeing helter-skelter, but the Kalinga caste people without for giving them, continued to attack and many were injured. One Dalit person, Chintala Ramaiah succumbed to injuries.

For a long time, the peasant castes rejected the constitutional right "right to vote" to Dalits. During 1986-87 election, at Korasavada village of Patapatnam Mandal, the Dalits voted for Congress. The angry weaver community attacked the Dalits for not casting their vote favouring the candidates of their will. In these villages, the weaver community were the land owned and of formidable. This caste belongs to "B" category of the backward castes.

During the 1981 co-operative elections, in Kuppili village a Dalit person contested in the election against the whims and pleasures of the village "caste elders". Immediately the caste people rallied the village against the Dalits and Dalits ran in terror. The group destructed their huts and whisked them. Dalits ran to nearby villages and town to save their lives. Here, the majority caste is Reddika and were the category "A" of backward castes.

Piridi, a village became famous for its development in the education sector. Here, Koppulavelama was the peasant caste under the D category of backward castes. During the early 90s, the caste people rallied the whole village and attacked a Dalit Street. Here, the sub-sect of Dalits, Madiga used to carry the dead animals. On the day of village goddess festival, they were on that work. They were required to beat the drums during the festival. Since they were on other work, they could not come on time. The angered sarpanch asked for the explanation and while he was answering, the sarpanch manhandled him.The Dalits expressed their displeasure over this then the peasant castes started beating the Dalits and attacked their houses carrying out social boycott on Dalits. Cases were booked against peasant castes, but eventually the caseswere closed with a compromise.

Kapushambham is a village in Garividi Mandal. The village sarpanch went to a street where Dalit lived to solve a family problem in that street. A rumour was floated that the sarpanch was attacked by Dalits. Without ascertaining the credibility of the rumour, the Toorpukapus attacked the Dalit Street and physically assaulted the entire Dalits, and they did not even let them go to the hospital. At last, the news spread to other areas and the democrats and civil society entered the scene and saved Dalits.

Brundavanam is a village in Santabommali Mandal where even until 2004-2005, there was no polling booth. The polling booth was in Kashipuram village. The Dalits of Brundavanam village supported Congress party. Kalingas and Yadavas of the Kashipuram villages did not let them vote and started attacking them physically. The Dalits ran away to escape from the attack and complained about the attacks. The case is still in the court. However, polling booth was established in the village. Here, Yadavas belonged to "D" category of backward castes.

As long as the Dalits kept quiet on the indecorous behaviour of the peasant castes, they were not resorting assaults. Whenever Dalits tried to defend their rights, they were attacked. In this way, every village had the foot prints of brutal attacks of backward castes on the hapless Dalits. However, of late the attacks had scaled down. The social awareness, the education above all, changing occupation pattern and the migration provided a checkmate to the unrestrained assaults.

A noticeable fact was the backward castes which had a control on the means of production, had resorted to such vicious attacks on the Dalits. In the fight against upper castes, the peasant castes could gain control on the means of production, but this did not happen in the case of Dalits. Hence, the Dalits, particularly the Dalit youth, left their subjugation of the menacing atmosphere of villages.

Education and Employment

For a long time, the Dalits of the country as a whole and particularly in this district was caught in the jaws of illiteracy. Orthodox Hindu social order legally proscribed education to Dalits. It was only after the advent of colonial Rule, could they learn constitutional rights. Though the constitutional provisions allowed them, the stark reality of poverty and impoverishment prevented them from going to school. The absence of ownership on the means of production made them wage workers. In such a situation, they could not send their children to schools.

In the surveyed villages too, the situation was not unusual. While the children of the land owned families were going to school, the malnourished children of the Dalits were engaged in earning two square meals in their houses as cattle keepers. Hence, in the surveyed villages, the gap among these social groups was extraordinary. There prevailed almost a three generations difference in the development angle. The following Table indicates the statistics of literacy among Dalits in India.

Table 8. Comparative Literacy Data on Dalits vs. National Literacy Level

Sl. No.	*Year*	*Total Male*	*Total Female*	*Total*	*Dalit male*	*Dalit female*	*Total*
1.	1971	39.45	18.7	29.5	22.36	6.44	14.67
2.	1981	46.89	24.82	36.2	31.12	10.93	21.38
3.	1991	64.1	39.3	52.2	49.91	23.76	37.41
4.	2001	75.3	53.7	64.8	66.64	41.9	54.69
5.	2011	80.89	64.64	72.99			

Source: Census abstracts and National S.C. Commission Reports.

Table 9. Comparative Literacy Data on Dalits vs. State Literacy Level

Sl. No.	*Year*	*Male*	*Female*	*Total*	*Dalit male*	*Dalit female*	*Total*
1.	1971	33.2	15.8	24.6	13.43	3.4	8.47
2.	1981	39.3	20.4	29.9	15.9	5.3	10.7
3.	1991	55.1	32.7	44.1	24.88	10.25	17.7
4.	2001	70.3	50.4	60.5	41.88	20.92	31.6
5.	2011	74.88	59.15	67.02			

Source: 50 years of Andhra Pradesh compiled by A.K. Farida, I.A.S., Table 21 and 2011 census data.

As seen from the statistics, during the year 1971, the national literacywas recorded as 29.5 whereas the literacy of Dalits was only 14.67. In fact, during 1961, it was only 10.27. By 2001 census, the national literacy reached 64.8 where as Dalit literacy reached only 54.69. In fact, the dropout rate among Dalits was alarming. As per the human resource ministry report, 70.57 per cent of Dalit children were dropping out at secondary level. Dropout rate among girl children was much higher than Dalit male children with females recording 73.42 while male children, it was only 68.42.

Gross enrolment ratio (hereafter GER) of Dalits in the higher education sector was showing dismal performance. As per 2000 data, the total GER recorded 5.09 per cent males 6.63 per cent and females 3.08 per cent. Rural figures were more disturbing in this aspect. The total GER recorded was 3.40 per cent with males 5.07 per cent and females only 1.70 per cent. (*Source:* Higher education in India issues related to Expansion, inclusiveness, Quality and Finance: University Grants Commission, New Delhi).

The state of affairs in Andhra Pradesh was more disturbing when compared with the other parts of the country.

It is seen from this data the lower rate of literacy in general and particularly the Dalits. By 2001, Dalits at national level achieved 54.69. However, Dalits could achieve 31.6 per cent of literacy in this state with Dalit females faring badly in this state. Their literacy was just 20.92 per cent. As per the human resource ministry report, 70.24 per cent of Dalit children dropped out at secondary school level with dropout rate among girl children was higher than the Dalit male children withfemales recording 72.24 while male children recorded 68.41.

As said earlier, in Adivasi chapter, the magic in the data is to be uncovered. In fact, the literacy rate of Scheduled Castes is calculated based on scheduled castes population. Hence, it appeared that literacy gained encouragingly. The formula of the statisticians is like this.

$$\frac{\text{Literates in Dalits}}{\text{Total Dalit population}} \times 100$$

Table 10. Literacy Rate of Dalits in the District

Sl. No.	*Census Year*	*Percentage of SC Literates with SC Population (official statistics)*			*Percentage of SC Literates with Total Literates*		
		Male	*Female*	*Total*	*Male*	*Female*	*Total*
1.	1971	14.50	3.30	8.84	4.84	3.16	4.40
2.	1981	23.08	7.25	15.16	7.07	5.55	6.64
3.	1991	31.93	13.56	22.79	8.04	6.99	7.70
4.	2001	63.64	40.53	52.05	9.29	9.31	9.30

Source: Primary Census abstracts.

However, the comparison between Scheduled Castes literates vis-a-vis total literates were showing startling official figure as per the formula below.

$$\frac{\text{Literates in Dalits}}{\text{Total literates in the district}} \times 100$$

The following table reveals both the figures.

As seen from the Data, the status of literacy of Dalits in this district was disappointing. In the year, the literacy rate stood at 8.84 per cent. Until 1991, there was no progress. During 1991-2001, it recorded massive leap from 22.79 to 52.05. If the following formula was applied, for every 100 literates, the Dalit literates were only 4.40 in the year 1971. The figure reached only to 9.30 in 2001 census.

During the decade 1970-80, the state and union governments consistently proclaimed that the development of Dalits was closely linked with the judicious re-distribution of land. As per the governments review, the schemes were unsuccessful. Hence, during 1990-2000, succeeding governments planned to uplift Dalits through quality education. The budget speech 1999-2000 proclaimed this target. It read, *"The basic development need of the Scheduled Castes families being Education, the Government is constantly improving the spread and access to better quality education."* *(Budget speech 1999-2000).*

Table 11. Employment Pattern in the Surveyed Villages

Sl. No.	*Employment Category*	*Men*	*Women*	*Total*
1.	Teachers	44	6	50
2.	State government	34	5	39
3.	Central government	12	1	13
4.	Defence	13	0	13
5.	Paramilitary	7	0	7
6.	Police	18	0	18
7.	The Public sector	37	1	38
8.	Reputed Private sector	3	0	3
Total		168	13	181

However, this statement also did not yield any result as seen from the above data and the empirical data of this district. The data indicated the actual employment structure of Dalits in this district. In the surveyed villages with Dalits residing in 78 villages. Out of a total 4,855 families, only 181 employees emerged. Dalit streets produced only one doctor and three engineers.

Out of 78 villages surveyed, 49 villages were in *the present Srikakulam district* and 29 villages, were in the *carved out* area,15 villages out of 49 villages could not produce even a single employee.16 villages out of 29 did not have any representation in the employment sector. 31 villages could not get a secured job. One can assume that the public sector had provided jobs to the deprived. Unfortunately, majority of them were working in Andhra Pradesh State Road Transport Corporation Ltd. as conductors and drivers or as messengers in the banking sector. The central government jobs were nothing but E.D. staff of the postal department. All these employees came from 175 families. Only 3.6 per cent of families could produce employees in the surveyed villages. Majority of the employees are in the Department of Police working as either Constables or Home Guards. Only one doctor is working in the state government. Out of three engineers, each one is working in Electricity Board, state government and in the private sector. Mostly the employment generation among the Dalits started during the early 80s.

As seen from the situation, there was an enormous gap in the education-based employment among the Dalits and land owned peasant families. Dalits were lagging behind at least three generations. Empirical evidence confirmed the chasm between the social groups. During early 70s, the children of the rich peasantry could get the employment in the government sector as teachers or as clerks. The rich peasantry could send their children to good schools and they had become technocrats and even crossed the national borders. However, the Dalits of 70s could not imagine the school and they were compelled to make use of their children as attached labour. The children of this attached labour in the third generation with a poor educational background were searching for their livelihood in urban centers. Thus, they reached from their Dalit streets to urban slums. In other words, the land owned peasant families who could utilise the surplus besides enjoying reservations climbed the ladder. However, despite having constitutional safe guards and reservations, the people of these Dalit families could not even touch the ladder.

The situation was reflecting the national situation that prevailed throughout the country. The National Scheduled Caste Commission report 2004-05 too revealed the same observations. It read, *"Economic development in India after five decades of Planned development has bypassed Indian Poor. For the members of scheduled castes who are doubly disadvantaged, the gap between rich and poor has been widening despite technology changes and galloping globalization."* (Chapter three of the report).

Migration

Dr. B.R. Ambedkar described the village, *"The intellectual Indian for the village community is of course infinite, if not pathetic... What is a village but a sink of localism, a den of ignorance, narrow mindedness and communalism?"*

Dalits had stuck on to this wretched atmosphere for centuries. They faced the wrath and oppression there. They could not get decent food for their work. Their wages were so minuscule that they could not meet even their minimum needs of life. This situation had continued until early 90s in the countryside. The openings of villages to the world outside made them flee from the miserable conditions. Hunger and rudeness haunted them. The minimum workdays and the pitiful wages could not make them to live as a human being. Until the late 80s, they used to wait for food at the functions of the peasant houses even without any invitation. They used to remain at the cattle-sheds for the completion of the lunch of the invitees after which the peasant castes used to give the remaining food to Dalits. The Dalits were made to satisfy with that "large heartedness". The children of the current generation Dalits could not tolerate this. The slightest opportunities in the urban and semi-urban areas made them to leave the villages. As already mentioned, in the population pattern, their migration slowly started during early 90s and reached its zenith over the time. The National Commission on Scheduled Castes noted, "*The reason for the decline in SC population seems to be extremely complex which might include methodological deficiency in Census Data collection, migration of SC population to urban from rural areas and a host of other factors. Migration of the scheduled caste population from usual place of residence to other State(s) can affect the number of the scheduled caste population whichis not enumerated "in the place of migration" because the state SCs list is valid only within the jurisdiction of the state or Union territory.*" (Chapter three of the report).

The migration of the Dalits was a common phenomenon at the national level. The empirical data was also in agreement with the National picture.In the surveyed villages, the migration of Dalits ranged from 50 to 75 per cent. The youth had almost left their dwellings. From every family, at least one earning member was migrating. Rarely in some villages the Dalits have a piece of land. However, this too did not prevent them from migrating. The lack of certainty on harvest and the social oppression made the youth to leave the village.

However, there is gloomy aspect of this migration. They were scattered as unorganised agrarian labour class in the villages. They were almost treated as semi-serfs in the rural areas. The migration did not guarantee them a luxurious lifestyle like their counterparts of the offspring of rich peasantry. Here too, they were leading harsh life in urban slums working as unorganised and unskilled workers in construction and transport sectors. They are caught "between Scylla and Charybdis". Despite all these, they preferred urban slums to rural Dalit streets. The minimum guarantee of work days and the dignity made them choose the urban slums. The ministry of social justice released the poverty data of the country as per which, among SCs, the rural poverty recorded 15.4 and in the urban, it recorded 39.9 indicating the transformation of rural poverty as urban poverty for these deprived.

15

The Fishermen and the Sea

The geographic base of Indian marine fisheries has 8118 km. coastline, 2.02 million sq. km. of exclusive economic zone (EEZ) including 0.5 million sq. km. of the continental shelf and 3937 fishing villages. (*Source:* Comprehensive Marine Fishing policy, 2004: Government of India, Ministry of Agriculture, Department of Animal Husbandry and Fisheries).

Indian fishers are leading their life along the seacoast. For a long period, their livelihood depends on the natural source that is sea. Their pattern of life can be compared with Adivasis since they had also depended for along time on the forests, which are a natural resource. However, both their lives encountered severe stress in the wake of development pattern that pursued over a period.The colonial rulers came to the country through the seaways but fortunately, they did not touch the wealth of the sea. Hence, the lives of fishers were largely peaceful. The history did not reveal any significant uprising of fishers like in forest terrains. The British had made a comprehensive survey on the wealth of the seas and oceans in India and Burma. The then Inspector General of Fisheries, Francis Day made a detailed survey and published a report named, *"Report on the sea fish and fisheries in India and Burma"* in the year 1873. Fortunately, the British were contended with forest and wealth of soil. Hence, the lives of the fishers were broadly peaceful. However, the British made an Act namely the Indian Fisheries Act of 1897. They left the subject to provinces.

Andhra Pradesh has a coastline of 982 kilometres. As of now, nine districts have the coastline. Andhra Pradesh has the second largest coastline in India. This district has the longest coastline with 194 kilometres. This district stood first in the number of the fishing village with 107, and it has third place in Indian districts. History proves that the traditional rights on the fishing rested with the fishing communities. In Andhra Pradesh, modernity has not invaded the seawaters until the late 70s. The Government of Andhra Pradesh made efforts to modernise the sea during 1970-80.

Demography of Fisherfolk

As per the national marine census in India, the total marine fishermen population is about 4.0 million comprising 8,64,550 families. Nearly 61per cent of the fishermen families are under BPL category. The average family size is 4.63, and the overall sex ratio is 928 females per 1000 males. Almost 58 per cent of the fisher folk are educated with different levels of education. About 38 per cent marine fisher folk are engaged in active fishing with 85 per cent of them having a full time engagement. About 63.6 per cent of the fisher folk are engaged in fishing and allied activities. Nearly 57 per cent of the fisher folk engaged in fish seed collection are females with 43 per cent being males.

Social Composition of Srikakulam District

There are three fishing communities in this district. Those are Vadabalija, Pallekaru or Agnikulashatriya and Jalari. Government recognised all these castes as backward castes and categorised them under "A". As a profession, Vadabalija used to fish in the sea. In only one village, Pallekaru as profession, go for fishing in the Sea. However, in the surveyed villages, they indicated that they were not doing fishing as a profession. Jalari caste conducted their activity in inland waters.

In this district, the coastline touches nine Mandals namely Ranasthalam, Srikakulam, Etcherla, Santabommali, Gara, Vajrapukotturu, Polaki, Kaviti and Itchapuram. All the villagers of these 107 villages, for a long time, had sustained with the sea resources. Majority of them are illiterates and practically they lived a tribal lifestyle. They did not know the policies that were framed, but they experienced the heat in the sea.

Means of Implements

In this state, the fishers used to make fishing with traditional implement until the early 80s. The same process prevailed in this District. Boat and the net were the main implements in fishing for the traditional fishers. Many changes took place in the manufacturing process of these implements.

Raft

The primitive implement in the fishing was raft (local dialect Teppa) which was made of either using the wood of Oleander or Silk cotton tree. To push the water back, they used a stick called Talabadda, which was made of Tada wood available in the forest. At that time, it used to cost about Rs. 3000 only. Almost every village had 50 such implements but disappeared by early 70s.

Kattumaram (Locally Kutlu Padava)

It is made of 4 or 5 solid logs lashed together in two or three pieces. When assembled, they take a boat form with a rockered bottom, sharp and narrow sterns. The dimensions are: length 4.5–7.5 m and beam 1.0–1.5 m. Wood with good buoyancy is preferred for construction and includes Melia dubia and Albizzia stipulata. The paddles, oars and other accessories are usually made of bamboo and casuarinas. It is propelled by oars or paddles while crossing the surf and by sailing in the open sea. The cost of a Kattumaram ranges between

Rs. 2,500–5,000 depending on the wood used, size, type of accessories, etc. It operates up to 35 km from the shore and up to 50 m depth, carrying a crew of 3–5 persons.

Kattumaram with Thermo Coal

The manufacturing process is one and same for both these categories. In the previously mentioned implement, they used hay of the paddy crop to stitch the logs. Now they are using thermo coal instead of hay. It enabled them to make a journey easily. They also use plastic and nails in the construction. The cost went up to Rupees 10,000.

Fibre Boats

During the early 80s, the government wanted to modernise the fishing sector to increase the catch and hence, introduced fibre boats. At the same time, the fishermen used to attach motor to the previously mentioned implements. Both the implements were being operated simultaneously in this district. The government in the initial phase supplied fibre boats on 25 per cent of subsidy. In this way, the government supplied five fibre boats in Donkuru village, one each to Kovvada, Manchineellapeta and Nuvvularevu. All the fishermen contended that they were not of good in quality with the hoses being damaged within a short period. The villagers of Nuvvularevu did not take the boat and asked the government to supply those boats to every fisherman.

Fibre Boats with Engines

Engines were subsequently attached to these fibre boats. In essence, the district took 40 years to taste the fruits of industrialisation. In this process, the number of implements had decreased. The ownership right on the implements

Table 1. Trends in the Usage of Implements in the District

		1980	*2005*	*2010*
	(A) Non-motorised			
1.	Plank built boats	898	686	2875
2.	Dugout canoes	285	2	16
3.	Catamarans	7555	4168	2081
4.	Ferro cement boat	2	0	6
	Total	8740	4856	4978
	(B) Motorised			
1.	Plank built boats	0	50	3
2.	Fibre glass	0	251	35
3.	Ferro cement	0	12	0
4.	Catamarans	0	0	65
5.	Dugout canoes	0	0	2
6.	Career boat	0	0	3
7.	Teppa	0	0	17
8.	Others	0	0	4
	Total	0	313	129
	The total	8740	5169	5107

Source: National marine census: 1980, 2005, And 2010.

was also showing a diminishing trend. The Table 1 indicates the trends in the number of implements used in this district.

As seen from this table, up to 1980, the implements were not even motorised. Ground level survey too indicated that the motorisation process started during early 90s in this district. Kattumaram was the principal implement in the year 1980 numbering 7,555. It was slowly dwindling, and as per 2010 census, it stood at 2,081. The net decrease over the span of 30 years was 5,474, the net percentage decrease being 72.45. Over a span of five years during 2005-2010, the strength of Kattumaram was halved. Total traditional implements dropped from 8,740 to 4,978 with the net decrease being 3,762.

The strength of motorised implements in this district as per census 2005 was 313, which later dropped to 129 during 2010 with the net decrease being 192 and the percentage decrease as 61.34.

The table indicated that there was rapid dwindling in the number of implements thus the fishermen were losing the foothold in the means of production.

Nets

For a long time in this district, the raw materials for making the net were cotton yarn and jute twine. 600 kilograms of cotton yarn was being used in making one net. In the local dialect, those were called Pedda kalavala vala, and Chinnakalavala vala. Fishermen used the first type of net during March-July and the second type of net during July-November. The government introduced nylon nets in the fishing villages on a low scale during the late 70s.

There were many types of nylon nets. The cost ranged from Rs.10,000 to 4,00,000. In the coast of Srikakulam district, the fishermen were unable to use the expensive nets, which were called in the local dialect as Allivala and Ringvala.

Implements in the Surveyed Villages

The Table 2 indicates the official data on the implements in the surveyed villages.

The empirical data showed some difference with the official data. The difference in the figures was small but in the case of Nuvvularevu village, the official information appeared to be incorrect. In Nuvvularevu, the Data showed one motorised boat and 232 traditional crafts. However, as on the day of the survey, the fishermen told that they had left fishing profession and hence they had no implements with them.

During the traditional period too, there was no complete ownership of the implements. However, the pace of modernisation alienated them from the means of using implements. The ordinary fishermen could not afford the increasing cost of the implements. As per 2005 census, 29 per cent of the fisher folk did not have any right on the implements. 46 per cent of the fishermen did not have any ownership right on the boat and 30 per cent of the fishermen did not possess any right on the nets.

In the surveyed villages too, the alienation was rapidly increasing. In Pedaganagallapeta, until the year 2000, there were 450 rafts. The number had

Table 2. Means of Production in Surveyed Villages

Sl. No.	*Village*	*Mandal*	*Population*		*Means of production*			
			2005	*2010*	*Motorised*	*Non-motorised*	*Motorised*	*Non-motorised*
					As in 2005		*As in 2010*	
1.	Idduvanipalem	Kaviti		2140			0	185
2.	Bandaruvanipeta	Gara	3111	3136	64	141	14	13
3.	Donkuru	Itchapuram	1187	1137	18	141	3	42
4.	Pedakovvada	Ranasthalam	1330	2009	0	68	0	155
5.	Chinakovvada	Ranasthalam		1843	0	118	0	226
6.	Chepalagollagandi	Sompeta	501	1032	0	104	0	81
7.	Chinaganagllapeta	Srikakulam	750	700	2	37	2	29
8.	Pedaganagallapeta	Srikakulam	806	794	0	47	0	34
9.	Manchneellapeta	Vajrapukotturu	2047	2262	32	192	7	179
10.	Nuvvularevu	Vajrapukotturu	4024	6026	0	92	1	232
11.	Pukkallapeta	Srikakulam		628	2	59	2	40
		Total						

Source: National marine census 2005 and 2010.

drastically decreased to 100 as per the survey. However, the official data indicated the figure to be 34.

In Chepala Gollagandi village, once there were 1000 rafts, but the total number of implements stood at 108.250 families were residing in the village but later, 50 families had no ownership right on the implements.

In Idduvanipalem, almost every household had ownership right on a raft until the dawn of 21st century. Later, the number of rafts had fallen to ten. 670 families were residing in this village. There were 100 fiber boats and five motorised fibre boats. 300 families did not have any ownership right on the implements.

In these fibre boats, normally 15 persons used to go for fishing. Almost all the fishermen were caught in the debt paying 15 per cent of income to the moneylender. They gave half the remaining amount to the boat owner. They distributed the remaining amount equally among themselves.

In the non-motorised and motorised rafts, four to five persons used to go for fishing. In that fishing income, the boat and net too had an equal share with the boat owner too getting a share.

There were also absentee owners of these implements by renting the implements. As per 2005 census, there were 566 absentee boat owners and 1,149 net owners.

Mechanisation

To exploit the fishing on a large scale, the successive governments proposed mechanising the fishing sector due to which, mammoth capital entered in the fishing sector. There was no mechanisation in the sea until 1972. In the process of mechanisation, the government planned to construct fishing harbours on one hand, and on the other, they looked at the foreign vessels to exploit the fishing resources. The Budget speech 1971-72 indicated this process reading, "*Exploitation of marine fisheries by mechanised craft is a prerequisite for development of fisheries*." Further, it is elaborated *"In the field of marine fisheries, the government is assisting in the establishment of fishing and processing industry, which would help improve the income of the fishermen considerably while it also augments foreign exchange earnings. A beginning has been made by leasing out the shore facilities at Visakhapatnam to a reputed firm. The establishment of a six crore Deep-Sea Fishing Project in Andhra Pradesh by a private company is under active consideration. Yet another firm proposes to operate two of its imported trawlers from the Visakhapatnam Harbour and to increase the number gradually to twelve in the due course. Other institutions and persons interested in starting deep-sea fishing industry are being encouraged to operate from Andhra Pradesh.*

It is proposed to construct nine fishing harbours in the State and as a first step, the U.N.D.P experts in Narsapur have taken up survey work and Nizampatnam harbours. Simultaneously, steps have been taken for the construction of fishing harbours in Visakhapatnam along with the outer harbour." (*Source:* The budget speech in Andhra Pradesh Assembly, 1971-72).

This is the end for the traditional fishing sector in this region. The proposed beginning had reached to its zenith by 2005. As per the national marine census

2005, the mechanised trawlers (in the local dialect Sona Boats) increased in Visakhapatnam to 550. In Kakinada, it reached 713. By 2010, the marine census, it further increased to 579 in Visakhapatnam. However, as per the empirical survey, the figure had reached beyond 600 in Visakhapatnam.

As per the deep sea fishing policy 1991, the foreign deep-sea fishing vessels have entered the Indian seawaters. They did not restrict their hunt only to the deep-sea waters. They violated all the provisions and Acts and exploited the demersal and pelagic fish. The large-scale agitations of the fisher folk forced the government to appoint a committee under the chairmanship of Murari, which recommended scarping the policy in unanimity. Subsequently, the policy was scrapped. However, 49 per cent of foreign direct investment was allowed in this sector. The foreign fishing vessels not only entered officially but also were encroaching the fishing grounds and were continuing the exploitation ruthlessly. In the words of a fisherman of Idduvanipalem "Sea is turned into mud."

In this process, the traditional fishermen with lowest economic background could not sustain with the competition of capital-intensive machinery and succumbed to the pressure.

Finance

"Beggars, we are, and cannot be borrowers" sardonically laughed off a fisherman of Donkuru. With low catch and low returns, the fishermen always remained a famished lot. They bred on borrowings. They borrowed at typical terms like the value of 15 per cent catch was to be given to the creditor as interest, on each occasion of fishing besides claiming share of the finest of the variety. Moreover, the entire catch was to be sold to the creditor only and at lower than market rates. The creditors were unwilling for many reasons. The life of the debtors was uncertain with having no assets of their own. Thus, the fishermen had to form a group to be able to borrow. They did so to some extent until the advent of Sona boats and mechanised trawlers. Nobody lent them the huge money needed, on whatever terms, and the sea was left to the big companies and the fishermen were left in the sea.

Never did they receive any financial assistance from any institution. The "social lending institutions" as they proclaimed, treated the fishermen at par with nomads. "Not a rupee, not a rupee, not a rupee"– they said in unison- did they receive from any Government. Institutions were banking on securities and guarantees and hence they were much pleased to lend to the businesspersons and big companies for purchase of mechanised fishing boats and trawlers. Increase in number of such boats threw the fishermen away from the sea like dead fish. Insurers were not far behind that, all the large vessels were taken care of while the traditional vessels were left high and dry. The lack of financial support to them was widely discussed in a report, and it yielded no results.

As per the national marine census, only three banks were available to them. However, no bank was lending to them. A report of the experts also confirmed these words reading, "*The weaknesses are that the outreach is poor due to apathy towards small borrowers, the transactions costs are high and they are highly rigid in lending policies. Insistence on collateral security leads to exclusion of most fisher folk from formal credit. The efforts of the government agencies have been focused more towards aquaculture and inland fisheries. Within the marine fisheries the focus is on mechanisation of traditional crafts. This has resulted in over exploitation of the fishing area due to the limitation of the craft to go beyond a particular distance into the sea.*" (*Source:* Credit availability for marine artisanal fisher folk: Andhra Pradesh and Orissa: overseas development administration post-harvest fisheries project: Information Bulletin Number 6).

Marine Fish Production

In this coast, there was a ban on fishing during 15th April-15th June. January to April months was considered as the best season in the coast. In the pre-modern phase, two persons used to go for fishing on a raft. Subsequently, five persons were accommodated in a Kattumaram. Later, in the fibre boats, 15 persons were going for fishing.

These traditional fishermen could get many varieties of fish in the pre-modern period. Some of those were Vanjaram, Konam, Chinna Konam, Vadimeeni, Tellachanduva, Nallachanduva, Royyalu, Sora, Kommulakonam, Erragurivindalu, Vanagarlu Talepara, Kavvallu, Gorakalu, Mulavaallu, and Kojjakavvallu. As per them, many species had disappeared from the sea. Some of those were Polasa, Tallekalli, Porabada, Pillasorachepa, Pillorijella, Ulavalu, Sorralu, Eraava, Attukoiah, Yangala, Savaadalu, Ballachepa, Aareyya, Erraengili, Ellisi, Vanametta, Errisorava, Poorvuriengili, Peddachavadi, Soosapariga, Kotibanadi, Kalireyya and Nallareyya.

As per the scientists of this sector, there were 1000 and above species in the seawaters. However, the diversity was rapidly decreasing. The scientists of the Fisheries Survey of India (FSI), Visakhapatnam, and the ground level fisher folk were contending that the diversity of the seawaters had almost halved.

During the year 1955, only 0.53 million tons of fish were exploited from the seawaters. The successive governments wanted to exploit the marine fish to earn foreign exchange and with this concept; mechanisation was introduced on a large scale. The hunting was on rapaciously. It is not only reflected in the depletion of resources but also in perishing of bio-diversity of the oceanic wealth. The table shows the trends in the marine production.

As seen from the Table 3, the marine fish production was 0.53 million tonnes in 1951. However, it had a share of 73.33 per cent in the total fish production. With almost on a war footing, the policy interventions made the sea as a hunting ground. Hence, the productions were continuously on the rise. During the year 1999-2000 alone, it showed a decrease in production. From that year, the pace of increase dropped down and almost reaching a plateau. Way back in 1986, the scientists of the Central Marine Fishery Research Institute

Table 3. Trends of Fish Production in India

Year	*Marine*	*Increase*	*Percentage of increase*	*Inland*	*Increase*	*Percentage of increase*	*Total*	*Percentage of marine*	*Percentage of Inland*
1950-51	0.53			0.22			0.75	71.01	28.99
1960-61	0.88	0.35	64.79	0.28	0.06	28.44	1.16	75.86	24.14
1970-71	1.09	0.21	23.41	0.67	0.39	139.29	1.76	61.85	38.15
1980-81	1.56	0.47	43.19	0.89	0.22	32.39	2.44	63.68	36.32
1990-91	2.30	0.75	47.91	1.54	0.65	73.17	3.84	59.96	40.04
2000-01	2.81	0.51	22.22	2.85	1.31	85.22	5.66	49.70	50.30
2004-05	2.78	-0.03	-1.10	3.53	0.68	23.94	6.31	44.08	55.92
2007-08	2.92	0.14	5.04	4.21	0.68	19.31	7.13	40.97	59.03
2008-09	2.98	0.06	1.99	4.64	0.43	10.27	7.62	39.10	60.90
2009-10	2.69	-0.29	-9.70	4.86	0.22	4.81	7.55	35.61	64.39
2010-11	3.22	0.53	19.75	5.07	0.21	4.24	8.29	38.85	61.15
2011-12	3.20	-0.02	-0.62	5.07	0.00	0.06	8.27	38.69	61.31

Source: Working group on fisheries on twelfth five-year plan.

(Hereafter CMFRI) commented, *"In spite of the increase in efforts expended for fishing, there has been no relative increase in the catch, which indicates a limitation of the present exploited grounds."* (*Source:* CMFRI special bulletin number 29, November, 1986 Page 2).

In that paper, they suggested for exploitation of new fishing grounds in the sea. Policy shift naturally tilted towards capital-intensive hunt. It had yielded results after about 10 years. With intervention and exploitation during 1985-93, the marine fish catch had increased. In 1994-95, the irresponsible catch had shown its ramifications, and for the first time, it showed a negative growth and a net decrease in the catch. From then onwards, the increase was minimal and again during the year 2009-10, the production had drastically come down recording a net decrease of .029 million ton.

Anticipating the threat of deterioration of marine fish production, Blue revolution occupied the field. Inland fish had a limited production of 0.20 million tons in 1951. It was always a junior partner in the total fish catch. For the first time, it had crossed its counterpart in 2000-01 netting a share of 50.30 percent. Later, it reached 61.31 per cent in total production.

The pace of diversion and the policy interventions can be seen from the Planning Commission report. *"The main objective of centrally sponsored scheme is to utilise the country's vast brackish water resources for fish/shrimp culture. Other subsidiary objectives are to increase foreign exchange earnings through increased shrimp production, generation of employment opportunities and increase of income of fish farmers/fishermen in coastal areas. With a view providing technical, financial and extension support to shrimp farmers in the small scale sector, 39 Brackish Water Fish Farmers Development Agencies (BFDAs) had been sanctioned in all the coastal states and the UT of Andaman and Nicobar Islands. During the first four years of the Ninth plan, an area of about 5000 ha has been developed for shrimp culture in the country by the Agencies. State-wise list of BFD is at Table 15. Against an allocation of Rs. 15.24 crore, an expenditure of Rs. 5.84 crores has been incurred by the end of the fourth year of the Plan period."* (Working group report on Tenth five-year plan).

The diversion of seacoast and paddy fields to harvest the fish had wider ramifications. The indiscriminate diversion of lands led to imbalance in nature with indiscriminate use of pesticides causing substantial harm to the nature. To earn some foreign exchange, the social cost was virtually ignored. The apex court intervened and directed to rectify the process. The working group on fisheries for tenth Planning Commission commented on this *"The performance of the programme has been affected due to the Supreme Court judgement of December, 1996 prohibiting non-traditional shrimp culture within the Coastal Regulation Zone (CRZ), i.e., 500 meters from the high tide line. The matter is currently sub-judice".(Working group report on Tenth five-year plan).*

However, the agricultural field has been transformed as fish fields. The aqua culture replaced the fertile rice belt of Andhra Pradesh. Interestingly, once the green revolution belt of Andhra Pradesh turned Blue in this process.

The Supreme Court intervention stopped the allotment of seacoast. However, the directives cannot prevent the indiscriminate transformation of traditional food basket.

Blatant Violation of Acts in the Seawaters

On paper, there were some restrictions on the hunting of mechanized trawlers. In reality, they were not functioning. The global and the Indian fleets also served in violation of the Acts and provisions. International exploitation in the Indian seawaters has a long precedence. Way back, Shri S.S. Dan reported in the Marine Fisheries Information Service which read *"Poaching by foreign vessel in India's Exclusive Economic Zone, particularly in the northern part of the Bay of Bengal, has become a grave problem. Five Thailand trawlers including one mother vessel were captured on 18-11-1981 by Indian coast guard from the sea close to the mouth of the river Ganges, 18 miles south of Sandhead Operations of Thai trawlers were reported by fishermen from Contai and Balasore coast. The number of trawlers operating in this area during 1981-82 are reported to be 75 to 100 and sometimes they are found even at a distance of 30 km from the shore at depths 40-45 m. These operations close to the shore cause damages to the drift nets operated in these waters by local fishermen. These drift nets, varying in sizes from 3,200 to 4300 ft long cost Rs. 20,000 to 30,000. Large quantities of dead fish of different varieties floating in the waters in these areas indicate that these boats only keep the skippers of Indian trawlers operating in this area often complained about the foreign trawlers that they do not abide by international rules, moving in zig-zag routes and without navigational lights in the night. Shri G. Mayabhan, skipper of trawler 'SuniYaRant reported to his base at Visakhapatnam about citing 40 Thai trawlers operating along the coast between Sandhead and Dhamra River on 2-10-1961. The skipper of another trawler Blue Anget' Shri C.M.A. Rashid reported to Visakhapatnam about seeing 30-40 Thai trawlers fishing at 40-45 m depth region in between Sandhead and Paradeep.These foreign trawlers are mostly 25 m to 50 m in length and equipped with powerful radars, which help detection of Indian coast guard vessels at very long distance and enable escape to waters of neighbouring countries or deeper areas. With the limited number of patrol vessels and equipment."* (Issue number 36, March 1982, CMFRI)

This situation aggravated further in the wake of allowing deep-sea vessels in the Indian seawaters, which never followed the existing stipulations. They not only captured the matured fish, rather, during the course of poaching, unprofitable fish and even eggs were also caught into the jaws of the nets. They never followed the stipulated mesh size. Hence, the juvenile fish and eggs were caught in these nets and thus the illegal hunt made the sea a burial ground to the juvenile fish.

Shri Ganapathiraju Pramod made a research on this illegal, unreported and unregulated fishing in the India seas. The data on this subject baffles even the common reader. The following table indicates the discards in the Seawaters.

Table 4. Discards in the Seawaters by the Mechanised Trawlers

State	*Average discards at sea by mechanised trawlers tonnes*	*Range*	
		Lower limit	*The Upper limit*
West Bengal	4440	1268	7,612
Orissa	99,247	67,076	1,31,418
Andhra Pradesh	2,07,232	1,34,826	2,79,639
Tamil Nadu	2,12,969	1,79,274	2,46,665
Kerala	4,29,074	3;51,778	5,06,371
Karnataka	1,61,042	1,11,985	2,10,099
Maharashtra	90,307	68,807	1,11,268
Gujarat	690	360	1,021
Andaman and Nicobar	13,200	99,600	16,800

Source: Illegal, Unreported and unregulated catch in the Indian economic zone: Ganapathiraju Pramod.

Further, the report said, "*Illegal catches by foreign as well as domestic trawlers were also estimated through interviews with trawler crews in all maritime States and Government enforcement staff in some States. Preliminary estimates reveal that such crafts comprise anywhere between 5-9 per cent of the total fishing crafts operating along the India's maritime zone. Estimates from this fieldwork on illegal catches by trawlers in the 8 km artisanal zone give an estimate of 1,300 to 2,600 tonnes for Andhra Pradesh.*" (*Source:* Illegal, Unreported and unregulated catch in the Indian economic zone: Ganapathiraju Pramod).

Srikakulam coast was also not an exception to this illegal exploitation. All the villagers told that the trawlers from Kakinada and Visakhapatnam came like army into the waters and destructed all the nets and even carried away the fish that were in the nets. In this illegal activity, they were not only losing their yield but also the implements. When reminded them about the protective measures, Mr. Kantarao of Donkuru classically told, "Imagine a cyclist dashing against a lorry."

Pollution is a serious cause of concern: *The term 'marine pollution' is defined as "introduction by man of substances into the marine environment resulting in such deleterious effects is harmful to living resources, hazards to human health, hindrance to marine activities including fishing, impairment of quality for use of sea water and reduction of amenities*" (FAO. Fish. Rep. No. 99. Conference on pollution, Rome, Dec. 1970).

Mainly the pollution is a result of Industrialization and indiscriminate usage of fertilisers and pesticides in the agriculture. Way back in 1972, the marine scientists warned on these issues. It read, "*Agricultural pesticides poison and kill millions of fish and other forms of aquatic life. The role of the oceans and seas as vital links in the life-giving cycle on the earth may one-day end if they continue to be polluted at the present rate. Pesticides like DDT, Dialdrin, Malathion and Parathion are harmful to aquatic animals.*

The major sources of pollution by industrial wastes are the effluents from chemical factories and refineries. In many cases, these are discharged directly into the rivers, estuaries and the sea. In pulp mill wastes, there are usually sulphur-containing compounds, arising from the wood digestion process and chlorinated phenolic compounds as a result of bleaching of the pulp. The effects of industrial organic wastes are often of a long-term nature. These interfere at various toxic levels of the food chain, and ultimately lead to a gradual depletion of the coastal marine resources. Thermal pollution or warm water discharge from industries and power plants also has a deleterious effect on the aquatic life. The worst offenders seem to be the atomic reactors, fertilizer and rayon factories." (*Source:* Aquatic pollution: V. Kunjukrishna Pillai and P.G. Jacob: CMFRI)

Basing on the definition and the observations of the marine scientists, it is useful to make an account about the pollution in this district.

As per the District Handbook of Statistics, the usage of fertiliser and pesticides is almost nominal in this district up to late 70s. As already enumerated in the chapter of fertilisers, the usage has no bounds in this district. As cropping pattern and in the illusion of enhancement of productivity, the peasantry is using these two lethal weapons indiscriminately. In a year, the peasantry is using on an average 1, 50,000 Metric tons of fertilisers and 15000 tons of pesticides.

As already said, the peasantry does not follow the norms of fertiliser usage because of the lack of proper guidance with the excess fertilisers running out of the fields and eventually contaminating the seawaters.

Until the onset of early 90s, this district had no significant industries. In Patancheru and in Telangana, some major Pharma and chemical industries have been functioning for a long time some of which are running even now. However, the environment awareness made the people to resist the establishment from running to expand the units. With this, the governments and judiciary intervened and applied pressure on them. Actually, the Capital was transferred to another place. Cheap labour, cheap land, unawareness of the effects of the pollution besides the concessions of the government in the name of development of backward regions made the Capital to come to this district.

The coast was then filled with Pharma, chemical, paper industries besides fish feed, and poultry farms. All these units have been mercilessly dumping their waste in the seawaters. Many field reports indicated the veracity of this state of affairs. In the current survey too, Kodulagumpa villagers of Komarada Mandal said, "because of the pollution created by the J.K. Paper Mill, the polluted water of the River Nagavali is so high that even the cattle are reluctant to drink the river water." In the village of Vanitamandalam of Polaki Mandal, the fish were dying because of the pollution of Vamshadhara Paper Mill at Madapam.

Interestingly the outsiders too had local sentiments on Capital. Hence, the factory was named after the famous river of the District "Vamshadhara". They were thinking that it was enough to keep the title on paper. Hence, they were trying to extinct the river from the natural purpose of its flowing. Even the national ıeports expressed concerns about the pollution being caused to the prime rivers of this district.

Along with these industries, the government had already permitted to establish five thermal plants and one nuclear power plant in this district along the seacoast. As already discussed in the chapter on allotment of land, the people were on the warpath in at least three places and already six persons were killed in these incidents. The main force in these battles is the fishing community.

Above all, the government of India proclaimed petrochemical policy and tried to implement it on a war footing. The PCPIR along the coast is covering Visakhapatnam and East Godavari districts. A number of Petrochemicals and chemical factories were in the process of beginning their work in this coast.

Cyclones and Storms

Had it been any other production pattern, the implements could have been preserved safely. However, in the case of the fishing sector, the traditional fishermen had to keep their implement at the seacoast. Sudden rains, storms and cyclones always played havoc with them. In every cyclone, they used to lose their implements, boat and nets. Immediately after the cyclones, many promises of rehabilitation reached them only on paper but nothing physically materialised.

Every profession has its risk factor and accident rate. This profession itself carried big risks, which were non-preventable. As per the national marine census 2005, the fishermen of this district had no life saving equipment with them. Hence, the death was very usual and frequent in these villages. There was a scheme of giving relief to the family of the deceased. However, as told by fishermen of Kovvada village, the amounts were not being sanctioned/ disbursed properly. The officials, in a written reply to the RTI question, said, "As per the official data, 58 fishermen were killed in the sea with compensation given to 21 cases."

Government Schemes

The governments were continuously promising many schemes for the welfare of these vulnerable sections. In the lean period, rice was to be distributed to these families. In the villages surveyed when asked about the scheme, many villagers expressed unawareness about the scheme while some villagers replied positive saying they had received rice once or twice. The officials also mentioned in a written reply to a RTI question "as per the official data, the department distributed the rice in 2008 and 2010"

The ongoing cyclones were damaging their dwellings. Taking this issue into consideration, the sub-group of fisheries of the Tenth Five Year plan recommended pucca-houses to all the fishermen living along the coast. The census data revealed that 42.77 per cent of the population had no pucca-houses. As per the information of officers of the department, they had sanctioned and built the houses for 9,430 families with the total households as per the census 2005 being 18,791. As per the official data, even half the households had no pucca-houses. Reality varied more than what the records showed/spoke. Even when the government sanctioned a house, they could not bear the additional expenditure for constructing the same.

The governments continuously preached about motorising the traditional craft only to get more yields. For this, the government promised to provide diesel at a subsidised rate of Rs. four per litre through earmarked supply units. Donkuru villagers had to go Chinabadam located at 70 kilometres to get the diesel on the subsidised rate. For this small subsidy, they could not go far to that village. However, the officials told in a written reply to a RTI question "in the year 2004-05, the department gave subsidy to 23 persons and by 2008-09, it reached 25."

There is another scheme for women. The government intended to supply iceboxes to all the women. However, the scheme did not reach its destination. In fact, 90 per cent of women are in the profession of selling fish. They used to start early in the mornings from their villages and move around the villages to sell fish. Live-fish fetched a better price over the dry fish. They were in a position to sell only the dried fish due to lack of preserving facilities. Taking into consideration of this situation, the policy makers were always insisting on the iceboxes. The officials told in a written reply to a RTI question "during 2004-05 - 2008-09, the department distributed 280 ice boxes."

Contribution of Marine Fish vs. Allocations to this Sector

Long ago, the government policies designed to earn the foreign exchange from the marine fish wealth. In this process, the technology and capital entered the scene. Fishing harbours were constructed to cater to this purpose. In all these process, the public investment was decreasing on one hand and on the other, foreign exchange earnings were increasing. In both the ways, Fish Capital survived in the seawaters with the small and under-privileged perished. The following table shows the foreign exchange trends in the marine fish sector.

As seen from the table, the export of marine fish during 1961-62 was only 15,732 tons. The foreign exchange earnings stood at Rs. 3.92 crores. The exports

Table 5. Foreign Exchange Earning through Marine Fish Wealth

Year	*Quantity in Tonnes*	*Value in Crores*
1961-62	15732	3.92
1970-71	35883	35.07
1981-82	707105	286.01
1991-92	171820	1375.89
2001-02	424470	5957.05
2005-06	512164	7245.3
2007-08	541701	7620.92
2009-10	678435	10048.53
2010-11	813091	12901.47

Source: Draft Detail Project Report NFDB and MPEDA.

have reached to 8,13,091 metric tonnes during 2010-11. The net increase in the export was 7,97,359 metric tonnes with the percentage increase in the tonnage being 5068. Even during the last ten years, the exports were almost doubled.

On this buoyant growth, MPEDA in a joyful mood declared, *"During 2011-12, for the first time in the history of Marine product exports, the export earnings have crossed USD 3.5 billion. This is also first time export has crossed all previous records in quantity, rupee value and US $ terms. Exports aggregated to 862021 tonnes valued at Rs.16597.23 Crores and USD 3508.45 million. Compared to the previous year, seafood exports recorded a growth of 6.02 per cent in quantity, 28.65 per cent in rupee and 22.81 per cent in US$ earnings respectively."* (*Source:* www.mpeda.com)

Table 6. Allocation to Fishery Sector in the Five Year Plans

Sl. No.	*Plan Period*	*Total plan outlay (in Crores)*	*Outlay Agri and allied (in Crores)*	*Outlay fisheries (in Crores)*	*Percentage of allocation in total outlay*	*Percentage of allocation in Agri. and Allied*
1.	First Plan	1960	294	5.13	0.26	1.74
2.	The Second Plan	4600	529	12.26	0.27	2.32
3.	The Third Plan	7500	1068	28.27	0.38	2.65
4.	The Fourth Plan	15902	2728	82.68	0.52	3.03
5.	The Fifth Plan	39322	4302	151.24	0.38	3.52
6.	The Sixth Plan	97500	6609	371.14	0.38	5.62
7.	The Seventh Plan	180000	10524	546.54	0.3	5.19
8.	The Eighth Plan	434100	22467	1232.82	0.28	5.49
9.	The Ninth Plan	859200	42462	2070	0.24	4.88
10.	The Tenth Plan	945328	21068	765	0.19	3.7
11.	The Eleventh Plan	2156571	50924			

Source: Various plan documents.

No doubt! Traditional fishermen could not draw much from this. The logistics needed for the utilisation of resources was inconceivable to the artisan fisherfolk. Hence, the capital-intensive operations started, and it reached its peak. On the other hand, the public investment either had decreased or had become stagnant. Hence, the commercial capital played a pivotal role in the grabbing of this wealth.

As seen from this table, the highest percentage of allocation to this sector was during fourth five-year plan, which, it was 0.52. In reality, the funds were allocated from agricultural budget. In the eighth plan, it recorded 5.49 per cent and thereafter it dropped to 3.7 per cent during tenth Five-Year plan. In fact, the destination of these meagre funds was required to be analysed. However, due dearth of full information, it was not possible to do that exercise.

Four million people were living on the seawaters. The only source of livelihood for a long period rested on the nature. Instead of extending a helping hand, the policies continuously encouraged the ambitious entrepreneurs to go to the battle ground. Because of this, the traditional fishers are in a position to fight unarmed to earn their livelihood in the sea. The erosion in the public fund drastically damaged the artisan fisherfolk. In fact, the sea is not only an earning source, but it is also strategically crucial. Unfortunately, this crucial aspect is missed out in the allocations, which is a tragedy on any term.

Fisherfolk and Sea

At least up to early 80s, sea and fisherfolk were indivisible. Almost as reports indicated, the entire catch belonged to the artisan fisherfolk. Prior to 1947, there was no proper data collection on the fish landings. As CMFRI told, *"The first attempt to build up a planned survey of fish catch was on all-India basis was made by this institute in 1948-49. In the estimates of total fish catch in India, The landings of the mechanised boats and of the big trawlers account for about 20 per cent."* (*Source:* 25 Years of Marine fisheries research: CMFRI published in 1972. Page 15 and 16).

During the said period, Andhra Pradesh did not witness any mechanised boats and hence, it could be construed that the entire catch belonged to the traditional fisherfolk. However, the post 70s drastically changed the scenario. The share of traditional fisherfolk was becoming marginal year after year. The official and non-official reports only indicated the traditional fishermen to be fish out of the water. At the same time, the wealth was being extracted in the manner that the basic character of renewable nature itself was fallen in the quandary.

Migration

Scientists said that the aquatic species were used to migrate from the existing place to keep alive from the pollution. Since, pollution spreads all over the sea, the life of the various species became endangered. Scientists declared that the major cause of this pollution was attributed to industrial effluents. In other words, the capital played the main role in the extinction of biodiversity in the seawaters.

In case of fisher folk too, the capital re-enacted the same process as they could not withstand the logistics of these big entrepreneurs and hence, they surrendered their head to the capital thereby losing the status as independent earner. In fact, their lifestyle resembles tribe life style, and they never were exposed to the remaining society. They did not expect the alienation of sea from them. Many people had to do away with their smaller vehicles as they could not compete with larger besides costlier ones. Businesspersons and then large companies owned modern boats, Sona boats and mechanised trawlers. The capital required was too large, that the fishermen were afraid of, even to hear, let alone venture. These big boats needed men to carry out fishing activities and employ the fishermen on wage basis. The entire process drove out the fishermen out of their profession/vocation and they migrated. Now, the cost of

Table 7. Occupational Pattern of Fisher-folk in the District

Year	*P=Population*	*Active fishermen*	*Marketing of fish*	*Making and repairing of nets*	*Curing and processing*	*Peeling*	*Labour*	*Others*	*Total*	*Other than fishing*	*Total in occupation*	*Percentage of people in various occupations*
2005	81,381	20,829	5920	6336	6841	126	13,135	2,003	34,361	532	55,722	68.47
2010	98,450	23,559	8697	3421	3596	782	13,181	267	30,644	1011	55,214	56.08
Changing pattern	17069	2730	2777	-2915	-3245	656	746	-1736	-3717	479	-508	

Source: National marine census, 2005 and 2010.

nets increased manifold and the number of nets used for fishing increased, necessitating additional money. While no one from the district was able, even to think of big vessels, capital from other places flew through and inundated the fishermen. Vessels harboured in Visakhapatnam and Kakinada tore through the shores of the district en route to Paradeep in Odisha and Kolkata. High-end vessels like Sona Boats, Trawlers, Gill Netters, Deep Sea fishing vessels, etc., grew in leaps and bounds washing the traditional fishermen ashore blowing a "the death knell" to the hapless fishermen which spurred migration.

The Table 7 indicates that the subsidiary occupations of the fishing are decreasing with considerable decrease in the category of making and repairing nets too. It reduced from 6,336 to 3,421. Hence, the net reduction in the figure is 2915. Similarly, the strength in curing and processing dropped from 6,811 to 3,421 with a net decrease by 3,245. The main subsidiary occupations of the fishing are negligible compared to these two categories. The reduction in the number indicated the main activity not being very healthy. On the other hand, here too the labour increased and showed an overall increase of 746. In total, the fishing and fishing related activity showed an overall decrease of 3,717. The percentage net decrease is 10.81.

Illiteracy and ignorance are twins in a social paradigm. 65 per cent of the fisher folk is illiterate. Both exist in this sector. They have a reservation of backward classes and they are categorised under "A". In the absence of formal education, their share in employment is in single digit. In the surveyed villages, Vaddithandra, Kovvada, Donkuru villages could not produce even single government employee. Each four persons from Bandaruvanipeta and Manchineellapeta joined the army. One person from Chepala Gollagandi and two persons from Idduvanipalem are also serving in the Army.

Gandhi told that because of the extinction of the employment opportunity in the countryside the Punjabis are joined the British army and tangled in the web of war and killing the peace-lovers of other countries. Kautsky in his book agrarian question recorded *"the peasantry is the ideal breeding-ground for a plentiful supply of children: this is of inestimable value where labour-power and soldiers are in great demand"*. (The agrarian question: Page 169: Karl Kautsky)

Both are told that, in the absence of independent bread earning opportunities, the rural offspring has to join the army or in industries as proletarian. The backward region Srikakulam district proved this fact, and it is supplying industrial labour and soldiers. In this process, only those who have lost their control on means of production joined the army. Even this opportunity also did not knock all the doors in the fishing villages. Hence, they are travelling from East coast to the west coast as wage labourers in the sea as seamen, drivers and labourers.

Migration is not a new subject to this district. Interestingly, the central government encouraged the migration of fishermen from this district way back in early 70s. A research report indicated this fact. It read, "*The Central Government encouraged the fishers from Srikakulam district to settle down in the Andaman Islands in the 1970s in an effort to improve the fisheries of the islands and provided the migrants with incentives like free accommodation and assets for fishing. Mostly fishers from Sompeta, Kaviti and Mandasa Mandals took advantage of the programme, and took their families along with them. They were provided with the traditional Burmese-type boats called Durga, fishing gears and even some working capital assistance to begin fishing operations. Of all the migratory routes that the fishers of Srikakulam have undertaken over the decades, the migration to Andaman is considered to be the best not only because it allowed the fishers to shift into an occupation that they understood well, but also made them the owners of their fleet, besides providing them with free accommodation and other perks (including concessions for travel)."* (*Source:* Micro finance in fishing enterprises -its impact on economic development of Andaman Islands: M. Suresh and Dr. Mohan; BIZ n BYTES—a quarterly published Journal of Applied Management and Computer Science - ISSN No. (0976 - 0458) Volume 3 - August 2011.

Helping hands society, a voluntary organisation of Srikakulam with the aid of Child rights and you (shortly CRY) has conducted a micro level survey on the migration of fishermen in Etcherla Mandal. The results of the study are given in tabular form hereunder.

As seen from this Table 8 it is clear that the migration has touched even 90.87 per cent in one village. The minimum percentage of migration is 45.12 per cent. In the surveyed villages, the average migration is 75.43. Interesting fact is long-term migration is showing higher percentage.

However, the scene has reversed lately. The fisherfolk left their dwellings in search of livelihood in a distressed condition. FAO reported this fact which read, *"The large-scale migration of men where traditional fishermen have not been able to cope with the unfair competition from trawlers has disrupted family life and put new burdens on women (e.g. 68 per cent of fishermen in the Srikakulam district of Andhra Pradesh were involved in distress migration in 2002 for employment outside the district and state)."* (*Source:* Report of the National Workshop on Best Practices in Microfinance Programmes).

The national media are also reporting the spree of migration in the fishing villages. The Hindu reported, "*Several fishermen of Ranasthalam, Etcherla, Gara, Polaki and Srikakulam Mandals have settled down in Gujarat while encouraging others to join them. "We could clear all our debts as my son is sending Rs. 10,000 every month from Gujarat. He could not have earned even Rs. 5,000 here. That is why I am encouraging other family members to either go to Maharashtra or Gujarat to earn more," said A. Ramana, a fisherman of Ranasthalam. With the large-scale migration, officials of the Fisheries Department could not take details from fishermen for issuing biometric cards. They are urging them to provide all the details whenever they come to their native place so that it would be easy to issue the cards which are necessary even to take up fishing activity in the Arabian Sea."*

"The West Coast has natural advantages for fishing. Many marine companies in Gujarat are recruiting fishermen from Srikakulam district, as they

Table 8. MicrolevelSurvey on Migration in Etcherla Mandal

Sl. No.	Name of the Village	Total Number of families	Number of Families					
			At home (%)		<3 months (%)		>3 months (%)	
1.	K. Mathyalesam	190	54	28.42	1	0.53	135	71.05
2.	Jalari Koyyam	124	33	26.61	7	5.65	84	67.74
3.	Rallapeta	101	27	26.73	0	0.00	74	73.27
4.	P. Dibbala Palem	20	9	45.00	0	0.00	11	55.00
5.	Musavanipeta	92	22	23.91	3	3.26	67	72.83
6.	S. Dibbala Palem	94	18	19.15	3	3.19	73	77.66
7.	Buchhivanipeta	416	34	8.17	4	0.96	378	90.87
8.	D. Mathyalesam	517	99	19.15	4	0.77	414	80.08
9.	Ginnivanipeta	63	15	23.81	2	3.17	46	73.02
10.	K.D. Palem	159	39	24.53	9	5.66	111	69.81
11.	Budagatlapalem	512	212	41.41	69	13.48	231	45.12
	Total	2288	562		102		1624	

are good at voyage. More than 10,000 fishermen from this region have already been engaged by several companies in the West Coast," said Lal Mohammed, Assistant Director of Fisheries Department-Srikakulam" (*Source:* The Hindu dated 3rd January, 2011)

Field reports are saying that there is an increase in their earnings when compare with their rural earnings. However, the illiteracy and ignorance made them vulnerable to exploitation. The villagers of Chepala gollagandi told that many people from their village migrated to various places. Some of them went to Goa for work. The company had not paid them stipulated wages. However, another person from Srikakulam District organised them in a union and made struggles to get their wage.

Global Examples of Preserving Traditional Fisheries

The capital all over the world made seawaters as a battleground with its natural character of greediness. Initially, the native companies eroded the traditional fisheries and in course of time, the global capital entered the picture and the oceans have otherwise become reserved for the technology-based machinery. In this struggle, naturally, only the influential people could survive with the weaker sections being perished.

Many foreign governments were trying to save the traditional fisher folk from the onslaught and tried to take corrective steps. A research report indicated, "*The Lofoten islands were characterised by many rules and regulations that hoped to resolve the conflict among fishermen using different fishing techniques. These regulations included gear and net specifications and timings for fishing, but could not ease the conflict. The rules were made and withdrawn repeatedly, as pressure from different groups increased. Ultimately, it was recognised that the only way to reduce the conflict was to hand over the decision making process to the fishing community. Today, the seas of Lofoten are divided into fishing grounds that are meant for different types of gear loglines, gillnets and Danish seines. The division of the fishing grounds is determined by the fishermen themselves. Boats are required to remain strictly in their area, and the fishery inspectors help the community by patrolling the areas to ensure that boats do not stray.*"

"Alanya in Turkey is yet another example of how communities are able to resolve the problem of overfishing and livelihood opportunities effectively (Berkes, 1986, pp. 215-29). The fishermen draw lots for fishing locations at the beginning of each fishing season, and then rotate to a new position each day. This ensures that the number of fishermen on a spot is controlled, at the same time ensuring equitable opportunity to all. Use rules govern the behaviour of the fishing" (*Source:* Briefing paper on fisheries policy: H.B. Soumya and Partha J. Shah)

They gathered many examples from Indian states. Even in japan, also the cooperative societies are playing vital role in saving the seawaters from indiscriminate utilisation of the resources. Finally, the paper recommended for, "*It is important to recognise the importance of such systems. When people form rules for them, they are most likely to follow them. Also, fishermen want to ensure that the fish population survives, so that they have a source of livelihood tomorrow. When they are given the right to take decisions for the resources that they are dependent on, they would automatically make sure that the resource in question is sustained."(Ibid).*

In India too, the fishing co-operatives have a long history, those were started and functioned during the colonial period. Moreover, the work ethic made them united and their unity developed distinct characters. However, at any point of time, these co-operatives were not taken into consideration in framing the schemes and Acts. In this District, there are cooperative societies in the fishing sector even from the colonial period. It is an essential factor to take the aspirations of the traditional fisher folk while making the policy decisions. Unfortunately, policies and schemes are not going in that direction. The pro-people intellectuals commented that the first comprehensive national marine policy 2004 did not travel in that direction.

16

Handloom Weavers

The next essential thing after the food for mankind is cloth. In Indian community production, so many professions emerged to cater to the needs of the society. In this process, weaving had emerged. Initially, like any other commodity, production and consumption limited to that village or nearby villages. Slowly, the market entered the scene, the market expanded, and it even crossed the national boundaries.

Professor Tirthankar Roy told in his paper about the textile trade, *"Early industrialisation is one example. At 1750, India supplied about a quarter of the world's industrial output"* (*India: Tirthankar Roy: a paper presented in National overview India: Textile conference IISH, 11 to 13 November 2004*) He also said, *"In 1950, India was the second largest cloth exporter in the world after Japan."* Weavers were the architects for this whole production structure. In this process of development, the life of the wavers is to be estimated.

Historical Background

Gandhi said, *"Agriculture and hand-spinning are two lungs of the national body. They must be protected against consumption at any cost" (Young India: July 13, 1921)* Though, East India Company, and the Manchester cloth tried to destroy one of its lungs, it did not achieve its success in every sphere. They got their success in the fine muslin. As Marx said, *"In 1824, the export of British Muslin to India hardly amounted to 10,00,000 yards, while in 1837, it surpassed 6,40,00,000 yards"*. (*Source:* Marx on India : page 14)

In this process, the main urban centers were destroyed and the rural industry survived for a long time. Indian textile business worried the Britishers, and they even declared an embargo on selling Indian textiles in Britain. The traders used to bring precious metal in exchange of their earnings in the textile sector. This was the primary reason for imposing the embargo. As per the British calculations, the annual worth of the precious metals stood at £30,000. Marx quoted this data and said, *"by the Act 11 and 12 William III, cap, 10, it was enacted that the wearing of wrought silks and of printed or dyed calicos from India, Persia and China should be prohibited, and a penalty of £200 imposed on all persons having or selling them"* (*Source:* Marx on India : page 26).

However, the capitalist did not lose the marketing opportunities. Marx said on this *"And thus, during the greater part of the 18th century, Indian manufactured products were generally imported into England in order to be sold on the continent and to remain excluded from the England market itself"* (*Source:* Marx on India: page 26).

Throughout the colonial period, a lot of debate continued on this sector and the Magazine "Young India" set a platform for this debate. It is interesting to read the whole debate in the light of current global debates for a student of political economy. At that time, on this issue, a debate between Rabindranath Tagore and Gandhi had been held which is worth while to read even now.

Post-Independence Period

Gandhi advocated for handloom sector persistently during the colonial period. In fact, he made it a national symbol of pride. However, the first blow of large magnitude came on the Indian weavers and that too not from the foreign capital, but from Indian manufacturers. Gandhi noted this fact and admitted that the cloth imported from the manufacturers of Britain was not competing with the coarse cloth produced by the Indian ordinary weaver. He also admitted that the Indian manufacturers were making inroads into the weavers market. He advocated the people to wear coarse handmade cloth made by Indian handmade yarn.

The first Indian mill was established in 1851. The first blow to the Indian ordinary weaver started in the samc year. Immediately after independence, the government appointed a committee under the chair of Kanungo. He made several recommendations on this sector, which read, "*The committee recommended a phased programme and suggested that at the end of 20 years, the handloom should be converted into improved semi-automatic handloom or decentralised power loom."* (Quoted in Growth and prospects of Handloom industry: Dr. Soundarapandian: NABARD Publication. 2002).

The crux of the report was advocating modernity in the handloom industry. The report instantly bore the brunt of the handloom sector, which necessitated another committee. The Planning Commission appointed popularly known Karve committee in the year 1955 whose report laid stress on the development of cottage industry in this sector. Thus, hordes of committees and reports emerged. Every second report expressed divergent opinion on this sector. Some argued in favour of small capital while some argued for the need of a big push. However, the dynamics proved the following option naturally and the people in the handloom sector came near to extinction.

Handloom Sector in Srikakulam District

There was a need to enumerate the history in respect of this district. N.K. Meera conducted a research on this sector, which included this district. Prior to 1950, Srikakulam district was a part of the then Vizagapatam district. As per that research, in Vizagapatam district, at that time, 61,228 weavers were earning their bread in this profession. 14,875 weavers were in the agency tracts. The necessary raw material, i.e., cotton was also cultivated in this district.

Social Fabric of Weavers

In this district, there are three communities in this profession. Those are Pattusali, Padmasali and Devanga. Government recognised all these three castes as backward classes. Government categorised them as "B". Inter-caste marriages are not allowed among these castes. Pattusali usually made silk weaving and the other two are in cotton weaving.

Means of Implements

The production was continuing in hand looms only. These looms needed many spares and accessories like Heads, Pickas, Reed, Brush, Hand brush, Shuttle. Charkha, Cloth warping Beam, warping machine, etc., and the list was not exhaustive. Many castes other than these three were used to manufacture and repair these spares and parts. Muslims, Erukula, Singam and carpenters were engaged in making these instruments for a long-time. Of late, all these have become industrial products. Prasadarao of Ampolu Weavers Society said, "earlier it was difficult to get these spares and parts in time. Now if, we order the item from a dealer at Hyderabad, the material was reaching the village within one or two days."

Entrepreneurship

Primarily, two types of entrepreneurship were continuing in the district - one under APCO. As per the official report, the structure of the society was described in their website, which read, *"The Handloom Societies in Andhra Pradesh are organised as a two tier structural societies in the village called Primary Handloom Weaver's Co-operative Society. The APEX society at the State level called A.P. State Handloom Weavers' Co-operative Society Ltd. (APSHWCS), popularly called as APCO".* (*Source:* www.apcofabrics. com). The village society used to take the raw material from the apex body and return in the form of finished product. In other words, independent entrepreneurship did not exist in this activity.

The second Apex body is Khadi and Village Industries Commission. The primary societies used to supply their finished product to this body. APCO used to supply the basic raw material that is factory made Yarn to the primary societies. In the second case, the weavers used hand spin yarn.

Raw Material and Final Products

In this district, cotton was the main raw material for producing the final product. For a long time, the weavers used to make the intermediary product yarn with hand. In turn, they manufactured the cloth with this handmade yarn. However, the machine made yarn replaced this handmade yarn and in the initial period, the colonial capital supplied the machine made cotton yarn to the Indian rural industry. In other words, the predominant intermediary, which is an integral part of manufacturing cloth, was occupied by capital-intensive industry. Marx noted on the supply of twist to India. It read, "From 1818 to 1836 the export of the twist from great Britain rose in the proportion of 1 to 5,200". (*Source:* Marx on India: page 14).

Gandhi vehemently opposed this trend and he continuously argued for hand spunyarn. However, the preaching of Gandhi did not sustain in the storm of Capital. The cheap and easily accessible yarn had virtually replaced the hand spun yarn even in the colonial rule. As mentioned by the weavers of this district, they have been buying the factory made yarn even during the colonial rule. At that time, it was called in the local dialect as "SEEMA NOOLU" (Seema is a synonymous term to foreign). Hence, in respect of raw material, the village rural industry gave way to Capital and therefore, it lost its dominance on the pricing mechanism of the necessary input. The fortunes of the village industry thus depended on the Capital.

Changing Pattern in Raw Material Ownership

The profession was linked with the yarn. Unfortunately, the thread was becoming a noose around the neck for innumerable weavers in the country. Since the raw material is linked with the Capital, Capital is playing havoc with the small entrepreneurs. Mill made cloth sector could not produce sufficient cloth for a long time. During that period, rural industry flourished. As soon as the urban industry dominated the production pattern, the looms had become obsolete and the lives of the weavers strained.

In the colonial rule, some argued that shortage of cotton cultivation was also one of the reasons for the dependence on imports. They argued that due to the shortage, the cotton and cotton yarn mill owners were forced to import yarn. However, over a period, this argument proved incorrect. The cultivation of cotton and productivity increased enormously in the country.

As seen from the data, the area under cotton crop has been continuously increasing with the yield too increasing from a mere 92 kilograms to a whopping 524 kilograms at one point and currently stabilised close to 500 kilograms a hectare. The production was continuously increasing, and it started at 30.62 lakh bales during the year 1950. Currently it reached 334 lakhs bales. The country is exporting cotton and is earning foreign exchange in this front. Unfortunately, the increased production did not bring any change in the plight of peasantry. Moreover, the development in the cotton production brought suicides in that sector. It appeared that there was no link between the enhancement of production and the welfare of the producer.

During the "Swadeshi" movement, many complained to Gandhi that the mill owners were taking the opportunity of boycott call of foreign goods for increasing the price of the coarse cloth. Gandhi pleaded with the "indigenous industrialists" to restrain from that greediness. At the same time, he advocated for hand spun yarn on Charkha to thwart the plans of greedy mill owners. However, both the suggestions did not materialise forever.

Table 1. Cotton Production Trends in India

Year	*Area in lakh Hectares*	*Production in lakh Bales of 170 kgs*	*Yield kgs per Hectare*
1950-51	58.82	34.30	99
1960-61	76.10	60.12	134
1970-71	76.05	56.64	127
1980-81	78.23	78.00	169
1990-91	74.39	117.00	267
2000-01	85.76	140.00	278
2001-02	87.30	158.00	308
2002-03	76.67	136.00	302
2003-04	76.30	179.00	399
2004-05	87.86	243.00	470
2005-06	86.77	241.00	472
2006-07	91.44	280.00	521
2007-08	94.14	307.00	554
2008-09	94.06	290.00	524
2009-10	103.10	305.00	503
2010-11	111.42	339.00	517
2011-12	121.78	353.00	493
2012-13	116.14	334.00	489

Source: Cotcorp.gov.in, 2012-13 figures are provisional.

After the colonial rule, the Indian governments established co-operative spinning mills to supply the yarn to the weavers to protect them from the mill owners. Andhra Pradesh government established cotton yarn mills under two types of co-operatives. One was under consumer co-operatives (Weavers are the consumers here), and another was farmer co-operatives. However, these co-operatives had shown losses and the mills were completely denationalised. The proceedings on this process were interesting to hear. In the words of Virupakshaiah, a veteran handloom activist of Draksharamam, of East Godavari District "in this state, under the category of consumer co-operative societies six mills were established in Hyderabad, Karimnagar, Guntakal, Nellore, Chirala and in Rajahmundry. The first two come under Telangana region and the remaining four under Seemandhra region. The government took a decision to sell these four mills of Seemandhra region. Against the proposal, Virupakshaiah of East Godavari Handloom Society approached the High court for stopping further proceedings. The court told him to restrict himself for Rajahmundry mill since it was under the jurisdiction of East Godavari. In that process, the court ordered a general body meeting to take a final decision. However, the general body accepted the proposal of the government giving clearance for sale. While establishing the mill in the year 1964, Virupakshaiah had purchased the land at Rs. 1800 per acre. The entire land was 40 acres. Hence, the cost of the land in 1964 was Rs. 72, 000. During 2002-03, the land was sold at Rs. 13 Lakhs per acre and the sale price was Rs. 5.20 Crores. Later, the price of land stood at Rs. two crores per an acre. Thus, the private entrepreneurs earned Rs. 80 Crores on the land. An interesting thing was the government did not even pay the shareholders money so far." (*Source:* Interview of Shri Virupakshaiah. Veteran activist of Handloom weavers)

Thus, the experiment of the co-operative process made some persons as billionaires while the shareholders lost their minimum capital.

Supply of Yarn

Various committees appointed by the government in the broader welfare of the handloom weavers recommended for a continuous supply of cotton yarn in hanks. Governments not only made stipulations in this regard and declared sops for this supply of yarn, it also stipulated the mill owners that they had to supply 50 per cent of the hank yarn to the handloom weavers. Later, the slab was reduced to 40 per cent. However, the mill owners did not follow this stipulation but they were getting the sops from the government by showing fictitious data. Many committee reports unearthed the malpractices of the mill owners, but the pernicious practice could not be arrested.

The expert committee (popularly known as Satyam committee in the handloom sector) noted, "Despite the reduction in number of handlooms, consumption of hank yarn has increased. This clearly indicates that power looms, more particularly those run by ex-handloom weavers, are consuming hank yarn in significant quantities. In fact, a survey undertaken by the Office of the Textile Commissioner has indicated that about 39 per cent of the hank yarn is being consumed by the power loom sector for production of yarn dyed fabrics and made-ups." (Report of the expert committee on textile policy: Ministry of textiles, GOI,1999 page 65).

Instead of recommending the arrest of such practices, the committee amazingly took the stand against poor weavers recommending, *"Another problem faced by the spinning industry is in the form of hank yarn obligation scheme. The production of hank yarn is uneconomical, wasteful, very much labour-oriented and impacting adversely on the economic viability of the spinning units. Though supply of yarn to the vulnerable handloom sector is no doubt necessary but it should not be done at the cost of the spinning sector, more so in the context of the on-going integration of world textile market. To ensure supply of yarn to the vulnerable handloom sector, the mill industry has to bear the burden of hank yarn obligation and restrictive export policy with regard to their finished product, i.e., cotton yarn, though they are permitted cotton import freely.* To improve the economic viability of the spinning mills, there was unanimity in the views of the members of the Committee that HYO Scheme should be done away with, with suitable arrangements for maintaining deliveries of required quantities of yarn to the Handloom weavers at reasonable prices." (Emphasis added) (*Source: Ibid* Page number 65).

The government did not accept this recommendation, but the ceiling was reduced to 40 per cent. However, the local handloom weavers were telling that

Table 2. Changing Pattern in Cotton Yarn Consumption

Sl. No.	Year	Production	Consumption						Export	
			Mill sector	Percentage of mill sector	Powerlooms	Percentage of power loom sector	Handloom sector	Percentage of Handloom sector		Percentage of the export sector
1.	1970	965	—	—	—	—	—	—	30.45	3.16
2.	1975	989	—	—	—	—	—	—	3.87	0.39
3.	1979	912	—	—	—	—	—	—	5.9	0.65
4.	1990-91	1464	248	16.94	556	37.98	342	23.36	90	6.15
5.	1995-96	1894	159	8.39	567	29.94	504	26.61	261.5	13.81
6.	2000-01	2267	154.5	6.82	534	23.56	530	23.38	513	22.63
7.	2005-06	2521	130	5.16	710	28.16	422	16.74	552	21.90
8.	2006-07	2824	135.5	4.80	773	27.37	461	16.32	616	21.81
9.	2007-08	2948	138	4.68	796	27.00	490	16.62	664	22.52
10.	2010-11	3465	—	—	—	—	—	—	720	20.78

Source: Compiled from various reports and commissioner textiles Mumbai, figures in Million kilograms.

the stipulations worked only on paper and the yarn was being supplied to power looms in the guise of handlooms.

There were two obvious reasons and one hidden reason for the non-cooperative attitude of mill owners. As Satyam committee noted "The conversion of cone yarn to hank yarn is highly labour intensive and mills have to incur an additional cost of about Rs. two to Rs. 10/kg". This is the first reason. The other reason is export of yarn. As Marx noted, India was a predominate importer of mill made yarn in the colonial rule. Now the Indian mill sector is emerged as an exporter of the yarn. The Table 2 indicates the export trends.

The export earnings and labour cost in the manufacture of hank yarn were the transparent reasons for the disinterest towards the supply of the hank yarn to the vulnerable handloom sector. Hence, it was proved that whatever be the capital, its interests were with their profiteering only but not with the vulnerable sections.

The other prominent inexplicable reason rested in the formulation of Marx. A general question may have appeared to a reader why these manufacturers are supplying intermediary product yarn to the international market rather than final products. Marx formulated, *"We therefore find that speculators make it a rule when such sudden changes in value occur, to speculate in that material on which the least possible quantity of labour has been spent: to speculate, therefore, in yarn rather than in cloth, in cotton itself, rather than in yarn."* (*Source:* Capital, Volume I, page 144/543: www.marxist.org)

Hence, the export of yarn and even qualitative cotton was crossing the national borders to make profits to the entrepreneurs. Even Satyam committee encouraged to export qualitative cotton to the international market to earn foreign exchange. It recommended for the encouragement of using non-cotton fibre cloth in place of cotton fibre cloth to release the cotton from the manufacture of less value clothes. In the words of Satyam Committee, "Indian textile industry is predominantly cotton based. In contrast to the consumption pattern of textile fibres in the world, which is tilted heavily in favour of non-cotton fibres with a ratio of 44:56 of 'cotton' to 'non-cotton' fibres, the consumption ratio in India is 66:34 in favour of cotton. The Textile Policy of 1985 had stated that the predominant position of cotton will be maintained though the consumption of man-made fibres/yarns will be augmented. The Committee is of the view that the time has come to attach equal importance to cotton and non-cotton fibres. It may not be possible or even necessary for India to reach the consumption pattern of world which is heavily in favour of non-cotton fibres, due to the climatic conditions and cotton advantage that India enjoys. It would be reasonable to provide additional thrust for consumption of non-cotton fibres, particularly in value added blended textiles and technical textiles, to release the demand pressure on cotton and make it more cost competitive. More importantly, it will release high value cotton for value added textile exports. In the final analysis, the market forces should determine the relative fibre balance." (Satyam committee report: Page 19 and 20: Emphasis added)

During the period of colonial rule, Gandhi argued for the usage of coarse cotton cloth in the place of mill made clothes. Now the system had virtually transformed to consumption of non-fibre cloth. The younger generation of the country is not even willing to use the cotton-stitched clothes.The recommendations of the committee by the turn of 2012 had almost come in reality at least in the case of the current generation.

In fact, the yarn exports during the year 1970 were 30.45 Million kgs. By 1979, even exports were reduced to 5.9 million kgs. The dawn of 21st century saw the persistent increase in exports. In the year 2010-11, it reached the upper limit of 720 million kgs. In fact, government imposed quantitative restriction on the export of yarn with the maximum limit fixed at 720 million kgs for that financial year. The industry did reach that magic figure. The expert committee had made its strong remarks on the quantitative restriction on the export of yarn. It read, *"It is, therefore, recommended that quantitative ceiling on export of cotton yarn should be removed and exports of cotton yarn are placed under OGL"*. (*Source:* Satyam Committee report, page 64-65)

The committee appointed by the government carried out the interest of the capital. The clarion call of the committee was reflected in the representation of outgoing president of Northern Textile Mills Association to the textile commissioner Mumbai. The media carried the news verbatim and read, "A minimum export of 1280 million kgs should be allowed during the year 2011-12 to prevent the spinning mills from going into red and ultimately closing down one after the other. This will also help the industry to strive to achieve the country's larger goal of doubling its exports by 2015." (*Source:* cottonmarket news.com)

Handloom Co-operative Societies in this District

Producer-consumer pattern had long been continued in this district. There was no scope for the intermediaries. The expansion of business paved the way for the intermediaries. The pattern was changed to producer-intermediaries-consumer. This framework naturally leads to profiteering of intermediaries.

In this district, the co-operative societies enjoyed a long cherished history. During the colonial rule, the onslaught of indigenous capital in the textile sector made an onslaught on handloom sector. The British rulers also formed committees to enumerate the problems and remedies. Royal commission on agriculture recommended for the co-operative sector during 1928, but they did not materialise. Subsequently, Haynes recommended for the establishment of co-operatives. Slowly the process had been started and it appeared that the co-operative societies were formed in this district.

In almost all the villages surveyed, the co-operative societies functioned well for a long time. However, these societies were slowly becoming non-functional and were at the verge of extinction. To recollect the history, few examples related to this process are narrated.

Bontalakoduru is a village in Etcherla Mandal where Pattusali caste is a major weaving caste. Almost 300 families used to dwell here in four streets. It was famous for hand-spun cloth. They used to produce silk clothes, and they earned much profit for a long period. They formed a cooperative society in 1944. They named the society "Bontalakoduru Weavers co-operative and Wheels Society". They opened a shop in the District Headquarter Srikakulam in the year 1946. They could almost sell the product in the entire state. With the surplus, some of them could buy agricultural lands in Vadada village of Gara Mandal. The shop earned profits up to 1976. Slowly, the decline of margins and increase in the cost of the establishment had forced closure of the shop. Almost 130 weavers from 300 families used to work in that society with 130 looms at that time. During 1988-2001, they had decreased to 60. During the date of survey (2011), there were only 15 looms in that village.

Weavers' societies, which used to produce cloth with the factory made yarn, were also considerable in number. In those societies, Zinkibhadra Society had a long history. Once, 400 Devanga families lived in this village. They formed Someswara weavers' co-operative society on 18/11/1944. Along with Zinkibhadra, the weavers of Sompeta and Palavalasa took membership in the society. They gave membership to the loom owners only. Hence, the membership was restricted to 305, by 2006, only 44 looms remained and the number had decreased to 37 in the year 2011. As already mentioned, the apex organisation APCO is supplying raw material to this society.

Products

During the colonial rule, the British textile sector could not damage the Indian made coarse clothes. The Indian weaver was damaged mainly due to the competition from the Indian industrial sector. The coarse clothes made by the Indian weaver needed more labour and the cost of labour was cheap when compared with British clothes. Even the cost of labour in the rural areas was less when compared with the Indian urban centers. Added to this, the cost of transportation also had its effect on the survival of Srikakulam weavers.

At that time, they used to produce 26 number count saris, towels, coarse Dhotis when 20 number and 60 number count towels and dhotis were the prime products of this district.

Weavers after Independence

The weavers had almost lost their independent entrepreneurship. They joined the co-operatives or worked under master weavers. The apex organisation is the supplier of raw material who took back the finished product. APCO fixed the wage rate for the weavers. The wage rate was Rs.10 for every one meter of fabric up to the year 2007. In the year 2007, the wage rate was revised and was fixed as 12 for every one meter of cloth. The weight of the meter fabric was fixed at 106 grams with the quality of the yarn as 2/60.

Wage Rate of Weavers and the Earnings of Weavers in this District

Before the actual weaving process, the children or the old aged parents of the weavers made the spindles with the hank yarn to manufacture the cloth

Table 3. Changing Pattern in Cotton Yarn Consumption

Sl. No.	Year	Production	Consumption						Export	
			Mill sector	Percentage of mill sector	Powerlooms	Percentage of power loom sector	Handloom sector	Percentage of Handloom sector		Percentage of the export sector
1.	1970	965	—	—	—	—	—	—	30.45	3.16
2.	1975	989	—	—	—	—	—	—	3.87	0.39
3.	1979	912	—	—	—	—	—	—	5.9	0.65
4.	1990-91	1464	248	16.94	556	37.98	342	23.36	90	6.15
5.	1995-96	1894	159	8.39	567	29.94	504	26.61	261.5	13.81
6.	2000-01	2267	154.5	6.82	534	23.56	530	23.38	513	22.63
7.	2005-06	2521	130	5.16	710	28.16	422	16.74	552	21.90
8.	2006-07	2824	135.5	4.80	773	27.37	461	16.32	616	21.81
9.	2007-08	2948	138	4.68	796	27.00	490	16.62	664	22.52
10.	2010-11	3465	—	—	—	—	—	—	720	20.78

Source: Compiled from various reports and commissioner textiles Mumbai, figures in Million kilograms.

where two persons were required to work continuously on the loom. Generally, the wife and husband shared the work. In that process, they could weave eight meters cloth. In the entire process, they could earn Rs. 96 only for a whole day.

Rajeev Vidya Mission is intended to provide education among school going children. It prescribed a school uniform. The government supplied the uniform to the school-going children. Many committees recommended to the government to provide contract work to the handloom workers. A part of the plan the committees recommended was giving public sector work to these weavers to enable earn their livelihood. As a part of it, the government allotted the work of weaving school uniform cloth to APCO. The raw material cost and the wage earned are shown in the table.

Table 4. Pattern of Expenditure and Wage Earned by a Weaver of Suiting Cloth per Meter

Sl. No.	*Material*	*Expenditure*
1.	Yarn, 276 grams	51.61
2.	Wage	19.58
3.	Total	71.19
4.	Allotment of APCO to the society	72.60
5.	Net earnings of society	1.41

Source: Interview with Kashina Prasadarao, weaver's society, Ampolu.

As per this table, the society earned a rupee and forty-one paisa for weaving a meter of cloth.

It was necessary to calculate the earnings of a member/worker of this society. The society gave Rs. 13.50 for every meter to the member/weaver. Chandarakala, a woman weaver in this society, mentioned that she could weave six meters in a day and hence could earn the daily wage with that much of hard work only Rs. 81. For this earning, she had to work 10 to 12 hours in that society. This Table shows the pattern of shirting cloth.

Table 5. Pattern of Expenditure and Wage Earned by a Weaver of Shirting Cloth per Meter

Sl. No.	*Material*	*Expenditure*
1.	Warf 55 grams	14.41
2.	Weft 55 grams	8.84
3.	Raw material cost	23.25
4.	Wage	15.83
5.	Total	39.08
	Allotment of APCO to the society	38.40
6.	Net loss of society	0.68

Source: Interview with Kashina Prasadarao, weaver's society, Ampolu.

For every meter of weaving a shirting cloth, the society incurred a loss of Rs. 0.68 paisa. The president of Ampolu society had given this data. When asked about incurring loss on the weaving of the shirting cloth, he replied in a voice of despair, "*We can adjust the loss with our gain in the suiting cloth.*" In this government activity, a society was earning Rs. 0.73 paisa per meter. A weaver/member could weave 10 meters of cloth in nine hours and as per the norms, he/she got Rs.17.50 for a meter of cloth and could earn Rs. 171.50 per day.

Prior to weaving, the yarn was required to be prepared in bobbins. In case of shirting cloth, a worker could do two to two and half kgs. of yarn. A worker earned Rs. 27.50 per kg. Thus, the workers' earning varied between Rs. 55 and Rs. 68.75. In case of suiting cloth, a worker could do two to five kgs. of yarn. A worker earned Rs. 14.40 per kg. Thus, the worker earned only Rs. 72 per a day.

They were even prepared to work in miserable conditions that prevailed in the countryside. However, the government was not allocating the work to them. The president of Ampolu society Kashina Prasad Rao lamented, "The government was not even allotting this work to the weavers. In 2009-10, they gave a work order for 25 crores to the societies. In the year 2011-12, they dragged on this allotment to the societies and in the last minute, they allotted this work order to the textile giant Aurobinda mills to the tune of 125 crores. It is nothing but imposing starvation on the voiceless weaver community".

Bankruptcy of Co-operative Societies

As already told the apex organisation APCO is supplying raw material to this society. The Government had introduced Janata clothes scheme. The scheme had two objects. One was to supply the clothes to the poor at a subsidised rate, and the other was to provide work continuously to the weaving community. However, in practice, the weaving societies made this scheme as a mockery and ultimately it paved the way for large-scale corruption. Weaver activist Manchu Krishna Rao of Korasavada village narrated the modus operandi. In his words, "people do not purchase saris and dhotis every month. Hence, they were piled up in the godowns. The then government made it compulsion on the fair-price dealers to lift the clothes along with the other essentials. They told that people are not purchasing the clothes. In spite of that, the government threatened them of non-supplying of other essentials. Dealers inevitably lifted the commodity and kept in their godowns. Practically it is impossible to them to keep the clothes for a long time. Then the idea emerged. The weaver's societies, the officer of civil supply and APCO employees colluded and paper transactions took place in the place of real supplies. Hence, the cloth is being lifted on paper and the weaver did not have any work to do. In this way, the managements of the societies benefitted a lot, but the weaver did not even earn a square meal in this process."

The president of Ampolu society had narrated another modus operandi "the government introduced 20 per cent rebate on the sale of cloth at the door of societies. In this process, some societies had shown fake transaction and got the rebate amount from the government. In this way too, the intended purpose did not serve and the weaver could not get even the minimum work."

When asked about the reasons for this fraudulent practice, which ultimately affected the weavers community badly, Mr. Krishna Rao said, "the changes in the societies Act caused the harm. Initially, the Act prescribed the attendance of 75 per cent of the member as mandatory to take the decision. Slowly the limit decreased and only 10 members were sufficient to take the decision. Hence, the president along with his directors was enough to take any decision. In this process, the society lost its true character of people's participation in the decision-making. Hence, the fraudulent practices emerged."

As per the official data, "there were 72 co-operative societies in this district during the year 1980 out of which, seven to eight were non-functional. During the year 1983, the co-operatives were re-organised and re-structured to make them run profitably. In this process, mergers and closures had taken place. By 1997-98, these came down to 50. Official membership of these societies was 12,426. In the year 1995-96, the membership was 14,223." (*Source:* Report on growth of Handloom industry: Planning commission, 2001)

Later, as per official data, there were 42 co-operative societies in this district. The official membership in the societies was 5,381. However, Mr. Krishna Rao told that the real membership did not exceed 2,500. The staff of the department told that six societies were almost on the verge of closure. The news of Eenadu dated 28/02/11 revealed that out of these societies, only five or six were functional. Planning commission report also indicated that the state of affairs all along the state was identical. In Andhra Pradesh, though there were 812 societies on paper during the year 1996, only 551 societies were functional.

Dr. Soundarapandian in his research report concluded, "Co-operation, though considered as the best form of organisation for a decentralised industry like handloom, has not been successful in the weaving industry." (Growth and prospects of Handloom industry, occasional paper 22, NABARD: Dr. M. Sounadarpandian.)

Policy Interventions and the Handloom Sector

Right from 1947, the successive governments kept on talking on this sector. Primarily, it was a rural industry. Handloom sector was the second largest producer of employment after agriculture in this country. In 1947, even the employment was more. Moreover, the early governments had national movement fervour. The prime objective of the movement was saving the rural industry in general and handlooms sector in particular. In this backdrop, the share of each clothing sector in the overall production had to be viewed.

As seen from the table, the percentage of handloom sector was decreasing. Interestingly mill sector too was travelling in the same direction. Power looms occupied the textile sector. In the year 1961, the power looms produced 5 per cent of the total produce. By 2011-12, it reached 60.77 per cent.

Though the handloom sector was contributing 6,903 million square meters of cloth annually, the hunger of the labour did not end. As per the national handloom census 2010, "the annual earning of Andhra Pradesh rural weaver's

Table 6. Sector- wise Production of Cloth

(In Million square meters.)

Year	*Mill*	*Hand-loom*	*Power loom*	*Hosiery*	*Khadi, wool and silk*	*Total*
1950-51	3727 (73)	742 (14.5)	636 (12.5)	0	0	5105 (100)
1960-61	5127 (69.3)	1900 (25.7)	375 (5)	0	0	7402 (100)
1980-81	4533 (36.4)	3109 (25)	4802 (38.6)	0	0	12444 (100)
1990-91	2589 (11)	4295 (18.4)	13348 (57.2)	2696 (11.6)	402 (1.8)	23330 (100)
2000-01	1670 (4.15)	7506 (18.66)	23803 (59.16)	6696 (16.64)	558 (1.39)	40233 (100)
2010-11	2205 (3.52)	6907 (11.04)	38015 (60.77)	14634 (23.39)	798 (1.28)	62559 (100)

Source: Various Textile reports, Ministry of Textiles, India (Figures in bracket indicate percentage).

family was Rs. 29,314. In the case of allied household, the annual income was Rs. 22,851. In the case of All India average, they were 38260 and 29,693." (*Source:* national Handloom census 2010. Table 6.7, Page 148/178)

As seen from this data, the average daily earnings of the rural weaver were Rs. 80.32 and for the allied worker, Rs. 62.60.

In fact, numerous committees and reports were created in this sector with a basic question faced by all these committees being whether the handloom sector could be continued in a same old pattern. Various committees expressed divergent opinions on this. While some committees argued for a radical shift, some argued for the status quo and some argued for via-media solution. Dynamics could not wait for long. Hence, only the natural selection was resorted once again in this sector.

Even the colonial rulers appointed a fact-finding committee for this sector during 1941. This was the beginning of appointing of committees and creating bundles of reports on the plight of the weavers. All the committees found out many problems with no solution in sight for the rural handloom industry. As said earlier, Kanungo committee recommended for radical transformation to protect the sector. However, the national sentiment did not accept the truth as such and Karve committee recommended for traditional development pattern. However, all the schemes and societies only strengthened the industrial lobby and finally the Capital engulfed the handloom sector.

Protective Measures for the Weavers

As already said, the principal raw material was linked with the capital-intensive industries with the successive governments only tried to supply the raw material by making stipulations. Not only in the sphere of raw material but many measures were proposed and implemented for the welfare of handloom weavers. However, every step in this direction in real terms was conducive only to increased concentration of Capital. The government reports and independent research reports only revealed this fact and because of the rampant misuse, the governments only could scrap those schemes. There was a necessity to recount some of the examples.

Excise Duty and Import Duty

Immediately after independence, the government proposed import substitution measures and in this direction, the government imposed quantitative restrictions on the cloth imports. These measures were, as noted in the research paper, "The immediate post-Independence years; therefore, saw a rapid expansion of cloth production in India. It is seen that cloth production in Indian mills increased by more than a thousand million meters in the five-year period 1951-56." [*Source:* The issue of small versus big in Indian textile industry, an analytical and historical survey: Deepak Majumdar: World Bank Staff working papers: Number 645].

The government levied excise duty in various slabs for the mill sector and handloom sector. This process also led to the destruction of the handloom sector while favouring cloth production in mill sector as indicated by a research report. In this system, the duty was reduced on fine yarn cloth and the duty was almost the same for all the sectors in the case of coarse cloth. In fact, Indian handloom industry survived on coarse cloth even from the onslaught of colonial industrial cloth. However, the tax concessions on the fine cloth made the handloom sector to cut their basic production to earn some profit. In view of this, production of coarse cloth hampered, and shortage of production emerged. Ultimately as concluded by the report, "It is clear that the policy of production of subsidised coarse cloth in the nationalised mills runs counter to some extent to the policy of protection of handlooms in so far as the latter supply, a large share of the output of course cloth." (*Source:* The issue of small versus big in Indian textile industry, an analytical and historical survey: Deepak Majumdar: World Bank Staff working papers: Number 645 page 17).

To curb the concentration of production in the mill sector, the measure taken by the government always encouraged the power loom sector. This sector had utilised all the gaps in the Acts and thrived. The crux of this process was reflected in many research reports and even in government's reports which read, *"First, the two instruments of control on mill-made cloth – the excise duty, and the reservation of specified lines of production for the decentralised sector—were not applied to power loom units employing less than five looms until 1974.*

Secondly, the lines of production prohibited have always been a much longer list for mills than for power looms. At the same time, as we have seen, the excise duty has been much heavier on mill cloth.

Thirdly and probably most importantly, although powerlooms (like new loom capacity created in the mills) are supposed to be set up only after a license has been granted by the government, the government's ability to enforce this policy has been meagre. "Unauthorised" power looms have mushroomed all over the country. Sometimes they are nominally broken up into units of less than five workers to give some legal validity to their evading the heavier controls and duties on units of larger sizes." [*Source:* The issue of small versus big in Indian textile industry, an analytical and historical survey: Deepak Majumdar: World Bank Staff working papers: Number 645).

The NABARD sponsored report revealed, *"To strengthen the competition of Handloom sector, the excise duty was imposed on the other two sectors namely, mill sector and power loom sector. It was first introduced in 1953 by the Handloom Act (1953) by which an additional excise duty was imposed on all cloth produced by the mills except for export. Later in 1956, it was extended to power looms also with a lower incidence. Here again, for all practical purposes power loom units with less than four looms were identically treated with that of handlooms on the plea of smallness and decentralisation. This resulted in deliberate fragmentation of units in power loom sector, which intensified competition to the handlooms.*" (Growth and prospects of hand loom industry: "NABARD sponsored report" Dr. Soundarapandian)

The above report stated that to get the concessions, the textile lobby plunged into action and installed many power loom units to get the concessions. Ultimately, as the report indicated *"the scheme was discontinued in 1961, as it was found that large beneficiaries were not handloom weavers due to the opportunity largely seized by the mill owners."*

As already mentioned, there is a stipulation that the spinning mills have to supply hank yarn to the handloom sector. For this, the government had extended central excise duty exemption on the sale of hank yarn to the handloom sector. However, the chairman of Andhra Pradesh Spinning Mills co-ordination Committee, in an interview to Times of India revealed, *"In 1974, the center had made it obligatory for the spinning mills to produce 50 per cent hank yarn and had given it an exemption from the excise duty as an incentive. But now the handloom units have gone down and there is not much of demand for hank yarn. Some smaller mills, according to Rao, are misusing this point to avoid 100 per cent excise duty by showing cone yarn as hank yarn.*" (*Source:* Times of India dated 02/09/2001)

Mr. Virupakshaiah also revealed the same fact. He told, "The mill owners are supplying cone yarn in the guise of hank yarn. Thus, they are evading the value added tax and it has two effects. On record, they are showing the clearances are made to handloom sector. In reality, the state exchequer is losing the revenue."

Initially, the successive governments chanted co-operative mantra for all the problems. However, the mantra proved to be a concentration of wealth in few hands over a period. In Andhra Pradesh, all the cooperative mills were privatised and the capital interests replaced the co-operative sector. In other words, the innumerable individuals who shared the public money in the shape of tax earnings were handed over to private big entrepreneurs in a public bidding. The process that took place in Andhra Pradesh was reflected in news stories. It read, *"The Andhra Pradesh government has drawn up plans for privatization of 10 co-operative spinning mills and sugar factories in the state by the end of the current year. Disclosing this in Hyderabad on Saturday, the Implementation Secretariat—the high-powered body constituted by the state government to oversee and implement public enterprise reforms—said that 15 out of the 19 enterprises identified under Phase I privatisation programme are likely to be restructured, wound up or privatised by the year-end."* (Business line: dated 27/10/2001)

As mentioned earlier, in the absence of sufficient supply of coarse cloth, the government made it mandatory on big mills to manufacture the coarse cloth to cater to the needs of the public. As observed by Deepak Majumdar, this resulted in the big mills incurring losses besides the sick units getting nationalised. The saga of this nationalisation could be seen from the official website of National Textile Corporation. The website narrated the version on its web page read, *"The National Textile Corporation Limited (NTC) is a Central Public Sector Enterprise under the Ministry of Textiles, which was incorporated in April 1968 for managing the affairs of sick textile undertakings in the private sector, taken over by the Government. Starting with 16 mills in 1968, this number gradually rose to 103 by 1972-73. In the year 1974, all these units were nationalised under the Sick Textile Undertakings (Nationalisation) Act 1974. The number of units increased to 119 by 1995. These 119 mills were controlled by NTC Ltd with the help of 9 subsidiary Corporations, with an authorised capital of 10 crore (US$1.81 million) which was raised from time to time and which is now about 7,000 crore (US$1.27 billion) and the paid up share capital of the corporation is about Rs.4,000 crore (US$ 727 million)."* *Source:* (www.ntcltd.co.in)

Again, the disinvestment mantra replaced the nationalisation mantra and was applied to National Textile Corporation. In that process, 78 mills were closed and 63,057 employees went on voluntary retirement scheme and the corporation spent an amount of Rs. 2,322 Crores on this scheme. (*Source:* FAQs in www.ntcltd.co.in)

For modernisation of the corporation, it sold the mills and lands to the private sector. The lands were alienated from public enterprise to private real estate tycoons. The total proceeds from sale of assets (Land, Plant and Machinery, and Building Structure) were Rs. 6551 crores. The total area of land sold was Rs.1533.09 acres. (*Source:* FAQs in www.ntcltd.co.in)

In this way, the entire protective measures laid the way for concentration of capital and displacement of handloom weavers in the country.

Can Casualty Prevent the Epidemic?

During the survey, when asked a handloom weaver of Korasavada village, if they would survive the onslaught of capital-intensive industries, he retorted, "Can casualty prevent the epidemic?" The lamentation of the ordinary handloom

Table 7. Sectorwise Production of Cloth during the Colonial Period (cloth in Million Yards)

Years	*Indian Mills*	*Handloom Sector*	*Imports*	*Total*
1900-1903	482.80	792.8	1967.7	3243.30
1912-1915	1187.0	1048.5	2738.7	4974.20
1918-1920	1575.8	712.4	1132.0	3420.20
1927-1930	2195.6	1155.5	1916.3	5267.40
1936-1939	3629.6	1420.5	654.7	5704.80

Source: The issue of small versus big in Indian textile industry, an analytical and historical survey: Deepak Majumdar: World Bank Staff working papers: Number 645.

weaver made the reader understand the situation. However, official statistics and reports are required to understand the fact. In fact, the mechanisation process in India had its origin in the late 19th century.

During the colonial period, the handloom sector dominated the cloth production. The Table 7 indicates the production pattern of that period.

This table shows the handloom sector's survival from the foreign capital. In the relevant period, the imports had even shown negative trend during 1917-1939. However, the mill sector was continuously making inroads in this manufacturing sector. During the period, the mill sector started its production with a modest 482.80 and reached 3629.60 million yards. The net increase in the production was 3146.80-million yards. The percentage of increase was 651. At the same time, the imports were decreasing continuously. Imports were registered the highest figure during 1912-15 to be 2738.70. By 1936-39, it fell down to 654.7 million yards. As mentioned earlier, the imports mainly comprised fine cloth. Hence, the imports were not the main contention to the handloom clothes.

By 1879, in this country, there were 56 mills in the textile sector. Those had 1.43 million spindles and 13,000 looms. By 1913-14, the number of mills increased to 150. The number of spindles increased to 6.62 million and looms were increased to 96,688. The concentration of mill sector led to the concentration of proletarian and led to industrial agitations. Hence, the mill sector had skilfully floated power loom sector and shifted the production to that sector. In this process, they obtained double advantage as already indicated. The number of looms recorded decreasing from late 80s. By March 2000, they decreased to 1.23 lakhs and further decreased to 0.52 lakhs by 2011. As seen from the cloth production data at table 109, the power loom sector produced more than the combined production of mill and handloom sector. Their combined production was 9,112 million square meters of cloth whereas the power loom sector produced 38,015 million meters of cloth. The overall difference was 28,903 million metres. (Data compiled from Annual report of Ministry of Textiles, 2010-11)

In the name of decentralisation, centralisation of power looms occupied the scene. These looms increased in leaps and bounds. The backdrop of the development of powerloom sector has been described in the handbook on powerlooms which read, "The growth of the decentralised powerloom sector was also encouraged by the experiences and success story of M/s Reliance Industry, Ahmadabad, which had installed powerlooms, discarded by M/s Mafatlal Industries Ltd., Nadiad in the year 1966 at Naroda Village of Ahmadabad (Gujarat). This is also known as a turning point in the history of Indian textile industry." Handbook on powerlooms: publication of Textile commissioner, Mumbai)

Table 8. Development Pattern of Power Loom Units

Sl. No.	*Year*	*Power loom Units*	*Spindles*
1.	1942	15000	
2.	1986-87	NA	638000
3.	1990-91	296035	1134000
4.	1995-96	333017	1412000
5.	2000-01	374076	1661000
6.	2005-06	377588	1926000
7.	2010-11	5,10,100	

Source: Handbook on power looms and the annual report of Ministry of textiles 2010-11.

This was almost a beginning of the low pressure in the textile sector. By this time, it turned as whirlwind, the artisan weavers had lost their grip on the production and on their profession. The growth of power looms can be seen from this table.

During the year 1942, there were only 15,000 power looms broadly restricted to the then Bombay presidency. By 2010-11, there were 5, 10, 000 power loom units and they had 22,69,469 power looms. The workforce in these units was 57, 29,158. In Andhra Pradesh, there were 45,402 power looms with the workforce to be 1,13,504. These power looms were considered as decentralised or small-scale sector on which pretext, they were getting concessions. They were not satisfied with those concessions and they made inroads into handlooms sector to grab the profits. Profits were directly proportional to violating Acts and Laws.

As already observed by the researchers, the inception of the power loom was started with intention of violating the law. At any point of time, they did not stop the malpractices and they were always busy in devising novel modus-operandi to mint money.

Expert committees and many research reports widely discussed these factors and nothing has stopped them. In fact, there was no such machinery to control malpractices of such voluminous units. They were drawing concessions without providing the yarns. However, on paper, the suppliers were shown as supplies to handloom weavers in view of which, it appeared that handloom-weaving sector was producing 11 per cent of total cloth since the production of cloth figures were based on the consumption of yarn. In fact, in real terms, the handloom sector did not produce even that much of cloth.

The government had reserved 22 items exclusively to protect the handloom sector by virtue of 1985 handloom Act. Subsequently, the number was reduced to nine items. However, the power loom sector produced all these goods and sold them in the market. Thus, it violated the Acts and Rules.

Korasavada Handloom Weaver's Society president Manchu Krishna Rao had worked as a member of implementing reservation committee. He narrated his experience on this issue and said, "I worked as a member of reservation committee during 1999-2001. I wrote a detailed report on the violations of the power loom sector. We went to Nakirekal of Nalgonda District for seizing the power loom unit. They got the tip off and emptied all the godowns. They were producing Ponduru brand cloths. Officers were also with us. In one of the units, we could find the illicit goods. Immediately, the management of that unit surrounded us only to thrash us. Immediately, we ran away only to save our skin. Ultimately, the government could suspend the Assistant Director of the department."

Though there was the enforcement machinery, the culprits were not being booked. The visits were being shown in big numbers but the cases were very nominal. The figures told the tale of these case bookings.

Table 9. Physical Progress of Inspections on Power loom Units

Sl. No.	*Physical progress*	*2007-08*	*2008-09*	*2009-10*	*2010-11*
1.	Targets for power loom inspections	209290	2,15,575	2,29,040	2,52,103
2.	Number of power looms inspected	249462	2,37,111	1,97,210	1,34,609
3.	Number of FIRs lodged	12	5	12	6
4.	Convictions	11	3	14	2

Source: Annual report, 2010-11 of Ministry of Textiles, Page 144.

It is clear from the table that there was no need to make any further analysis on the statistics. Either the entire power looms are genuine in their operations or they are capable to conceal their activity by hook or crook.

However, one thing was clear. The mushrooming of power looms and the veracity of vigilance cases booked on them proved the proclamation of an ordinary handloom weaver's outburst of epidemic in this sector.

The violations were not restricted to work places. The official government exhibitions had also set a platform for these violations. The power loom sector used to bring their clothes to the exhibition and they were selling their clothes in the guise of handloom clothes. In the surveyed villages, every handloom weaver complained about this. This was also not a new phenomenon for the trading sector. The mill sector tried to cash the national handloom sentiment even during the national movement. Gandhi expressed helplessness over the fallacious intentions of Indian mill owner to cash the national sentiments and he opined that the full-fledged hand weaving and the awareness of public only put a checkmate to this fraudulent practices.

Gandhi expressed these views in the year 1925. However, Gandhi's aspirations had not fulfilled and the same old techniques were continuing in a large scale. A news item revealed the same old practice in Andhra Pradesh. It read, "*Handloom and power loom, the two sectors of textile industry, are in a brush, though the present situation is too subtle to be handled by Government. The cloth is generally made on either power looms or handlooms. Whatever is the method of production; the cost of yarn and chemicals is the same. Power looms use electricity and less manpower whereas handlooms use more manpower and no electricity. The end result is the handlooms are costlier than the power looms because of higher wages. The topic of interest for consumer is the sales of power loom cloth as handloom cloth. Most of the unscrupulous persons were passing power looms as handlooms, making unreasonable profits, and cheating the consumers.*" (*Source:* www. fibre 2 fashion.com, Dated:16/05/2007)

Finally, the steering committee report of twelfth planning commission also corroborated the ground level reports. It read, "of particular concern in this scenario is the steady erosion of livelihoods in the crafts and handloom sectors due to increased competition from machine manufactured products." (*Source:* Report of the steering committee report, constituted for twelfth Five-year plan, 2012-17, Page 7)

Employment Pattern Weaver Community

There was a need to observe the changing employment pattern in the surveyed villages. Surveyed villages were 12. In these villages, once 1072 Devanga families, 75 Padmasali, and 439 Pattusali families resided. Out of these families, 723 families had permanently migrated. 663 families were earning their livelihood on non-weaving profession by the daily migration.

In the surveyed villages, Boddam, Murapaka, Ampolu, Bontalakoduru were nearer to urban. The first village was nearer to Rajam, an industrial centre and the other three were nearer to the district headquarter Srikakulam. Almost 100 men from Boddam village were on daily migration, 135 men from Bontalakoduru, 80 men from Ampolu, and 100 men from Murapaka village eked their livelihood in the urban non-weaving profession.

Normally, majority of these families were landless and they eked out their livelihood on their traditional profession with meager earnings. In view of this, they could not send their children for a better education. In the surveyed villages, only three villages Bontalakoduru, Korasavada, and Murapaka could produce some employees.

Korasavada village produced many professionals and majority came from two families who had blood relation and the rivalry. They succeeded in the business as well in education. 17 were in the doctor profession in that village and four were doing their graduation in medical colleges. In all the 12 villages, five villages did not knock the door of government employment though they had reservation under backward classes. These villages produced 147 employees. The following table reflects the employment pattern of these villages.

Table 10. Employment Pattern in the Surveyed Villages

No. of Villages surveyed	*No. of families*	*Employment*			
		Doctor	*Engineer*	*Teacher and Teaching profession*	*State gov.*
12	1173	30	17	66	9

(*Table Contd.*)

No. of Villages surveyed	*No. of families*	*Employment*				
		Public sector	*Private*	*Defense*	*Police*	*Total*
12	1173	6	5	13	1	147

Migration

As seen from the survey results with the news reports of this district amply revealing that they were under a distressed migration. Their houses were in dilapidated conditions. Many streets had become vacant. As seen from the villages, the houses of Brahmins and weavers were in a sorry state. Since migration was common in all the communities, nobody was interested to live in these houses.

Eenadu carried a news item about migration in this community in detail on 28/02/2011, which read, "Once, Sompeta handloom society had flourished with 360 members. Now it is running with 35 looms. The remaining is going to nearby towns in search of livelihood. Majority of them are working in construction sector as collies."

Buragam was a village in Kanchili Mandal. Once there were 50 looms but later only ten looms were working. The remaining had vanished from the village employed as construction workers or as security guards at apartments.

Byrisarangapuram was a village in Mandasa Mandal. Once, 200 looms were busy in making cloth. Later, only 70 looms remained and the remaining families migrated.

Rajapuram was a village in Kaviti Mandal. Once, 90 families eked out their livelihood from this profession. Since it is not even providing the sufficient food, only six looms were working and the all other families changed their profession by migration to other cities.

Baruva was a major Panchayat in Sompeta Mandal. Once, it was a hotbed of Swadeshi movement in this district. 100 families used to get their food on loom. Later, only seven families have stuck to the profession.

Rattakanna was a village in Itchapuram Mandal. Once 80 families were busy in this profession, but later, only four families were trying to survive on the profession. Majority of them were working as construction labour and as rickshaw-pullers in the urban streets.

The surveyed villages were also revealing the same truth. In the surveyed villages, there were 1321 looms. Later, there were 311 looms. In fact, working looms were much lower. Landlessness was also a major reason for the distressed migration. Out of total 1896 families, (pre-permanent migration) 1844 families were landless. The twin attack on the handloom sector in the shape of landlessness and decaying of their profession made them to flee. Nobody was interested to continue his/her children in the profession.

The national handloom census 2010 revealed, *"During the Third Handloom Census, the respondents were asked for their opinion on whether they believed that their children would continue with handloom activity. The majority of them responded that they were not sure (35.7 per cent) or that they did not believe that children would pursue the activity (24.5 per cent). Only 25.3 per cent of the households were positive about their children continuing in the trade.*

The states where the number of households believing that their children would continue with handloom activity was less than the national average are Tamil Nadu (9.2 per cent), Andhra Pradesh (10.9 per cent) and West Bengal (16.4 per cent). This shows that households in states primarily into handloom production do not believe that their next generation would continue the activity, as the work was hard, time consuming and yielding low remuneration." (Handloom census 2009-10: Page 37: Ministry of textiles: GOI) {Emphasis added}

The member of Planning Commission Syeda Saiyidain Hameed expressed her deep anguish over this process and told the media: *"Since 2004, the handloom sector has been assigned to me as a Member of the Planning Commission. In most of the clusters I visited, there was deprivation and exploitation. I looked at their skilled hands, which were pounding stones or digging earth. Children were not learning skills of their parents. Instead, they were pulling rickshaws, picking rags, building roads... doing anything but weaving. I rued that these youth would never see a himroo weave, a kaani shawl or know the kamkhwab fabric, which was woven for the Mughal royalty. India's post-Independence USP is getting lost. Without a massive effort it will be the end for most weaves—jamdani, Kanjeevaram, tangail, kota doria, tanchoi, Bhagalpuri, ikat, gadwal, paithani."* (*Source:* Business Today, 06/03/2011)

As told by the Planning Commission member, the children of the weavers were settling in the activities other than weaving to earn their livelihood in this district too. The process made to recollect the words of Satyam committee, which read, *"The aim of the policy basically should be to prepare the sector to face the imminent competition as a result of opening up of the market and move out those that cannot cope with the competition to other more viable options*." (Expert committee report, Page: 93).

The committee used these words about the progeny of handloom weavers. By the turn of first decade of the 21st century, the fate of the progeny proved the writings of the committee. They were out only to join the urban army of petty uncertain "professions" as construction workers, wage workers in decentralised sector, auto drivers and even as rickshaw-pullers.

Later, the leftover women took over the responsibility of weaving. In the surveyed villages, Ampolu Co-operative Society is quite healthy. In this society too, the women replaced the men. Men are going to nearby towns as industrial labour or to work in service sector, which was inevitably feminised. In Boddam village, a woman weaver told that her husband is working in Rajam and on all the days excepting Sunday she is busy in weaving to earn Rs. 80 per day. The same story was repeated in Ampolu. Chandarakala, a woman weaver, had shown a loom and told that the loom belonged to her husband. In the holidays, he used that loom to earn some money. During the weekdays, the loom used to be lying idle.

The national scenario too was reflecting the same reality. The following Table indicates the feminisation of Indian handloom sector.

Table 11. Feminisation of Indian Handloom Industry

Census Year	*Men*	*Women*	*Total Workers*
1987-88	15,55,270	26,38,947	41,93,767
1995-96	12,22,201	21,03,887	33,26,088
2009-10	8,48,473	29,08,362	38,46,835

Source: Handloom census, 2009-10.

The decrease was in the men workforce, which had drastically come down from 15, 55, 270 to 8,48,473. The overall decrease was 7,06,797, by 45.44 per cent. In other words, one out of two could not cope up with the competition. The share of woman workers rose from 62.92 per cent to 75.60 per cent over a period of 25 years.

Welfare Schemes and Handloom Sector

So many schemes were introduced for the welfare of handloom weavers. Here too, the policymakers were in dilemma. The schemes were to be aimed at societies or to individuals which had come to fore as a question. Many opined that societies were intended to make the weaver beneficial. However, as per estimates, not even 30per centof the weavers were in these societies. It did not mean all the members in the society got benefits. As already indicated, the vocal sections of the society bodies credited the benefits.

The handloom societies and the weavers were caught in a severe debt and they had resorted to the extreme step due to which, the Andhra Pradesh government declared moratorium on the debts. In view of the factious data, many society bodies swallowed the money while the lives of weavers could not see the light. On hearing about the moratorium, the handloom weavers of Zinkibhadra village had stopped repayment of their loans. The bank authorities of Sompeta seized the savings amount of Balla Bhîma Rao to the tune of Rs. 6,091 that he kept for his daughter's marriage. In this way, they also seized an amount of Rs. 52,000 on 5/6/2010 of the weavers of that village.

Every citizen of this country knows about the non-productive assets of these banks and big wigs were involved in these issues. However, the banks considered the handloom weavers to be the culprits in the enhancement of these amounts and took the legal steps to realise the amounts only to reduce the bad debts as non-productive assets.

When asked about the performance and benefits of the welfare scheme at Zinkibhadra village, a weaver, Simhachalam lamented, "forget about the recounting of all the schemes.....let the government issue Antyodaya cards. Antyodaya cardholder is entitled to receive the rice on free of cost from ration shops. Forget about the vegetables at least we expect the rice with starch."

Even the apex court had directed several times to distribute the food grains to the poor people.

The question is whether the directives of the apex court or the hapless voice of Indian rural weaver can move the civil society of 21st century.

Bibliography

1. A.M. Simons, The American Farmer, Charles H. Kerr and Company, Chikago, 1908.
2. Barry Pavier, The Telangana Movement (1944-51), Vikas Publishing House Pvt. Ltd., Sahibabad, 1981.
3. Bharat Dogra, Seed Industry in India: Seeds of Plenty or Seeds of Discontent, Navdhanya and News from Fields and Slums (NFS) India.
4. Bharat Dogra, Crisis In Indian Fishery, Navdhanya and News from Fields and Slums (NFS) India, 1993.
5. Bharat Dogra, Farm Research: Important Areas of Concern, Navdhanya and News from Fields and Slums (NFS) India.
6. Chao-KUO-Chin, Agrarian Policy of Chinese Communist Party, Asia Publishing House, 1960.
7. Compiled by S.C. Ray, Agricultural Indebtedness And Its Remedies: Being Selections From Official Documents, Calcutta University Press, 1915.
8. Compiled by W. Francis : ICS, Provincial Gazetteers of India, Madras Vol. I, Oxford, 1908.
9. Complied and Published by Chief Planning Office: Vizianagaram, District hand books Vizianagaram (1990-91 to 2010).
10. Complied and published by Chief Planning Officer, Srikakulam District handbooks Srikakualm (1979-2010).
11. D.D. Kosambi, An Introduction to the Study of Indian History, Popular Prakashana Private Limited, Mumbai, 2011.
12. D.D. Kosambi, Exasperating Essays: Exercise in the Dialectical Method.
13. Compiled and edited by D.F. Carmichael M.C.S, A manual of the District of Vizagapatam in the Precedency of Madras, William Thomas, 1869.
14. Daniel Thorner, The Agrarian prospect in India : Five Lectures on Land reforms delivered in 1955 at the Delhi school of economics, University Press Delhi, 1955.
15. Dr. B.R. Ambedkar, States and Minorities, www.ambedkar.org.
16. Dr. B.D. Sharma, Wither Tribal Areas, Sahayog Pustak Kutir, New Delhi, 1995.
17. Dr. B.D. Sharma, Agricultural Credit An Unpardonable Fraud With Farmers, Sahayog Pustak Kutir, New Delhi.
18. ED: N. Venkataswamy and T. Nageswarara rao, Paatikella Andhrapradesh (In Telugu Language), Telugu Academy, Hyderabad, 1981.

19. Ed: S.N. Dubey and Ratna Murdia, Land Alienation And Restoration In Tribal Communities In India, Himalaya Publishing House, Bombay, 1977.
20. Ed: Jag Parvesh Chander, Teachings Of Mahatma Gandhi, Narain Das Kumar, Lahore, 1945.
21. Fabian Society, Capital and Land, Fabian Society, 1904.
22. Frederic Engels, The Peasant Question In France and Germany, www.marxist.org.
23. Frederic Engels, The Present War in Germany, www.marxist.org.
24. G.G. Campbell, Modern India a Sketch of the System of Civil Government, John Murray, London, 1852.
25. Henry Summer Maine, Village Communities in the East and West, John Murray, London, 1871.
26. ICAR: New Delhi, Resource Analysis for Integrated Development: Rai Bareli District, ICAR, New Delhi.
27. Karl Kautsky, Agrarian Question, Zwan Publications, London, 1988.
28. Karl Marx, Marx on India, Tulika Books, New Delhi, 2006.
29. Karl Marx, Pre-capitalist accumulation, www.marxist.org.
30. Liut-Colonel A.T. Eetheridge, Report on the Past Famines in Bombay Presidency, Printed for Government, 1868.
31. M.K. Gandhi, Khadee Ardhasastram (In Telugu Language), the government Press, Madras, 1958.
32. M.N. Roy and Abani Mukharjee, India in Transition, Edition de la Librairic J.B. Target, 1922.
33. P. Anderson Graham, the Rural Exodus, Methuen and Co., 1892.
34. Pannalal Patel, Jeevitame Oka Naataka Rangam (Gujarati Novel in Telugu Language), Kendra Sahitya Academy.
35. Rahul Samkrutyayan, Olga Nunchi Gangaku (In Telugu Language), Visalandhra Publishing House, Viziawada.
36. Romesh Dutt, Indian famines and their causes and prevention, P.S. King and Son, London, 1901.
37. Romesh Dutt, Open Letters to Lord Curzon on Famines and Land Assessment in India, Kegan Paul, Trench, Trubner and Co., Ltd. London, 1900.
38. S.C. Dubey, Bharateeya Gramam (In Telugu Language), Telugu Academy, Hyderabad, 1974.
39. S.S. Rameshan, Srikakulam District Gazetteer, The Director Printing and Stationary, Hyderabad, 1979.
40. Sir Richard Temple, India in 1880, John Murray, London, 1880.
41. Sydney Herbert, The Fall Of Feudalism in France, Frederic A. Stokes Company, New York, 1920.
42. Theodore Morison, The Economic Transition In India, John Murray, London, 1911.

43. Theodore Morison, Industrial organisation of An Indian province, John Murray, London, 1918.
44. Thomas Southhall Dymond and Digby C pedder and Edward Carpenter, Socialism and agriculture, Fabian Society, London, 1908.
45. V.I. Lenin, Capitalism in Agriculture, www.marxist.org.
46. V.I. Lenin, Marxist Views On Agrarian Question in Europe and in Russia, www.marxist.org.
47. V.I. Lenin, The capitalist System in Agriculture, www.marxist.org.
48. V. Pavlov, V. Rastyannikov, G. Shirokov, Problems of Third world: India : Social and Economic Development (18th-20th Centuries), Progress Publishers, 1975.
49. Venkat, Srikakula Girijana Rytanga Udyamam (In Telugu Language), Tarimela Nagireddi Memorial Trust, Viziawada, 2007.
50. Waltar Burr, Rural organisation, Macmillan Company, London, 1921.
51. Wolf Ladejinsky, Agrarian Reform as Unfinished Business, World Bank, Oxford University Press, 1977.
52. Fifth Report From The Select Committee of House of Commons on the Affairs of East India Company: 28th July 1812, Black, Parry and Co., London, 1812.
53. Maxim Gorky, Nagaram (In Telugu Language), Prajashakti Publications.
54. Srinivasa Raghavaiyange, B.A., Dewan Bahadur, C.T.E., Memorandum on the Progress of the Madras Presidency During the Last Forty Years of British Administration. Superintendent, Government Press, 1893.
55. Madras Land Revenue Report 1855, H. Smith, 1858.
56. Madras Land Revenue Report 1865, H. Morgan for Board of Revenue, 1866.
57. Manu, The Laws of Manu, G. Buhler (Translator).

Research Reports Official and Unofficial

1. Agricultural diversification towards high value commodities: A study in food surplus states in India with a focus on Punjab and Andhra Pradesh, International Food Policy Research Institute (IFPRI).
2. Agricultural statistics 2010-11.
3. Andhra Pradesh Crop Report 1955.
4. Annual Reports, Ministry of Textiles Government of India.
5. Annual Reports, J.K. Paper Mills.
6. Annual Reports, Ministry of Fertilisers: India.
7. Annual Reports, Department of Petrochemicals.
8. Basic Animal Husbandry Statistics; 2010.
9. Broucher of Nuziveedu Seeds Company.
10. Budget speeches of Andhra Pradesh (1970 to 2011), Ministry of Finance, Andhra Pradesh.

11. Census Reports 1971, 1981, 1991, 2001, 2011, Registrar General of India.
12. Clean Development Mechanism Improving Rural live and flrogh carbon sequestration by adopting Environment friendly fact orology based agro forestry (reforestation practice).
13. Contract Farming- Efforts on for educating farmers, A.P. State government Power Point Presentation.
14. Economic surveys of India (1970-2010), Ministry of Finance, India.
15. Economic Potential of Biological Substitutes, Indian Council of Agricultural Research.
16. Election Results of General Elections, Chief Election Commissioner, India.
17. Forest wildlife Statistics 2004.
18. Growth and Prospects of Handloom Sector in India : NABARD Mumbai, DR. M. Soundarapandian.
19. Land Committee Report (known as Koneru Rangarao report).
20. Land holding survey 1986 and 1992, National Sample Survey Office.
21. Long Term Partnerships with Emerging Players, International Finance Corporation.
22. National Agricultural Policy, 2000.
23. National Commission on Agriculture 1976.
24. National commission on cattle 2000.
25. National Commission on Farmers: Towards Faster and More Inclusive Growth of Farmers' Welfare: Fifth and Final Report, Chaired by Swaminathan
26. National S.C Commission report:1994-95.
27. National S.C Commission report: 2004-05.
28. Official India Textile Statistics 2010-11, Ministry of Textiles: Govt. of India.
29. Performance Audit on Fertiliser Subsidy, Comptroller and Audit General of India (CAG).
30. Performance Audit Report on Land Allotments, Comptroller and Audit General of India (CAG).
31. Replies from various Government Departments under RTI Act.
32. Report Number 24184, World Bank.
33. Report of Expert Committee on Prevention of Tribal Land and Its restoration, Planning Commission, Govt. of India.
34. Report of Steering Committee on Handlooms and Handicrafts Twelfth Five Year Plan (2012-17), Planning commission: Govt. of India.

35. Report of Sub- Group on Land Related Issues, 12th five year plan: Planning Commission.
36. Report of the Committee on State Agrarian Relations and the Unfinished Task of Land Reforms, Planning Commission, Govt. of India.
37. Report Of The Expert Committee on Textile Policy @ Satyam Committee Report, Ministry of Textiles, Govt. of India.
38. Report on Growth and Prospects of the Handloom Industry: A study conducted by Planning Commission, Seemanthini Niranjana and Soumya Vinayan.
39. Speech of Shri Sharad Pawar, NDC meeting on 27th June 2005.
40. Strategy Paper on Welfare of Scheduled Caste and Scheduled Tribe Population, Government of Andhra Pradesh.
41. TATA Agri Company Broucher.
42. Working group reports of various five year plans, Planning Commission, Govt. of India.
43. World Bank Report on Community Forestry: report number 00001464, World Bank.
44. National Marine Census 1980, Central marine fisheries research India (CMFRI).
45. National Marine Census 2005, Central marine fisheries research India (CMFRI).
46. National Marine Census 2010, Central Marine Fisheries Research India (CMFRI).
47. Report on the sea fish and fisheries of India and Burma, Major Francis Day.
48. CMFRI Bulletins.
49. Booklets by Bay of Bengal Programme.
50. Illegal Unreported, Unregulated Marine Fish catch in Indian Economic Zone- A Field Report, Ganapathi Raju Pramod.
51. Export of Marine products from India 2010-11: export Trend, CMFRI.
52. Mining Leases in Srikakulam District, www.srikakulam.nic.in.
53. Minutes of Public Hearing, APPCB.
54. Briefing paper on fishing policy, H.B. Soumya and Partha J. Shaw.
55. National Marine Fishing Policy 2004.
56. Union budgets From 1970 To 2010.
57. Andhra Pradesh State Budget From 1970 To 2010.

Articles

1. Agricultural co-operative finance and business management, Dr. P.S. Badal.
2. A strategy for improving land administration in India, Klaus Deininger.

3. An Analytical Study of the Functioning and the Problems of the Powerloom Industry in Maharashtra with Special Reference to Malegaon Dist. Nashik, Arif Anjum and D.V. Thakor.
4. Attached and Casual labour wage rates, Rakesh Basant: EPW March 3,1984.
5. Dedly crop : Difficult times Indian cotton farmers to desperate action, Jonathan Cart.
6. Indian handlooms in 20th century, Tirthankar Roy.
7. Land Para-professionals as a last mile solution to land issues of the poor, B. Rajasekhar, I.A.S.
8. Le Socialis me et Limpot, Karl Marx.
9. Migration and Human Development in India : Human Development Research Paper 2009/13, Priya Deshingkar and Shaheen Akter
10. Paper on Land Revenue Administration- An Historical Outlook, C. Umamaheshwararao I.A.S.
11. Real wages of agricultural labour in Andhra Pradesh: Two decades of stagnation, G. Parthasaradhy, EPW July 31 ,1982.
12. Sham of Minimum Wages, EPW June 14-21 1980.
13. The changing agricultural demography of India- evidence from a Rural youth Perception survey, Amrita Sharma and Shaheen Akter.
14. The Nationalisation of the Land, Karl Marx.
15. The private deliver of public crop varieties : Rice in Andhra Pradesh, Rob Tripp.
16. Who will speak for the village? Agrarian change and marginalising Realities in contemporary India, Surinder S. Jodhka.

Periodicals and Dailies

1. Deccan Chronicle
2. Eenadu
3. Economic and Political Weekly
4. Frontline
5. Seminar
6. The Hindu
7. Times of India

Websites

1. www.agcensus.nic.in
2. www.ambedkar.org
3. www.apdes.ap.gov.in
4. www.apfdc.nic.in
5. www.apfinance.gov.in
6. www.aplands.nic.in
7. www.aptribes.nic.in
8. www.chemicals.nic.in

9. www.cmfri.nic.in
10. www.cotcorp.gov.in
11. www.dahd.nic.in
12. www.eci.nic.in
13. www.fao.org/fishery
14. www.finmin.nic.in
15. www.fsi.nic.in
16. www.icar.org.in
17. www.mansantoindia.com
18. www.marxist.org
19. www.mospi.nic.in
20. www.mpeda.com
21. www.ncsc.nic.in
22. www.nfdb.ap.nic.in
23. www.nuziveeduseeds.com
24. www.planniningcommission.nic.in
25. www.rural.nic.in
26. www.tataagrico.com
27. www.texmin.nic.in
28. www.tribal.nic.in
29. www.txcindia.nic.in

Annexure 1: Villages Surveyed in the Undivided Srikakulam District

Sl.No	*Name of the Mandal*	*Name of the Vilalge*	*Priorty of Selection*	*Persons Helped*
1.	Sompeta	Gollagandi	Anti thermal agitation	B. Sundara Rao, Raghavulu, Kodandam
2.	Palasa	Kambirigam	Land Struggles	Barla Sundara Rao and D. Anjaneyamurty
3.	Saluru	Kurukuti	Non Schedule Tribal/Land Struggle	Prasad
4.	Palakonda	Annavram	Once a social hegemony village	S. Raminaidu and Srinivas
5.	Kotturu	Ponnaturu	Unofficial Submerged Village	Surya Rao
6.	Rajam	Boddam	Weavers/un irrigated	Ganapati rao ,Kishor, Srinivas
7.	G.Sigadam	Devaravalasa	Weavers/un irrigated	Kishor and Hemasundar
8.	Palakonda	Malliveedu Singupuram	Adjacent to Tribal area	S.Raminaidu and Srinivas
9.	Regidi Amudalavalasa	Adavaram	Anti zamindar Struggle	S.Raminaidu
10.	Kaviti	Borivanka	Coconut Plantations	R.Ramakrishna
11.	Merakamudidam	Gopannavalasa	Dalit struggle and murder of Dalit leaders	Shodhana and M.Ramkumar
12.	Hiramandalam	Pedasankili	Displaced	Simhachalam
13.	Hiramandalam	Duggipuram	Displaced	Simhachalam
14.	Garugubilli	Naviri	Displaced	Ganteda Gourunaidu
15.	Garugubilli	Kotavanivalasa	Displaced	Ganteda Gourunaidu
16.	Pachipenta	Madavalasa	Displaced Tribal Village	Prasad
17.	Pachipenta	Kodikaallavalasa	Displaced Tribal Village	Prasad
18.	Cheepurupalli	Ramalingapuram	Dry village and Land Alienation	Shodhana and M. Ramkumar
19.	Bobbili	Piridi	Education and unirrigated	Kolli Ramakrishna, Jakku Srinivas, S.G Prasad
20.	Itchapuram	Loddaputti	Effected by Odisha Irrigations Project	R. Ramakrishna, Paila Harishreddi
21.	Srikakulam	Ganagalalpeta	Fisher folk village	Boddepalli Kranti
22.	Gara	Bandaruvanipeta	Fisher folk Village	Hemasundar

(Contt...)

23.	Sompeta	Chepala Gollagandi	Fisher folk Village	Kodandam
24.	Vajrapukotturu	Nuvvularevu	Fisher folk Village	Kalidas
25.	Vajrapukotturu	Manchineelapeta	Fisher folk Village	Kalidas
26.	Itchapuram	Donkuru	Fisher folk village	R.Ramakrishna
27.	Kaviti	Idduvanipalem	Fisher folk village	R.Ramakrishna, Barla Sundara Rao
28.	Ranasthalam	Kovvada	Fisher folk village	Mylapalli Polisu
29.	Sarubujjili	Yaragam	Flood effect village	Banna Ramarao
30.	Balijipeta	Ajjada	Inamdari/endowment lands	Reddi Krishnamurty Naidu
31.	Terlam	Nandabalaga	Inamdarri village	Varahabhatla Bhaskararao
32.	Santabommali	Vaddithandra	Inland fishery/threat of displacement	Venkatarao
33.	Vangara	Maddivalasa	Innamdari village and Irrigated	K.H.S.Sharma
34.	Veeraghattam	Chalivendri	Irrigated	Sambashivarao
35.	Gara	Vadada	Irrigated	B.Naveen
36.	Polaki	Mabagam	Irrigated	Attada Appalanaidu
37.	Santabommali	Brundavanam	Irrigated	Venkatarao
38.	Ponduru	Boddepalli	Irrigated	Duppala Govindarao
39.	Garugubilli	Lakhanapuram	Irrigated	
40.	Jiyyammavalasa	Parajapadu	Irrigated but not receiving the water	Ganteda Gourunaidu
41.	Ramabhadrapuram	Gollalapeta	Land alienation	Jakku Srinivasa rao
42.	Ramabhadrapuram	Appalarajupeta	Land alienation	Jakku Srinivasa rao
43.	Seethanagaram	Ippalavalasa	Land alienation	
44.	Cheepurupalli	Viswanathapuram,	Land alienation	shodhana volunteers with the questioner
45.	G.Sigadam	Batuva	Land alienation	shodhana volunteers with the questioner
46.	Garividi	Kapushambham	Land alienation	shodhana volunteers with the questioner
47.	Garividi	Baguvalasa	Land alienation	shodhana volunteers with the questioner
48.	Garividi	K.Palavalasa,	Land alienation	shodhana volunteers with the questioner
49.	Garividi	m.duggivalasa,	Land alienation	shodhana volunteers with the questioner
50.	Garividi	chukkavalasa,	Land alienation	shodhana volunteers with the questioner

(Contt...)

97.	Gumma Lakshmi Puram		Boddidi	Tribal village In Scheduled Area Ganteda gourunaidu, Mallipuram Jagadeesh and tadangi Satyam
98.	amudalavalasa	chintala peta	un irrigated	Bendi Ravi, Pedada Krishna
99.	Burja	Thotavada	un irrigated	Boddepalli Kranti , Rajanikant
100.	Regidi Amudalavalasa	Kandisa	Un irrigated	S.Raminaidu ,Ganapati Rao and Kishor
101.	Santakaviti	Ponugutivalasa	un irrigated and adjacent to industries	S.Raminaidu ,Ganapati rao and Kishor
102.	Lakshminarasupeta	Karakavalasa	Unirrigated	Banna Ramarao
103.	Lakshminarasupeta	Chorlangi	Unirrigated	Banna Ramarao
104.	Nandigam	Turakalakota	Unirrigated	B.Kishor, Todarmal,Venugopal
105.	Kanchili	Jaadupudi	Unirrigated	Barla Sundara Rao
106.	Mandasa	Cheepi	Unirrigated	Barla Sundara Rao and Madina Raghavulu
107.	Badangi	Veerasagaram	Unirrigated	V.Venkateswara Rao
108.	Bobbili	Chtrakota boddavalasa	Unirrigated	Kolli Ramakrishna and Kolli Ramarao
109.	Parvatipuram	Chinabondapalli	Unirrigated	J.Shivaji
110.	Komarada	Dalaipeta	unirrigated	Ganteda Gourunaidu ,Mallipuram Jagadeesh
111.	Komarada	Kodulagumpa	Unirrigated/Pollution of J.K.Paper Mill	Ganteda Gourunaidu ,Mallipuram Jagadeesh
112.	Ranasthalam	Saragadapeta	Weaver	
113.	Laveru	Murapaka	Weaver	Koona Ramu
114.	Etcherla	Bontalakoduru	Weaver	Boddepalli Sudhakar
115.	Srikakulam	Alikam	Weaver /Recently irrigated	Bhaskara Rao
116.	santakaviti	Pullita	Weavers	S.Raminaidu ,Ganapati rao and Kishor
117.	Santakaviti	Mamidipalli	Weavers	S.Raminaidu ,Ganapati rao and Kishor
118.	Gara	Ampolu	Weavers	T.Sunil
119.	Sompeta	Jnkibhadra	Weavers	
120.	Patapatnam	Korasavada	Weavers	Anand,
121.	Ponduru	Tolapi	Weavers/ Kalinga education	Duppala Govindarao

Index

E

F